"Ten years ago we provided support t(⋯ ⋯ ⋯ ⋯ ⋯ ⋯ ⋯ ⋯ ⋯ ⋯ ⋯ ⋯)
family and group. At that time the social silence about the reality of RAT was deafening. Kathleen Sullivan is continuing to break this silence by speaking of the atrocities she experienced as an infant, child, youth, and vulnerable adult. Her writings are an important contribution to a civil and human rights movement focused on developing a child friendly world."

— Linda MacDonald RN, BN, MEd &
Jeanne Sarson RN, BScN, MEd

"I met Kathleen Sullivan near the beginning of my healing as a ritual abuse survivor. We connected through PARC-VRAMC. It was early in the survivor movement, but Kathleen was already there reaching out to others and sharing her knowledge of recovery issues. I purchased one of her books, *Lessons We Have Learned: A Survival Guide*, and found it full of valuable information. She told me about her living memorial garden to honor the dead and comfort those who had survived. I was able to see some of the gardens, walkways and monuments in her newsletters and on her website.

"When I considered starting my own non-profit organization, it was Kathleen who pointed me in the right direction and assured me I could succeed. With determination, I found my way through the stacks of government forms. Kathleen has remained a courageous and outspoken advocate to this day. She is an example of strength and fortitude. I wish her much success with her new book. She has earned that success. May her book be a means to educate the public and assist survivors around the world.'

— Jeanne Adams,
founder of Mr. Light & Associates, Inc.

"Kathleen Sullivan makes the critical connection between the communications industry and the mind control projects. Her ability to see through the pain and horror to the truth, the actual reasons behind the systematic abuse of children, is exceptional. I highly recommend this book for those interested not only in what happened, but why."

— Patty Rehn,
US Contact
The Advocacy Committee for
Human Experimentation Survivors (ACHES-MC)

"We all look for the purpose God gave us to be put on this earth. Sometimes we come to find out that purpose. If I have one thing to teach from my experience, it is that we must be knowledgeable so we don't continue to make the same mistakes and allow bad people to take advantage of us and our children. The answer is there. Dig for truth and then share it."

— Jackie McGauley, Advocate,
Affirming Children's Truth (ACT)
TunnelReport@aol.com

"As a criminal justice trainer and consultant on cult crimes and crimes against children, one of the difficult tasks is coming to terms with the unacceptable evils that are done against little ones. One has a choice: ignore it and pretend it isn't real or face it and do something about it. The second way is more painful and difficult; but to do nothing is to let the evil flourish. Ms. Sullivan's book is a book that demands a response. Read it only if you are prepared to be responsible for the awful truth you will learn, and brave enough not to turn away."

— Dr. Gregory Reid, DD
Occult Research and Crime Consultants

Unshackled:

A Survivor's Story of Mind Control

Unshackled

A Survivor's Story of Mind Control

Kathleen Sullivan

A Dandelion Books Publication
www.dandelionbooks.net
Tempe, Arizona

A Dandelion Books Publication
Dandelion Books, LLC
Tempe, Arizona

Library of Congress Cataloging-in-Publication Data

Sullivan, Kathleen
    Unshackled: a survivor's story of mind control

Library of Congress Catalog Card Number 20033108619
ISBN 1-893302-35-0

Cover art by Mary Bach-Loreaux; cover and book design by Amnet-Systems Private, Limited, www.amnet-systems.com

Dandelion Books, LLC
www.dandelionbooks.net

In Memorium

Penny
Cindy
"Momma"
Molly
Daddy K.
J. Hodges
David
Deborah
Peter D.
Rose
Grandma S.
Lola D.
Valerie Wolfe
Lorraine B.

I am grateful for having had the opportunity to spend a bit of time with each of you. I thank you for having shown me—in your unique ways—the better path. I look forward to seeing you again in the next life. Until then, God bless and keep you.

With all my love,

Kathleen

Contents

It is from numberless diverse acts of courage and belief that human history is shaped. Each time a person stands up for an ideal, or acts to improve the lot of others, or strikes out against injustice, he sends forth a tiny ripple of hope, and crossing each other from a million different centers of energy and daring, those ripples build a current which can sweep down the mightiest walls of oppression and resistance.

— Robert Kennedy

Foreword

By H. Michael Sweeney[1]

What is mind control, this curious force that is rarely mentioned in the mass media? Mind control can be traced back to the earliest of ancient history, in the sacrificial rites of the worshipers of Baphomet and other Satanic idols of Biblical times. It is also a tool that has been scientifically developed and cultivated by the CIA and other intelligence organizations; it is ultimately an instrument of political control.

The focused and intentional abuse of a small child can result in forcing the mind to split into multiple personalities, a phenomenon that under normal circumstances has traditionally been thought of as rare. Those who use it as a tool to program people want us to believe that Multiple Personality Disorder, or Dissociative Identity Disorder, as it is now known, does not exist, or that patients who display its symptoms are either prompted to do so by dishonest therapists, or are imitating something they have seen in a book or movie.

In reality, the mind of a normal child readily splits into alter-personalities when repeatedly and inescapably subjected to unspeakable terrors. The split-off alter contains the memories of the terrors behind a veil of amnesia. Though deeply scarred, this terror-ridden fragmentary personality will be suppressed, leaving the primary self relatively free to continue in life without further displaying any symptoms of the suffering the victim has endured. Sadly, this desperate form of self-preservation can be manipulated with evil intention.

In mind-control programming, this effect is achieved time and time again, creating dozens, hundreds, or even, as with Kathleen Sullivan, thousands of fragmented alter personalities. Each tormented alter has a unique identity, life experience, personality, set of moral values, skills and capabilities, fears and weaknesses, and even a unique understanding of reality itself. In fact, some can be so detached from reality that they believe they are objects or animals, not even human at all. These beliefs reflect their programming. How they are actually used is up to their programmers or handlers.

Programmed operatives are not fictitious entities invented for theatrical productions. Take *The Manchurian Candidate*, an action-adventure-spy thriller. It is considered a form of imaginative entertainment; however, the book and film were based on top-secret, classified information involving the intelligence activities of Red China, Korea, and the United States. This knowledge is in the hands of other nations, too, including the "good guys" in England, Canada, and Australia. As early as World War One, countries on both sides relied on early "prototypes" for spy work, ever advancing the technology and learning by its use as they went.

Through methodical manipulations via drugs, hypnosis, torture and training, it is possible to create a Manchurian Candidate; a programmable person with absolute obedience. There seems to be no limit to the complexity and ingenuity employed in this process. Handlers pick and choose alters, assign them duties, and give them their own set of memories, instructions, triggers, and fail-safe booby traps, to ensnare anyone attempting psychological reconstruction of the self. Once the ability to fragment has been established, other alters are cultivated to amplify their skills and taught how to best serve their master. Examples of controlled programming can be found among serial killers, mass murderers, and even terrorists whose "inexplicable" crimes explode in living color on our television screens.

As much as I would like to, I cannot discount the vastness of this phenomenon. The sad fact is, the technology is so well-researched, and so easy to employ, it is being used in truly creative ways. I estimate there are now tens of thousands of "sleepers" in place and certainly hundreds of active programmed operatives with experiences comparable to Kathleen Sullivan's. Other experts in the field mention even higher estimates.

Evidence of the perpetration of mind control by agencies of the United States government has found its way into the Congressional Record and proposed state and national legislation. Government documents from MKULTRA and Project Paperclip have been released under the Freedom of Information Act. Patents for devices that allow control of the mind have been filed. Articles in medical journals and scientific papers discuss advancements in the technology. Interviews with medical professionals who are dealing with the aftermath of uncontrolled experimentation and manipulation have been published. Themes involving mind control are found in fiction, music, television and film, and documented in confessions by perpetrators and victims. Brazen bragging by the likes of Satanist and military psyops expert, Michael Aquino, has placed valuable confirmations on the record.

Those few brave victims of mind control who have come forward, typically report being used as lab rats in bizarre experiments, and in many cases, sent on missions. What makes Kathleen Sullivan's story so remarkable is that she reluctantly admits having been used to kill. In the course of relating how that came about, she reveals unique and invaluable insights into the infrastructure, the methodologies, and the purpose behind it all.

Our first instinct is to turn away from any ugliness. Although the experiences revealed in *Unshackled* are painful and often repugnant, we dare not turn away, for this is not only a bold and courageous revelation; it also serves notice that just as we are all victims of these atrocities, so we all have the potential to free ourselves from their insidious influence, to resist and transcend them.

Our whole society is affected by the sanctioned use of our own non-consenting citizens as programmed assassins. Insofar as we are persuaded by propaganda not only to tolerate such a practice, but also to endorse it, we all become enmeshed in the machinery that makes mind control work.

In becoming aware of the baneful influence of propaganda, it is helpful to bear in mind that our world history is not the random happenstance as presented in what they call the "news." I am skeptical of messages purveyed by the mass media because these corporations are largely owned by military contractors and have been compromised by CIA interests ever since Operation Mockingbird; at this point you will find thousands of intelligence operatives in key positions of what you may believe to be our "free press."

Thus, whenever some explosion, assassination or other tragedy seems to "just happen," especially when there are unasked and unanswered questions, there is a very good chance that a programmed operative was involved, either as the doer of the deed, or as a patsy set up to take the blame for it. The questions that should be asked will become readily apparent. To unravel the clues, always start with the question, *"Cui bono?"* Who benefits, or whose agenda will now be less encumbered? Then ask what social changes are being promoted by opinion-makers, often citing reports of polls. Connect the dots, and a recognizable picture of mind control will emerge.

Most victims of mind control programming are not assassins. Many have been used less dramatically to infiltrate and manipulate the development of corporations, foundations, agencies, and other socially influential infrastructures. Many more seem not to have been used at all; as sleepers, they may simply be awaiting some future event requiring them to be triggered into action.

While historically, the CIA has been the most significant developer of programmed operatives, today it is clear that the same technology has been widely used by other groups, including intelligence agencies of other nations, various mafias and occult groups, select "elite" families, and perhaps most frightening of all, certain churches and fraternal organizations. What makes the latter so frightening is that many of them operate networks of hospitals and clinics that specifically involve themselves in the creation of programmed victims, as well as the recapture and reprogramming of those whose control mechanisms seem to be slipping.

In my first book, *The Professional Paranoid*, I listed over 400 CIA fronts and CIA-influenced companies and institutions. Fully half of these are involved with mind control. Half of those seem bent on convincing us that mind control does not work, and that complaints of ritual abuse are nothing more than false memories induced by bad therapists. I'd rather that was true. But in point of fact, nearly a third of all my clients turn out to have suffered ritual abuse and/or programming, though when they initially reached out for help, they generally had no concept of what lay behind their problems. Virtually every one of these people has had some exposure to cults, military intelligence or the CIA. None had been to therapists, except those belonging to these groups—their programmers.

Mind control is a covert crime perpetrated by covert means. There are organizations which have been established to rush in and ensure any exposure of the crime is dealt with quickly, and effectively covered up with disinformation. It thus remains the perfect crime, reduced to nothing more than a mysterious bump in the long, dark night of our political and social nightmare.

Victims of mind control often do not realize they are victims. They are even less likely to wake up to their own reality if there are people deliberately put into their lives to ensure the secrecy–people disguised as friends, relatives, or coworkers–their handlers and programmers. In my book, *MC Realities*, I offer a long list of symptoms and clues to help identify such unhappy states, as well as advice on how to fight back.

It is not a hopeless journey, but it is a perilous and difficult one. This book is testimony that success can be had.

Unshackled will cause many readers to question whether we are being told the truth about the political and social landscape of our world. If you value the purpose of our laws and our constitutional rights, if you treasure free will and the pursuit of happiness, you will realize that these rights are in jeopardy for all of us, when they are denied to anyone.

Notes

1. H. Michael Sweeney is the author of the following publications:

   - *The Professional Paranoid: How to Fight Back When Investigated, Stalked, Harassed, or Targeted by Any Agency, Group, or Individual.*
   - *MC Realities: Understanding, Detecting, and Defeating Mind Control and Electronic Weapons of Political Control Technology.*
   - *The ProParanoid Newsletter.*
   - *The ProParanoid Reference CD-ROM: A collection of materials useful to victims, investigators, and students of the intelligence community, mind control, and political intrigues.*

These publications are available from his website, http://www.proparanoid.com. Readers may request a sample newsletter by sending an email to theprogrammedassassin@proparanoid.com.

Author's Introduction

By way of introduction, I am above all a dedicated American. A physician might describe me as a "well-nourished Caucasian female of average height and weight," and note that I have naturally brown, short straight hair and gray-blue eyes. I am neither beautiful nor ugly, which means that most people would scarcely notice me in a crowd–an important asset during my covert past.

As far back as I can remember, my IQ has tested toward the high end. I'm grateful for my intelligence because I have been able to use my mind analytically to come to terms with what was done to me.

Because of the traumas I sustained for more than three decades, I spent most of my life severely dissociated. From one day to the next, I didn't know who I was. Although I'm now fairly integrated, I may continue to have occasional flashbacks and may shift more in my moods than those who have never been prone to dissociation.

As of the date of *Unshackled's* publication, I continue to study Social Work at a local university, with an additional minor in psychology. Although I struggle with an anxiety disorder (PTSD), I've managed–thus far–to keep a high grade point average.

My initial vocational goal is to become a Licensed Clinical Social Worker (LCSW). I hope to help other trauma survivors find their way to richer and fuller healing, and to teach mental health professionals how to work more effectively with severely dissociated clients.

In part, my healing process has focused on finding positive value in the years of trauma that I endured. If I didn't believe that I could turn evil into good, I would not have fought so hard to survive the pain of my past.[1]

Unshackled has not been easy to write, nor will it be pleasant to read. Much of my past was ugly and brutal. Although I have done my best to remove any gory details that do not go to the very essence of my story, some sections will still be difficult to read. If you feel uncomfortable with any information in this book, please feel free to skip that section and go on to the next.

Although the traumas I describe may seem more than any human can endure, I assure you I not only endured them, but am now healing from their long-term effects. I hope that in a way, this book will be a testament to the strength and creativity of every ritual abuse and mind control survivor. We've been through hell and have lived to tell you about it–if you're willing to listen.

Too many TV shows, books, and movies promote the idea that being a professionally trained operative is exciting and adventurous. Nothing could be further from the truth. Assassinations in particular take assailants to a place in their souls where no mentally healthy person would want to go.

One of the reasons I have chosen to tell my story is my anger at the people who broke my mind and conditioned me to become a mentally controlled slave, and at those men and women who used me to harm precious innocents at the risk of my own life. I am angry that I have needed many tens of thousands of insurance benefit dollars to heal. I am angry that I am (as of the date of publication) still legally disabled because of what was done to my mind, body and soul. I am especially angry at detractors, some with "M.D." or "Ph.D." after their names, who publicly label ritual abuse and mind control survivors "fabricators" and "liars"–while hiding the fact that they (the detractors) have ugly covert reasons for attacking us.

I am going public about my past because I have run out of patience with those who perpetuate the following lies:

- Ritual crime does not occur in North America, or
- Ritual abuse in North America is a phenomenon that has suddenly appeared out of thin air;
- Because survivors' stories are bizarre, they cannot possibly have occurred (in other words, bizarre equals impossible);
- Hypnosis cannot be used to influence people to perform acts against their will, or
- Hypnosis doesn't exist;
- Dissociative Identity Disorder (DID), formerly known as Multiple Personality Disorder (MPD), is fabricated, rare, and/or bizarre;
- Dissociation is caused by demonic possession;
- Pagans and occultists are demonically possessed or spiritually evil;

- People commit evil acts because they are driven by evil spirits;
- Recovered memories of childhood abuse are unreliable, fabricated, or have been implanted by unethical therapists;
- Repressed memory doesn't exist;
- People who remember, in therapy, that they were abused as children, are likely to drag the abusers through the court system and destroy their reputations;
- Child sexual abuse survivors are not responsible for their decisions to remove themselves from unsafe family members, when they remember what those individuals did to them–their therapists are;
- Child sexual abuse survivors are solely responsible (or maybe their therapists are, too) for "destroying" their childhood families if they say what was done to them; and therefore,
- The child molesters and rapists are not responsible for the long-term effects of their crimes within the family and the lives of their victims;
- People who claim to be survivors of child abuse are sick and want to stay in a fake victim role;
- People who claim to have been abused by family members are playing a "blame game" to avoid taking responsibility for their emotional problems;
- If FMSF spokespersons say that alleged child abusers–who have been successfully prosecuted–are not guilty, then they are innocent of all charges;
- Because the victims cannot prove what had been to them, they have fabricated their memories of the abuse;
- Sexual assaults against children are acts of love;
- Children want to be sexually assaulted;
- Children are not harmed by sexual assaults;
- Documented ritual abusers always work solo—they are not usually part of a larger criminal occult group that remains hidden;
- Even though Timothy McVeigh and Eric Rudolph were certainly brainwashed by the leaders of isolationist Aryan cults that encouraged violence, these young men and others like them have not been mentally controlled and manipulated to commit terrorist crimes;
- The CIA's MKULTRA program never included experimentation on, or traumatization of, children;

- The CIA's mind-control programs ceased in the mid 1970s;
- Such experimentation was unsuccessful and didn't go to the next step of creating mentally controlled slaves;
- Only the CIA has used mind control techniques against nonconsenting citizens;
- Those who claim to have recovered memories of having performed crimes in altered states of consciousness are seeking attention or want to be punished for crimes they never committed;
- People who recover memories of having been abducted and harmed by aliens are psychotic or insane;
- The CIA and US presidents never authorized illegal assassinations before 9/11;
- The CIA created assassination techniques and tools but never used them before 9/11;
- The worst of criminals can be identified by odd or deviant behaviors, isolationism, criminal records, a clear disinterest in participating in the local church, mosque or synagogue, making children uncomfortable by their presence, and so on;[2]
- The worst of criminals work alone–they can't get along with other criminals and therefore cannot successfully network and do business with other criminals;
- Pedophiles work alone–they don't meet as groups to share deviant materials and to assault children;
- Only males sexually abuse children;
- The worst of criminals don't operate in our neighborhood/town/county/state/country.

Most citizens in North America are still unaware of the existence of a large network of pedophiles and black-marketers who buy, sell, and use child and adult slaves in our continent and beyond. Because many of these slaves' bonds and chains are mental, they are invisible and difficult to prove in a court of law. Regardless, mental slavery is a clear and flagrant violation of our civil rights and should be addressed as such.[3]

Although this book includes information about my having been used in controlled alter-states as an assassin, I am not suggesting that all, or even most, mind-control survivors were trained or used to kill. I do not know what percentage of us have. I fervently hope that we are a small minority within the mind-control survivor community; if not, our country is in serious trouble.

Several people have suggested that I and other mind-control survivors could have used information from fictional movies and television shows to create "false memories." Although a few people may have done this, many mind-control survivors recalled specifics about techniques, agencies, types of programming, and more–*years* before such material was made available through television shows and movies. Most likely, scriptwriters used our stories that were available to the public in books, magazines, postings and websites to create their quasi-fictional stories.

Although fictional mind-control characters may appear sexually titillating, exciting, and appealing, our real experiences have consistently been demeaning and horrific.

I will share a *few* of my verifications with you. The remainder will remain in my possession as "life insurance," to ensure the safety of my loved ones and myself.

Until the early 1990s, I didn't know that I had a dissociative disorder and amnesia. My split-off altered states of consciousness (henceforth known as "alter-states" or "parts") had efficiently functioned away from my conscious awareness. Some people call this condition a "split personality," although it would be more accurate to say that my personality was shattered.

Contrary to popular opinion, Dissociative Identity Disorder (DID) is not schizophrenia. Schizophrenia is a lifelong, hereditary chemical imbalance in the brain that is often successfully treated with psychotropic medications. Although a genetic component may increase a person's ability to develop DID, it isn't necessarily a lifelong disorder. It can be reversed, given the right kind of therapeutic help and support–in a safe environment.

A common, knee-jerk reaction to hearing the stories of survivors of ritualized abuse and mentally controlled slavery is that–because our stories are bizarre to the extreme–they cannot possibly be true. I've also observed a secondary reaction to our horrific stories: after claiming our stories are fabricated, these people openly deride us. (I find this reaction bizarre. Would they also roll down their windows, then point and laugh at victims of serious car wrecks as they drive by?)

I ask you to please keep in mind that we survivors have been exposed to hardcore criminal minds for whom what is considered bizarre in normal society, is their acceptable norm. Most of these criminals (mostly men) are intelligent sociopaths who have zero conscience and no fear of the law. My primary tormentor, a brilliant and creative man, often said to his criminal associates, "If it works, why not?" In other words, he wasn't mentally and emotionally constrained by written and unwritten social mores and rules. He and his associates had no limitations, other than their humanness, and therefore did *anything they chose* to reach their goals.

When deciding which life-information to incorporate in *Unshackled,* my litmus test was that I must be so certain about that information's validity, I would be (and still am) willing to swear to it in a court of law.

I am reasonably certain, and am therefore willing to testify, that the CIA was the agency primarily responsible for my having been experimented on and traumatized in controlled settings as a child, to eventually be used against my conscious will as a covert slave-operative.[4] I do not, however, want the CIA to be scapegoated. Other federal agencies and groups, including criminal occult leaders and Mafia organizations, also use mind control techniques on unwitting victims. I still value most of the services the CIA provides for our country. Those of its many thousands of employees and contractors who genuinely seek to do what is right for our society and the world should not be held accountable for the actions of criminals who secretly operate among them.

As I relate my past interactions with various organizations and groups, I am not suggesting that all of their members or employees would follow the examples of those individuals I was forcibly exposed to. Decent, caring people, as well as people of ill intent, can be found in every social and professional milieu.

Where I mention the False Memory Syndrome Foundation (FMSF), I am not suggesting that all of its members are former CIA MKULTRA perpetrators, child molesters, and/or criminal occultists. Some members may have been falsely accused of crimes against children. Others may be so dissociated that they truly do not remember having hurt innocents. And some of the FMSF's supporters may have accepted the clever lies fed to them by more unsavory members–particularly its founders.[5]

Although I do mention mind-control techniques that I've witnessed in several Christian denominations, I am not suggesting that all, or most, of their ministers and pastors choose to use mind-control techniques on their congregations. I sincerely hope that those who do, will remain a small minority.

The opinions that I express in *Unshackled* are not the opinions of PARC-VRAMC [Positive Activism, Remembrance and Commemoration for Victims of Ritual Abuse and Mind Control], an advocacy organization I founded, nor are they the opinions of the book's publisher or editor. They are mine alone.

I do not want it to be used as a tool to recklessly slander or libel any person. For that reason, regardless of the ways that certain individuals harmed me in the past, I will not name most of them. I am, however, willing to testify in court about them if their identities are made public, and about those perpetrators I do name. Although human nature tends to sanctify the dead, history should not be unnaturally revised or contorted to meet the emotional needs of surviving family members.

Varying perspectives about an event or an individual can be equally valid. I ask that my childhood family respect my right to speak out about memories and recollections that may understandably differ from theirs. I regret any pain I stir up in the minds and hearts of those who know they were also victimized. And yet, I must remind them that I am not responsible for their pain; those who harmed them are. I hope that, if needed, they will seek professional help to cope with their painful pasts.

After learning of this book, other family members who are active perpetrators may try (again) to callously assault my mind and my character in an attempt to silence me and to dissuade other observers in the family from remembering, breaking free, and speaking the truth. To these perpetrators: I have the right to speak out about what was done to me, and by whom. Although I have not named some of you, I reserve the right to do so. If I am challenged in court, I will gladly testify against you. I'm sick unto death of carrying the back-breaking burden of the knowledge of our family's sins against the innocent. I'm laying that burden down and will not pick it up again. If going public means losing any remaining ties to the family, so be it. I'm worth it.

Because I focus attention on the behaviors of certain perpetrators who negatively changed the course of my life, I readily concede that the information I present about them may appear biased. I am not, however, suggesting that this is all they were and did. Some parts of their personalities were not destructive, and they may have even enriched the lives of others. No one is all good or all bad.

To protect the privacy of family members who acknowledge that they, too, were victimized, I will not reveal information from a number of their documents in my possession that directly verify some of my memories. Their stories belong to them.

While I have my stepmother's express permission to name and write about some of my experiences with my father, I have not released the names of my stepmother, mother, ex-husband, maternal grandparents, or surviving daughter. If you happen to know their names or identities, please do not reveal them to others. My goal with this book is not to shame them–even though those who are perpetrators deserve to feel ashamed. I also ask that the privacy of my father's adult children be respected.

To protect the identities of people I prefer not to name, I've given them the following aliases: Dr. J, Dr. T, Dr. X, Albert, Emily, Clyde, Dee, Fritz, Geena, Gerrie, Grandma M., Grandpa M., Grant, Dr. M, Helen, Janie, Jessie, Joan, Lucian, Pam, Pete, Poppa, Rose, and Therese.

To trauma survivors: this is a non-fictional account of my life, no one else's. If you sense that certain sections are similar to your own history, please skip those sections to avoid possible memory contamination.

Information about the criminal network within which that I was forced to co-exist may seem new and strange to some of you. My suggestion is to think of the groups and organizations comprising that network as a hidden co-culture that has operated, largely undetected, in Europe and North America since at least the 1940s.[6]

Not unlike the mafias, these organizations have rules and mores that are drastically different from those of "normal" society. And yet, as a full-fledged co-culture, their world has existed in plain sight, totally interconnected with mainstream society, politics, religion, academia, business, banking, entertainment, and more.

Although the leaders of this co-culture do not want the public to know that it exists, I hope *Unshackled* will help you to recognize some of their ideas and intentions, their activities and their endangered victims.

In my past, I was extensively exposed to individuals and groups who practiced the occult religions of Druidism, Satanism, Paganism, Rosicrucianism, and Luciferianism. Although at times I may appear to be biased against occult practitioners, I beg you to take my expressions in context; it was certain practitioners of these beliefs who hurt me and others.

In a similar way, I ask you to remember that not all Aryans and Neo-Nazis are like those who it is my regrettable duty to describe in this book. And please remember that most Germans are not Nazis.

Although I have written about a series of related crimes that I witnessed in Reading, Pennsylvania and in Cobb County, Georgia, I am not suggesting that local residents supported such activities, nor am I suggesting that local law enforcement personnel helped to conceal such crimes. The criminals were clever and well-financed, and had numerous high-tech resources that would have made detection and prosecution extremely difficult, if not impossible.

Since 1991, I have met other survivors of ritual abuse and mind control who independently verified my memories of experiences that we'd shared. Because they have reason to fear for their lives, I will not reveal their identities.

To protect myself legally and to preserve my life and the lives of my loved ones, I will not provide any identifying details of any crimes that I was forced to perform in the past.

Wherever you see the word "I," please be aware that I may be relating experiences that I'd had no awareness of, before I connected with split-off parts of my personality and mind.

Because I am only one limited person, and because I value my privacy, I am not willing to provide one-on-one support for those who read this book or learn of my history in other ways. If you need support or information, please feel free to utilize the resources listed at the end of this book.

What I experienced in my past, no other ritual abuse or mind control survivor has experienced in exactly the same way. And yet, much of what I describe in this book has also been experienced in a comparable way by many trauma victims and survivors. I gratefully dedicate this book to them.

Kathleen A. Sullivan
Tennessee, USA
http://www.kathleen-sullivan.com

Notes

1. " . . . positive reinterpretation of a traumatic event requires the victim to think about whatever positive gains or lessons can be gleaned from the horrific experience, and to focus on them in readjusting to the future . . . such positive reinterpretations are therapeutic, since they allow victims to see meaning in the world and to improve their self image, feeling stronger and more capable of confronting adversity." (Bower and Sivers, pg. 647)

2. If you are a parent or grandparent, daycare operator, school teacher, law enforcement officer, therapist, or minister; if you're none of the above and still want to know more about pedophile mentality; I strongly urge you to purchase Dr. Anna Salter's *Predators: Pedophiles, Rapists, and Other Sex Offenders* and keep it close at hand. *Predators* explains pedophile behaviors and mentality in a way I've not found in any other piece of literature. It breaks every entrenched myth about child molesters that can keep us from recognizing one in our midst–one who right now, this minute, may be hurting a child. I believe it should be required reading for anyone who has responsibility for the care of children.

3. Article XIII of the *Bill of Rights* states: "Neither slavery nor involuntary servitude, except as a punishment for crime whereof the party shall have been duly convicted, shall exist within the United States, or any place subject to their jurisdiction."

4. I am amazed that journalists and reporters still ask CIA spokespersons and Directors, "Did your Agency perform assassinations?" and then report their negative replies as gospel truth. Wouldn't they look ridiculous if they were to interview alleged murderers and then report *their* claims of innocence as true–simply because they said they were? The same holds true for those who accept–at face value–the CIA's claims that it didn't employ or use certain individuals, because it has "no records" of them.

5. Dr. Colin Ross wrote: "The FMSF is the only organization in the world which has attacked the reality of multiple personality in an organized, systematic fashion." (Bluebird, pg. 115) Why would they do this? I believe some of the doctors who perpetrated crimes as CIA mind-control contractors became afraid when their former victims started to remember. I believe this is why some of these perpetrators formed or joined the FMSF–to use it as a disinformation mechanism to discredit the victims *in advance*, by convincing the public that recovered memories and MPD/DID are "fabricated" or "implanted." Perhaps they knew that their victims would be less likely to remember the crimes against their humanity if public opinion was turned against them:

   > It is far harder for memories to be recovered when there is a threat of social retribution or powerful social or political determinants of shame about what is recalled . . . a more comfortable survival can come

naturally into being when conditions mean that the unspoken is given a social voice. (Woodcock pp. 147, 149)

6. In their leaflet, *Seeing Inside the Ritual Abuse-Torture Co-culture*, Sarson and MacDonald wrote:

> We have named the culture of these destructive families/groups as a co-culture versus a sub-culture because the ritual abuse-torturers exist among us, undifferentiated from the neighbour next door. They draw no attention to themselves by way of unique clothing, body piercing, or hairstyle, or by race, or by living in a commune, or by openly advertising their evil-based beliefs and behaviours, hence the reason we have entitled our book, a work in progress, *The Torturers Walk among Us*. Perpetrators of RAT [ritual abuse/torture] can be living successful lives, making a living "legally" employed, hold positions of extensive positional power and community status, others have class and wealth, others are "simply common folk." (pg. 1)

Government Programming

What Happened?

In the summer of 2001, I reached a critical crossroads in my life. For the past several years, I'd tried to follow the examples of a large part of the ritual abuse/mind-control survivor population–a community with whom I had the good fortune to connect. Due to their fear of being cruelly ridiculed or harmed again, most of those brave men and women have chosen to quietly get on with their lives, never speaking about their remembered experiences outside of their personal support networks.

I've tried silence too, but it hasn't worked well for me. I felt like a counterfeit when I mimicked others around me, hiding my past while presenting myself as a "new" Kathleen. Because I wasn't being authentic, I was miserable.

When I opened up to one of my professors about my past, she said I ought to write an autobiography. Blushing, I told the professor that a prolific author, Gordon Thomas, had already suggested the same. "Then why are you hesitating?" the professor asked.

Accepting that teacher's challenge, I took a year off from my studies to do what I'd dreaded the most: to review thirteen years worth of hand-written journals that were full of my memories of traumatic events that I'd previously blocked out. I had stored the journals out of sight in my basement in six white plastic file cartons. The task of piecing together my life story from the journals still seemed impossible.

As I slowly worked my way through them, I was troubled by how fragmented my memories still were. Most of those I'd recorded had, in reality, lasted only between ten seconds and a minute or two.[1] Assembling and connecting the memory fragments was like trying to reassemble a ten-thousand-piece jigsaw puzzle.[2]

Day and night for over a year, as I reviewed the journals, an uncanny urgency drove me to absorb every bit of the memories–only to block them out again when I put the journals down! Determined to remember this time, I read them again and again, typed them onto diskettes, and reviewed them verbally in therapy.

Although those memory reinforcement techniques seemed to help, I was horrified to rediscover some of the deeds I'd committed in the past, under the direct control of professional handlers. How could that have been me: so brutal, so cruel and heartless? How could I have actually wanted to hurt people and make them feel–in their bodies–the pain I had felt in my soul? *What had happened to me?*

Agencies and Organizations

Another question plagued me: who and what were the groups and facilities I remembered having been exposed to? Certainly, none of them had been part of my "normal life"!

My journals indicated that I had performed illegal acts for a network of organizations, groups, networks and agencies. My alter-states knew most of them by code names.

Various spook handlers referred to the CIA as *the Web, the Agency, the Organization, the Family,* and *the Company.* A former CIA Director, George Bush Sr., was sometimes called *the webmeister.* Some CIA employees who had also previously been in the OSS referred to themselves as the *Old Guard.*

Several self-identified NSA employees I met in Atlanta in the late 1980s and early 1990s alternately referred to their agency as *the Net* and *the Dragon.*

I was exposed to several Mafia members, beginning when I was a young child. Dad sometimes took me with him as his cover when he met with mobsters who may have been members of the Colombo-Profaci crime family that operated in the Northeast. As a young adult, I met mob members in Chicago. Later, I met members of Trafficante's organization and was taken more than once to a compound in Florida that I knew as Marina Del Largo–not to be confused with Donald Trump's resort, which has a similar name. I also met and interacted with mobsters in Atlanta. (I will not provide any other details about my experiences with any of these groups or individuals.)

I knew NASA by its official name.

I was taken to meetings of groups known as the "Golden Dawn" and the "Illuminati." At those gatherings, I learned that some members of Illuminati were also members of the Golden Dawn. They exposed me to a mish-mash of Luciferian and Pagan beliefs. The members of the international Illuminati organization seemed to be covert "Rosicrucians." The words, "the Illuminati" alternately referred to the group and to its individual members. Although I used to be in awe of the Illuminati, I now consider it to be one of many secretive cartels.[3]

I was also exposed to a mob-connected occult network, headquartered in New York City, code-named "Satanic Hierarchy." (Again, I will not provide further details about my interactions with this organization.)

As an adult, I repeatedly encountered members of a large, national Aryan network–"The Brotherhood." Another Aryan group, perhaps part of that same network, was called "The Order." Another, Western Mysteries, was especially involved in publishing literature. I met representatives from many smaller Aryan groups over the years–each had a code name that was known only to insiders.

Alleged CIA handlers referred to male Secret Service personnel as *bus boys*. Self-identified Secret Service agents called one of my highly trained bodyguard alter-states, *plain Jane*.[4]

I was also forcibly used by members of an international network, code-named the Octopus, that included alleged CIA employees and contractors, members from several *Mafia* families, and more.

Government Facilities

I was taken to numerous US military bases and government facilities over a period of more than thirty years. I have since been able to identify several of them, first-hand.[5] These are the names of some that I believe I was taken to for programming and/or training:

Fort Payne, Alabama. After our family moved to Atlanta, Georgia, I was taken to a military base that I was told was Fort Payne. Female teenagers and women were given special training there. I was called a "Golden Girl" and received what was code-named "Black Claw" physical training.[6]

Redstone Arsenal, Alabama. There, I believe I received MKNAOMI biochemical black op conditioning, briefings, and debriefings.

Juvenile Facility in North Carolina. When I was sixteen, I was taken by my parents to a facility near Morganton and Marion, North Carolina. The grounds were enclosed by a high chain-link fence. A separate observation

tower was attached to an above-ground enclosed walkway that led to
the main building, where I and other youths received specialized ops
training, and where I was also brainwashed about the Aryan, Pagan
Golden Dawn belief system. Those who didn't follow orders were brutally punished. I first remembered this facility in the early 1990s when
an emerging alter-state drew a crude map of the buildings and grounds.
A social worker from North Carolina recognized the drawing, and said
that she'd known the facility as the "Western Carolina Adolescent
Correctional Center." (I've not yet found a verification of a facility having
that name.)

Great Lakes Naval Base near Chicago, Illinois. My first husband,
Albert, took me to a large building on the base where I and other adult
female "patients" wore hospital gowns and endured extensive mental
programming and training in a psych ward setting.

Fort Gillem near Atlanta, Georgia. I was repeatedly driven there by
a man who escorted me into a set of underground corridors and rooms
where he seemed to be in charge of local spooks. He and other professionals sometimes briefed and debriefed me there.

Fort McPherson near Atlanta, Georgia. After I'd had several vivid
memories of that base in the 1990s, my second husband, Bill, drove
me there to see if any of the buildings looked familiar. I immediately
recognized the large, white Forcecom building where, in a below-ground
room, a female programmer had forcibly reconditioned me after a
failed op (by threatening to shoot me), so that I would continue to do
assassinations. I had also remembered a one-story cafeteria building
behind it, where I'd been taken by a male handler who had been hungry.
As Bill and I sat in the Forcecom parking lot, we saw several casually
dressed individuals leave the smaller flat-roofed building, carrying
Styrofoam take-out food containers.

Fort Benning, Georgia. I believe that, as an adult, I received limited
training at this Army base. At that time, a male handler told me that I was
the only woman receiving it there. I was told that I was given specialized
training to familiarize me with how Rangers worked together on ops.
(Over the years, I developed tremendous respect and deep appreciation
for those men; unlike most spook handlers, they remained gentlemen.)
I was also put through brutal mock torture/interrogation sessions to condition several of my alter-states to respond in specific ways if I were ever
caught and interrogated while overseas on an op.

Edgewood Arsenal, Maryland. When we lived in Maryland, my father took me to a sprawling government facility code-named "Edge-of-the-Woods." There, I endured the unexpected effects of a hallucinogen and mind-shattering mental programming.

The Farm. When I was a teenager, Dad took me to this spook-run facility to have me trained for black ops. It may have been at the CIA's Camp Peary; it may have been at a CIA/Aryan-run "counterterrorism" camp in Powder Springs, Georgia; or it may have been at an entirely different location.[7]

Fort Campbell, Kentucky. I reported to this huge Army base several times to be briefed for special ops and to receive limited conditioning and training.

Dobbins Air Force Base, Georgia. When I lived near Atlanta, I was often transported from this base by jet to other locations for covert ops, and then was brought back to the base before being transported home.

Goddard NASA facility near Washington, DC. I believe I was taken there in approximately 1968, to be mentally programmed.

Huntsville NASA facility in Alabama. I believe that mental programming was done to me at that facility after my family moved to Georgia in 1969. During a tour in the mid 1990s, I easily identified several of the buildings.

"Meadowlark" Air Force Base, exact location unknown. I was flown there from Dobbins AFB in 1985, and was interrogated in underground rooms by military intelligence personnel.

Black Ops

The years of programming and conditioning at these and other government facilities prepared me to become a covert slave-operative. When I fell asleep at home in my adult years, my nighttime alter-states emerged. Because these alter-states were adrenaline junkies, ops were their drug of choice.

Sometimes I was first taken to a local cult meeting. After the horrific ritual, other parts were triggered out to be transported. Most of my op-trained parts were more than willing to go on far-away assignments. It was what they existed for.

These are some of the activities that my covert op programmed alter-states performed while under the control of professional handlers:

- Protection, body-guarding, and escorting
- Assassinations
- Hostage interventions and rescue
- Arms smuggling, including transportation of small rockets
- Bombings and sabotage
- Teaching children how use standard and makeshift weapons against mock adult attackers
- Kidnapping
- Taking out snipers
- Surveillance
- Torture and interrogation
- Clandestine photography
- Clandestine search of an organization's files
- Killing assassin-programmed individuals who had gone out of control and were an imminent danger to those around them. (Because they were so dissociated they felt no pain when injured, I was trained to kill them in a particularly gruesome way.)

Professional handlers used a succession of my pre-programmed covert op alter-states to successfully perform each operation. Afterwards, I was transported home with no memory of the event.

My black op (assassin) trained alter-states were even more specialized. Through hundreds of repetitive acts, each was conditioned to kill in at least one of the following ways: zip wire, gun, knife, or chemicals. Other methods were also used on certain ops. The zip wires were sometimes sewn into loosely-basted hems of garments, particularly blouses and jackets, with soft ends to protect my hands from being sliced through.

Each black op alter-state was trained to use at least one type of weapon. Some were also trained to select a certain number of objects or surfaces in any environment to use as makeshift weapons.

In the early 1990s, I was severely re-traumatized as I remembered the crimes that I'd been forced to commit. As I resuscitated the dead parts of my soul, I felt the immense emotions of pain, grief, and horror that I hadn't felt during the actual ops.

Travel to Exotic Places

To give you an idea of what remembering was like, I'll share from two days of journals that I wrote in January, 1993.

First, I relived a series of emerging traumatic memories in bits and pieces, starting with a childhood memory of my father driving his chisel into my skin to lift my kneecap–just enough to frighten me. Then he used a drill to wound my feet–again, not enough to leave a lasting scar.

As I remembered this, I slipped into the same kind of trance state that I'd gone into as a child, to escape the pain. When I came to, I found that I had written many pages of memories. Several were especially upsetting:

In a teenaged training session, I held a long sharp knife and plunged it deeply into the front of someone's torso. I was being taught that there were two ways I could do it. I could either do the "T," which was to cut from below the belly button up, and then–at an angle—do the upper stomach and heart, or I could do it with one deep, lower slash from one side to the other, through the intestines.

I was taught that either way was extremely effective. The lower slash would leave the person in pain for a while before the actual death, if that was what was intended. To simply kill, the "T" was preferred. Before doing it to live adults, I was made to do it on upright adult cadavers. Each time, I wiped the fatty tissue off my long knife. I was taught that it was important to keep the knife clean; and anyway, I didn't like looking at it.

Then I remembered standing in a room with white walls. I saw an intense, slim woman, average height, with short, dark hair and eyes. Other people stood in the room, too. On a table to my right were objects that could be used to attack and kill.

I had no choice; the woman held a knife and kept reaching out as if to slice at my forearms. When I finally got tired of parrying, jumping back, and moving my arms away from her, I went after her full-force. I grabbed her knife and cut her neck deeply–from one carotid artery, then right through her throat to the other artery.[8]

In the next memory, another adult was fighting me. I grabbed a knife from the table. Unfortunately, because it was dull and serrated, I couldn't use it on the attacker's neck. After I successfully took the attacker down, a slim, friendly, middle-aged man with curly, graying hair took the knife from my hand and pushed it down hard on the victim's fingers–cutting several of them off.

When I came back into consciousness and read these journaled memories, I was devastated. I felt solely responsible, even though the gray-haired man had instructed me. After all, the knives had been in *my* hand.

(Nearly every day, similar heart-pumping, gory memories emerged in my dreams and waking hours. They followed me to the store and to the post office, to church and to school. The memories were clearly telling me that I had been trained to kill. Why me? Having no answer, I felt a heavy weight of guilt.)

That afternoon, I decided to shake off the effects of the memories by going to a nearby shopping mall. While investigating a sale at a pharmacy, I found a bin full of bumper-stickers. I bought several: "JOIN THE ARMY! Travel to exotic places . . . meet unusual people . . . and kill them." "I'M A VIRGIN . . . but this is a very old bumper-sticker." "TOTO, I don't think we're in Kansas anymore." "I'd kill Flipper for a tuna sandwich." "I'm Glad I'm Not You."

My favorite was, "In spite of the cost of living, it's still popular." Although I was remembering horrible things that I'd done in the past, I was determined to survive.

When I returned home, I tried to get some sleep. Instead, I struggled through one vivid dream after another.

Early the next morning, my husband left for work in his pickup truck. Alone in the house, I placed several pillows between my back and our queen-sized bed's wooden headboard. I grabbed the spiral-bound notepad that I'd placed on my dark brown wooden nightstand, and wrote whatever came to mind. Soon, I felt as if I were falling asleep, although my eyes remained wide open. I didn't understand that I was capable of putting myself into a trance state, thereby allowing split-off alter-states to emerge and write in my notebook.

When I came back into consciousness, I found that I'd written about a covert operation in a foreign country. As usual, this memory had no beginning and no end.

Even if it should someday be proven to me that this particular episode was an implanted screen memory, I still feel grateful that I was able to recall it. After being so emotionally battered by horrifying memories, this recollection restored my sense of inherent goodness.

Firefight

I have no idea how I arrived there, who took me, or how I got back home, nor do I know the year the event unfolded. I suspect that it occurred between 1982 and 1987.

Based on the architecture and the vehicles, the angle of the sun and speech patterns of the natives, I can venture a guess that we were in a South or Central American nation.

It was daytime, warm outside. I was inside a battered, old, two-story clapboard residential retirement home not far from a downtown area. It had lots of bedrooms occupied by a number of elderly Caucasians. The kitchen was on the first floor in the right rear, the living room in front. A porch, bordered by a wooden railing, was in front of it. The residence wasn't fancy, but it was livable and clean. The residents were taken care of by a small team of professionals, including nurses.

Several of the bedrooms were downstairs in back. Some of the residents had to sleep in them because they couldn't walk up the stairs. One, an older man, was very slim with thinning brown hair on top of his head. He seemed quite ill. I helped put him on his back in the smallest bedroom. We covered him with a colorful, handmade, pastel pink, block-style quilt. He was in a lot of pain–I think it was his heart.

Some kind of political action was taking place in the vicinity. I was at the residential home with a makeshift team of CIA agents, mercenaries, and others–anyone in the area who was available had been called in to help. The elderly folks were in danger, and our assignment was to protect them.

Had we not been in imminent danger, the professional handler who had brought me there would probably have taken greater care to ensure that I did only what he gave me orders to do, nothing more. This time, however, I was free to follow my own instincts, because he was too busy doing other things.

During the late afternoon, we received a directive from a young, slim, fiery man with thick, curly, dark-brown hair. We were told that he'd commandeered the downtown area, and wanted to use this house as his base of operations against soon-to-arrive military forces who we prayed would kick his ass. Unfortunately, the elderly residents couldn't be transported away in time.

Some of the aged males had served in previous wars. They knew how to fight, but most of them could no longer shoot straight, due to shaking hands or poor eyesight. Others were quite senile, and there was no safe place to take them.

As more residents returned to the house, we gathered them in the center of the house, with groups upstairs and downstairs.

Two elderly gentlemen who still had good eyesight were asked to carefully hide by the windows and alert us if they saw any movement coming up the dirt streets.

We knew that the action would be coming from the downtown area. The military leader had already ordered filled burlap bags to be stacked in piles across the dusty street from the front of the house, his men guarding them. An "SOS" had gone out for more of our folks to find their way to the house to help us defend the elderly residents.

We were told to hold our fire, due to insufficient weapons and ammunition.

My dark-haired, short handler handed me a shotgun and ordered me to use it. I explained to him that I didn't know how.[9] Several rifles and pistols were quickly taken up by the others. They had a sweet automatic machine gun–a newer model. Big and black, it used brass projectiles. All I had to do was aim and pull the trigger–it would do the rest. After I tested it, I didn't want to use anything else, and they didn't take it away.

The real trouble didn't start until dusk. We turned off all the lights in the house, so nobody could see where we were when we fired. Some men started approaching the house by pushing what looked like rectangular plywood dollies on wheels, stacked with filled burlap bags. They seemed to be using them as moving shields. Our lookouts warned that it was time to start firing.

The enemy had a lot more ammo than we did. We only shot when we had a good chance of hitting one of them.

We couldn't afford for even one of those men to get into the house. Too many people could get killed too fast. If we could just keep them at bay! More men came in droves through nearby buildings, settling down behind the stacks of bags. Typically, they had flat, dark-skinned faces and wavy dark hair.

Although they had automatic weapons, they must have been drugged or drunk or both, because they couldn't shoot straight. It took a while for us to realize this. I was genuinely frightened, and didn't expect to live through the night. I tried my best to shoot the crowns of any heads that rose an inch or two above the tops of the bags, but they were too small a target and I didn't want to waste my ammo.

Several male spooks and mercs hid behind furniture that we had stacked behind the wooden rails on the porch. One man and his partner, both American businessmen, had come by earlier in the day to volunteer their services.

I went from window to window in the house when the lookouts told us they saw movement outside. We were quite nervous, because there were several roads–it was hard to see everything going on.

Unfortunately, we weren't paying attention when the sick elderly man, clad in a light-colored terrycloth robe, unexpectedly walked out onto the porch. Several of the men tried to grab his robe to stop him. I went berserk and ran out onto the porch. A middle-aged, brown-haired man helped me force him down onto the wooden surface, while the others remained hidden behind the furniture. Unfortunately, we three were now in plain view of the enemy.

I knew the color of the robe made the man an easy target. I saw several men behind the bags rise up, as if to get a better shot at him.

Without thinking, I stood up with my black machine gun and started firing at their heads. There was some light on their side of the street, perhaps from the moon, and I could see a black substance fly through the air from two of the men who had crouched side-by-side. They deserved it for shooting at that innocent, senile man!

After that, we were more aggressive and held them off through the night. I don't remember how long I kept firing. When I went into the house to get more ammo, it suddenly hit me: I had stood out there on the porch in full view of those men across the street as I had fired at them, making myself a very easy target! I shouted to the others, "Did you see what just happened! I was standing right there, and they were shooting at me, and none of the bullets hit me!" My preoccupied handler agreed it was a miracle.

One man seemed to be in his sixties. In the kitchen, he offered me some of his cartridges. He had several different shapes and sizes in a clear plastic box. I didn't even know which kind to use. When I grabbed a bunch, he stopped me and showed me how to select the right ones. I put the others back and thanked him. A black, long "drawer" pulled out from the lower side of my machine gun. He showed me how to insert the projectiles. He said all I had to do was point and shoot.

Time lapse. I woke up in the early morning, startled, wondering why everything was so silent. It was dark in the house and nearly everyone was sound asleep in chairs, sofas, and on the floor. Only one other person seemed to be awake–one of the old vets who had posted lookout the night before.

He whittled a piece of wood as he sat at the old cloth-covered kitchen table. I was beginning to feel the emotional impact of what had happened. I asked, "Are they gone?" He nodded, then told me about the elderly robed man, who had been shot in the leg. We talked quietly for a while, so as not to wake the others. I felt very comfortable with him. He was a man of few words. I thought of him as the kind of person I hoped to someday become.

Later that morning, the others started to wake up. While they chose food from the refrigerator, I opted for a peanut butter sandwich. I was deeply touched when the old gentleman quietly gave me one of the bullets that he said I'd shot the previous evening. It was rather flattened and a little bent. It meant more to me than any medal that may have been given to me. I sensed it was a symbol of his personal respect and his way of honoring my help. I put it in my right jeans pocket, vowing never to lose it.

As always, my handlers did a full-body search before they transported me home. Although they took away the memento, they couldn't completely erase the memory of another mission accomplished–this one, with satisfaction.

Validation

After I read this journaled memory, I told my husband, Bill, what I'd remembered about the ammunition that I had used. As I spoke, his face registered shock. A retired Army NCO, he explained that the elongated brass bullets were called 7.62 gauge, 30-caliber universal projectiles because they could be used in a number of different weapons. From his extensive experience with ordnance, he told me that yes, the gun I used *was* a machine gun, and yes, those projectiles *would* have been used in such a gun, and yes, the way I described loading it really *is* the way it would have been done.

After that, he shook his head and chuckled about what he called the Shootout at the OK Hilton. He said, "What kind of woman am I married to?" Calling me his "Pistol-Packing Mama" he declared, "You were a *hero!*"

When he called me a hero, my face crumpled and I started to cry. "Yeah, I was a hero, all right . . . but I was also the worst monster there could be." I wished so bad that the way I had behaved on that particular op had been the way I'd behaved on *every* op. Soon, more emerging memories reminded me that this simply wasn't true.

Notes

1. "Fragmented encoding of a traumatic event makes voluntary retrieval and reconstruction of a trauma in explicit memory difficult, if not impossible." (Spinhoven et al., pg. 263)

2. "More compelling and less consciously available dimensions of denial are when memories of gross violations are so threatening to the psychological and physical integrity of the survivor that recollections are literally split off from consciousness . . . the shattering manner in which torture and atrocity violate the physical and psychological boundaries of survivors frequently causes their recall of events to emerge in ways that may be fragmentary, disconnected and bizarre." (Woodcock, pg. 144)

3. I am not opposed to participation in secret, invitation-only organizations. I am, however, concerned when such groups use tax revenue to create governmental policies, agreed on at those meetings, that are diametrically opposed to the will of most taxpayers and voters.

4. I think one reason I was also chosen and trained to perform protection services for targeted individuals was that I'd done a number of very successful hits and snuffs, and therefore had a better feel and sense of how a person might go about killing the client. I was acutely alert to the body language, eye expressions, hand movements, and vocal inflections of potential assassins.

5. I've not yet tried to validate the memories of other bases and facilities, because if I go to any of them, I risk being re-accessed. I'd rather be without some validations than be hurt again.

6. I repeatedly remembered that the boys and girls who were trained to become Aryan super-warriors were called "Golden." After these memories emerged, my stepmother gave me copies of letters that Dad had sent to her while attending Purdue

University in Indiana. I was astonished that, in a letter dated 6/25/79, he'd written: "I went to see *Golden Girl* Friday night–about a big blond test-tube baby raised by 2 scientists from Hitler Germany who was trying to prove his theories about the superiority of white, blond, Republicans. He kept sprinkling super vitamins and growth hormones on her grits, then convinced a group of rotten capitalists with mustaches to finance an Olympic training facility for her. If she wins three golds in Moscow, they have her name for their living bras, cereals and panty hose, and the professor gets to prove that blonds can do anything better."

7. Camp Peary, A.K.A. The Farm, is a CIA Directorate of Operations "spy school" near Williamsburg, VA. Another facility code-named The Farm was a 60-acre estate in Powder Springs, south Cobb County, in Georgia. It was owned and run by a spook named Mitchell "Mitch" WerBell III. This counter-terrorist training camp, COBRAY-SIONICS Training Center, contained a "clandestine factory developed to perfect the tools and techniques of sniping, counterinsurgency, and the *coup d'etat.* (*New York Review,* pg. 2) WerBell III was a highly respected "OSS Captain, guerilla fighter, military advisor, soldier of fortune, paramilitary expert, silencer designer and weapons wizard." (*American Ballistics*, pg. 1)

8. Some of my black op trainers called the resulting gash a "smile."

9. Because my trainers didn't want me to use my weapons training on my own volition, I was only allowed to touch a gun when it was given to me with specific instructions about what to do with it. Each time, it was already loaded.

Early Years

Good Times

Although I endured many traumas that I mercifully blocked out over a period of more than thirty years, I also lived a reasonably "normal" life that I was comfortably able to remember. These are my favorite childhood memories from that part of my life.

Almost every year, our family–consisting of Mom, Dad, two younger brothers and I, went to the annual Shriner circus that was held in a large building in downtown Reading, Pennsylvania. We were each allowed to buy one souvenir. My favorite was a brown, furry, toy monkey on elastic strings.

Once in a while, Dad took us to the "band shell" in the city. The concrete structure, shaped like a giant opened clam shell, sheltered orchestras and bands that played free concerts. I especially enjoyed watching big goldfish as they swam in a murky pond in front of the stage.

After we moved to the nearby suburb of Reiffton, my brothers and I discovered how to climb a huge pine tree in our back yard. When Mom removed the lower branches, we nailed boards to the trunk and scampered up again. Climbing to the top, I could see forever!

On warmer days, we met with neighborhood boys at a creek below a huge, grassy hill near Exeter Township Junior High School. We spent many lazy summer days catching crayfish, chewing on watercress, wading barefoot on big slippery rocks in the cold water, and occasionally falling in while the others laughed.

In the winter, the big hill above the creek was our favorite sledding spot. Adventurous souls used wooden sleds or round, metal saucers with handles to hurtle down the packed white snow to the edge of the creek.

We dubbed our favorite neighborhood play area, the "rock pile." It was really a large cluster of boulders. I played Jane when the boys took turns playing Tarzan. When they were knights storming our rock castle's turret, I was the damsel in distress.

In the winter, we built snow forts to hide behind during snowball fights. Our snowmen had carrots and raisins for their noses, eyes, and mouths, and sticks for arms. Sometimes we lay on our backs and moved our arms and legs to make "angels" in the snow. Tired and cold, we went inside and placed our wet snowsuits, scarves and gloves on radiators until they were toasty dry.

We regularly attended a Lutheran church several blocks from our home. It was just down the road from the elementary school that my brothers and I attended. Although Dad and several other church members ritually abused me in the church buildings, especially at night and on traditional Christian holidays (Dad had keys to all the buildings), I enjoyed attending Sunday School classes and participating in the children's choir. We proudly sang, "Praise Him, praise Him, all ye little children . . . God is love . . . God is love," *Beautiful Savior*, *Onward Christian Soldiers*, and other music that made God and the church seem non-threatening and beautiful.

On warm summer days, we walked to a nearby A&W drive-in restaurant. I loved the frosty, ice-cold glass mugs that the root beer was served in.

When we visited Mom's parents in the nearby town of Laureldale, we sometimes went to a large carnival at the Reading Fairgrounds several blocks down the road. I usually ate a red candied apple or pink cotton candy as I went on slower rides, or stood and watched my brothers ride faster, higher ones.

At night in the hot summer, my maternal grandparents' windows stayed open. I often stood next to their living room window that faced the direction of the fairgrounds. Feeling the cool breeze on my face, I enjoyed listening to the screams of race cars and excited crowds.

When Dad drove us on Sunday afternoons into the countryside, I looked for brilliantly colored hex signs painted on barns. Most were based on superstition; locals believed they brought good fortune or provided protection from witches and demons.

Once in a while, we went to Crystal Cave in Kutztown. I was awed by its gorgeous, natural quartz formations.

Dad stored rock specimens in several cardboard boxes in a closet in our basement. Sometimes he encouraged me to handle them. My favorites were embedded with rough gemstones and chunks of iron pyrite, also known as fool's gold.

Dad occasionally drove us to Pittsburgh, Pennsylvania and nearby Zelienople to visit Mom's extended family. A great-aunt and her husband lived in a small brick house. Behind their back yard was a single-wide, white trailer. One day, my great-aunt walked me to the trailer to introduce me to a big, black-haired woman who lived there alone. My great-aunt explained that Nellie had been a nurse, and was paralyzed from the waist down from a car accident.

Fascinated, I watched as Nellie swung her legs in either direction through the long trailer, balancing herself on wooden rails affixed to its walls. She showed me woven potholders and other items she'd hand-crafted, as well as her collection of postcards that friends sent her from their travels all over the world.

When I expressed an interest in the postcards, she offered to give them all to me. I was stunned by her kindness, more so when she offered to be my pen-pal. After that, I wrote back and forth with her on a regular basis. Every time we visited my great-aunt, I immediately went to Nellie's trailer to spend more time with her.

Sometimes, when we visited my mother's parents in Laureldale, we walked at night to a nearby miniature golf establishment. I looked forward to buying a cone of swirled, soft-serve ice cream from a nearby food stand.

One summer in Reiffton, my oldest brother's best friend gave us a large roll of red tickets for a carnival in a nearby wooded area. We sneaked to the carnival one night, fascinated by the dancing women, small gambling trailers, and other attractions that were clearly meant for grownups. The people there were nice to us. When Dad found out, however, he forbade us to go again. He said it was run by "filthy gypsies." Still, I was glad we'd gone–it was an adventure!

Because my oldest brother's large bedroom was in the attic, we often played up there for hours at a time, when we couldn't go outside. One Christmas, our parents gave him a hobby kit that included a miniature oven, metal molds, and tubes of Plastigoop. We spent countless hours making colorful rubbery bugs, miniature snakes, and other Creepy Crawlers.

One August, I was with Mom at her parents' house. My birthday was in a couple of days. She said that my present was on the back porch. When I opened the storm door and looked out, I saw a white cardboard box. I cried as I heard mewing and saw a tiny paw poke through a hole. I named my black and white kitten "Snoopy," because he investigated every piece of furniture in our living room. I dearly loved him.

One of my favorite school field trips was to the chocolate factory in Hershey, Pennsylvania. I was fascinated at how the little Hershey Kisses were manufactured by big machines, then wrapped in silver foil. At the end of the tour, each visitor received a big chocolate bar. Afterwards, we went to the amusement park. Even the street lights looked like giant Hershey Kisses!

When Dad drove us home from Laureldale to Reiffton, we often stopped at the Pagoda, a seven-story building atop Mount Penn. We climbed several sets of stairs to look at the city of Reading far below. If we were below the mountain at night, we could look up and see the Pagoda's multiple roofs outlined by bright red-orange horizontal lights. On some of my worst nights, its consistent presence was soothing.

On warm summer days, I always looked in our yards for four-leafed clovers. I shared them with my brothers so they would have good luck, too. I also liked to observe and play with bugs. I especially looked for praying mantises, because they were supposed to bring good luck.

Every spring, tent caterpillars invaded the stunted crabapple trees at a nearby high school. I kept the squiggly creatures in a big glass jar in my bedroom until I gagged from the inevitable stench.

I often caught fireflies in the small yard behind our paternal grand-parents' house in the upper end of Laureldale. Grandma gave us glass jars to keep the bugs in. I marveled at how they blinked in the dark. Sometimes my brothers, younger cousins and I played kick the can and freeze tag in the yard.

In the daytime, we stood behind the house and waved to the men who stood in the engines and cabooses of passing trains on a railroad track beyond the back yard. We jumped and shouted happily whenever they waved back.

Buttercups grew wild in the grass near our house in Reiffton. I rubbed the small yellow blossoms' pollen on my nose and upper lip, fascinated by the petals' shininess. Our next-door neighbors' cherry trees were full of lovely pink blossoms in the spring. Sometimes, when they gave me permission to break off a small branch, I took the cloud of blossoms to my favorite school teacher.

Large maple trees flanked both sides of our street. My brothers and I called the seed pods "helicopters" because they rotated in circles as they floated to the ground. We opened the sticky pods and placed them on our noses, pretending to be rhinoceroses as we playfully charged at each other.

Sometimes in the summer, locusts flew up into the tall trees to attach themselves to the bark and shed their shells. The night was often filled with their rhythmic buzzing. We would sell their empty shells to neighbors for five cents apiece.

Mom's mother grew roses and other lovely flowers in her yard. Each summer, we plucked colorful snapdragon blossoms and pinched them between our fingers to make their "mouths" talk.

My favorite flowers, Queen Anne's Lace and chicory, grew wild along roads and highways. The blue chicory flowers nicely contrasted against the tall green grass. Each white Queen Anne's Lace blossom was really a large cluster of hundreds of tiny, individual flowers. The blossoms reminded me of snowflakes–so delicate and intricate!

This is how I preferred to know my life. Although I thought this was the whole story, I lived another life that I was unaware of.

Infancy

My birth certificate states that I was born in the Reading Hospital in August of 1955. I was first child in my generation of our extended family. My first home was a second-floor apartment in downtown Reading.

Although some authorities on memory claim that people cannot retrieve memories of infantile experiences, I believe they are in error.[1] I've had many flashbacks of lying on my back in a wooden crib in a room. When I turned my head to one side, I saw a dark brown door frame surrounded by a light colored wall. I explored with my eyes and mind. Although I couldn't talk, I could observe and anticipate. Sometimes my mother entered the room and walked towards my crib, avoiding my eyes as she silently changed my diaper.

When the shadows grew longer, my gut spasmed as I recognized the tall outline of my father in the doorway. His eyes were cold and gray; his hair short, straight and dark blond. His posture was erect, his figure lean. He changed my diaper and more. I looked into his eyes as he gently caressed my tiny genitals with his fingertips. I enjoyed the pleasurable sensations.

Sometimes his eyes were expressionless as he looked into mine, while pushing a diaper pin into my tender flesh. I quickly learned that crying was useless, and endured the torture in silence.

Although my mother breast-fed me at the beginning, one day, Dad introduced the head of his penis after I'd suckled at her breast. Because I was a sucking machine, I did to the head of his penis as I had to Mom's nipples. Because Dad put sweet liquids on his penis at first, I enjoyed the sugary taste and soon adapted to the secondary taste of a clear, slightly sticky liquid. I acclimated to that taste before I could crawl.[2]

When I look at early pictures of myself, I do not see a child who was apathetic. For the first couple of years, especially when away from home, I still smiled and was curious about my environment. I don't think I would have done as well if Dad hadn't made regular, direct eye contact with me as he sexually stimulated me.

Dad sometimes volunteered to change my diaper, pretending to be a helpful father. As time went on, he pushed soft items into my tiny vagina, including dark red, canned Vienna sausages, then his pinkie finger, then his larger fingers–while using other fingers to manipulate my clitoris. That created waves of vaginal contractions that were so powerful, they hurt. As my vagina stretched, Dad gradually inserted grapes, hot dogs, bananas, and eventually his large, long penis.

By the age of four, I sometimes jumped up and straddled one of his legs. If we were in the presence of other adults, Dad pushed me away and said quietly: "Not now, not now." Later, if he had time, he took me to a private room and pleasured me. By then, I was totally addicted to his scent and touch, and to the orgasms.

As I grew older, one of the results of the ongoing sexual abuse was incontinence. Sometimes, when I played outside with my brothers, I wet my pants. They made fun of me as I ran home and hid my clothes in the washing machine.

Although I enjoyed vaginal orgasms, Dad also inserted his penis into my rectum. He used Vaseline and later, KY Jelly, as lubricants. Still, I felt immense pain and was often constipated.[3]

Early Childhood

In 1957, after my first brother was born, we moved to a rental home on Bellevue Avenue in Laureldale, several blocks up the street from my maternal grandparents' home. Because my parents didn't own a car at that time, Grandpa M. took Dad and me at night to meet with small groups of men in their homes. Grandpa M. seemed to know them well.

Some of the men digitally penetrated me as the others watched with lust or amusement on their faces. Because Dad didn't smoke or drink liquor, I was repulsed by their odors. When I wasn't being molested, I quietly watched and listened as they talked and joked. I noticed that Dad's laughter was different–the noise came out of his mouth in bursts that ended abruptly.

I also noticed that he seemed agitated when he didn't know what to say, or how to say it. Although he did whatever Grandpa M. ordered, Dad's body was extra stiff in the presence of those men.

Elementary School

After my second brother was born in 1961, we moved across town to a two-story, red brick home on East 36th Street in Reiffton, a sedate community. Already a tomboy, I found lots of places outside to play and hide.

I was painfully shy when I attended Reiffton Elementary School, a red brick building several blocks from home. Although I made good grades, I was frustrated when teachers wrote on the backs of my report cards that I was shy. I couldn't help it!

My inability to socialize created other problems. I was usually the last child chosen to be on a dodge ball team during recess. I tried not to cry when the leaders of the two teams argued about who would have to take me.

Still, school was important to me. It was my safe place. I do not yet have any memories of having been abused by any of my elementary teachers. They were my lifeline to sanity and morality.[4]

Because I received positive attention from the teachers, I worked hard to please them. They treated me as a good girl, worthy of attention and praise. From them, I learned to treat others fairly and to obey rules. They proved to me that some adults were fair and honest. I'm grateful that they cared about me, because they laid the essential foundation for my sense of morality and social responsibility.

Middle School

I transferred to a distant middle school for fifth and sixth grade, after being tested and placed third highest in its top, accelerated class. For the first time, I rode a bus to school. Although I was proud of my good grades, I now became the daily target of a snobbish clique of girls. For two years, whenever they harassed and belittled me in front of the other students, I didn't know how to respond assertively. I did try to become friends with the blond leader, but when she just laughed at me, I wished the floor would swallow me up.

One afternoon at home, I sobbed to Mom that I couldn't take their torment anymore. Instead of comforting me, she said I should do as she had in school: "Laugh with them; then they won't know they're getting to you." The next day, the clique made fun of me for laughing at myself when they did. Every day after that, I cried and stayed as far away from my classmates as I could.

Although we were told to eat lunch together at the same table in the cafeteria, no one in my class would allow me to sit with them. I made books my new friends, because they didn't hurt me or make fun of me. I went to the school library and checked out every book I could, regardless of its content. I read each one from cover to cover. I read every encyclopedia and book in our home, including Mom's adult *Reader's Digest Condensed Books*. I read cereal boxes at the breakfast table. I read books during lunch in the school cafeteria, pretending that I preferred being alone.

Even when I went to Girl Scout meetings and troop campouts, I still had difficulty socializing. I continued to read books at every opportunity. They were my escape when reality was too painful to endure.

Ritual Abuse

Although I was almost always in emotional pain and had difficulty connecting to others, I successfully blocked out all memory of why I was that way. I still believed I led a normal life.

Although I had only one close friend, I did have my extended family. Whenever he could, Dad drove us to Laureldale on Sundays after church to visit with my mother's parents in the afternoon and with my father's parents at night.

On most weekdays (except for the summer), I went to school, then came home to feed and pet my cat, do my homework, perform chores for Mom, and then play outside with my brothers and the neighborhood boys–if they'd let me.

I didn't know that I had amnesia about psychopathic Friday night rituals that Dad officiated.[5] In most of those rituals, cats or dogs or humans were tortured and sometimes killed; adults raped me and other children and even animals with abandon; blood was smeared and drunk after it was mixed with opium and red wine; and knives and stabbings were an integral part of the group structure.

When I was only four years old, Dad started making me kill babies, his hands forcing mine. Each time he made me kill a precious baby (really, he killed it), he said that either I would do exactly as he said, or he would kill the baby himself, after giving it additional pain. Dad never made an idle threat. When I resisted, he immediately tortured the infant and laughed, forcing me to watch.

Although the guilt of killing the babies was unbearable, I knew they were better off with my killing them as quickly and painlessly as possible, than if my father tortured them first.

I couldn't possibly live in both my home and ritual worlds with a single mind and consciousness. I'm certain I would have either gone insane or died from the cumulative emotional shock and physical pain.

Since he kept me up late during those rituals–going to bed around 3:00 AM was the norm–I was often sleep-deprived the next day. Exhausted, I sometimes accidentally slipped into a trance state. When I did, I had flashbacks of the rituals. The strange words spoken at them poured out of my mouth. To a psychiatrist unfamiliar with ritual chants, my words might have sounded like "word salad," a kind of gobbledygook spoken by some people who suffer from schizophrenia.

Each time I did this, either Grandpa M. or another relative drove me in his car–usually a station wagon–to a flat-roofed, one-story facility some distance from the city. Mom usually sat in the front, passenger seat while I lay down on the back seat to keep from throwing up from motion sickness.

The driver usually parked just beyond a dull-colored, plain metal door on the right side of the building, near the back. Each time, I was whisked through that side entrance, then a short distance down the narrow corridor into the first empty room on the right.

Each time, I was made to lie on my back in that private room on a single-sized hospital bed, with my wrists and ankles in leather restraints. Up to my left, in a cement wall, was a white-covered window. The door to the corridor was across the room. It was also made of dull-colored metal with a small, criss-crossed, wire-reinforced window that a tall, putty faced, brown-haired man in a white medical coat occasionally peered through.

Whenever Grandpa M. brought me there, he talked to me alone in the room, reminding me that I had to stay there until I stopped "talking." After he was gone, the room became my safe place. Alone and undisturbed, I was able to remember what I unconsciously repressed at home.[6]

In that private room at the facility, I fully remembered the secretive, occult rituals. I remembered that Dad took me to several different buildings in the Reading area. I remembered a large, encircled hexagram on the floor of each ritual room–white if the floor was painted black, and black if the floor was light colored. I saw the flickering white candles that were placed carefully on each point of the star, where it touched the circle. I heard the otherworldly chants of my relatives and other adults who walked around the circle, clad in long black robes with pointed hoods.

I recalled ritualistic activities that my father and other adult cult members performed in those buildings. Their "sacrifice" might be a child to be raped, an animal to be killed, or–on special days–a (pure) infant or a child to be slaughtered. Afterwards, during the inevitable anticlimatic orgy, I was ordered to sexually service the adults.

I remembered another night when Dad took me into a large wooded park near our neighborhood. There, he bound me, naked and inverted, by my wrists and ankles to a big wooden cross that he'd laid on the ground. After he restrained me, he inserted a cattle prod into my stretched vagina and electrically tortured me in a way that quickly broke my mind, creating an alter-state that compartmentalized a deep and powerful rage.

During some of the indoor rituals, Dad told me that child sacrifice was sanctioned by God, because He had commanded Abraham to sacrifice his son. He also said that unholy communion–cannibalism and drinking victims' blood–was sanctioned because, after all, Christians professed to drink Jesus Christ's blood and eat His flesh during communion.

Dr. Black

Alone in the private room, I remembered more: Dad and Grandpa M. transported me to private meetings comprised of men who spoke fluent German. All of them boasted about being a Nazi, and bragged about their special heritage. One Nazi was neatly groomed with an erect posture. I knew him alternately as Dr. Schwartz, Dr. Black, Joseph, and Yusef, depending on which adult was talking to him.

The doctor (whom I'll call Dr. Black) was slim with short, slightly wavy, shiny black hair and dark, glinting eyes. He was intelligent and seemed to have a scientific mind. I once saw a narrow, gray metal slat (a brace?) beside his inside, right ankle. His shoes were shiny and black, and he usually wore a plain, neatly pressed black business suit.

These Nazis provided Dad much-needed respect and acceptance. He seemed unusually happy and relaxed in their presence, whereas most other groups of men made him stiffen.

In English, Dr. Black emphasized the importance of my learning their traditions and beliefs. He said that I and other children were bred to carry on their traditions, and to fight for their cause. He and an older man with straight, gray-blond hair recited phrases in German that I was instructed to repeat, verbatim.

Because I felt stressed from being with those men while also being conditioned at school to be pro-American, my mind developed two separate entities–a brown-haired American girl who only spoke English, and a blond-haired Nazi boy who spoke only German. I didn't have enough emotional strength to consciously be both at the same time.[7]

Undamaged

Still lying on the bed at the facility, restrained and unable to move, I also remembered that Dad forced me to participate in child pornography. When I was two years old, he had driven me to a town not far from Reading. As usual, he didn't explain where he was taking me. The sun shone brightly outside. We entered a building that had a large room with a high, white ceiling. In it was a large, white, possibly circular stage. Beside the stage stood a short man with wavy brown hair. He held a megaphone and called out instructions.

Across the hall from that big room, two beautiful, long-haired women dressed me in a sheer blue robe with a matching sequined border, and applied makeup to my face. As I walked onto the stage, I saw Daddy standing behind the middle-aged director, watching me silently. As ordered,

I lay down on my back. One of the pretty women rubbed herself atop me as if she were masturbating. Then a slim, blond man in a skin-tight, leopard-print suit did the same.

After that, one of the women led me into an unlit hallway and left me standing there. Alone for a minute, I tried to kill myself by beating my head against the hard, ceramic tiled wall. When that didn't work, I remembered how my favorite cartoon character, Casper the Friendly Ghost, made himself invisible and flew away without anyone seeing him. I instinctively developed a male child Casper alter-state that felt disappointed when the woman took him back to the dressing room. People weren't supposed to be able to see him! My Casper alter-state went under, and I came back into consciousness.

Again, the two women dressed me–this time in a sheer purple gown with a thin, purple-feathered border. I was again told to lie on the white stage, this time with my face to the floor and my stomach propped up on a pillow. The blond man from the first scene walked towards me with a small, black Scottish terrier. He flicked the tip of a black whip to either side of my face whenever I tried to move away, as the dog penetrated me from behind.

I felt great pain and tried to make my heart stop so the dog would be removed. I may have fainted, because when I awoke, a man wearing a white lab jacket held the round, cold metal end of a stethoscope against my little chest.

After that, I was dressed in one more robe–orange with a matching sequined border. While on the stage, I was told to walk towards a huge, muscular, brown-haired man with a handlebar moustache. He held a metal bar way above his head; old-fashioned barbells hung from either side. His engorged penis poked through a hole in his strongman circus costume.

When the director told me to hold the penis with my hands and suck it, I was confused. I was accustomed to doing that to Daddy in private! Ashamed, I obeyed. One brown-haired, clean-cut man standing beyond the stage was visibly upset. His facial expression helped me to know that what was being done to me was wrong. Because of that, I kept my sense of inherent goodness–in spite of my shame.

Afterwards, Dad drove me to a veterinarian's office, where I was examined and pronounced "undamaged." Wordlessly, he drove me home, never mentioning what had just been done to me.

Nazi Meetings

In the psychiatric facility, remembering and reliving the clashing memories of rituals, porn shoots, and secret Nazi meetings was too much for my young mind. Between school and church and these secretive events, I was being exposed to too many groups with opposing belief systems. Exhausted and lonely, I believed there was no one I could safely confide in. (Dad and Grandpa M. had repeatedly threatened that if I told a teacher about what they were doing, they'd kill him or her. This was another reason why I seemed shy at school.)

I felt despair as I reviewed what Grandpa always told me before he left me alone in this room: no one would believe me if I *did* talk, because the attending doctor (male, Caucasian, middle aged, short, balding with brown, straight hair) had written in my chart that I was schizophrenic. Grandpa repeatedly reminded me that "nobody believes schizophrenics–everybody knows they're crazy."

As I lay on the hospital bed, unable to move, I felt trapped. I had no escape and no chance of being rescued from the rituals and bestiality and the Nazi men. A major part of my core personality went down into my subconscious and didn't emerge again until the late 1990s.

In the interim, I allowed my father and other perpetrators to chip tiny pieces off the thick, concrete shell I built around that part of my original core self. They could have the outside, peripheral parts of me, but I would never again allow them to touch that part of me. I instinctively knew if they ever reached and broke my core self, I would die.[8]

Dr. J

When I was about four or five, Grandpa M. and Dad took me to meet with another man. Unlike most of the CIA MKULTRA-contracted psychiatrists I was subsequently exposed to, Dr. J didn't use an alias.[9]

Dr. J was probably the most proficient practitioner of mind-control I ever met. He was nearly emotionless when he conditioned me. Over the years, he told me that he wasn't defeated by mental defenses, because he used them to advance his own purposes. He either agreed with me or he totally ignored my resistance. He knew what my worst traumas were, and he also knew which spoken words would trigger my memories of them.[10]

He seemed to quickly pick up on and use people's psychological vulnerabilities against them. He noticed that I had the need of a father's love, since the only "love" I got from Dad was in the form of pain, terror and sex.

Dr. J took over where Dr. Black left off, as a "fatherly" doctor-figure in my life. Dr. J would pat my head and say, "Good little girl." Dad had never said those words to me. And so, despite all that Dr. J did to me, I looked forward to seeing him again.

Before I entered kindergarten, Dr. Black had tried to use the tactic of becoming my "loving father" substitute, but he wasn't successful because he was always emotionally cold–a true Nazi. And he enjoyed raping me, which made him too much like my real dad.

In my earliest recovered childhood memory of being with Dr. J, I sat alone and naked in a fetal position in the middle of a whitish linoleum floor in a fairly large, white-walled laboratory room, alternately screaming and crying, snot and tears flowing unchecked. I didn't understand that I just had been dosed with a hallucinogen. Nobody came to comfort me. It was such a horrible feeling, knowing that something terrible had happened in my mind and in the room, while fearing that it would come again soon.

Dr. J sometimes wore strange costumes. He even dressed in drag (women's clothes and makeup)–something I saw no other MKULTRA psychiatrist do. This time, he entered the lab wearing an adult-sized cat costume with no face mask. As he approached me in that costume, I hallucinated again. His face changed and I felt that I was going insane.

As the "cat," Dr. J said English words to me in nonsensical patterns, as if creating his own language that he expected me to remember. I can't remember the words now, but they sounded as if he had adapted them from Lewis Carroll's children's classic, *Through the Looking Glass.*[11]

After Dr. J left the room and I was alone again, I saw things that one would only see in nightmares, never in daytime reality. I knew that what I saw was not possible, yet I saw it clearly.

Then suddenly he was back. He'd changed costumes–this time he was a big white rabbit with long, white and pink ears. He talked about following the white rabbit and going down into the rabbit hole.

Then he picked up a real, dead, full-grown white rabbit by its ears from a silver metal table and swung it, slamming it again and again against the shiny white ceramic tiled wall until it was smeared with the rabbit's blood. I trembled violently as I wondered, would he do the same to me?

Then he walked towards me and stood in front of me. As I stared at the blood on the tiles and at him in the absurd white rabbit costume, he said, "There is no white rabbit." . . . as if to say, what I had seen did not exist, so there was no point in telling anyone, because only I saw it and therefore for everyone else, it simply did not exist.

I knew that Dr. J was the crazy one, not me, because of what he did to the rabbit, and because he wore those costumes and acted especially crazy when he wore them. The man had no more shame or embarrassment about his bizarre behavior than the Mad Hatter.

At home after that, I sometimes had hallucinatory flashbacks. When things "changed," taking on a form I could see but no one else could, Grandpa M. again smirked and ordered one of several relatives to take me to the side entrance of the facility to be restrained.

Even at that age, I knew I was not crazy. I decided that I must be having "daymares." But because they weren't nightmares, *I had no way to stop them.* When I had nightmares, sometimes I could tell myself in the middle of one, "This is a nightmare; I need to wake up now." But when I was drugged and hallucinating, or having hallucinatory flashbacks, I couldn't stop it until it wore off. Sometimes I was assaulted for hours by the worst visions and experiences possible. No escape, no way out. And because I was regularly taken to rituals where I saw killings and dismemberments, my small mind had a lot of horrific material to process during those bad trips.

Notes

1. In *Memory and Abuse: Remembering And Healing The Effects Of Trauma*, Dr. Charles Whitfield explained the ongoing debate over recovered infantile memories:

> A common tactic of FMS advocates is to attack the credibility of survivors who remember having been abused before age three or four–whether or not they have always remembered it. They use the "infantile amnesia" variation of the "false memory" defense. But many

people can and do remember traces, fragments or even the majority of traumatic experiences from this early age. (pg. 25)

2. When I remembered this event, I wondered if I'd unconsciously fabricated it. Several years later, I read *Trance Formation of America* and discovered that Cathy O'Brien, one of its authors, had remembered that her father had done the exact same thing to her as a baby. (pg. 81) Why did our fathers do this? Was it strictly for their own pleasure? Were they hoping we would bond with them instead of our mothers? An even more horrifying thought flitted through my mind: was this an early phase of our sexual programming?

3. One of the ways the FMSF and other detractors have tried to discredit survivors of childhood abuse, is by claiming they have no medical records to prove their stories. I have remembered, as have many other mind control survivors, that our parents took us to doctors who, for whatever reasons, helped to cover-up for them during our medical examinations.

4. Bobbie Rosencrans, MSW explained why school became my safe haven: "Although some were initially wary of school, some daughters found they loved the safety, structure and basic fairness of most elementary school classrooms. School may have been their retreat from painful family life." (pg. 180)

5. "More compelling and less consciously available dimensions of denial are when memories of gross violations are so threatening to the psychological and physical integrity of the survivor that recollections are literally split off from consciousness." (Woodcock, pg. 44)

6. Carla Emery explains this form of memory recall:

> Revivification is not based on current memories, recollections, or reconstructions. The present itself and all subsequent life and experience are blotted out during this type of hypnotic event. The memory tape plays. The subject relives the experience. Revivification is very different in subjective experience, and objective significance, from reenactment. The reliving of revivification is compelling, vivid, and experienced as "now." (pg. 234)

For more information about memory recovery and hypnotic programming, see Emery's website at http://www.hypnotism.org.

7. In *Bluebird: Deliberate Creation Of Multiple Personality By Psychiatrists*, Dr. Colin Ross presented information about the CIA's and US Army's joint project PAPERCLIP and two other related projects, NATIONAL INTEREST and PROJECT 63: "Through these programs, over 1000 German scientists and their families were secretly brought into the United States without State Department scrutiny or approval. Recruitment of German scientists through PAPERCLIP and related projects continued into the 1980s." (pg. 3)

When I remembered the secretive meetings in the 1990s, I was willing to accept that Nazi war criminals had been brought into the US by our government. However, I didn't want to believe that some of them could have been the men I'd met at those meetings. I mentioned my concern to a journalist who tracked Nazi activities in America. In February, 2002 he told me about an article he'd found on the Internet, "New Jersey and the Nazis." Its author, Hans Wolff wrote:

> . . . an important segment of the New Jersey Germans were pro-Nazi before the war and also gave safe haven to Nazis after the war. As we will see, these Nazis also included many Eastern Europeans and Russians, including the elite and largely White Russian SS VorKommando Moskau, which organized the killings of Jews and Slavs in Nazi occupied Eastern Europe and Russia. (pp. 1-2)

This article helped me to understand that even if the Nazis I met didn't actually live in Reading, Grandpa M. and Dad could have easily driven to nearby New Jersey to meet with them there. It also explained several other odd memories I'd recalled, in which Grandpa M. had taught me about White Russians, their political importance, and their plans to regain control of Mother Russia.

8. "The dimension of life-threat may be primary for symptoms of fear, anxiety, hyperarousal, and intrusive memories. The dimension of social-betrayal may be primary for symptoms of dissociation, amnesia, numbness, and constricted or abusive relationships. High levels of both life-threat and social-betrayal characterize many of the most severe traumas." (Freyd and DePrince, pg. 142)

9. Because this book doesn't have enough pages to hold all of my memories of childhood programming sessions, I will mainly focus on four programmers: Grandpa M., Dad, Dr. Black/Schwarz, and Dr. J.

10. Laura S. Brown explained verbal triggers when she wrote that "memory is considered to be state-dependent, and recall is frequently contingent on the re-creation of certain internal or external cues associated with the original event or experience." (International Handbook, pg. 200) In *Memory and Abuse*, Dr. Charles Whitfield also explained state-dependent memory:

> We tend to remember better when we are in the same inner or experiential state that we were in when we first experienced or learned something . . . If our internal state is different in the present from what it was during the original experience, then we may have difficulty remembering the experience or event . . . memories acquired in one neuro-psycho-physiological state are accessible mainly in that state, but they are dissociated and less available for recall in an alternate state. (pp. 44-45)

11. Given how crazy-making Lewis Carroll's book can make readers feel, it's no wonder it was used extensively in mind-control programming. If, when

reading the following excerpt, you temporarily feel your mind short-circuit (even if only for a split-second), that is when you are most vulnerable to hypnotic suggestion:

"But I don't want to go among mad people," Alice remarked. "Oh, you can't help that," said the Cat. "We're all mad here. I'm mad. You're mad." "How do you know I'm mad?" said Alice. "You must be," said the Cat, "or you wouldn't have come here." Alice didn't think that proved it at all; however she went on, "And how do you know that you're mad?" "To begin with," said the Cat, "a dog's not mad. You grant that?" "I suppose so," said Alice.

"Well, then," the Cat went on, "you see, a dog growls when it's angry, and wags its tail when it's pleased. Now I growl when I'm pleased, and wag my tail when I'm angry. Therefore I'm mad."

Sexual Abuse

Dissociation

Because I endured many different kinds of trauma that were perpetrated by many different people over a period of more than thirty years, I also developed many different kinds of alter-states and personality fragments. Some were instinctively modeled after the *perceived* personalities and belief systems of the adults who hurt and betrayed me. For instance, I created a Dr. J part, numerous Dad parts (each one visualized as having dark blond hair and cold gray eyes), a Grandpa M. part, several Mom parts, a Dr. Black part, and more.

I also developed animal alter-states that were patterned after real animals' personalities. This was, in part, because Dad and other adults repeatedly put me in cages with the animals, instructing me to observe and become like them. By trancing and focusing on the animals' personalities, I was able to block out my fear of them until I was safely out of the cages.[1]

I also created alter-states that specifically compartmentalized the occult teachings from rituals. I believe that what I was forced to endure in those mind-shattering rituals was deliberate and pre-planned. Dad even assigned different names to the alter-states that he created during them.[2]

Orgies

At many of the rituals, especially those held on Friday nights, I observed the adult members as they seemed to use orgies to release their tension after the gory ritual sacrifices. I figured that they must fear Dad as much as I did; after all, what guaranteed that he wouldn't become angry at them and use them as the next sacrifice? I knew this was possible, because we'd watched him murder several adult members, always using the excuse that because they'd betrayed him, he killed them to "teach" the rest of us not to talk to outsiders about what we witnessed in the rituals.

During the orgies, I created alter-states that blocked out unpleasant scents, sounds and memories by focusing both on my sexual pleasure, and on successfully pleasuring the adults–male and female. What they did to me sexually was wrong, but because two of the men showed me small kindnesses, I emotionally bonded with them.

Parental Dissociation

Although I may have been genetically predisposed to dissociate during times of great stress, switching into separate alter-states was also modeled to me by both of my parents.[3]

When we lived in Laureldale, I stayed at home with Mom while Dad went to work at a factory. On at least two occasions, Mom took me up a flight of stairs into what was probably the attic of our rental house.

Each time, she used a twisted, white bed sheet to hang me by my neck from an exposed wooden rafter.[4] When she did this, her voice became a little girl's. She seemed to verbally reenact what someone had done to her when she was a child. Then her voice became a strange, older adult's and she said ugly things to me. Each time I started to pass out, her voice changed back to normal and she asked me what I was doing up there.

She also repeatedly put me inside a wooden peach crate in what may have been our basement. Sometimes I stayed in it for hours, cramped and in pain. When she came downstairs to look for me, she "rescued" me from the crate, asking how I got in there. Because she didn't seem to remember, I saw no reason to tell her that she was responsible.

Because Dad was an electrical, chemical and mechanical engineer, he was familiar with electricity and its many types of conductors. After we moved to Reiffton, he used some of his tools and live electrical wires in the basement to torture me. At those times, his voice and facial expressions changed. He grinned oddly and his voice went up about half an octave. He often sing-songed as he tortured me. Even though he hurt me badly, I felt protective towards him. Because he was not an adult at the time, I mentally took his place, convinced that *someone* had to fill that role! (This was how I created several "Dad-the-torturer" alter-states that were later used by professional handlers to interrogate others.)

The telling factor in each of these situations was that my parents became amnesic strangers and did things that they didn't seem to remember afterwards. For this reason, I believe that both parents had alter-states that perpetrated some acts that they had no conscious knowledge of.

Unbeknownst to Dad, I developed many "home" alter-states in a futile attempt to adapt to my parents' unsettling changes and shifts in personality.[5] This was a good thing, because those child alter-states preserved my sense of being good and decent when adults poured their shame on me.

The effects of my parents' dissociation continued to influence me when I was an adult. Because I had felt protective towards Dad when he regressed into a sadistic child alter-state, I later gravitated towards men who switched into child alter-states, feeling equally protective and maternal towards them. If they hurt me, I blocked out their abuse in the same way I had, when Dad had switched and then tortured me.

Pedophilia

Dad raped me regularly after we moved to Reiffton. To keep me in bed at night, he convinced me that alligators lived under it. He said that they would bite my feet if I left it.

My heart pounded when I had to go to the bathroom in the middle of the night. I nearly screamed as I bounced off the bed, landing as far from it as I could, then sprinting into the bathroom. When I prepared to crawl back into bed, I first lifted the covers and bent down to see if any creatures waited to snap at my tender little feet. I became so afraid of the alligators that no matter what the temperature was in our house, I covered my feet with a blanket.

If I left the bed, the alligators might bite my feet. If I stayed in bed, Dad might rape me again. I developed a child part named Annie (based on my middle name) that compartmentalized the feeling of utter hopelessness and the memories of Dad raping me in my own bed.[6]

Although Dad continued to sexually assault me, he seemed more interested in molesting boys. He often used my unsuspecting brothers to lure neighborhood boys into playing touch and tackle football on a grassy upper field at the nearby high school. Behind our house, Dad also erected a basketball goal. Again, he encouraged the children to play with him. At the time, I didn't understand why Dad didn't encourage the boys' parents to play with us. Now, I believe he wanted every possible opportunity to touch the children's bodies, undetected.

According to a letter that Dad wrote in 1989, he was also an advisor to the Catholic church's St. Catherine's Orphanage in Reading from 1960 to 1964. He taught Math and English to some of its child residents, and repeatedly invited his favorite male student to spend nights in our home. I believe that Dad used his volunteer work at the orphanage for the primary purpose of accessing more child victims.[7]

In the summer, we often walked several miles from Reiffton to a membership swimming park. When he wasn't swimming in the adult section, he lay on a big towel on the grass, propped up on his elbows. In the same way that some men like to watch beautiful women in swimsuits, my father lusted after the innocent children.

He had a certain look when he was sexually aroused by them. His upper eyelids closed halfway like a contented feline's and his lips became full and soft. Many years later, I grew nauseous when I found an old photo of a trusting young female cousin sitting on Dad's lap . . . he had the same expression.

When I was an adult, Dad sometimes forced me to attend secretive pedophile meetings where he told the listeners, mostly men, that he chose to cultivate a six-month "relationship" with a boy before he made his first sexual move. He said once the boy believed that Dad loved him, he knew the boy wouldn't tell anyone that Dad had "approached him sexually."[8]

Sex Equaled Love

Although they'd had plenty of opportunity, neither Mom nor Dad ever–to my memory–privately held or caressed me in an unselfish, nonsexual way. Mom also never told me that she loved me, although she did sign, "Love, Mom," on letters and greeting cards when I was an adult.

Mom didn't say good things about me, other than that I was smarter than she and that I resembled my father's only sister. I considered that a compliment, since Dad's sister was warm and loving towards me in a respectful way.

The only holding and touch I received from Dad, other than spankings and torture, was sexual intercourse–although gradually I also blocked out those memories.[9] Sometimes, after he had finished raping me, Dad would say, "I love you, daughter." Because this was the only time that he said he loved me, I mentally paired love with sex. Lying beside him on the bed he normally shared with Mom, I felt warm and wonderful inside. I believed I was lucky to have a dad who gave me special love and attention!

My sexually conditioned alter-states looked forward to our "special times." Whenever Dad made fun of Mom, as we lay alone together in the bed, my alter-states felt superior to her. Dad encouraged me to believe I was his wife, and that Mom was the usurper.

Kiddy Porn

Even more unacceptable to society than parental sexual abuse of children, are the actions of parents who film their children being sexually abused, and then sell or swap the pictures and videos with other perpetrators.

I have repeatedly remembered that as a child, I was often given to adults to be sexually violated, both in and away from rituals. I've also clearly remembered being raped by a succession of men for porn shoots that Mom, who was there to supervise me, called "soap operas."

I was used in a lot of pornography, both as a child and later as an adult. Dad told me that some of the kiddy porn films that he forced me to participate in were sold for a profit on the black-market to other voyeurs and pedophiles. Most people do not understand that pornographers can make big money by selling illegal pornography that can include bestiality, snuff (murder), and kiddy porn.[10]

I'm glad most parents are genetically "programmed" to love and protect their children. Unfortunately, a healthy emotional bond never existed between me and my parents. They were both broken on the inside, and had turned to sexual perversions to physically and emotionally satiate their desires. They had found and associated with other broken people for whom what was unacceptable to society, was eerily "normal."

I still mourn the loss of not having had a mother and father to love, protect, and make me feel good about myself. I sometimes wonder what my life would have been like if they had. I also think about the many children in our country who are being hurt in frighteningly similar ways. Although I am free to heal my wounds, tragically, many victim-slaves are still imprisoned in one of a number of brutal pedophile and black-marketing networks.[11]

Some people may want to believe that these predators, and groups of predators, are rare. I believe this is a fallacy, because I have met many career pedophiles who seemed to network in sophisticated ways. I was present at some of their secretive meetings, where Dad was so brazen, he happily presented information on how to sexually ensnare children and then use them for pornography. Kiddy porn, child prostitution, and child slavery continue to be highly lucrative trades.[12]

Comfortably Numb

Because of the sexual assaults and torture, I became physically numb. Even when I walked into furniture, I felt no pain and later wondered at my bruises.

In the early 1990s, when I began to remember, my body woke up in tandem with my mind. The following changes in my body suggest to me that at least some of the memories were real:

Before I began to remember the rapes and torture, my blood pressure usually hovered somewhere between 90/60 and 80/50. Now, my blood pressure averages about 120/80.

Before recovery, I couldn't sweat–this was dangerous in hot weather. Now, I sweat as easily as most people.

Before I remembered the abuse, my hands and feet were constantly cold. I always wore socks to bed. Now, my extremities stay warm most of the time.

In the past, I rarely felt physical pain. Now, I feel pain as soon as I hurt myself. This change angered me; dammit, I didn't want to feel pain! A therapist helped me to understand that feeling pain is important, because it signals when I am injured, so that I can attend to the injury.

Before recovery, most of my sexually addicted alter-states required pain to be able to experience sexual pleasure. Now, because my body is much more sensitive to touch, and because I've remembered the source of the original pain, I no longer need pain to enjoy an intimate relationship with my husband.

These and other physical transformations have indicated that I was in a trance-state before I remembered. Physical disconnection had been important, because I couldn't dare to feel my body during sexual assaults and torture sessions–the pain could have killed me. I feel grateful that at those times I was able to dissociate and numb my body.

Notes

1. One of those experiences was unexpectedly beneficial: Dad put me in a cage with a relaxed, older lioness. Although I initially feared that she would eat me, she instead let me lie in front of her elongated torso, my back to her abdomen, and then

she put her large right paw atop my left side. Feeling her closeness and warmth was probably the closest I ever came to experiencing maternal nurturing.

2. In *The Osiris Complex*, Dr. Colin Ross wrote:

> The only time personality states are deliberately created and named by parents, according to the information we are getting from MPD patients in North America, is in cults. In Satanic and other types of cults, apparently, personalities are deliberately created to carry out certain ritual tasks, to hold post-hypnotic instructions, and for other purposes. (pg. 137)

Some self-described "authorities" on ritual crime and recovered memories–including Kenneth Lanning (an FBI employee) and FMSF spokespersons–have publicly insisted that no proofs of ritual crime in the US exist, and that alleged survivors and their therapists are fabricating "false memories." I find it difficult to believe that these professionals are so inept that they are unable to locate proofs that are openly available to the public.

In the 1990s, a pro-survivor organization, Believe the Children (BTC) published a long list of documented occult crimes, most of them perpetrated within the US. To review an online version of the BTC's Ritual Abuse Report, go to the PARC-VRAMC website at http://parc-vramc.tierranet.com and click on "BTC RA Report." Karen Jones' "Satanism and Ritual Abuse Archive" contains newer information about such crimes. It can be found at http://www.newsmakingnews.com/karencuriojonesarchive.htm.

3. Carla Emery explained the process of spontaneously switching from one altered state of consciousness to another: A fugue is a spontaneous, complete dissociation. Persons with split personality are in fugue when being an alternate persona. The original personality is amnesic for the fugue period. M.H. Erickson called such a trance an example of posthypnotic behavior which erupts from the unconscious up "into the conscious stream of activity and fails to become an integral part of that activity" (*Nature of Posthypnotic Behavior*)—unless the subject later manages, or is enabled, to remember. (pg. 230)

4. Because of this and other physical traumas, the muscles in the back of my neck are always tight and painful. Some professionals now believe that fibromyalgia can result from injuries done to muscles, ligaments and tendons during physical and sexual assaults.

5. Dr. Colin Ross wrote: "It is common for adult women in treatment for MPD to describe clear evidence of MPD in one or both parents, which can include clear descriptions of switching and names of parental alter personalities." (*Osiris Complex* pg. 199)

6. For the child who depends on an abusive caregiver, the situation demands that information about the abuse be blocked from mental mechanisms that control attachment (bonding) behavior... the closeness of the victim-perpetrator relationship

impacts probability of amnesia. Amnesia rates across a variety of studies appear to be higher for parental or incestuous abuse than non-parental or non-incestuous abuse. (Freyd and DePrince, pg. 142)

7. Like other pedophiles, Dad sought physical contact with as many children as possible. In the late 1980s, Dr. Gene Abel and his associates interviewed sex offenders who were clients, guaranteeing them confidentiality. Few people were prepared for the results of their study:

> Two hundred and thirty-two child molesters admitted attempting more than fifty-five thousand incidents of molestation. They claimed to have been successful in 38,000 incidents and reported they had more than 17,000 total victims. All this from only 232 men. Men who molested out-of-home female children averaged twenty victims. Although there were fewer of them, men who molested out-of-home male children were even more active than molesters of female children, averaging 150 victims each . . . Despite the astounding figures, most of these offenses had never been detected. In fact, Abel computed the chances of being caught for a sexual offense at 3 percent. (Salter, pg. 11)

8. Why would Dad brag to other pedophiles about the techniques he used to entrap and sexually molest children? Anna C. Salter, Ph.D. explains:

> The truth is that many sex offenders like to talk about their exploits—
> if it can be done in some way that doesn't hurt them in court. They are
> proud of what clever fellows they are. Narcissism is their Achilles'
> heel. (pg. 5)

9. I not only blocked out memories of feeling terror, pain, and horror; I also blocked out memories of having felt very ashamed. This often occurred when I was forced to do something that I knew was socially unacceptable–especially if I enjoyed the activity. This included orgasmic "sex with" Dad and other adults. Some pedophile organizations claim that children's enjoyment of sexual stimulation is "proof" that children want sex with adults, and that children shouldn't be kept from "doing it with" adults. These molesters seem to miss the point.

Children and even adolescents are grossly underdeveloped–sexually, physiologically, emotionally, and even mentally. I firmly believe that any adult who willingly and repeatedly takes advantage of a vulnerable child's natural inclination towards pleasurable sexual stimulation should be kept completely away from children until and unless that adult is sufficiently rehabilitated and truly understands the depth of the pain and damage he or she caused in the child victims' minds and lives.

10. In the 1990s, when I remembered decades of forced participation in porn shoots, I felt embarrassed and worried that some people might still own revealing films or pictures of me. I also feared that someone in my new life might accidentally come across them. Another fear arose from threats that Dad and other handlers made

when I was an adult: they would send porn pictures to my neighbors and co-workers if I didn't stay silent. My way of dealing with that last fear is that if such pictures ever surface, I'll use them as verifications of my past enslavement.

11. In August 8, 2002, the Associated Press reported arrests made for crimes, perpetrated by a group of adults, that were painfully familiar:

> WASHINGTON – A group of parents sexually molested and photographed their own children and swapped pictures over the Internet, forming what one man called "the club," said US Customs Service officials who announced charges Friday against 10 Americans and 10 Europeans.
>
> Forty-five children were victimized, including 37 Americans ranging in age from 2 to about 14, said Customs Commissioner Robert C. Bonner.
>
> "These crimes are beyond the pale," Bonner said. "They are despicable and repugnant."
>
> The suspects are men except for Bente Jensen of Denmark, who was charged along with her husband . . .
>
> "What is particularly disturbing about this case is that the majority of the people who have been charged were actually the parents who were sexually exploiting their own children," Bonner told a news conference.

As I read the article, I wept for the children and also for myself–for the hell we've all endured. I also felt grateful that someone cared enough about their welfare to intervene on their behalf. Now they have a chance to experience normal childhoods.

12. To learn more about the child black-marketing trade, read *The Commercial Sexual Exploitation of Children in the US, Canada and Mexico*, published in September of 2001. It can be obtained via the Internet at http://caster.ssw.upenn.edu/~restes/CSEC.htm, from the University of Pennsylvania, School of Social Work, Center for the Study of Youth Policy, 4200 Pine St., 3rd floor, Philadelphia, PA 19104-4090, or by phone: (215) 898-5531.

Two websites, http://parc-vramc.tierranet.com and *The Finders Case* at http://www.gregoryreid.com/id87.htm provide information about an investigation (reportedly thwarted by the CIA) into organized child sexual abuse, black-marketing of children, criminal occult ritual abuse, and kiddy porn, allegedly perpetrated by members of the CIA-connected Finders cult in Washington, DC.

Family Matters

Physical Conditioning

Before I was born, Dad was a celebrated cross-country runner. (Albright, pp. 96, 104–105) In 1960, he barely missed representing the United States at the Olympics in Rome. I suspect because he saw his children as extensions of his own ego, he wanted each of us to also become star athletes. He took us almost every day to the race track at the nearby high school and used a stopwatch to time us as we sprinted in the grassy field or ran long distances on the encompassing oval cinder race-track. He also entered us in local children's track meets. My brothers did fairly well, but because I was overweight, I came in last every time. Each time, Dad berated and belittled me in front of the other participants and their parents.

My Father's Sadism

Although I always knew Dad had a cruel streak (forcing me to run when I hurt was a good example), I wasn't able to remember the rituals, the torture sessions, or the rapes. Still, I always felt fear and anxiety in his presence. I knew something was very wrong with him.

After we'd moved to Reiffton, Mom bought a record album, *The Best of Spike Jones & His City Slickers*, from a city bus driver for Dad's birthday. Delighted, Dad constantly played the record. He especially played a parody of *My Old Flame*. In that song, the singer pretended to set fire to his lover. As Dad listened, he grinned in a childlike way, baring his teeth. His laughter and facial expression scared the crap out of me. His other favorite song on the album was *You Always Hurt the One You Love*. It could have been his theme song. Another song, *Der Fuehrer's Face*, made fun of Hitler. I think Dad may have enjoyed that particular song because he sometimes chafed against his Nazi mentors' rigid control.

Over the years, he amassed a large collection of long-playing record albums. He especially loved big bands, jazz, movie soundtracks, and classical music. He repeatedly forced me to sit in the living room and listen to some of them. One was an orchestral version of the *Red Shoes Ballet.* Each time he played it, he told me the story of the girl who found a pair of magical red shoes that she believed would help her become a good ballet dancer. When she couldn't remove the shoes, they made her dance until she died from exhaustion. Dad said the girl was punished for being selfish. After that, I stopped asking for anything from my parents—I didn't want to die!

Another record included the *1812 Overture.* Dad laughed as I froze whenever I heard a set of notes that signaled the cannon blasts were coming. He turned up the bass so the walls reverberated, forcing me to listen to it again and again until I wasn't afraid of the booming sounds anymore.

Sometimes he unscrewed my bedroom's ceiling light bulb. I don't know how many times I entered my bedroom at night, terrified of the dark, and flipped the switch—to find it didn't work. He often hid in my room in the dark, waiting for me, then hurt or raped me. He sometimes unscrewed the light bulb after he tucked me into bed and laughed as he walked out of the room, knowing that I'd be too terrified of the dark to try to run to the bathroom.

Until I remembered those frightening experiences, I had recurring nightmares of entering my dark bedroom, the light switch not working, my heart thudding as I felt the presence of great evil in the darkness, then physical pain.

My cat, Snoopy, was the only warm-blooded creature I fully trusted. I don't remember how old I was when Mom gave him to me, but I probably had him for at least ten years. (When I was about to leave home and marry my first husband, she made me leave Snoopy beside a road far away from home, next to an opened can of tuna.)

Snoopy never betrayed me. Feeling his soft fur and the vibration of his purring kept me emotionally soft and connected. He often pulled me out of bad moods by rubbing against me and meowing, demanding to be held and petted.

Unfortunately, Dad decided to use Snoopy to control me. He knew that I dearly loved my cat and felt personally responsible for his safety. I was a constant nervous wreck, because I knew Dad could hurt or kill him at any time. He used my fear of what he could do to Snoopy to ensure that I obeyed him and didn't tell neighbors about our family secrets.

Whenever I showed a spark of defiance towards Dad at home, he picked Snoopy up and petted him while baring his teeth at me. When my shoulders drooped, he put Snoopy down. I got the message; he didn't need to say a word.

Dad also knew I was especially concerned for my youngest brother's safety. Sometimes I felt as if I were his mother. Although I feared what Dad could do to Snoopy, my greater fear was that Dad would kill my brother. Recognizing my instinctive drive to protect him, Dad repeatedly threatened that if I didn't do exactly what he said, or if I ever told outsiders what went on in the house, he would kill him. Although I didn't remember Dad's threats after a while, I still felt the terror. I remained hyper-vigilant whenever my little brother and I played together in the house. Alert to the sound of Dad's heavy footsteps, I usually tried to distract Dad and keep him in a good mood by telling him about my good work that day at school.

Whenever Dad caught us saying an unacceptable word, he made us stand in front of the basement sink as he rubbed a bar of soap, hard, on our teeth and sometimes on our tongues; then he told us to stand there. When I cried and begged him to let us wash our mouths out, he grinned at my discomfort. Even now, I cannot stand the taste of soap or shampoo.

By punishing us for cussing, he magically made himself appear moral. Because his behavior created cognitive dissonance in my mind, I unconsciously blocked out contradictory memories of the times when he was amoral and dangerous.

Dad's favorite form of sadistic abuse at home was "spanking." The sexually voyeuristic abuse usually went like this: first, Mom was angry about something we did. When Dad came home from work, she told him we needed a spanking. Dad called us into their bedroom while Mom went into another part of the house. He made us stand in a row beside their bed and then told one of us to get his brown, plastic hairbrush from their medicine cabinet. I shook and cried when he told me to bring it to him. (One day, I hid the brush. I learned not to do that again.)

One at a time, he made us pull down our underpants and bend over the bed. He said in advance how many spankings he'd give us. His arm was strong and the spankings were very painful. On one occasion, he lost control of his anger, and used the bristle side of the brush to make hundreds of bleeding pinpricks on my buttocks and upper legs.

(Mom was upset about that–not because he'd hurt me, but because he'd made noticeable marks.)

Usually, Dad kept control and spanked us very slowly. He'd hit us once and then wait until we felt the full intensity of the pain.[1] That increased our fear of being hit again. I usually cried and begged him to please not spank me anymore. He usually responded by saying, "You'd better stop crying or I'll give you something to cry about!" His words made me feel crazy, because they suggested that I had no reason to cry when he hurt me.

After Dad spanked us and went into another part of the house, Mom hugged us and angrily said that Dad was a bastard. And yet, the next time we misbehaved, she started the cycle again.

When we attended Sunday morning services at our nearby Lutheran church, we always sat with our parents on a hard, uncomfortable wooden pew. We were not allowed to wiggle or talk as the pastor's voice droned on. Once in a while, Dad let Mom bring coloring books and crayons to keep us quiet. More often, Mom shared a small pad of blank paper from her purse that we were allowed to doodle on with tiny church pencils. Sometimes, Dad allowed us to draw on our church bulletins.

He often fell asleep during the sermon–sometimes he snored. And sometimes, when he awoke from his nap, he drew odd heads of Indians with lumpy, slanted foreheads, feathers coming out of the tops of their heads. He laughed when he showed us those pictures. I felt relieved when he drew them, because then I knew he wouldn't hurt us.

Sometimes, however, he grew angry as we wiggled, whispered, or dropped a pencil on the floor. That was when the mental torture began. With every movement or sound that we made, he raised a finger and wordlessly counted with his lips, staring at us. Each finger raised meant how many "spankings" he would give all three of us as soon as we got home. Of course, that upset us and we cried. Our tears meant even more spankings.[2]

When we lived in Pennsylvania, we only had one car. Sometimes on Saturday afternoons, Dad drove all of us to town. He usually dropped Mom off in front of a store, telling her he'd drive around the block while waiting for her. When Mom emerged from the store with packages in her arms and tried to open the locked passenger door, Dad moved the car away. Mom walked towards the car and tried again, fussing at him through the closed window. He again moved away. She tried again.

Eventually, he drove around the big city block while Mom waited by the curb, humiliated and angry.

When he finally stopped and unlocked the front passenger door, Mom climbed in and yelled at him. When Dad laughed at her, baring his crooked teeth, I laughed too. Then she turned her rage onto me, sometimes reaching over the seat and furiously hitting me as Dad kept laughing.

Dad's sadism spilled over in other settings, away from rituals and home. When he was given permission to torture me and other children in controlled laboratory settings, his sadism increased exponentially. With the CIA allegedly backing him, he could do anything he wanted, knowing he didn't have to worry about being arrested for his crimes against humanity.

This is the main reason why I am so angry about the CIA's MKULTRA program. Although it may have initially been created for good, it also basically gave carte blanche to sadists and pedophiles who took advantage of defenseless children in secretive settings.

One of Dad's programming techniques that he used in a building where he held rituals was to attach ropes to cages. Then he put me and other naked children in them (one per cage). He would use the pulleys he'd attached to the ceiling to pull the cages up into the air, jiggling us occasionally by jerking on our ropes to keep us off-balance and helpless. Sometimes he kept us in the cages up in the air for days. By doing this, he conditioned me to believe he had total control over me and my body.

He also took me to a laboratory in the Reading area that I suspect was in a Bell Lab building. The following is a journaled childhood memory that explains one way Dad successfully programmed my mind in that lab:

Pain, isolation, deprivation. Torture, training, total isolation in a dark, not black, soundless box made of metal. Dad poured his pain into me (via electrical torture). I became the repository for his pain. Pain kills. I was alone in that box . . . no one to talk to, no one who cared. *NO ONE.* He was master of horrors. He cut the kitten open alive, starting with its sweet tender stomach. It trusted him. It trusted him and he killed it. He said he was teaching me not to care. Then he put me in the box that was too small to stand in; I had to sit in it, one side open.

I saw the lab. I saw my father. The box was my only respite. And he let me decide when to come out again. He kept busy and patiently waited until I decided to come out again – to *HIM*. He forced me to choose to come to him, to be with him, no matter what pain he gave me. I became Frankenstein's lab assistant. His creation. Cold. Uncaring. Wooden. You are what is done to you. Do unto others what was done unto you; give out as has been given unto you. These were Satan's laws and he was Satan in the flesh. Satan is human pain-giving. Hate hate hate let the whole world hate. Kill kill kill let the whole world kill . . . all should have to feel as I feel and yet it is never enough. Never enough. I'm always back in the box. With the knowing and the pain.

The way that box worked, I sat in it with a roof, front and two sides completely closed, the "door" side behind me–my father left it open just enough so light from the lab came in between the top of that side and the roof of the box. The light from the lab was inviting and I was never totally in the dark. Dad knew I was scared of totally black places. It was like he was saying, "See how kind I am to you? I even make sure you have some light! And see, I'm not dragging you out–you have to want to come into the lab–you have to want to be with me." I had to turn around and crawl out on all fours.

When I opened the box and came out, I chose to be with him, with those men, in the lab. Tortured in the lab, then put in the box, no torture, then go back into the lab for more; tortured again. And no, I never learned to like it. I never liked the pain. Sometimes they didn't torture me–and when they didn't, it was even worse, because then I felt like I was becoming one of them.

Grandma M's Kindness

Unlike my parents, my maternal grandmother was often kind and attentive when I visited with her in her home in Laureldale.[3] When Mom started working as a secretary at a nearby insurance agency, Grandma took care of me, especially when I was ill. Every time I eat chicken noodle soup and saltine crackers, I still remember how good Grandma made me feel as I lay on her rough-textured living room sofa and watched afternoon soap operas with her. If not for Grandma and the kindness and positive attention I received from my elementary school-teachers, I might have broken all the way and become a willing sadist like my father.

Perhaps the kindnesses I received from others is also why I'm unable to hold onto my hatred towards Dad for what he did to me and so many others. I suspect he didn't have anyone to love and cherish him when he was hurt as a child. Maybe this is why he broke all the way and became a human monster.

I often visited my maternal grandparents in their old, two-story house. One day, as Grandpa worked in a small repair shop near the house, I grabbed a handful of roasted peanuts from his jar in a kitchen cupboard. I couldn't understand the fear on Grandma's face when she caught me. She begged me not to do it again, but I couldn't resist–they were so delicious! Fortunately, Grandpa never seemed to notice.

Grandma seemed to do whatever Grandpa told her to do. Sometimes she shook when she told me that I must be careful not to make him angry. Mom often called Grandpa "king of the hill," albeit never to his face. Although Mom seemed bitter and angry towards him, she still insisted that we go to their house at least once a week.

I didn't understand Mom's anger when Grandpa ranted about "niggers" and "kikes" and "Pollocks." I was too inexperienced to know that his words weren't part of a normal person's vocabulary.

Sometimes, I sneaked down their wooden, enclosed stairway that led from the kitchen into the basement. I sat quietly on a narrow, painted step and listened as Grandpa talked to men on his elaborate ham radio set. Although he often spoke in English, he occasionally spoke in German and several other languages that I didn't recognize. Although I didn't understand much of what the men said, I felt proud of Grandpa for talking to men who lived so far away. How many grandfathers could do that?

One day, he caught me sitting there. Angry, he yelled at Grandma to make sure I didn't spy on him again. Since I didn't want Grandma to get into trouble, I reluctantly stayed upstairs and gave him his privacy.

The family's need to protect Grandma from discomfort seemed extreme. When I became an adolescent, a teenaged male relative sexually molested me, several times, in their basement. When Mom asked me why I didn't want to go to Grandma's house anymore, I told her. Instead of comforting me or expressing anger that I'd been molested, she said, "You mustn't tell Grandma–it will break her heart." She never mentioned it to me, again.[4]

Grandpa M.'s Control

Before 1990, I didn't know that I had altered states of consciousness. I also didn't know that Grandpa M. had created several of them for his own future use. He had used a rudimentary form of torture to split my personality by holding the lit end of his ever-present cigar against my forearm when we were alone in his repair shop. The pain put me into a trance state. He then verbally implanted hypnotic suggestions. When he finished, he gave another suggestion that completely blocked out all memory of the torture–if I noticed the pain, he either said I accidentally brushed against his cigar, or burned it on another hot surface.

Back inside the house, he gave me a paper band from one of his cigars. I wore it proudly on my finger. Sometimes he even gave me an empty cigar box to take home. Because he tortured me sometimes and was friendly at other times, I both feared him and was loyal to him.

That loyalty was used frequently by professional handlers when I was an adult. I was conditioned to call Grandpa at home if I was on a state-side op that went awry. Whenever he answered the phone, I told him what had happened, and then he told me what to do. My child alter-states were always excited when handlers tricked them into believing we were going to Pennsylvania to see Grandpa.

Grandpa told some of my child alter-states that he worked for "The Company." He said he had been part of the O.S.S., which he called the "Old Guard." He seemed angry about certain changes that had been made within the Company. He told me he had personally recruited my father for them. From what I have remembered, Grandpa also seemed to have covert connections to at least several high-ranking politicians.

Racism

When I was a child, I only interacted with Blacks one time. At Dad's urging, our Lutheran church had donated its old wooden pews to a Black inner-city congregation. They responded by sending their choir to our church to give a concert.[5] Although I would like to believe that Dad had a soft spot for Blacks, I think he more likely went out of his way to seem supportive, even contributing money to a Black arts organization, so if anyone ever tried to accuse him of affiliating with local Nazis, those witnesses would effectively be discredited.[6]

At Aryan and neo-Nazi meetings in Pennsylvania, and later in Georgia, Dad often talked about Blacks' inferiority and their tendency towards violence–as if he had none.[7] Because I believed him and other Aryan leaders, I irrationally feared anyone with dark skin. Even when I was an adult, I was convinced (although I couldn't remember why) that Black men would want to hurt me because I was a white woman.

Dad and other local handlers occasionally transported me to run-down parts of large cities, making me meet alone with Black men for drug transactions. Sometimes the handlers drove away, leaving me alone with those strangers. Each time, I was terrified that the Black men would kill me. Although I blocked out those memories, the irrational fear kept me from interacting with Blacks.

Unlike Dad, Grandpa M. openly expressed his bigotry at home. And yet, he seemed to change in his later years. When I was in my thirties, Mom told me a lovely story: because he was a volunteer fireman, Grandpa was sent into the home of an elderly Black woman who had fallen out of her bed, breaking her hip. She was in great pain and cried out every time Grandpa tried to move her. He surprised himself by being gentle and empathic towards her. That experience changed his life and his attitude towards Blacks in general.

He also became more gentle and compassionate towards Grandma after she was stricken with Alzheimer's disease. Several relatives told me that Grandpa visited her almost every day in a local nursing home, doting on her.

Grandpa's changed behaviors proved to me that anyone has the capability to change and become a better human being. How ironic that the same man who I believe set me up to become an MKULTRA slave, eventually showed me how to recover my soul through his own life-example.

Interpreter

Although Grandpa M. told me that he had introduced Dad to the CIA, and also seemed to be Dad's primary handler in Pennsylvania, Dad told me that Dad had been "tapped" by the CIA to act as an interpreter for some of the Nazi immigrants that the CIA and US Army had secretively brought into the US. He said that because he was a native American who spoke German, he wasn't considered a security threat.[8] If Dad told me the truth about his recruitment, then I suspect it occurred after he enrolled at Reading's Albright College, where he earned a Bachelor of Science degree.

Although he had listened to weekly German radio programs as a child, and although his mother spoke fluent German at home, Dad hadn't seemed comfortable with the language until after he'd joined two clubs at Albright that focused on German language and culture.

The meetings of the first club, *Delta Phi Alpha*, Beta Psi chapter, were conducted in German and focused on "important and interesting aspects of German culture."

The monthly meetings of the second club, *Der Deutsche Verein*, included "folk songs, student talks on Germany, Christmas caroling, and films." Dad was vice-president of the second club for one year, and participated in both clubs during his last two years at Albright. (Albright, pp. 40, 70–71, 125)

This may have been a marked change in Dad, because his earlier 1948 Muhlenberg High School yearbook states:

> Bill . . . delights in chemistry . . . would rather run than study . . . member of "mad" track team . . . Mixed Chorus standby . . . plays bass horn in band . . . prefers Jarrof and Como records. . . *struggles in German class* [italics added]. (Muhltohi, pg. 43)

Nazi Recruitment

In 2003, when President George W. Bush ordered the US military to invade Iraq, he did so against the wishes of the majority of the United Nations, including two of its most powerful members, France and Germany. As a result of their governments' unwillingness to support our President's actions, many US citizens joined together to boycott their imports–some restaurants even changed their menus to show "Freedom Fries" instead of "French Fries!"

Although the animosity was strong between our countries during that time, it paled in comparison to the hatred most Americans felt towards Germans during WWI and WWII. Because Dad's mother was a

German-American, she and others in their community protected themselves by hiding their heritage. They did this by claiming that they were "Pennsylvania Dutch." Because I didn't remember being taken to meet the Nazi men and didn't know I was part German, I believed Grandma when she told me that I was instead part Dutch.

This was the environment Dad grew up in. He heard people call Germans "dirty Krauts" and worse. Some of the neighborhood boys even targeted him for brutal beatings, possibly because of his heritage.

Dad was forced to hide half of who he was. And yet, he was regularly exposed to German radio programs at home that surely would have encouraged him to feel proud of his heritage. The schism between who he was, and who he feared to let people know he was, must have been painful and crazy-making.

I believe this is the primary reason why he so quickly aligned with the Nazis he later introduced me to. Whereas he'd been made to feel dirty and ashamed for being half German, these men helped him to feel proud of his heritage. They also provided a form of paternal nurturing and acceptance that his own father hadn't been able to give him.

Once Dad emotionally aligned with these hardened Nazi immigrants, he never seemed to want to be anything else. And yet, because our country was still understandably biased towards Nazis, Dad again hid who he was.

Paternal Grandparents

According to family lore, Dad's father, a Welsh immigrant, was sold as a boy by his mother to a ship's captain, to pay the family's property taxes.[9] As an indentured servant (really, a slave), Grandpa was brought by ship to America, where he was eventually adopted and raised by an uncle who changed the boy's last name from Chirk to Shirk.[10]

I believe Dad's long-term minimization of the seriousness of Grandpa's mother's betrayal, and of Grandpa's subsequent slavery, may be one reason why Dad saw nothing wrong with using me and other children as objects to be bartered, sold, and abused.

When I was older, Dad told me more about his tumultuous childhood. (He also told the story to several other relatives.) When Dad was a child, his father was sometimes in a dangerous rage when he came home drunk at night. Dad said that more than once, his mother locked herself in the basement while Dad led his four siblings into the woods to hide all night. As the eldest child, he also seemed to suffer the worst of his father's abusive rages.

I believe Grandpa Shirk was a complex and wounded man. I believe he drank heavily to medicate deep emotional pain. Heaven only knows what the men did to him, a defenseless boy slave, on that long overseas voyage. And if his mother had sold him to strangers, what else did his childhood family do to him?

Still, Grandpa Shirk often gave me positive male attention–something I never received from my own father. Grandpa usually acted as if he liked me, and sometimes he talked to me as if we were the only two people in the room. Because he was often kind to me (although not always), I emotionally bonded with him, more than I did with Dad.

In the summer of 1968, I vacationed at my paternal aunt's house. One sunny day as I played in the back yard, she received a phone call. A relative told her that Grandpa had committed suicide in front of the church where he worked as a janitor. When she told me, I went into shock: "No! He can't be dead!"

The next day, after I'd returned to Laureldale, Grandma Shirk told me that Grandpa had stuffed a towel in the tailpipe of his car and had "gone to sleep" by inhaling the exhaust fumes. She said Grandpa had killed himself because the pain from his recent stomach cancer was too much to bear. Unfortunately, because Grandma didn't add that what Grandpa had done was wrong, I believed committing suicide to avoid pain must be an acceptable family tradition.

During the funeral service, Grandma led me and several younger cousins to Grandpa's coffin in the front of the room. She encouraged me to touch his cold, hard cheek with my finger. As I did, I realized that the one man I truly loved was gone forever. And as I rode with Grandma in the black limousine, my heart shattered. He really was dead. He was gone.

At home, neither of my parents ever discussed Grandpa or his death with me. It was if he had never existed.

For a long time after that, I had grief-filled dreams in which strangers drove me on a city street. Each time, I saw Grandpa walking along a sidewalk. I tried to break the car window with my feet so I could call out to him, but I was always too late. When I escaped from the car, he'd already disappeared. Each time I awoke, my pillow was soaked with tears.

Notes

1. Anna C. Salter, Ph.D., explained why sadists like Dad liked to prolong the agony of their victims:

    > The point of sadism is not indifference to pain. It is the deliberate infliction of pain and terror . . . Often sadists will tell their victims in advance what will happen to them in order to increase the terror . . . Rather than being indifferent to how others feel, they are exquisitely attuned to it. But suffering in others does not produce the same feeling state in them. Instead, it produces the opposite. Other people's helplessness makes them feel powerful. Other people's vulnerability makes them feel invincible. Other people's dying makes them feel alive. Other people's submission makes them feel dominant. (p. 108)

2. It's not as easy as one might think, to pick a sadist out of a crowd. I do not find it strange that most people didn't know Dad was one. Anna C. Salter explains why:

    > If you think that the sadists and the Ted Bundys of the world must somehow look different and can be spotted on the street, think again. Despite an extraordinary level of deviancy and callousness, they are often well ensconced in communities . . . Those sadists who were termed "more severe" (defined as killing three or more people) were considerably better adjusted and more successful than those termed "less severe" (defined as killing only one person), according to one study. For example, 43 percent of the more severe sadists were married at the time of the offense, as opposed to 7 percent of the less severe ones; 33 percent had military experience as opposed to none of the less severe; 43 percent had education beyond high school as compared to none; and a full one-third had a reputation as a solid citizen, as opposed to none of the less severe." (pg. 113)

3. Rosencrans explained how an adult survivor of child sexual abuse can have a poor relationship with her mother, and yet the girls in the next generation can have a positive relationship with the same woman:

    > Some . . . may be viewed and experienced by their grandchildren as much more positive maternal figures than the adult daughters have ever experienced them to be. This transformation may be a relief for the now-grown daughters, but it can also be painful. Their children may get from their grandmothers the nurture and safety that the daughters never received. The grandchildren may trust and love their grandmothers, even though the daughters may never be able to trust them, accept positive information about them as grandmothers, or love them. (pg. 80)

4. In my early twenties, I confronted that male relative by letter. In response, he apologized for what he'd done to me. This is the only apology I have ever received from a sexual abuser.

5. I mean no disrespect when I use the word "Black" instead of "African-American." I prefer to use that word when necessary, because some Blacks have told me they do not want to be called African-American since their ancestors emigrated to the US from other countries.

6. Throughout my life I have met many people, some of whom were politicians or ministers, who publicly professed to support Black rights while also being heavily involved in secretive Aryan organizations and activities. The same has held true for individuals, including ministers, who claimed to be staunch Christians while secretly practicing occult religions. My rule of thumb is this: the harder a person consistently works to "prove" how unbiased or Christian he or she is, the more likelihood I think there is, that the person is the opposite.

7. In 2001, I found a verification about racism and neo-Nazism in the Reading area. The article by Mark Stuart Gill was published in *Ladies' Home Journal.* Gill wrote about Bonnie Jouhari, a Black woman who had worked at the US Department of Housing and Urban Development (HUD) in Reading:

   > Through her work, she had discovered that 98 percent of minorities in Berks County lived in a ten-square-mile radius in the city of Reading. The other 864 square miles, with better, more affordable housing, were almost entirely white. Minorities who tried to move outside of the urban neighborhood met with stiff resistance . . . [Jouhari stated that] "there is a deeply entrenched prejudice that people here accept as a matter of daily life." (pp. 118–122)

   Because of Jouhari's work at HUD, she was targeted by two white supremacist leaders. She and her teenaged daughter were cruelly harassed as they fled from one state to the next. Although Jouhari eventually won a lawsuit against one of the leaders, she and her daughter were, at last report, still living in hiding. (pp. 118, 122–124, 190)

8. In the 80s and 90s, Dad continued to speak German fluently. At least once at its AT&T factory in Norcross, Georgia, Dad served as a tour guide for a group of visiting Germans.

9. In a 1989 letter to his second wife, Dad wrote: "My father was sold as a child." That part of Grandpa's history was confirmed to me in a subsequent letter from a relative who wrote: "Thomas Curtis Shirk was an orphan. His father died when he was a young boy. His mother hired him out to be an indentured servant. Then she died also." I have since learned that most Whites refer to their enslaved ancestors as "indentured servants" to avoid the feeling of shame that is attached to the label of "slave."

10. Dad often bragged that his father's side of the family had partial inheritance rights to the "Chirk family castle in Wales." I thought these claims were pure fantasy until I found proof of the castle's existence through the Internet. Although I found nothing that indicated that it had ever belonged to Dad's family, information about the owners' family coat-of-arms raised the hair on my arms:

> The Red Hand of Chirk
>
> There are interesting myths or legends about the origin of the red hand in the Myddleton coat-of-arms. One story tells of a dispute which arose between two youths of the family in the distant past, over inheritance of the castle. To settle the dispute it was agreed that the two youths would run a race, to finish with the winner touching the Castle gates. It is said that the first youth to reach out to the gate at the finishing line was deprived of victory by a supporter of his adversary, who drew his sword and cut off the youth's outstretched hand–thus the "bloody" hand. Another version of this story tells that they swam across the castle lake, and the first hand to touch the far shore was cut off.
>
> The second legend says that the red hand was put as a curse on the Myddleton family. It was said that the curse would only be removed if a prisoner succeeded in surviving imprisonment for 10 years in the Chirk Castle dungeons. The red hand still survives as part of the Myddleton coat-of-arms, proving legend says, that no one in history was able to live longer than 10 years in the terrible conditions of imprisonment at Chirk Castle.
>
> Another version of this story says that if a prisoner could stay alive for 12 years (without cutting his nails) he would inherit the Castle. A further story tells that one of the early Myddletons who was leading a battle, was badly injured. He placed his blood-covered hand on the white tunic he was wearing and left the imprint of the bloody hand. This then became his heraldic symbol (http://www.chirk.com/castle.html).

Basic Programming

Western Electric

Dad worked at the Western Electric (WE) factory in Reading for about thirteen years. I have a wood-framed "good luck" caricature of Dad that one of his co-workers drew for Dad when he was preparing to transfer to a position at another WE factory in Baltimore, Maryland. Most of his Reading plant co-workers added their signatures in pen. Occasionally, as I look at their names, I wonder if any of them were Nazi immigrants.[1]

I've had numerous recurring memories of one of my father's co-workers. The big, black-haired man, also named Bill, had a German last name. He was Dad's best friend for many years. Our family spent a lot of time with him, his wife, and their two sons who were about the same ages as my brothers.

I've repeatedly remembered that Bill's wife was one of Dad's long-term advisors, especially when Dad programmed my mind. She also attended some of his occult rituals. Although Dad despised women in general, he did whatever she said without balking. He genuinely seemed to respect her. I've had no memories of their having an affair, and don't know whether she truly cared about him or was merely controlling him.

Sometimes, when Dad wanted to take me to meet with the woman, he first instructed me to drug Mom so that she'd sleep while we were gone. Dad kept a small, brown glass container of liquid in an old paint can in a narrow basement closet with a green wooden door. As instructed, I used the dropper to surreptitiously put one or two drops of the liquid into whatever Mom was drinking–usually coffee. That always seemed to work.

Even away from cult settings, Bill's wife seemed to have a lot of power over our lives. Mom often depended on her for help and advice, from one mother to another. Bill's wife seemed to have endless patience with Mom.

Because Bill's wife was nice to me at times, I didn't hate her. I was not, however, emotionally connected to her–she was cold as ice. I did like her husband; he was often funny.

Because I didn't remember that couple's involvement in Dad's cult activities, I felt sad when Mom eventually decided we mustn't socialize with them anymore. When Mom told Dad (and us children) that Bill had asked her to have sex with him, Dad angrily refused to believe her and blamed her for his loss of their friendship.

I have two good memories about Western Electric. In the first memory, Dad took my brothers and me to the factory whenever the Navy's Blue Angels–a precision aviation team–performed an air show over the city of Reading. He let us stand on the roof for a clear view of their performance. I jumped and clapped as the jets flew overhead in perfect formation.

In the second memory, Dad brought home vacuum tubes from the factory that he had helped to design. One weekend, for "show and tell" at school, he helped me fasten them onto a wooden board. I felt proud when I showed my classmates what Dad had made.

Unfortunately, he also introduced me to a darker side of his work.

Experimental Laboratory

Dad repeatedly drove me to a large, red brick building in the Reading area, telling me that his work there was connected to his work at Western Electric.[2]

The multi-story building housed at least one upper-floor scientific laboratory, where Dad and other men wore white lab coats. In that laboratory, he experimented on white rats and guinea pigs that they kept in large aquariums atop long counters. Whenever I went there with him, Dad told me I was his guinea pig. I believed him. We entered the lab through a guarded door with a rubber seal that whooshed when it slid open. We walked along a short encased corridor, then through another whooshing door, into the lab. The scientists in it seemed to perform chemical experiments. This may explain why Dad was involved–after all; he bragged that was a mechanical, electrical and chemical engineer.

One afternoon in that big lab, Dad forced me to stand and watch a Caucasian, blond, clean-cut man standing inside a glass-fronted, small, sealed room. As I stared, the man's skin turned red as a lobster. Because I didn't see what happened to him after that, I believed Dad when he said that he'd died from radiation.

That horrible experience generated a series of nightmares that I've never forgotten. In them, the blond, red-skinned radiation monster chased me up and down the streets of Reading because I'd watched him die and had done nothing to save him.

After that incident, some of the lab scientists conspired to play a trick on me. One of the white-coated men would look agitated and yell that the radiation monster was on the loose: "Run for your life; he's coming!" Each time, I left through the sealed corridor, then quickly ran down several open flights of metal stairs, and then out past a solid door where, just beyond, Dad usually parked the car. Then Dad inevitably exited and drove me home, using back roads to confuse me about the lab's whereabouts. As usual, by the time I returned home, I'd completely blocked out having been to that building.

That same evening, Dad would force me to watch the weekly *Outer Limits* sci-fi television show. Sometimes it was about a lab-created monster. Although I always cried and begged him not to make me watch the program, he didn't relent. I was so terrified of the radio frequency sounds signaling the beginning of each show that professional handlers played them over the phone when I was an adult, to put me into a controllable trance-state.

Chain Programming

At home, Dad-the-engineer drew flowcharts of my "systems" of alter-states, leaving them on his easel in our upstairs screened-in porch. Because he drew the systems in code, only he and some of my alter-states understood what the charts represented. Those parts believed him when he told them he knew me better than I knew myself.

Although non-traumatic hypnosis could have effectively been used to control my mind, Dad clearly preferred using trauma-based programming to split it. To create a new *system* (group) of alter-states, he first triggered (called out) a primary alter-state that he'd previously created. When that alter-state emerged, he traumatized that alter-state, sometimes using electricity, until that part couldn't take any more pain. That part "went under," leaving another part of my mind conscious to endure the next trauma.[3]

Dad called this technique *chain programming*. He traumatized one alter-state after another, verbally assigning each one an individualized code name, until I stopped functioning altogether. When that happened, he knew he'd gone as far as he could. He'd start the next session on another day, again calling out a primary alter-state and then traumatizing that part to create another succession of linked alter-states and personality fragments.[4]

Somehow, Dad knew that if a trauma was familiar, a previously conscious part would emerge that had coped with that type of trauma before. The only way he could create new alter-states and personality fragments was to expose me to traumas that I hadn't yet learned how to cope with.

Using this technique, Dad eventually created over a thousand alter-states and personality fragments in my shattered mind. He assigned each one a code name that was later used by him and other professional handlers to trigger them back out into consciousness. He also took me to spend time with other adults, allegedly working for the CIA, who used more sophisticated techniques to program and train many of these alter-states.

Some of those professional trainers taught me how to use various deadly weapons. They especially used repetition to condition the split-off parts of my mind to respond so automatically while using those weapons, that during ops I used them without even thinking–similar to driving a car without thinking about how to do it. Not having to think about how to hold and aim a weapon probably saved my life many times, because even a second or two of extra response time could have easily led to my death.

I had the bad luck of being raised by a father who enjoyed hurting and terrorizing me and other child victims. He was a sociopath with no moral brakes. He often boasted that the sky was the limit as to what he could do to children's minds. He repeatedly told me I was his prototype, and explained if a technique worked with me, he'd use it later on other children.

How could any group of adults torture and brutalize innocent children for years? I'm not sure I have an answer, because that reality is still so horrific to me. Nonetheless, some do enjoy it.

The following is a childhood memory about a professionally run programming facility that I and other children were taken to, mostly by our parents.

I was exposed to torture/kill training when I was no older than eight, in a "school" housed in the same building where I was taken by relatives when I had flashbacks. I believe it may have been set up, financed, or both, by the CIA to condition children in controlled alter-states, to become future assassins.[5] In special rooms in the middle of the same building, we were also forcibly exposed to radiation and more. Whenever he was present, Dr. Black seemed to be in charge of those forms of experimentation.

We slept in that middle section of the building until our training was complete. This seemed to take place in the summer because we wore warm-weather clothes. Mostly brick, two-story houses with slanted roofs were in a row across the road from the facility. The facility itself was tan or red brick on the outside, with a wide, mustard-colored band that seemed to have been painted around the perimeter of the recessed, upper external wall atop the building's otherwise flat roof.

I was taken there at least twice by my parents in the summertime for special training. Although my parents indicated they knew what was being done to me there, I do not know if all of the other parents were aware that their children were being traumatized. I believe the teachers and trainers were, in part, sifting through the groups of children to determine which ones would be likely candidates for future ops.

One of the most upsetting things they made us do there was to use sharp knives to gut teddy bears they had given us, in a big shower room in the back, left side of the building. (Sections of the building were given alphabetical codes–A, B, C, and so on.) The teachers also used modeling clay to fashion life-sized heads with faces, then taught us how to assault the faces with our fingers and hands–especially gouging the eyeholes.

More benign classrooms were in the front part of the building, where relatives brought the children and picked them up. Those adults may not have been aware of what went on in other parts of the building. During our classes in the front rooms, we were taught various subjects, including how to conduct ourselves at social events. One time, some of the girls and boys were taught how to behave during a mock tea party.

This is the first of several facilities I've had memories of having been taken to, as a child, to be programmed and trained for future use by– I believe–the CIA and some of its affiliates.

Wizard of Oz

Dad, Dr. Black, and other mental programmers often used movie and storybook themes and characters to create alter-states and systems of alter-states in the minds of their child victims. *The Wizard of Oz* was known among programmers as the "base program" movie for child victims in my generation.

Each year, Dad forced me to watch the movie on television, even though I cried and begged him not to make me. This was before the VCR was invented. The Wicked Witch of the West and her monkey soldiers always frightened me, as did the tornado that lifted and carried Dorothy in her house from Kansas to the Land of Oz.

Later, Dad hypnotically imprinted the identities and personalities of several of the movie's characters onto a succession of blank slate alter-states that he'd created through unusually severe torture. Several of these alter-states were later used on black ops.

One was given the name, *scarecrow*. This part of my fragmented mind was hypnotically conditioned to believe he had "no brain," and therefore was completely obedient and suggestible to whoever triggered him out.

My *cowardly lion* alter-state compartmentalized much of my fear, and never emerged outside of handlers' control. Keeping my fear separated was crucial on ops because otherwise, I might have hesitated or frozen instead of thinking and acting quickly.

The alter-state that Dad and Dr. Black seemed to prize the most was given the code name, *tin man*. That male alter-state was created for the sole purpose of performing assassinations in my adult years. Based on the movie's character, this part had "no heart" and therefore couldn't emotionally connect with other humans. (Because this part believed he was male, he also didn't feel intimidated when he went one-on-one against larger, muscular males.)

My Wizard of Oz programmed alter-states were also conditioned to believe that Washington, DC was *Emerald City*.

In the movie, the tornado transported Dorothy away from her homeland, Kansas–which represented my normal home life. The phrase "over the rainbow" was used to mentally "transport" me from my normal life to the ops world, with the symbolic rainbow hypnotically bridging them.

When I was an adult, I unconsciously identified my Wizard of Oz programming to potential handlers via personal checks with rainbows printed on them, and a rainbow sticker I had placed in my car's back window.

Dad also reinforced the programming by giving me, as a birthday present, a large, faceted Australian crystal that he told me to hang inside a window at home. Whenever the sun shone through it, many tiny "rainbows" moved back and forth on the opposite wall. (I also hung a crystal from my car's rear-view mirror.)

In the movie, Dorothy was told to click her ruby slippers and chant, "There's no place like home," to go back to Kansas. When a handler took me home and parked in front of my residence, he or she said that same phrase. As I heard the words, I mentally clicked my ruby shoes and switched back to my home alter-state. Believing that I'd been given a ride home by a coworker, I exited the car and walked into my residence. I'd already been conditioned to never look back at the car to see who was driving.

Although the *Wizard of Oz* was the primary movie that was used to program my mind, Lewis Carroll's books, *Alice's Adventures in Wonderland* and *Through the Looking Glass,* were also effective. Unique themes and phrases from the books and the subsequent Disney movie, *Alice in Wonderland,* were used to transport me mentally from my normal world into "Alice's World," where nothing was ever as it seemed, and insanity was always just around the corner. Anyone who knew that I had this particular mental programming could approach me in public, claiming to be the White Rabbit. Then, by saying "I'm late, I'm late," the handler–usually male–knew that I'd go into an immediate trance and follow him.[6]

Otherworld

"Otherworld" was another hypnotically implanted mental program that was used to convince many of my alter-states that when they emerged in strange places with spook handlers, they had been transported from my home life into another space-time dimension. This belief discouraged those alter-states from trying to find out where they were, and made them feel hopeless about trying to find a way back home.[7]

In "otherworld," nothing was real, and nothing had to reconcile with my regular world. Such knowledge kept me from being afraid. When I was in "otherworld," I believed I was safe from pain and mortal danger, because the programmer told me that no one ever was hurt or died in "otherworld"–after all, no one in it was real – including me!

An extra benefit to my handlers from this particular mental program was that, because I believed nothing in that world was real, I had zero fear of carrying out instructions on black ops. This was because I didn't fear being hurt or killed, and because I had no fear of being arrested–after all, the crime had never happened! This was probably the closest I ever came to experiencing what the mind of a sociopath must be like.

Greek Alphabet

When I became an adult, many of my programmed alter-states were "owned" or "time-shared" by groups and agencies who utilized my services. The rank of ownership went like this: first dibs went to a succession of individuals who held a high office in DC; then came individuals who allegedly worked within the CIA's Directorate of Operations; then came wealthy "owners," including a British tycoon and several influential DC politicians, most of whom had the power to (in some way) cover-up for some of the CIA's illegal stateside activities and its more questionable budgetary needs (most of these "owners" were connected to The Octopus); lastly came "lower level" covert associates such as occultists, pornographers, pedophiles, Nazis, and Mob members–they used me to do stateside activities.

This time-share plan was necessary because I only had one body. Those who personally "owned" some of my alter-states had to agree to wait their turn to use me. For this reason, some owners either purchased, or were given (for bartered favors), access to similarly programmed alter-states created in a number of adult slaves. This is why a surprising number of mind-control survivors reportedly had the same owners, and it is also why many of them have discovered alter-states having the same programming and code names.

To the best of my knowledge, Dad was put in charge of arranging my schedule and negotiating with those who used me.

Having access to a personal slave gave some of my owners a sense of power, prestige, and control that they might not have otherwise experienced. They were confident I would not be able to remember who had instructed me to perform the crimes, or how I got into each situation. They knew I would do both the crime and the time if arrested, while they'd remain free to use other disposable, amnesic slaves at their beck and call.

I'm grateful that I was not caught doing their dirty work. If I'd been put in prison for what I'd had no choice about doing, I never would have received the professional help that I desperately needed, to remember and heal![8]

Daniel Ryder was one of the first authors I told about my CIA mental programming. He verified that the code-names of several systems of alter-states I had listed in 1991 were later mentioned by Dr. D. Corydon Hammond, a psychiatrist, at a professional conference in the summer of 1992. At that conference, Dr. Hammond described the CIA's Greek alphabet coded systems of implanted alter-states, based on information he had received from a remarkable number of recovering mind-control survivors and their therapists.[9] (I have never talked to or consulted with Dr. Hammond.)

To the best of my understanding, my *Alpha* alter-states compartmentalized memories of my primary traumas. Dad created them first, and then traumatized each of them to create more fragmented alter-states as parts of my "chain programming." My Alpha system included personality fragments (information storage parts) that compartmentalized what were code-named *mind files*. To the best of my understanding, these parts of my brain stored information that was hypnotically implanted by several individuals operating at high levels in our government, to be retrieved by them as needed. This ensured that no paper trail would be left behind.[10]

Several of my Alpha-programmed alter-states also couriered verbal messages, diamonds, Krugerrands, illegal drugs, and arms. Unfortunately, some of these parts were also used to transport child slaves to several D.C. politicians who are probably still hard-core pedophiles.[11]

My *Beta* alter-states were sexually conditioned and trained. Some programmers referred to them as *Barbie* parts. Handlers used them in prostitution and pornography–particularly bestiality, kiddy porn, snuff films, and necrophilia. When I was a child, several of my Beta alter-states were used to sexually blackmail drugged or inebriated politicians. In my adult years, my Beta alter-states were used to sexually service and blackmail both men and women.

My *Delta* alter-states were trained to do covert operations. Although these alter-states often performed assassinations, they also participated in hostage interventions, protection of individuals who were in danger of being assassinated, body-guarding of politicians and other VIPs, and the training of future slave-operatives.

My *Theta* alter-states received specialized psychic training. Children like me were chosen for this training because, as abuse victims, we were highly sensitized to the moods and thoughts of others–especially of our abusers.[12]

I am convinced that certain individuals working within or contracted by the CIA were aware of the trauma-paranormal link long before most mental health professionals "discovered" it.[13] I believe the ongoing suppression of this information and the clever demonizing of these human abilities has occurred because the CIA, and other intelligence agencies that have also funded psychic research, have a vested interest in keeping the knowledge away from the public domain.

I've had recurring memories of receiving part of my childhood Theta training from James Jesus Angleton, a CIA counter-intelligence chief. Perhaps because he knew I attended a Christian church every week, he used New Testament scriptures to teach me to expand my consciousness.

He started my mental training by reminding me that Jesus Christ had said that anything He had done, we could do *more so*–with our minds. Angleton then taught me that the biggest block for people in accessing and utilizing their natural psychic abilities was their belief that they could not, or must not, do it. He taught me that if I chose to bypass that mental block, I could do anything I wanted with my mental energy, even telepathically moving a mountain, as long as I believed that I could.

To the best of my memory, Angleton worked intensively with me, one-on-one, conditioning my mind to process problems and experiences away from rigid societal rules and mores. He said this would always be my ultimate edge: while my adversaries would respond in ways in which they'd been socially conditioned, I'd use unexpected methods and weapons to attack and defend (e.g., using a concrete floor, a tiny, sharp stone, or a pen as a lethal weapon).

Sometimes he gave me a deck of cards and watched as I played solitaire. When I laid the king card down first, then the queen and jack, he asked, "Why not put the two on top of the king, then an ace? You can put the cards down any way you want." If we played checkers or chess, he made similar statements.

He said the human brain has potential that we haven't even begun to tap into. He encouraged me to use as much of it as possible.[14]

Other mental programmers further conditioned my Theta alter-states to believe they could read the minds of other people, communicate with some of them telepathically, and perform what is commonly known as remote viewing. Some of this training may have been successful.[15]

My limited experience with remote viewing involved sitting in a room while being observed through a two-way mirror. I was taught to send out my mental energy like a radio signal, to contact the mind of a person in another location. I was taught to assess that person's physical health and to see their environment through their eyes. I do not know, to this day, if it was my imagination or if I really "saw" what was occurring in the other person's life. At that time, however, I believed the ability was real.

I was also taught to place my palms on another person's body and channel the energy from my body into the person's body, or to draw out the person's pain or illness.[16]

When I was an adult, my Theta capabilities were fine-tuned as I served as an intercessor and prayer warrior in several Christian churches. If these abilities are legitimate, then I do not believe they are anything other than human. I do, however, believe they could be considered part of the forbidden fruit mentioned in the book of Genesis, since a person using them might feel godlike. I choose not to use my Theta training any-more–not out of fear of demons, but because I simply want to respect the mental, emotional and physical boundaries of others.

My *Omicron* alter-states were handled by Mafia individuals when alleged CIA employees from the Directorate of Operations wanted stateside hits performed. I will neither divulge details of those hits, nor will I identify any of the individuals who handled me within the Mafia. They are extremely dangerous people, and I intend to live a long and healthy life.

Notes

1. According to a Western Electric website at http://home.earthlink.net/~rhodyman/rdgworks.html, WE personnel in Reading, PA performed classified work for the US government, even in the early 1950s:

   > Operations in Reading began when Western Electric converted a nearby knitting mill in Laureldale into a factory that produced devices for the US government for use by the military and the space program.

2. When I told a private investigator (a former WE employee) about this building, he said that it may have been owned by Bell Laboratories. He further explained that engineers who worked for Western Electric were required to work for six months in Bell Labs facilities as part of their employment.

3. The CIA had experimented on the minds of its own employees, to create controllable, amnesic alter-states. In *Bluebird*, Dr. Colin Ross cited CIA Artichoke documentation about a "series of cases" in which alter-states were hypnotically created:

> A CIA Security Office employee was hypnotized and given a false identity. She defended it hotly, denying her true name and rationalizing with conviction the possession of identity cards made out to her real self. Later, having had the false identity erased by suggestion, she was asked if she had ever heard of the name she had been defending as her own five minutes before. She thought, shook her head and said, "That's a pseudo if I ever heard one." (pg. 33)

4. Carla Emery reported similar mental programming that Pavlov performed on the minds of dogs:

> The **breaking point** is a physiological event. Abuse causes the ego, the "I," to shrink, pull back, and weaken until, finally, exhausted, it gives up. Pavlov named that moment of giving up the **ultraparadoxical stage** . . . [William] Sargant argued that anything that causes temporary cortex overstimulation and collapse has the healing effect of loosening up old programming patterns, thereby allowing the implant of new ones . . . Pavlov stressed dogs, through deconditioning, into the ultra-paradoxical crisis. After the breakdown, he conditioned new habits into them. Sometimes, he put the dog through the whole routine again: stressing it into another breakdown, and then retraining into [it] yet another set of habits. (pg. 426)

5. In *Bluebird*, Dr. Colin Ross wrote:

> Manchurian Candidate [assassin programming] work was done under MKULTRA Subproject 136, which was approved for funding on August 23, 1961. *The deliberate creation of multiple personality in children* [italics added] is an explicitly stated plan in the MKULTRA Subproject Proposal submitted for funding on May 30, 1961. TOP SECRET clearance status for the Principal Investigator on Subproject 136 had been initiated by the Technical Services Division of the CIA at the time the Subproject was approved. (pg. 61)

6. Although the following links between the CIA and *Alice in Wonderland* might seem coincidental, please note that in both articles, this is the only book that was mentioned:

- "A Tour Through 'Hell Week': A Newsweek correspondent takes the CIA spy tests," by Douglas Waller 4/12/93: "Much of spying is making sense out of Byzantine secrets. One personality test has 480 true-false questions: 'I like *Alice in Wonderland* by Lewis Carroll'; 'I gossip a little at times.'" (pg. 33)

- AP Washington 4/30/94: "CIA chief plans to fix flaws in scarred agency: 'But I will not espouse the judicial philosophy of the Red Queen and *Alice in Wonderland:* sentence first, verdict after,' [James Woolsey] said."

7. A similar program was also installed in my mind by a stocky, brown-haired, brutal, alleged CIA programmer who used the alias "Spencer." His program was triggered by the phrase: "Spencer's World."

8. This is the main reason why I and other recovering mind-control survivors feel deep concern for slave-operatives who are arrested. Most of them are immediately approached by Company-contracted psychiatrists who pretend to befriend them (as Patty Hearst, Timothy McVeigh, and Jack Ruby were compromised by Dr. Louis Jolyon West and others). By being assigned a Company-connected psychiatrist, slave-operatives have no chance of experiencing true recovery through the help of *legitimate* mental health professionals—especially if they are put to death before they can receive such help.

9. To find an unauthorized transcript of Dr. Hammond's historic presentation on the Internet, use the words "Greenbaum Speech" as your search term.

10. When I found some of these odd personality fragments, I remembered that when they were previously activated, they had verbally given the information like ticker tape coming out of a machine. I seemed to have unconsciously memorized the information in such a way, that because I recognized that none of it belonged to me, it was kept totally separated and undisturbed until recalled. One of my dilemmas upon finding the stored information was: what should I do with it? I decided it will remain my personal property—after all, it was put in *my* brain!

11. I delivered verbal messages from US politicians to influential persons in other countries, and also delivered "messages from God" to mentally programmed Christians who accepted the orders as coming straight from God. The majority of these Christians were members of Charismatic, Baptist, and Pentecostal churches.

12. In *The Osiris Complex,* Dr. Colin Ross wrote:

> According to my model and data, speaking analogically, the genes for dissociation and the paranormal are closely linked to each other on the same chromosome . . . any extragenetic factor that activates one tends to activate the other, since they are linked. Severe, chronic childhood trauma is one such factor . . . highly psychic individuals tend to be highly dissociative . . . trauma opens a window to the paranormal. (pg. 70)

13. Dr. Ross wrote, "Although ESP is a universal aspect of human experience, it has been suppressed by the intelligentsia in the twentieth century, and is not a subject of mainstream psychiatric discussion or research." (*Osiris*, pg. 68)

14. When I first remembered having been trained as a child by Angleton, I thought I was fabricating these memories. How could I, just a child, have met with such a busy man? And even if I had, how could he have been connected to MKULTRA, when he'd overseen counterintelligence? Nearly a decade later, I found information that explained his connections to MKULTRA:

> The ARTICHOKE [pre-MKULTRA] Team must have been under the command of James Angleton, who was Chief of the CIA Counterintelligence Staff from December 1954, until 1974. Angleton was also involved in MKULTRA, as described in an article in the February 18, 1979 *Wilmington Sunday News Journal* entitled: "UD prof helps concoct 'mind control' potions." The article . . . mentions Angleton's involvement in MKULTRA. Angleton's name appears in "a list of all persons who have been briefed on 'Bluebird' [also pre-MKULTRA]." (Bluebird, pp. 27-28)

Several months later, I received a copy of an article, *James Jesus Angleton & the Kennedy Assassination*. Its author, Lisa Pease, explained one of Angleton's connections to Nazi war criminals, some of whom may have taught mind-control techniques to Angleton and other CIA personnel:

> . . . Angleton obtained access to the Ratlines the Vatican was using to move people out of Europe to safety abroad. Angleton and others from the State Department used the Ratlines to ferry Nazis to South America. (pg. 19)

15. In the early 90s, Keith Harary wrote a surprisingly honest article, "Selling the Mind Short: Exposing the Myth of Psychic Privilege," for *Omni* magazine. In it, he exposed the fallacies of several myths about "psychic" powers and abilities:

> Disseminating propaganda requires subverting rational thinking with seemingly plausible lies. I was a teenager when I first believed the lie that there was something about me or anybody else that could properly be labeled "psychic." A part of me felt sick when the label was used on me–the way I felt when I smoked my first cigarette. There was something compelling and forbidden about the experience, and something I also knew could eventually do me in down the line . . . the authority figures who sold me the bill of goods were parapsychologists at one of the field's major laboratories, who used the label "psychic" to explain my performance in a parapsychology experiment. That the mind is capable of remarkable feats is undeniable. Exploring the implications of this realization does not require resorting to extremes. It should encourage us to create a middle ground–one that defines human potential in human terms. If a higher perceptual, communicative, and thinking capability exists with us, then it cannot be destined to remain anomalous or denied by rational people or consigned to the realm of

the psychic and paranormal. It must be understood within the context of normal experience and achievable human potential and considered within the emerging framework of mainstream science. (pg. 6)

16. Frank Herbert's story, *Dune* and its subsequent movies were used by mental programmers to reinforce my belief in my ability to transfer my energy to other humans.

Horrification

House of Horrors

Richard Rhodes has written a fascinating book, *Why They Kill: The Discoveries of a Maverick Criminologist*, that presents the personal story of Lonnie Athens, a criminologist who specializes in the study of violent criminals. According to Athens, "dangerous violent killers" first must pass through "four separate stages of violentization": brutalization, belligerency, violent performances, and virulency.

Athens divided the process of the first stage, brutalization, into three sub-stages: "violent subjugation, personal horrification, and violent coaching." During violent subjugation, "authority figures from one of the subject's primary groups use violence or force [the victim] to submit to their authority." In the second sub-stage of brutalization, "personal horrification," the victim witnesses the violent subjugation of someone emotionally close to them. Finally, during "violent coaching," the victim is coached by a person in their primary group to perform violent acts. (pp. 112–120)

Unfortunately, I experienced all three sub-stages of brutalization in my father's occult rituals; my father was my personal coach.

Although Athens considers horrification to be the experience of witnessing brutal harm being done to others, I consider horrification to be more than that. In my opinion, it is a mind-bending experience that involves either witnessing harm done to others, or being harmed ourselves, by individuals or groups that either use horrific methods or perform the harmful acts within horrific environments.

I believe horrification is the primary emotional response of victims who are forced to participate in criminal, occult rituals–particularly children. During such rituals, both the methods used (e.g., intimidation, threats, torture, rape, ingestion of repulsive substances, mock or real killings of animals or humans) and the environments in which the rituals are performed (physical location, robed participants, candles, chants, frightening animals, ritual implements and symbols, and more) can easily horrify, scar, and even split the minds of child victims.[1]

During my childhood, Dad and several other cult members took me to numerous buildings and homes in the Reading area. One of the ritual locations was a large stone building on the side of what locals called Schuylkill Mountain, just outside the city of Reading. More than once, Dad ritually traumatized me in its underground dungeon.[2]

I have also vividly recalled that Dad made me crawl on my hands and knees into a large crawl space under a stone building, probably on the same mountain. The entrance into the ground-level crawl space was sealed by a square, flat-surfaced, hewn granite block that had been placed in the wall. Words were engraved on it. Behind the wall were bags full of the remains of many dead babies.

Dad made me lie atop the bags in the daytime while he met with men inside the building. As I lay perfectly still, I became one with the sweetly innocent dead. I felt safe because I believed no adult would want to crawl inside to hurt me. I desensitized to the pungent odor and became friends with it. This was a sad bonus when, as an adult, I was used to do body disposals. I can still easily differentiate between the odor of a dead animal and a human, because a decomposing human corpse smells sickeningly sweet.

Arson

Dad didn't limit his criminal activities to secretive rituals, rape, and pornography. Even outside the rituals, I saw more horror than any child should. He knew if he took me with him to commit crimes, nobody would believe he was responsible. He occasionally burned houses and other buildings at night, sometimes with people still in them. To this day, I detest the odor of gasoline.

He always seemed fascinated with fire. In the late 1960s, after our family moved to Georgia Dad set fire several times to a large wooded area near our house. Then he stood and watched excitedly as a fire truck came, its siren blaring. Each time, he claimed local teenagers had set the fire and acted like a hero as he helped the firemen put out the blaze.

When committing arson at night, Dad's prepared excuse for being in the locale was that I'd had a nightmare, and therefore he'd taken me for a walk or a drive. If he didn't commit the crime too late at night, he then took me to an ice cream parlor and bought me a butterscotch sundae.

The smell and taste of the delicious sundae blocked out the smell and taste of gasoline and smoke. By the time he took me home, all I could remember was the ice cream.

In the summer, after he'd performed a nighttime arson job, he sometimes searched fence lines for honeysuckle vines and encouraged me to inhale the blossoms' fragrance and suck on their nectar. This also blocked out previous smells and their attached memories. When we returned home, all I remembered was the blossoms' lovely fragrance.

Nightmares

Although he tried, Dad couldn't stop my repressed memories from seeping through into my dreams. I've never forgotten that most nights during my childhood, I awoke with a pounding heart and sweat-soaked sheets. Many times, my pillow was inexplicably soaked with tears. The bad dreams were so terrifying, I feared they would eventually kill me.

What I didn't remember during the day became my nemesis in the dark. I tried to avoid night terrors and dreams by reading books until I couldn't keep my eyes open. I cannot remember a single night that I did not have nightmares. I naïvely believed that everyone must have them as much as I did.

On at least two occasions, I woke up downstairs, standing alone in my nightgown. I had no memory of having walked down the stairs. Frightened, I screamed for my parents. Each time, Dad came and told me I had been sleepwalking, then carried me back up the creaking wooden stairs to my bedroom. Because I didn't understand what caused my sleepwalking, I felt embarrassed that I'd caused such a fuss.

Perpetrator Alter-States

I continued to compartmentalize unpleasant memories in alter-states, keeping them separate from my consciousness. I unconsciously fashioned some of them after the perceived personalities of adult criminals like my father. These parts were sociopathic, emotionally cold, and deadly.[3] Dad and other programmers called them "blank slate" alter-states, because they had zero memory of my life at home, church, or school. Having been created through extreme torture and mental duress, these parts initially emerged with only the most basic memories of how to dress, breathe, eat, walk, use the bathroom, and so on.

Because of their insane lust for ego gratification, my father and his cohorts seemed especially pleased to create alter-states that worshipped the ground they walked on. When I was an adult, these alter-states were used to perform crimes–always under the control of professional handlers–that I could not, and would not, have carried out under any other circumstances. Why is this?

For whatever reason, I was born with a naturally soft and caring heart. As a child, I cried and begged my oldest brother to stop when he pulled wings off of flies in the basement window as he laughed at them, or used the sun's rays through a magnifying glass to burn grasshoppers to death on big rocks.

I couldn't stand to see anyone, or anything, being hurt–and I especially would not allow myself to hurt them. Because of this, Dad and his associates used extreme torture and related trauma to break my mind and then create the blank slate alter-states that had no awareness of time other than the moments in which they existed.[4]

These alter-states were then conditioned to harm others without balking. I guess it takes a monster to create one.

Notes

1. In psychology classes, I learned that some of the early indicators of the development of anti-social personality disorder are: setting fires, cruelty to animals, property destruction, and an inability to emotionally attach to others. Antisocial personality disorder and *criminal* occultism may be directly linked, because such rituals often include fire and inhumanely sadistic acts perpetrated against animals, children, and even adults.

2. A correspondent who lived in Pennsylvania heard about my desire to find that building. In July, 1998 she sent me a pamphlet and photos of Stokesay Castle, a mansion that had been converted into a popular restaurant. The stone castle was located at Hill Road and Spook Lane, within walking distance of Reiffton. In an E-mail, she wrote:

   > There is a restaurant halfway up Schuylkill Mt. It's called Stokesay Castle. Before I ventured in there, I asked a waiter who was outside, how long it'd been a restaurant. He said 20 years. I went inside and

asked permission to look around and sure enough, there was your dungeon . . . Upon reading a pamphlet of theirs, I found that the castle was . . . kept as a summer home until 1956 when [the owner] sold it to "a group of individuals" who converted it into a restaurant.

3. Carla Emery wrote about eighteen "techniques of criminal hypnosis," as compiled by Paul Campbell Young. Young's "Technique #17" may explain why blank slate alter-states take on the perceived personas of perpetrators:

> *Assumption of Another's Identity*—Young cited M. H. Erickson's *"experiments on transidentification"* for this item. The hypnotic subject unconsciously incorporates wishes and attitudes of the hypnotist, like a child incorporates parental rules and views. Just as each adult has attitudes absorbed in childhood from their parents still influencing them, so each hypnotic subject acquires unconscious parameters and a role model from the hypnotist too. (pg. 353)

4. "It is a fact that memory becomes disoriented under hostile interrogation and that torturers aim at deliberately confusing recall. It is the torturer who not only determines real units of time under torture but who also damages historical orientation. The unit of time for torture remembered under intense emotions becomes stretched out and thus distorted. In the brain, fear of annihilation leads to a slowdown in the experience of time–similar to the impact of hallucinogens–that changes the synchronization between time as it is lived out and calendar time." (Graessner et al., pg. 192)

Adolescence

Junior High

As my trauma-based programming continued, I blocked out all memory of it so I could continue to cope with my "normal" life activities and responsibilities.

During my seventh and eighth grades, I attended Exeter Township Junior High School, less than a mile from home. There, I felt more secure. It was especially nice not to have to suffer any more mental and emotional abuse from the snobbish girls' clique at the middle school.

Dad insisted I play the French horn in the junior high school band. The heavy brass instrument was difficult to carry back and forth to school, and draining spittle from it certainly wasn't feminine. Still, I did what Dad wanted. As I played it, I noticed that my lungs' air capacity increased.

In the summer months, my brothers and I competed at the membership swimming pool to see how long we could remain underwater. I usually won, because I was able to do more than two minutes without great discomfort.

I believe I was obsessed with swimming long distances and holding my breath underwater, because I was unconsciously conditioning myself to survive drownings. As part of Dad's ongoing near-death trauma regimen, he would drown and then resuscitate me, creating even more alter-states that he had complete power over. I think it gave him the ultimate sense of power over me–"killing" me, then bringing me back from the dead.[1]

Dad arranged for a professional French horn player, Al Antonnuci, to be my tutor. I studied with the bearded man at night, once a week, in an old, multi-story building in Reading. After each session, I listened as Mr. Antonnuci played his shiny silver horn. The notes were so pure, I sometimes wept with joy.

At the new school, I emotionally bonded with a married German couple who taught classes in separate rooms on the second floor. The dark-haired husband was our science teacher. He kept a large black snake in an aquarium in his classroom's front wall. We often watched in fascination as the mounds of white mice slowly moved along the length of the snake's body.

I took two years of German from his gentle, tall, brunette wife. Although I spoke German fairly well at the time, I now remember little of the language, because of the horror of having been tortured and raped by German-speaking men. They made the language repugnant to me.

Cross-Country

In the summer of 1969, Dad transferred to Western Electric's plant in Baltimore, Maryland for a one-year assignment. We moved into a newly built, two-story house on Saxon Hill Drive in a recently developed subdivision not far from the town of Cockeysville.

Each morning, Dad woke my brothers and me up at 5:30, even in the middle of winter, to run up our steep street, then out into the countryside and back, for a total of three miles. Sometimes he made me run up a steeper dirt hill behind our row of homes.

Although running up the dirt hill made my calves burn like molten steel, I felt exhilarated as I reached the top. I'd finally found my runner's high. I've since learned that running increases the amount of cortisol in the brain, which probably helped me to fight off depression.[2]

Running with Dad was unpleasant. He insisted that I keep pace with him. Because he was a foot taller, it was impossible to match his long, loping strides. I cried when he wouldn't slow down. He usually stopped and waited as I cried, yelling at me or doubling back behind me and then hitting me on my back or buttocks, knocking me to the ground. When he did that, I cried so hard that I panicked and couldn't breathe. My pounding heart felt like it would burst. Each time, he looked at me with disgust and ran home, leaving me crumpled on the ground. I cried harder, my heart breaking. I knew I'd never be good enough to please him.

High School

Although I made good grades at our new school in Maryland, I again felt like an outsider. I met several other girls who also had difficulty socializing.

Although we ate together in the cafeteria, we didn't do much else together.

That same year, I developed adolescent "crushes" on several boys, especially a brown-haired, chubby, gentle boy named John. He also played a brass horn in the school band. He called me "Snaggletooth" because I'd accidentally broken one of my top front teeth in Pennsylvania and it had never been repaired. I felt embarrassed about it and rarely smiled. When John teased me into smiling, his kindness drew me to him. I felt devastated when I discovered that he had a steady girlfriend. Would any boy ever want me?

Once a week, Mom took us to the public library. It was a safe place where nobody hurt me. Still an avid reader, I always took home a stack of books. The stories took me where nobody could hurt or betray me. Sometimes, when bad things were done to me, I flew away into the stories in my mind.

I know that I participated in classes at Cockeysville High School. I have records to prove it. And yet, I've had numerous memories of exiting our regular school bus in the morning at the school, then boarding another yellow bus that took me and other students to several other locations. Each was a training facility set up like a regular school. Because these memories are vivid, consistent, and continue to recur, I believe they are of real locations and people. At these spook schools, the teachers taught subjects that never would have been allowed in a public school–including becoming familiar with holding and handling various types of knives, handguns, and other lethal weapons.

Notes

1. In his web-published memoir, *My Father the Serial Killer*, Steve Griggs describes an alarmingly similar pattern of behavior exhibited by his father, who was brought over from the Lithuanian Death Camps to serve in the United States Army, plausibly as a push-button assassin. A homicidal sadist, Steve's dad developed a taste for recreational violence on the side, and his children were not only witnesses, but victims. Steve describes himself and his sister as "a couple of MKULTRA kids who just wanted to get through the next 24 hours, every day." From *My Father the Serial Killer*:

   > In 1962, I was 10, my sister Dianne was 6, and we lived at Fort Devens, Massachusetts. I overheard my father tell my mother that he would

drown my sister while she took a bath. I went outside and sat next to her in the woods and spoke to her.

"If you want to live, you have to practice holding your breath every minute of every day, even when you are in school, even in the laboratory. Look at the clock, hold your breath and time yourself. What's going to happen is this: when you're taking a bath, he's going to come in and hold you under. You have to be ready with air in your lungs–but don't let him hear you take it in. At first you have to struggle but stay relaxed in your mind. Then let some bubbles come out, but not all of it, and let your body go limp. He'll stand there and look down at you for a while, so don't move or open your eyes. Nothing! Do you understand? Nothing!"

Dianne shook her head yes, and started holding her breath.

"I don't know exactly what's going to happen after this, but if we can get this far, there's a good chance that something else will happen to interfere with their plan because they haven't thought it out this far and they don't know that we know."

It worked.

The rest of the story of Dianne's drowning may be found along with other excerpts from *My Father the Serial Killer* at http://www.sondralondon.com/ tales/griggs.

2. The drug-like high of being on dangerous ops may have been due to a similar increase in cortisol levels, and may be why I grew addicted to ops. Dr. Zebulon Kendrick, Ph.D., a kinesiologist at Temple University in Philadelphia, Pennsylvania, explained:

> . . . produced by the adrenal glands during stress, cortisol rises during intense bouts of exercise and, unlike endorphins, crosses the blood-brain barrier. Cortisol has an anti-inflammatory and analgesic effect and dampens or hides pain and can give you a general feeling of well-being. (*Ladies' Home Journal*, February 2003, pg. 118)

Georgia Rebellion

Georgia

The following summer, Western Electric transferred Dad to an engineering position at its new cable factory in Norcross, Georgia. A growing industrial suburb, Norcross was a half-hour drive north of Atlanta. To anyone who would listen, Dad bragged that he'd been chosen to create the plant's new cable reel yard. I felt proud of him, and was glad that he was happy.[1]

Although I was disappointed that Atlanta was nowhere near the Atlantic Ocean, the big city was surprisingly clean and modern. The sky above it was startlingly blue, and the clouds seemed so huge and white that I fantasized I could reach up and touch them.

Our new, two-story, red brick house was built on Club Drive in Snellville, a tiny rural town about a half-hour from Norcross. The woods behind our home overlooked the town. With its white columns, our house looked like a Georgian mansion. It was built on the highest property in the area. Mom said that Dad liked the idea of looking down on everyone else; I think she was right.

The hill behind our row of houses was covered with tall pine trees. Their branches didn't start growing until about two-thirds of the way up the trunks. This was a problem, because in the winter during ice storms, some of the tops of the trees bent all the way down to the ground, their trunks snapping like huge twigs from the weight of the ice that coated the long needles. Still, the ice storms were spectacular. When the sun shone on an entire landscape coated with ice, the sheer beauty took my breath away.

Mom was hired as a secretary at the W.E. Norcross plant, so my brothers and I were left unsupervised at home after school and during the summer. In warm weather, we spent a lot of time at our subdivision's swimming pool. I felt peaceful as I lay on my back on the concrete, sunning and listening to the lapping, chlorinated water and the rock music from my portable radio.

Since my body was beginning to develop, I was embarrassed to let boys see me in a swimsuit. Mom told me they would only want me for one thing: my big breasts. Terrified, I stayed away from the boys as much as possible.

Dad also made nasty comments about my developing body, and weighed me on the bathroom scale at least once a week. Whenever I gained a pound, he accused me of not adhering to a diet that he'd created for me. Because I dieted faithfully, his accusations made me feel crazy.

Acting Out

Since we'd moved far away from our childhood family, Dad seemed freer to do whatever he wanted to us, while continuing to present himself to the outside world as a perfect father of a perfect family. As in Pennsylvania, Dad was active in church and several civic organizations. Again he went to an extreme to prove he wasn't a racist. This time, he intervened on behalf of a Puerto Rican neighbor who was being harassed by an elderly racist neighbor who drove through his manicured front yard, leaving deep ruts in it. Dad personally confronted the elderly man and ensured that from then on, the Puerto Rican man and his family would be treated with respect.

At the same time, Dad took me to Aryan meetings and occult rituals in Gwinnett County and in several other parts of northern Georgia. His shifts in behavior from one extreme to the other was one of the reasons I continued to be unaware of his darker side. I naturally preferred to know my father as a champion of the proverbial underdog instead of a dangerous racist.

Although Dad still terrorized me in rituals, I followed Mom's example at home by becoming more rebellious towards him. Then they started fighting openly, yelling and hitting each other. I soon spiraled into depression.

Within a short time, an unexpected source of relief entered my life. Tom, our teenaged lifeguard, was funny and cute. At first I hoped that he'd want me to be his girlfriend. I quickly noticed that many other girls also wanted to be with him. Ashamed of my developing body, I didn't think I could compete against them for his affections. Instead, I resigned myself to becoming a friend.

One hot summer day, while the afternoon rain pummeled the red clay dirt outside the fenced pool area, I found Tom and another teenaged boy huddled inside the pool's pump house. At first, I didn't understand what they were doing—smoking a joint of marijuana. Tom said I could try it, if I didn't tell anyone. I coughed when the harsh smoke burned my throat. After the rain stopped, we walked outside to the pool and sat on a roofed, wooden picnic table. As Tom played his twelve-string guitar, I was fascinated by the beauty of the chords. I couldn't stop laughing and smiling–I felt so wonderful!

When I returned to school the following fall, other students hooked me up with local drug dealers. Soon, I was smoking marijuana nearly every day. When I wasn't high, depression hit hard, leaving me lost and hopeless. Because all of my new friends were drug users, we shared whatever we could find with each other. And yet, because of all the horror stories I'd heard about hard drugs like heroin, I was careful only to take what I knew I couldn't get hooked on. To supplement my newly rebellious lifestyle, I also started smoking about two packs of cigarettes a day.

One reason why I preferred marijuana to alcohol was that my parents could easily recognize the smell of liquor. The only sure signs of my drug use were enlarged pupils, inappropriate emotional affect, and the munchies.

For a teenaged girl already suffering from compulsive overeating and low self-esteem, the munchies were an aftereffect from hell. Whenever my friends and I came down from our drug-induced high, we raided the local convenience store. Bags of Fritos and Doritos, Three Musketeer candy bars, and beef jerky satisfied our enormous cravings. When I was stoned, I didn't care if I ingested huge quantities of calories.

On the days when I couldn't find any marijuana, depression hit me over the head like an iron skillet. I was so desperate, I tried anything, including inhaling sulfuric fumes from lit matches.

Sexuality

As a newcomer to the South, I quickly learned that rules of conduct were drastically different from those in Pennsylvania and Maryland. Many of the students teased me about how I talked like a Yankee. I retaliated by calling them rednecks. Some of the boys affectionately called me "Socks," insisting that I must have stuffed my bra. Although I feared getting close to them, I did feel drawn to those who were emotionally troubled.

Several times, I mistook a young man's sexual advances for love. Because the thought of intercourse terrified me, I did everything I could to avoid it. And because I still blocked out all memory of having been sexually abused, I believed I was a virgin.

The first time I did have sex, I was disappointed by the lack of sensation. I was also concerned because I didn't bleed when penetrated. What had happened to the "cherry" everyone joked about?

Mom had recently purchased a paperback book, *Everything You Want to Know About Sex But Are Afraid To Ask.* She hid it in a small drawer beside her bed. Because my parents never discussed sex or birth control with me, this book was the extent of my official sex education.

Some of the teenaged drug users called themselves "freaks." They taught me how to rebel against authority figures. We called policemen "pigs" and oinked at them when they drove by in their patrol cars.

Feeling increasingly rebellious, I dressed outrageously to embarrass Dad–although never in his presence. Sometimes I secretly borrowed Mom's too-short skirts and dresses that she wore to work, and enjoyed wolf whistles from construction workers who were building new homes in our neighborhood. I also wore leather moccasins instead of shoes.

Because a local double standard permitted teenaged boys but not girls to smoke, I smoked cigarettes while walking beside the main road to and from the high school each day. Sometimes I took the tobacco out of my cigarette and smoked the marijuana in full view of passing cars. I didn't understand that I was unconsciously trying to draw attention to what was wrong in our home.

At sixteen, I wore blue jeans nearly every day. I even wore them to our Methodist church's Sunday night services, which was considered scandalous. That pleased me immensely. By then, most of the adults in our church had stopped asking me to baby-sit their children. Only one person seemed to see past my rebellious façade.

Pastor Hodges

Since a Lutheran church wasn't nearby, we'd joined the local Methodist church. Our pastor, Judson "Judd" Hodges, was a marvelous, black-haired mountain of a man. He became my saving grace during those dark teenaged years. Since he was taller and wider than Dad, I wasn't afraid to tell him about the constant fighting in our home.

The church was just off the main road between our wooded property and the high school, so I passed it every day as I walked to school and back. On many afternoons, I visited with Pastor Hodges either in his study in the church or in the living room of the next-door, red brick, one-story parsonage–when his gracious wife, Betty, was there. Pastor Hodges' consistent appropriate behavior meant the world to me. With him, I always felt safe.

When I wasn't numbed by drugs, I was in great emotional pain. During each visit to his office, Pastor Hodges sat quietly as I cried and talked about how miserable I was at home. He didn't try to shut me down and he didn't ask questions that I couldn't answer.

Instead of being judgmental, he gently tried to help me understand that my new friends at school weren't really friends at all. He knew most of them, and warned me that they were using me. He said they would drag me down with them. I wasn't ready to admit he was right–I still needed drugs to survive.

Pastor Hodges didn't try to preach down to me; instead, he met me where I was at. He didn't argue when I told him I couldn't stand going to Sunday morning church services "because of the hypocrites" (really, my parents). Instead, he invited me to use that hour to read Christian books that he'd placed on a set of wooden bookshelves in another part of the church. Instead of judging and chastising me, he helped me to feel loved and accepted.

Pastor Hodges wasn't just there for me. He was also supportive of my mother as she struggled to break free from Dad's brutal control. When she decided to have a medical procedure that would ensure she'd have no more children, Dad was furious and refused to drive her to the clinic. Having no one to turn to, she drove there herself. After the surgery, she was in so much pain, she couldn't drive. When Dad refused to come get her, she called Pastor Hodges, who transported her home. Dad hated the pastor after that, and never forgave him for "interfering" in their marriage.

Exercise Regimen

Still despising my developing body, Dad created a new exercise regimen. First, he cleared dirt paths in the woods behind our house by removing some of the pine trees. Then, at 5:15 each morning, he ordered me to get out of bed, get dressed, run down the steep path behind our house, then across the bottom of the woods and then back up to the top. My lungs burned and I cried from the pain in my calves, chest, and sides. At first he ran ahead of me, demanding that I keep up with him. Then he stood at the top of the hill and timed me with his stopwatch. Finally, he let me run with our family's dog, a half-collie/half-German shepherd he'd named Lassie. I preferred her company to his.

If the ground was muddy, I learned not to slide. I constantly watched for exposed tree roots and leaped over felled trees that blocked the paths. My calf muscles burned like fire every time I ran up the steep hill. When I sobbed from the pain and my inability to breathe, he ordered me to run the entire trail again. Pity wasn't a part of Dad's vocabulary.

He purchased a work-out bench and barbells, and trained my brothers and me to lift them in our big basement. He also made me exercise on a mat, where he sexually assaulted me when the rest of our family was either busy upstairs or away from the house. Even the way he approached sex with me had changed. Unlike the past, when he'd often convinced me that he loved me as he raped me, he now did it brutally. It was almost as if he hated the woman I was becoming.

One Saturday afternoon, as I did a set of sit-ups on the mat in the basement, the door to the upstairs kitchen was open. I heard Dad and Mom arguing loudly in the kitchen. Mom criticized Dad for being so strict with me. I wept bitterly when I heard Dad yell, "Kathy looks like a baby elephant!" I finally realized I could do nothing to make him satisfied with my body.

Violence

At home, Dad's physical abuse of Mom escalated. He beat and raped her so forcibly at night, I could hear her head banging against their headboard as she screamed, "Bill, don't! Bill, please stop!" I clenched my fists and cried myself to sleep, holding my pillow over my head, frustrated that I couldn't save her and angry that she didn't leave him. (In a deposition in 1989, Dad admitted he had beaten Mom, although he tried to convince the lawyers that he'd only done it two or three times.)

Mom started taking valium, and later told me she visualized a bubble around her that made Dad's cruel words bounce back at him as she smiled at him. She lost so much weight, she looked like a prisoner of war–I suppose in her own way, she was. Fortunately for her, the women's liberation movement was now in full force. Whenever we went out to eat at a truck stop in Norcross, Mom put a dime in the juke box and played Helen Reddy's hit song, *I Am Woman*. Dad fumed quietly as it played, while Mom smiled triumphantly at him. When we returned home, Dad usually beat her again, but she kept playing the song in restaurants and smiling.

LSD

I experimented with LSD three times, by choice. The first pill was a dud. The second time, I felt an almost uncontrollable urge to grab pruning shears from my younger brother's hands and stab him in the stomach with them. Frightened, I ran to an excavated area beside our subdivision's main entrance. I sat alone for hours and enjoyed watching Egyptian hieroglyphics that wavered and moved in the dirt until the acid wore off.

The third time I took LSD, I saw lines of tiny, colorful, Mickey Mouse cartoon characters move like miniature traffic grids on the dirt and trees behind our house. Each time they moved, they clicked. When the hallucinations wouldn't stop, I ran into the kitchen and drank milk to purge my stomach. The vomiting frightened me, so I drank some of Mom's refrigerated paregoric. The opium in it seemed to make the hallucinations worse.

I called my closest friend, whose boyfriend was a drug dealer, and asked them to come take care of me until I came down from the acid trip. Her boyfriend laughed when I threw up in his car on the way to my friend's house. Terribly ashamed, I vowed never to take LSD again.

Secret Investigation

As part of my rebellion, I started a sit-in demonstration with Tom's youngest sister in the corridor outside the office of our high school's principal. Our large, vocal group demanded that female students, like the males, be allowed to smoke at school if they brought a signed permission slip from their parents. Dad didn't tell me that the principal called him at work that day, to tell him what I'd done.

In 1989, Dad stated that when I was a teenager, he'd been asked to participate in a secret commission that, he claimed, had been organized to investigate drug trafficking in Snellville. He said he'd known that I was taking drugs daily, and had known who was supplying me.

Only once in my teen years did Dad indicate to me that he thought I might be taking drugs. That day in our living room, he showed me a magazine article about LSD. He said I should stay away from the drug because it could damage my brain. Then he walked away, signaling the end of our one-sided discussion.

Escalation

Dad still drove us to church every Sunday morning. Regardless of what went on at home, he wanted us to continue presenting ourselves as a model, upstanding family.[2] He now taught a Sunday School class and sang in the adult choir with Mom. I enjoyed singing in the junior choir. What the church members didn't know was that after church, as Dad drove us home, Mom yelled at him, calling him a "liar" and a "hypocrite."

Sometimes Dad stopped the car in the middle of the road and hit her; more often, he waited until we were inside the house and then beat her as she screamed in rage at him. The way they expressed their hatred towards each other broke my heart.

Mom secretly consulted with a divorce lawyer. He advised her that in Georgia, unlike in Pennsylvania, if she filed for divorce, she had the legal right to half the property value of the house and any attached land. She also learned that if Dad bruised her, she could have him arrested. After she told Dad what the attorney said, he used football tackles to push her against the refrigerator and walls with his chest and shoulders, laughing at her helplessness and outrage as he pinned her. Sometimes he deliberately tripped her and laughed as she fell on the kitchen floor.

Although I was horrified and feared for her safety, I did nothing. If Mom couldn't stop him, how could I? Sometimes when they fought, Mom shouted, "I'm not your squaw!" Dad retorted that he still owned her and she was his property. I felt confused by his strange words–surely he knew that men couldn't own their wives!

Running Away

The stress at home grew unbearable, especially at night and on weekends when Dad was home. Three times, I ran away from home to escape it.

The first time, I ran as fast as I could through the woods in the late afternoon, because I was afraid Dad would beat me for something I'd done at school.

I went to the house of Janie, a young friend from school. Her mother was the quiet epitome of a true small-town Southern woman. At dinnertime, the black-haired, dark-eyed woman introduced me to my first full Southern meal of grainy white corn bread, buttermilk, fried fish, and home-grown vegetables. After the wonderful meal, she welcomed me to spend the night in Janie's room. Not wanting to anger my parents, she called Pastor Hodges, who mediated with Dad to ensure I wouldn't be hurt when I walked home the next morning.

The second time I ran away, I again went to Janie's house. Her mother again contacted the pastor, who called my parents. After that, the gentle woman said that I was welcome to come to their home any time my parents fought, with the understanding that I had to return home after they'd had time to cool off. I wished I could live with her family.

The last time I ran away from home, I was afraid of Dad's temper because I'd quit the school's marching band and its female track team without his permission. Summoning up my courage, I hitchhiked to the nearby town of Stone Mountain, then took a bus to Atlanta. Being alone in the big city was scary. I didn't have enough money to spend the night in a hotel. What would I do?

A middle-aged, male, Caucasian pimp approached me and invited me to stay at his place for "just one night." He promised he wouldn't do anything. I followed him into his first-floor apartment and tranced as I stared out his bedroom window, watching a strong breeze blow through several big hardwood trees. He quietly walked behind me and caressed my buttocks. A protector alter-state emerged and screamed at him while running out of the building. When I was safely away, I reemerged. Not knowing where I was, I cried. Now what would I do?

I stopped at a tiny "greasy spoon" Huddle House restaurant to buy a sausage biscuit and soda, then called a classmate to tell her what I'd done. Although she couldn't help me, I felt better, knowing that she cared. I decided to keep walking until I could find a safe place to sleep.

Mission Possible

Early that evening, I talked to two young, blond women I encountered on a city sidewalk. Because they seemed nice, I asked if they knew a safe place where I could spend the night. One of them pointed to a large, upright white cross in the yard directly behind us. On it were the words: *Mission Possible.* She said she knew the older couple who ran the mission–they would give me safe shelter.

I was warmly welcomed by the Lands, who said they were Pentecostals. Mrs. Land said they provided a safe haven for male and female drug addicts and prostitutes who wanted help. She said she and her husband occasionally risked their lives to help enslaved prostitutes break free from their owners.

Mrs. Land asked my permission to call my parents, and said she'd make sure they wouldn't hurt me. The young female residents, who wore long dresses and skirts, led me upstairs to their large, shared bedroom. We stood in a circle and held hands as they prayed together in English and in tongues. Although their strange babbling frightened me a bit, I felt at peace and sensed that everything would be all right.

Mrs. Land walked into the room and said she had called Mom, who agreed to come for me and not harm me.

When Dad picked me up instead, I was frightened, but soon I relaxed–it was the nicest he'd ever been towards me. First, he drove through Atlanta's Piedmont Park, where he said hippies took drugs and slept on the grass. He talked as if they were filthy, and said I might have ended up there. I made a mental note to stay there if I had to run away again.

To my surprise, Dad offered a compromise: if I would do the best I could in school, he wouldn't ask for more. Although I continued to take drugs every day, I maintained a good grade average. That seemed to satisfy him.

School Intervention

At the high school in Snellville, my female guidance counselor seemed to be the only adult who sensed the depth of my pain. She had amazingly smooth, porcelain skin and shiny, short black hair. Her voice was soft and she was never confrontational. She was the only person at school I felt safe to open up to, although I didn't remember enough to be able to tell her about the more hidden traumas.

She arranged with all my teachers to let me leave my classes any time I wanted to meet with her. She also encouraged me to spend my study hall periods in her office. I read my assignments at a table while she worked at her nearby desk. Her quiet, unobtrusive caring provided another calm oasis in my troubled life.

Busted

In the fall semester of my senior (12th) year at school, I bought two unusually large, white Quaalude tranquilizer pills from a young blond student who was making a small fortune selling drugs in the school's parking lot. He said another teenager who had burglarized the local pharmacy the night before had sold him a large volume of the pills. I bought two, paying twenty-five cents for each. Later, my closest friend asked me to sell one to her. I did, for twenty-five cents.

That day, students who took the pills dropped like flies all over the parking lot and in the classrooms. To keep some of them from being arrested, we hid them in cooperative students' cars until the drug wore off. I made an unscheduled visit with the guidance counselor, and told her I was upset because my friends were getting sick. I didn't tell her I had bought two of the pills, because I didn't want her to think badly of me.

As we talked, my back was to the corridor outside her office. I heard a commotion and turned to look. Two men half-dragged my friend into the vice principal's office. I started crying because I was worried about her health. Soon, the vice-principal sent for me. In his office, he said my friend had told him I'd sold her the drug. He said if I told him who I bought the pills from, he wouldn't have me arrested.

I shook and cried. Then I said I'd tell him whatever he wanted, as long as he'd call Dad at work to smooth the way for me when I was home. I also asked him to call Pastor Hodges. Soon, the big man entered the small room and enveloped me in his strong arms as I sobbed uncontrollably. The vice-principal said I would have to be suspended from school for the rest of the semester. Then he said he'd make sure my record was kept clean if I told him who sold me the pills. He kept his word—my high school transcript doesn't indicate my suspension.

Turnaround

My friend's mother was furious that I'd given her daughter the pill. During a phone conversation with Mom that afternoon, the girl's mother accused me of being her drug supplier, and banned me from having further contact with her. I was incredulous, because the girl's much-older boyfriend had supplied both of us for years! I was relieved when Mom believed me.

That night, Dad angrily questioned me and asked who had started me on drugs. I told him about our lifeguard, Tom. Dad immediately went to Tom's house and confronted him. The young man lied and said he'd never given me marijuana. Because Dad was on the neighborhood's pool committee, he immediately fired Tom. That really tore me up, because I liked Tom and had become friends with his youngest sister. Within a half a day, I'd already lost three friends.

Later that night, Dad yelled at Mom and blamed her for my becoming a drug addict. He said if she'd remained at home instead of going to work, none of it would have happened.

Volunteer Work

To keep me out of trouble during my suspension, Mom and Dad decided I would do volunteer work away from home.

A neighbor invited me to spend several days a week with her at the large office of a regional magazine in downtown Atlanta. She was kind and respectful; I enjoyed riding in her car and talking with her. A huge room above the office area stored large stacks of magazines. Sometimes her boss asked me to look through them for defects. I also did small odd jobs in the office, and felt excited to be in a professional working environment. Although I looked a mess with my long hair and faded blue jeans, the young office workers went out of their way to make me feel welcome. Some of the men even let me bum cigarettes from them when my neighbor was away.

On my last day there, the editor-in-chief gave permission for her and another female employee to take me to an expensive French restaurant, the *Fleur-de-lis*, for my first fancy meal. They even ordered cherries flambé! Although I cannot remember the magazine editor's name,

I'll never forget his kindness. My neighbor also put a white carnation in a vase on my desk. I cried. For the first time in my life, I felt special in a good way.

My other volunteer job was with the Red Cross in the nearby, old town of Lawrenceville. A petite, elderly woman was my supervisor. Early each morning, Mom dropped me off on her way to work. I helped the supervisor tear donated, well-used bed sheets into bandages for soldiers in Vietnam–that was my only connection to the war.

During Thanksgiving, I went with her to deliver boxes of food to elderly shut-ins. I didn't know that so many older people were lonely! Back at the office, a local newspaperman took a picture of me in a white uniform, filling cardboard boxes with canned goods. I laughed when I saw it in the paper–I certainly didn't look like a "freak" now!

When I returned to school for the winter semester, my friends were disappointed that I didn't want to get high with them anymore. Some even accused me of being an undercover narcotics agent. That accusation hurt, but I understood their fear. I focused on doing well in my schoolwork and staying out of trouble.

When I met with the guidance counselor to discuss what I'd like to do after I graduated, she gave me a battery of vocational tests. After reviewing the results, I decided to go to college and major in either library science or psychology. When I told my parents what I wanted to do, they seemed pleased.

Divorce

One month after I'd returned to school, Mom secretly filed for divorce. She didn't tell anyone she was having an affair with Dad's best friend, a fellow engineer at Western Electric who was also married.

The night Mom arranged to have Dad served with the court summons, she told my brothers and me that she'd filed for divorce because Dad never spent time with us anymore. She ordered us to act as if nothing unusual was going to happen, when Dad came home from work.

My stomach hurt as I listlessly shoved scrambled eggs around the inside of a frying pan with a spatula for our dinner. I'd just been sucker punched; the runny eggs were making me nauseous.

When Dad entered the kitchen from the carport, he was excited in a childlike way. He said he'd purchased tickets for all of us to go to Disney World. Seeing the happiness in his face, I felt guilty for not telling him what was about to happen. I wanted to rescue him. When the sheriff's deputy came to our house in a police car, he handed Dad the summons and told him to leave. Dad must have been in shock, because he didn't argue.

We remained in the house in Snellville while Dad moved into an apartment with a friend, about twenty minutes away. Mom divorced him for "mental cruelty." Because Dad didn't contest the divorce, it was quickly finalized. For the first time in my life, I wasn't afraid of his walking into the house and hurting us. I felt the beginning of freedom and looked forward to a happier future.

And yet, at the same time, their divorce created a deep schism in the center of my being. As sick as our family had been, I'd felt more secure when their marriage was intact. Because Mom wouldn't allow Dad to have any contact with us, I'd suddenly lost my father. And because Mom now spent most of her free time away from home, I'd basically lost her, too.

Since my brothers and I were left to fend for ourselves, I cooked lots of rice, scrambled eggs, grilled cheese sandwiches, and tuna noodle casseroles–the extent of my culinary skills.

After I graduated from high school in the spring of 1973, I told Mom that I planned to go to college the following fall. I was stunned as she coldly said that since Dad had his own living expenses now, they couldn't pay for me to go.

I was hit by a tidal wave of fear. How could I build a new life? Because of my bad reputation as a former drug user, nobody in town would hire me. And because I didn't have a driver's license or a car, I couldn't work anywhere else! I had no viable way to plan for a self-sustaining future, and didn't know how to begin.

I couldn't discuss my fears with Mom, because she was always gone (secretly spending time with Dad's friend). Dad wasn't allowed to contact us. I didn't think Pastor Hodges could help me. And because I'd graduated, I didn't believe I had the right to talk to the school counselor any more. Feeling completely hopeless, I sank back into depression and started using drugs again.

Notes

1. Although Dad did do a great deal of work for Western Electric, which later merged with AT&T, he may have also used his position there as a cover for other activities. In a 1989 letter to his lawyer, he wrote, "In my job, I must travel to all points in the US and to many foreign countries at a moment's notice. We are under a company directive to use our AT&T [credit card] for these reservations."

2. Anna C. Salter, Ph.D. interviewed Mr. Woodard, an incarcerated rapist and molester, who explained how he'd gotten away with so many crimes before he was finally caught:

   > I lived the life of a chameleon or salamander, changed colors with the wind. I didn't just live a double life. I lived multiple lives. Whatever the situation called for, I lived it. If I hung around Christian people and I knew that they were Christian, then my actions and my mannerism were similar to theirs. And I adapted to whatever the situation required. (pg. 35)

   This was the same behavior I witnessed in Dad. Based on her years of interviews with sexual offenders, Salter gave a warning to her readers that we would be wise to heed:

   > Sex offenders are well aware of our propensity for making assumptions about private behavior from public presentation. They use that information deliberately and carefully to set up a double life. It serves them well but doesn't do much for the rest of us. (pg. 38)

Married

Albert

Shortly after graduating from high school, I met Albert. A native of Miami, Florida, he'd recently moved to the city of Atlanta to stay with an old friend in a Christian men's home. Seven years older than me, Albert was 5'7" with wavy, dark brown hair.

When we first met, I was spending the weekend with Cynthia, an older girl who worked with Albert at a factory in Norcross. She arranged for him and a male co-worker to go on a double date with us. The first night, Cynthia dated Albert and I dated his friend.

The four of us drove around in a small car for a while, talking and listening to the radio. Later that night, we stopped at a small park. While Cynthia and Albert kissed in the car, his big, shy friend sat next to me on a picnic table and tried to kiss me. Feeling nauseous, I pushed him away. We silently sat on the picnic table the rest of that long night, careful not to touch each other.

The next morning, Cynthia suggested we go out again that night. I said I would if we switched partners. That evening, as she and Albert's friend kissed in the car, Albert and I spent most of the night standing and talking on a bridge over a wide creek. I felt happy when he didn't try anything sexual. He encouraged me to share deep, personal thoughts and feelings. His interest in my life made me feel good.

Early the next morning, on the way back to Cynthia's house, I sleepily lay on the back seat with my head on Albert's knees, facing his stomach. I awoke to see his bulging zipper rhythmically poking at my face. As tears slipped out of my eyes, I turned my face away and pretended to still be asleep. I felt so degraded!

After the men left Cynthia's house, I felt so dirty and ashamed that I lied and said Albert had been a perfect gentleman. She said she knew I was lying, and warned that he was "nothing but trouble."

That afternoon, Albert called Cynthia and cried for at least an hour. He said he was depressed because his live-in girlfriend in Miami had broken up with him. As I listened, Cynthia told him he should forget about the past. I was drawn to the intensity of his emotions as he wept almost non-stop. Against Cynthia's stern advice, I agreed to go out with him on a real date.

When Albert learned that I was using illegal drugs, he said it was sinful and insisted that I stop. I did. Then he took me on "dates" to shoddy bars in the outskirts of Atlanta. I didn't drink to get a buzz or have a good time; I drank until all the sounds and lights and faces merged together. Drinking made my problems go away–until the next morning.

After several weeks of driving from the factory to our house late at night, Albert asked Mom if he could sleep in our living room on a pull-out sofa bed instead of going home. She readily agreed. Years later, she admitted to me that night after night, she'd heard me tiptoe down the stairs, and had heard us having sex on the pull-out sofa in the living room, leaving deep grooves in the wooden floor. She never indicated that she knew what we were doing, nor did she ever mention birth control to me.

The first time we had sex, Albert pushed my head down hard against him. I gagged and felt like I was suffocating. I went away for a while. When I came back into my body, I didn't know that I'd switched to a sexually experienced alter-state.

Albert probably thought that I'd remembered the entire experience, and was pleased with my skills. Soon, he spent almost all his free time at our home.

Albert's Family

Albert's English father had abandoned his wife and five children when Albert was very young. His mother, Virginia, eventually married Paul, a dark-haired, slim, short man who claimed to be a Nazi who had immigrated to the US via Spain.

Albert expressed hatred whenever he talked about Paul. His stepfather was a radio minister and blue-collar worker. Albert and one of his three sisters hinted that Paul had done terrible things to them and their mother, although they never shared any details with me.

When Albert drove me to Miami the first time to meet his parents, I was horrified that his mother wasn't allowed to drive several blocks to the grocery store or to church without Paul's express permission. Like Albert, Virginia had large dark circles under her eyes.

I was even more appalled when, upon Paul's command, their large black dog crawled across the small wooden living room floor to where he stood. For hours at a time, the dog lay on the wooden floor, not moving until Paul gave it permission. Huge calluses were on its legs.

Although going to Miami helped me to recognize that Albert's stepfather was overly controlling, I didn't understand how the horror that Albert had endured as his stepson had affected his mind and poisoned his soul.

Pregnant

Since Dad had conditioned me to be a sexual machine, when I was alone with Albert, I was like a sexual robot with no "off" switch. I felt secretly ashamed of my lack of control and wished Mom would intervene, but she never indicated that she knew what we were doing.

We also had sex in my bedroom during the day while Mom and my brothers were away. It was easier than trying to find something to talk about. When he was there at night and my family was still awake, we sat outside on the cool cement floor of our family's large screened-in porch. A Pentecostal, Albert played his Spanish guitar (he was tone deaf) while insisting that we sing Christian songs together. Sometimes he tape-recorded our songs to send to his older brother, Richard, in Illinois. Afterwards, Albert would lead me in prayer, then give me "prophecies from God." Because I believed that God was really speaking through him to me, I felt special and became dependent on Albert to facilitate a deeper relationship between me and God.

One night, Albert called from the factory. He said he had something important to discuss with me when he came to the house. When I told a friend, she suggested that he planned to give me an engagement ring. Believing her, I was excited as Albert drove up the cement driveway and parked in our brick-walled carport.

Mom and my brothers had driven to Pennsylvania, so Albert and I sat alone in the living room. We played my radio in the dark as candles illuminated the wood-paneled walls. I was disappointed when Albert frowned and said that we were sinning against God by having sex outside of marriage. He said that because I was causing him to sin, he didn't want to see me anymore. I was stunned and deeply hurt–all along, I'd believed that he loved me and wanted to be with me!

Just then, we heard Diana Ross's hit song, *Touch Me In The Morning*. Believing it must be a message from God, I told Albert, "Just this one more night. Give me this one more night." For the first time, we made love so gently, it squeezed the breath out of me. By morning, he decided to continue dating me.

Although birth control pills were available, I knew nothing about them. Instead, Albert used a less reliable method–condoms. He convinced me that as long as he used them, I couldn't get pregnant. One night in September, a condom was defective. Although Albert freaked out, I privately thought that God had caused it to happen, because He wanted me to become pregnant and marry Albert.

Within weeks, I felt more full inside than normal. Mom took me to a medical clinic in Snellville for a pregnancy test. The doctor smiled and said, "The rabbit died." Mom later explained that I was pregnant.

When I told Albert over the phone, he accused me of trying to get pregnant so he'd have to marry me. Then he tried to talk me into "shacking up" with him in Florida, as he'd done with his rich, blond ex-girlfriend. He said he'd even paid for a wedding announcement in a Florida newspaper, to con her parents into thinking he'd married her! That bothered me–I didn't want to marry a dishonest man. I was also troubled by his refusal to remove her picture from his wallet, no matter how much I cried and begged him to. I didn't understand that he was still on the rebound from their broken relationship.

All I wanted to know was that he loved me and would be happy with me as his wife–later, if not now. If having his baby was what it would take to rope him into marrying me, then I was glad I was pregnant.[1]

A year earlier, Mom had told me that if I should ever become pregnant, she'd fly me to New York to get an abortion. But now, she didn't make that offer. Instead, she encouraged me to marry Albert.

At the time, I wasn't aware that Dad had quit paying child support for me. I also didn't know that Mom was preparing to sell the house and move into a smaller rental home with her still-married lover–leaving no room for me in her life.

Illinois

Albert's older brother, Richard, was thin and lanky with red hair and a full beard. He was an elder of a small Charismatic church in

Waukegan, a sprawling, large, old city on Lake Michigan, about an hour north of Chicago. Waukegan was usually hot and humid in the summer and bone-freezing cold in the winter. Far above, its sky was almost always a dull color.

Richard's pastor, Bob, had perfectly styled white hair and a neatly groomed moustache. Bob's wife, Barbara, was large with a strong operatic voice and long, straight, thick blond hair.

Bob, Richard, and several other men were in the process of developing a new church that would be under the direct authority of Apostle John Robert Stevens, the leader of the Church of the Living Word in Anaheim, California. Members called the church network The Walk, signifying their unique walk, or relationship, with God.

When Albert told Richard that I was pregnant, Richard insisted that Albert bring me to Waukegan to be married before God. Albert decided that if he cooperated with Bob and Richard, he could convince them to help us financially. First, he sent me to Illinois for one week to spend time with the church members. He wanted to be sure that I'd be happy living there.

During a church service that week, Pastor Bob, Richard and other elders laid their hands on my head and shoulders and "prophesied God's word" to me. Bob, Richard, and one other man said they "saw" me coming back there to serve God, but not with Albert.

When I returned to Atlanta and told Albert what they'd said, he was furious. He reminded me that he was God's mantle of authority over me. Hadn't God given him many prophecies for me when we prayed together? Because Bob and other elders had also told me that God had revealed to them that Albert was a "chosen prophet," I continued to believe that Albert's prophecies were from God.

Married

In late November 1973, Albert drove us in his rickety old sedan to Waukegan. On December 2, we were married in the church's ranch style, one-story house that doubled as a residence for Bob, Barbara, and their two young sons. I felt excited that I was joining a community of Christians who would become my new family. Half a country away from Dad, I felt safe.

Mom and Dad traveled there separately for our small wedding. I wore a tight-fitting, long, yellow dress that a female church member had quickly sewn for me. Albert and I had written our own vows. In mine, I promised to follow Albert as Ruth had followed her mother-in-law, Naomi: "Thy people shall be my people, and thy God, my God."

Later, when I saw photos of the ceremony, I noticed that sunlight coming through a window behind Bob had seemed to make a white aura around his head. I believed this was a sign from God that He'd supernaturally blessed our marriage. (Bob taught us that a white aura indicated God's strong presence.)

For $125 a month, we rented a small upper-floor, government-assisted apartment at 2409 Dugdale Road, part of a large, low-income housing complex. Cooped up in the apartment in the frigid winter with no phone and no TV, I thought I'd go mad. Fortunately, Richard and his family lived in a nearby apartment building. I spent most of my free time with them, and quickly adjusted to the constant pandemonium in a household with five energetic children. I grew to love each of them and became one of their regular babysitters.

Nursing Home

Barbara A., a middle-aged brunette church member, offered to hire me as a weekday nurse's aide at the All-Seasons Nursing Home in Waukegan. After I was hired, I had to walk about two miles each way, sometimes wading through deep drifts of snow. Although I only earned $2 an hour, I felt better about myself because I had a job and wasn't lonely anymore.

Although most of the patients on the first floor of the two-story nursing home were elderly, one Black, male, paraplegic patient was middle-aged. Lonely and depressed, he said his wife refused to let him come home, and rarely visited him. His muscles were wilting from lack of exercise. As often as I could, I took him upstairs to the exercise area, where he began to bulk up his arms and upper torso.

My work at the nursing home was character-building. I was careful to show respect to bedridden patients as I fed and washed them, changed their urine-soaked bed sheets, and emptied their urine and colostomy bags. I also pushed heavy meal tray carts down the halls and helped patients turn in their beds and transfer to wheelchairs and back. The work was exhausting, but I loved it.

One winter day, a large, young, Black male patient–the paraplegic's roommate–had a grand mal seizure in the large first-floor community dining room. I was down the hall in an elderly patient's room when I heard the loud thuds as the young man's head repeatedly slammed against the linoleum covered floor. My sister-in-law, who had also been hired as an aide, witnessed the seizure. The man was taken by ambulance to a hospital.

When I walked into our dark apartment that night, I felt so exhausted, I left pots of macaroni and cheese and green peas on the stove. It wasn't much, but surely Albert would understand.

Although he drove to work while I walked, Albert constantly complained about having to be on his feet all day in the shipping department of a nearby store. When he walked into our apartment that night, he started complaining again as I lay on our mattress on the bedroom floor with a migraine headache.

Ignoring my discomfort, Albert screamed and cursed at me for leaving him a pan of cold pasta. He threw it against the kitchen wall and shouted, "Clean it up!" Then he angrily insisted that I get up and make him a decent supper. I cried as my head throbbed. I tried to tell him how upset I'd been about the patient. He didn't care.

What had happened to the man who had enjoyed talking with me late into the night? Frightened and hurt, I walled off my emotions. As I crawled on my hands and knees to wipe up the sticky mess, I decided I wouldn't let him hurt me that way again.

At the nursing home, I was angry at how badly the patients were neglected. I ended up doing the work of several nurses' aides. I also did chores I wasn't qualified to do, like changing patients' colostomy bags, and their surgical and bedsore dressings. Someone had to do it. While I toiled, the male orderlies hid in the laundry room and played poker. They often laughed at the cries of patients who lay in urine and feces on their stinking hospital beds.

Someone always tipped off our normally absent male supervisor when a state investigator was about to pay a "surprise" visit. Before each inspection, the supervisor handed us various colored pens to fabricate entries in patients' charts that "proved" we had done what was required by state law.

One day, a young female inspector came to the nursing home. No one was expecting her this time. As the first-floor staff played their daily poker game in the laundry room, unaware of her presence, I showed her how we'd fabricated the patients' records. She asked me to show her more.

I took her to the room of an elderly, petite, female, Black patient. The poor woman's tendons were so tight and hard, she couldn't move her curled arms and legs at all. Covered with large bedsores, she lay in a fetal position on her back with decaying food inside her clenched fists, her uncut fingernails growing into her palms.

The inspector taught me how to work with the elderly woman by slowly and gently moving her frozen arms and legs. As she did this, the woman, who was in agony, yelled in a hoarse voice: "Lord have mercy! Lord have mercy!" Although I understood that I had to cause her pain in order to help her, her cries broke my heart.

After that, I did what I could to give extra help to that elderly woman and several others. Unfortunately, I injured myself in my seventh month of pregnancy. An extremely overweight Black woman had repeatedly called out for help. She wanted to get off her hospital bed into the wheelchair so she could use the bathroom. Because the orderlies refused to help, I ran out of patience and tried to move her on my own. As I shifted her from the edge of her bed to the wheelchair, the chair moved away and she fell on her rump on the floor. Although she was uninjured, I felt something tear or split between my legs. Unaware that I should report the injury to the administration, I walked home, frightened.

That night, I was in so much pain, I had to crawl from our mattress to the bathroom. Albert accused me of faking an injury so I wouldn't have to work. My frustration and helplessness instantly turned into anger; I'd be damned if I would let his selfishness push me into losing my baby! Because Albert said we couldn't afford another exam with the obstetrician, I lay in bed for several days until the pain subsided. I never went back to the nursing home.

I couldn't understand why Albert was so distrustful and bitter towards everyone, including me. As much as he'd insisted on my moving with him to Waukegan to join the church, he now opposed my bonding with church members, and insisted we move back to Atlanta. I felt torn between my love for the church family and my duty to my husband. Pastor Bob, Richard, and other church leaders challenged me to put my devotion to God and the church first. I was already so brainwashed, I believed I couldn't have a relationship with God outside The Walk.

Albert was furious when I refused to move back to Atlanta with him. He said he wasn't willing to raise our baby in Waukegan because the city was "too depressing." When he told Dad what he wanted to do, Dad invited Albert to live with him in Atlanta while Albert searched for a job. Despite Albert's cajoling and angry threats, I stayed in Waukegan.

The Sisters

After Albert found a job in Atlanta, he refused to send me any money. He said I'd have to come to Atlanta since I had no way to pay the rent on our apartment. Instead, I sublet the apartment to two young men and moved into our church's two-story women's home on Greenbay Road, a wide, busy city street in Waukegan. For over a month, I subsisted on church members' charity. The women living there became my sisters. They gave me a private bedroom that had previously been occupied by Lynn, a friendly young, long-haired female who had recently birthed a baby girl. I enjoyed Lynn's company–she reminded me of a reformed Janis Joplin, my favorite singer.

Bob and the church elders continued counseling me to choose the church and God's will over my marriage. They said because Albert was staying away from his calling as a prophet in the Walk, he was in rebellion against God.

I cried every night, afraid I'd have to divorce the father of my baby. Although I couldn't remember what Dad had done to me, I feared going back to Atlanta. Pastor Bob and the elders said my baby and I were protected by God's umbrella of protection as long as I stayed in The Walk. I believed them.

Baby Rose

I told Albert that Barbara, the pastor's wife, had become my Lamaze partner and coach in his stead. Realizing I wasn't going to come to Atlanta, he gave up and returned several weeks before our baby's due date. He moved into the men's Greenbay house, two blocks away, and took his rightful place as my partner at the Lamaze classes.

Ever since I'd learned I was pregnant, I'd done everything possible to ensure that my baby would be healthy. I'd stopped smoking and drinking, and ate only natural foods. One female church member gave me a large package of expensive Shaklee prenatal vitamins. I walked two miles almost every day in the spring and the hot, muggy summer. I regularly had my baby blessed by Bob and the elders, who placed their hands on my swollen belly and head and prayed for both of us.

Pastor Bob and Barbara negotiated with a young newlywed couple, Bob and Ann-Marie M., who had recently received an old, two-story wood-framed house from Ann-Marie's parents as a wedding present. The couple agreed to let us live with them until we could afford to rent our own apartment.

Slim and bubbly with blue eyes and blond hair, Bob M. was our church's music leader as well as an elder. Quick-tempered Ann-Marie had coal black eyes and dark straight hair. Since she wanted to have Bob's baby, she hoped she could learn how to raise hers by observing me with mine.

One morning, when I was two weeks overdue, my obstetrician called. I liked the thin, dark-haired man because even though I could pay little, he remained gentle and respectful. He said he wanted me to go to the hospital so he could induce labor. Because I'd avoided all drugs–even aspirin–to protect my baby, I cried and asked God for help. As I packed my hospital bag, the contractions began on their own. I took this as a sign that God was blessing my baby.

In the hospital, my labor lasted twelve hours. A scowling gray-haired nurse walked into the labor room after several hours and demanded that I stop using the Lamaze method. She said because I panted like a puppy during contractions, I was depriving my baby of oxygen. I tried to breathe normally, but that made the pain unbearable. Physically para-lyzed by its intensity, I screamed that she could go to hell. As I resumed panting, she angrily stalked out of the room, shouting that I was killing my baby.

A few minutes later, a young, brunette nurse entered. She had a gentle, calm disposition and was comfortable with the Lamaze method. Dr. T. came in once in a while to see how much my cervix had dilated. Dissatisfied, he gave me injections that sped the contractions. They started coming every minute. I was so tired! A sterling Lamaze partner, Albert encouraged me and wiped my face with cold wet washcloths.

I cannot describe the happiness I felt when my precious baby, who I'll call Rose, came out of my womb. She had the most beautiful cry. Hearing her voice, I fell completely in love.

Love Lost

Although at first they'd been excited about having a baby in their new home, Bob and Ann-Marie weren't prepared for Rose's nighttime crying. Since our upstairs bedrooms were right next to each other, Ann-Marie insisted I put her in a borrowed, white wicker bassinet I kept in the downstairs living room. Ann-Marie said I should let my baby cry to keep from spoiling her. In my mother-heart, I knew she was wrong. My baby was crying because she needed me. Each night, I waited until they'd closed their bedroom door, then tiptoed downstairs and held Rose on my stomach until we both fell asleep on the sofa. I felt like the happiest woman on earth.

I was lucky to be able to stay home and breast-feed my baby with no complications. I wanted the best for her—La Leche members in our church taught that mothers' breast milk protected babies from many illnesses.

Rose was the only human I had ever fully bonded with. For the first time, I knew what true love was. We locked eyes every time she sucked greedily at my engorged breasts. I couldn't get enough of her. Her soft fuzzy skin fascinated me. She was brown-haired with blue eyes and had the most amazing, flowery-scented breath. I was blessed to experience a month and a half of bliss and bonding with her.

The rest of this chapter honors her memory, and Emily, the daughter who I unwittingly raised in her stead. It is a compilation from daily journals, written by many of my alter-states over a period of about five years. The death of my baby girl was so traumatizing that the memory shattered into little disconnected pieces that surfaced, decades later, one small piece at a time.[2]

I strongly advise ritual abuse survivors to avoid reading the remainder of this chapter–it can be extremely triggering.

Before Rose was born, I'd been transported in a vehicle (by whom, I don't yet remember) to secretly meet with a young couple I'd previously visited with Dad in their home in Virginia. The olive-skinned, black-haired, dark-eyed young husband was a lawyer. He bragged that he was a "dandy." Like Dad, he loved doing awful things to his victims; and like some hard-core Satanists, he stored human body parts in large glass jars of formaldehyde in white, wooden kitchen cupboards. His slim, lovely young wife was light-skinned with long, straight, light brown hair.

That Sunday, not knowing how I came there, I stood talking with the young couple in Chicago in an empty, below-ground parking deck with thick concrete walls. When the young mother held out her new baby to me, I saw the husband smirk. Not a good sign. I was doubly concerned when I saw the same ugly smirk on the young woman's face. I removed the thin receiving blanket from their baby's face.

At first, I couldn't comprehend what I saw. They'd put plastic wrap on the squirming, premature baby's face. Its complexion had turned unnaturally dark. Even though I knew I was in danger of being tortured if I dared to break that man's mental control, I snatched the plastic away. The baby screamed in absolute fury. I was so shocked by the experience, I pushed the memory away.

Several months later, in September, 1974, Dad secretly paid for me to fly with Rose to Atlanta to meet with him. The afternoon we arrived in Atlanta, the air was almost cool with just a hint of a breeze. The sun shone brightly. Dad seemed to drive aimlessly, then stopped and got out of his car. Carrying Rose in my arms, I followed him onto the middle of a large, dusty, sparsely vegetated piece of empty property. No people, buildings or houses were anywhere near us. I saw a treeless subdivision in the distance–all its homes looked alike.

Fear clutched my heart as I held my baby girl tightly. I felt doom, although I didn't know why. When I looked at Dad again, he held out a large, sharp knife with a black handle, similar to the knife he'd used in rituals when I was a child, putting his hands over mine and forcing me to kill precious babies.[3]

My mind short-circuited. Dad looked into my eyes and said, "If you don't kill her, I will." Instantly, a succession of ritually conditioned alter-states emerged. Each one frantically assessed the situation, trying to figure a way out. When one part saw no way out, that part went under and the next part came out.

They knew they could try to run with Rose to the distant houses and yell for help, but since Dad was a cross-country athlete, they couldn't outdistance him. They could try to fight him, but he was much stronger, and where could they put the baby to keep him from hurting her in the struggle? And if he killed me or I killed myself, there was no telling what he'd do to her.

A mother-part emerged and stared at my baby's sweet face. She tried to comfort herself with the knowledge that Rose would soon be with God in heaven, where He'd keep her safe and surrounded with His love. And even if it killed the mother-part, she was determined to be the one to do it with every ounce of love in her. She would not allow Dad's cruel, filthy hands to touch Rose's innocent body. She'd seen Dad rape baby girls to death. He was not going to do it to Rose! She'd kill her first, with love and gentleness. She wanted the love and reassurance in her own eyes to be the last thing Rose would see.

As she prepared to cut Rose's carotid arteries, she felt such piercing pain, she realized she couldn't go through with it. She couldn't kill the most important person in her universe. When she submerged and a ritually conditioned child alter-state emerged, Dad noticed the shift and grinned. As he'd done so many times in the past, he put his right hand atop mine and forced it to cut Rose's soft neck. I believe it was a mercy that the child alter-state didn't recognize Rose as her child. Dad forced my hand to cut Rose's carotid arteries, one at a time.

After the deed was done, the mother-part reemerged. She wanted to scream with wild grief as she saw the blood pulse and Rose's precious eyes faded to dull, then black. She was losing her baby, dear God, she was losing her baby. As Rose's eyes stopped seeing, she told herself, "She's with God now. She's safe." But the dark pain of her baby's leaving was unbearable.

She didn't move as she watched Dad carry Rose by her ankles to keep from getting her blood on him. He wouldn't allow the alter-state to bury Rose. He said that since the baby came from my body, she was garbage. He put her precious body in a black, plastic garbage bag and threw it into a nearby commercial sized, metal dumpster.

Within minutes, Dad had successfully destroyed the one relationship in my life that made me feel good as a human being. So many parts of me now felt pure hatred towards him, wanting to kill him. But deep down, they knew they could never go there. Because they were dependent on him to tell them what to do, think, and believe, if they killed him, they believed they would also cease to exist. Survival came first.

After putting her body into the dumpster, Dad raped me on the dusty ground, reclaiming me for himself.

I believe Dad tried to murder my goodness that day, to make me like him. When he ordered me to kill Rose, that was the closest I ever came to breaking forever and becoming a willing perpetrator. But by holding onto my love for her and my hatred towards him, I was able to preserve my truest self, deep inside. He could make me kill her, but he could never take away my love for her. It embodied my gentleness and kept me from becoming monstrous like him.

The darkness in him did not engulf the light in me that day, but my grief over losing my beautiful sweet baby was so great, I couldn't allow myself to feel softness and caring anymore. I erected thick concrete barriers around my love and my memory of her, so that Dad could never touch or hurt that essence inside me. Unfortunately, by walling up and preserving my deep love for her, I couldn't express love or caring towards anyone else.

Later that day, I walked along an open-air, concrete balcony to Dad's room at a hotel where we were staying. When I knocked on his dark, solid door, he silently opened it. Shirtless, he walked toward his bed. Because he had drawn his thick drapes shut against the bright sunlight, I couldn't see well at first.

As my eyes adjusted, I saw something moving beneath a white-cased pillow on his bed. I looked closer and saw the squirming legs of an infant. Dad watched calmly as I snatched the pillow off the infant, not caring if he punished me. I yelled, "How could you do this?" In an even voice he said, "No one will ever know she's not yours. She's physiologically compatible."[4]

In a sudden flash of insight and memory, I realized he'd set up everything that had occurred that day. But why had he chosen this particular baby? I felt cold as I picked up the screaming infant and looked at her face.

Although she was the same general size as Rose, her hair and skin were a bit darker. She was physically stronger and much angrier when she cried. As I looked closer, I remembered. The preemie in the garage. Dad grinned. I walked out to the open-air balcony, clutching her against my chest as she continued to scream. Although my heart felt like stone, I made a decision: by God, he was not going to kill her! Holding her tightly, I lost all memory of Rose and gave this baby my birth-daughter's legal name. (From now on, I'll call this baby "Emily.")

After I returned to Waukegan with her, to stay sane, I had to believe she was mine. Still, I felt cold every time I looked at her. Because she seemed different and was angry when she cried, I believed that demons had invaded my baby's body.

One day, in the church's nursery room behind the sanctuary, a young female member with short, curly, dark hair picked Emily up and cooed at her, laughing. When I told her my baby was demon-possessed, she looked at me in horror and said, "Why, she's an angel!" My stony heart couldn't accept her words. I believed my baby had become the epitome of evil.

Determined to save her from Satan, I followed the teachings from Apostle Stevens and Barbara. I constantly laid my hands on her and anointed her body with olive oil, commanding the demons to leave her body in the name of Jesus.

Because I focused on her, I didn't recognize that I, too, had changed. I was now ready to do assassinations. Each time I, in controlled alter-states, was sent to kill a targeted man, I unconsciously killed Dad. My fury and hatred were tremendous. And when I was ordered to do "disposal" and "clean up" (dismembering male bodies and more), I visualized cutting Dad completely apart so he could never hurt anyone again.

My professional handlers knew my rage at the targeted men was really about Dad. And although I was used again and again, my fury never abated. Because the adrenaline rush and the rage gave me additional strength, when I was pitted against larger, more muscular males with equal training and conditioning, I always won.

Something else happened during the day of Rose's murder. Several of my alter-states were now certain that Dad wanted me dead. Because he'd killed Rose, they knew that he'd really killed me by proxy since she came from my womb. I believe that in Dad's mind she was merely an extension of me. He couldn't have gotten closer to killing me without actually doing it. Some of my alter-states feared they might be next.

Why did he groom and train me from childhood to perform the most dangerous ops? I believe he hoped that someday I'd be killed on an op. That way, he wouldn't have actually killed me. My death would have been so emotionally sanitized, he wouldn't have felt any guilt. After all, such things happened.

Whenever my professional handlers sent me into situations to do assassinations, my own life was also at risk. Many of the targeted men knew they were in danger. Some were armed and ready; some had even hired professional bodyguards that I had to find a way past, usually by posing as a prostitute. Some of the targeted men were also seasoned professionals, which made them extremely dangerous. Each time, I fought hard to survive.

By keeping my emotional energy focused on Dad and visualizing him as I attacked those men, I preserved my sanity. Each time, I mentally fought like an animal against the greatest beast of all, knowing that he, the man who had killed my precious daughter, was also the man who now sent me to die. This knowledge gave me the strength I needed to fight, stay alive, and come home one more time.

Notes

1. When I told Dad the good news, he didn't respond at all. Later, he wrote a scathing letter to Albert, accusing him of "impregnating" me and taking me into a life of poverty.

2. Some readers may ask, how do I know this isn't a fabricated memory? My answer is this:

   > Although I initially chose to believe that the pieces of this memory were fake, I was consistently slammed by powerful attached emotions–especially grief and love. I also began to vividly remember the month and a half I'd spent with my baby *before* her death–those memories had been completely missing.

   > In 1994, I did try to have DNA tests done on me and my given daughter, Emily, with her permission. Unfortunately, the person we gave the samples to (later proven to be CIA-connected) reneged. Since then, Emily and I have both determined that I probably am not her birth mother, because our skin tone, hair color, eye color, and physical stature are dissimilar. Regardless, I carefully reminded her that, whether or not I'd birthed her, I had raised her as my child and loved her just as much.

3. This form of excruciating mental torture seems to have been used by other sadists as well. In their leaflet, *Acts of Torture*, Sarson and MacDonald reported that a knife was forced into the hands of Sister Diana Ortiz in November 1989, by one or more members of the Guatemalan army's counterinsurgency force. Her torturers forced her to continue to hold the knife "as they plunged it into another woman and this horror [was] videotaped for blackmailing purposes." (pg. 1)

4. Although I remembered well enough to know—to my great sadness—that this memory was valid, I still had difficulty accepting that my father would do such a horrendous thing to Rose, Emily, and me. I later learned that baby switching in Nazi/Aryan cults is not uncommon. By keeping the children from bonding with their birth mothers, the cult leaders can more easily bond with and mentally control the children.

AFTER ROSE'S 9/74 MURDER, 9/27/01

Brainwashed

Immersion

Even though I couldn't remember my sweet baby's murder, the immense emotional pain remained. If I didn't find a way to block it all out, I would die. My escape was to fixate on The Walk's teachings. I spent most of my waking hours in a trance state, making the cult's "spiritual" world my only reality. Nothing else mattered anymore. By then, the construction of our church's new, one-story building in North Chicago had been completed. Pastor Bob named it "Ecclesia Fellowship." Since Albert refused to go to church anymore, other members transported me and Emily as often as needed.

The congregation had become my safe family, and I felt at home whenever I was with them. Pastor Bob and Barbara became my spiritual parents. Because I believed they loved and cared about each of us, I did whatever they said. Some of the women taught me how to sew, cook, and do basic household chores. In effect, they became my mothers.

After about a year, Bob and Ann-Marie tired of how we took advantage of their free hospitality. They insisted we find another place to live. We found a cheap attic apartment in a large old house at 14 Jefferson Avenue in downtown Waukegan. Unfortunately, because we'd moved near Lake Michigan, the temperature changes were more severe. One winter's night, the outside temperature dropped to 60 degrees below zero with the wind chill factor.

Alone and isolated during weekdays, I grew paranoid about being attacked by Satan and his hordes of demons, especially the big, bad ones that Apostle Stevens called "Nephelim." Since I didn't have a job anymore, I did intercessory prayer for hours on my knees each day, prayerfully fighting invisible demons that our leaders said were constantly attacking us from the spiritual realm.

The leaders also told us that every word we spoke as sons of God had the power to become reality. For this reason, I feared if I said I felt like I might be getting the flu, I'd accidentally speak the illness into existence!

I didn't want to dirty my spirit with earthly information and demonic influences from "Babylon" (normal society). Now, at the leaders' encouragement, printed literature and taped sermons from the Walk became my primary sources of information about the outside world. I believed I was as happy as I could ever hope to be, since I was drawing so close to God.

Energy Exchange

During praise and worship services at Ecclesia Fellowship, we were told to raise our hands. We sang any way we wanted, especially in "tongues" that sounded remarkably like baby babbling. We were told that when we prayed in tongues, the Holy Spirit was sweeping into the building, filling our spirits like oil being poured into lanterns. We were told that this would prepare us, Jesus' spiritual bridesmaids, for the impending wedding of Christ and the Church. We were told that, by becoming more holy, pure and obedient–filling ourselves with the "living word of God" (mostly from Stevens), we would hasten Jesus' return to the earth to reclaim his spiritual bride (us), and to set up his new kingdom.

Sometimes, as we prayed together in church services, we were instructed to hold our palms outstretched toward whomever the leaders prayed for. We were told to send the power of the Holy Spirit from our bodies, through our hands, to them to give them strength, healing, or deliverance from demonic influences.

I often experienced a physical exchange of energy after church services. In the back of the sanctuary, Barbara and other seasoned female members hugged me and others, chest to chest. When they did, I felt strong energy flow from the center of my torso to theirs, and back again. As the energy flowed, we comfortably swayed back and forth in rhythm with it.

I never sensed that this practice was sexual–the energy transfer felt clean and pure. Sometimes the force of the flow was so strong, it knocked us away from each other. When it did, we stood there quietly, praying and swaying peacefully until we'd recovered our faculties. We were pleased that the Holy Spirit was channeling so strongly through us!

We were also instructed to pray for people who were not in the building, and to visualize where they were, what they were doing, and what their special needs were. If we had a "prophetic" vision about a person we prayed for, we were to walk up onto the stage where Pastor Bob and the elders stood and share the vision with the rest of the congregation. Because my heart pounded rapidly nearly every time I thought of walking up onto the stage, I usually remained silent.

One night, in a rented room in a small commercial building in downtown Waukegan, Barbara set up a meeting where church members viewed a film that showed how physical energy transferred from one human body to another. It focused on scientific Russian experiments, in which individuals were instructed to interact with each other while their energy fields were filmed. We watched energy move from one person to another. As one couple interacted sexually, their auras even changed in size, shape, color, and intensity. Fascinated, I wondered why more people didn't know about energy exchanges and energy-field auras.

Submission

Because I still believed Albert was God's mantle of authority over me, and because he continued to give me prophecies from God when we prayed in our large, airy, wooden-floored bedroom at night, almost everything he demanded, I did. Even when he told me to do things I didn't feel good about, I continued to obey him.

The only time I disobeyed him was when people with higher authority gave me different instructions. These instructions came from Pastor Bob, Barbara, the elders, and Apostle Stevens (through taped sermons and rare visits to Ecclesia).

I'd been conditioned throughout my childhood to obey Dad. Disobedience wasn't allowed. Now, because Albert was my primary male authority figure, I obeyed him.

Albert was often cynical, demeaning, and abusive towards me; he had a cruel temper. If I didn't immediately obey his commands, he screamed at me and made life hell until I fully complied.

Another reason for my obedience was that I was dependent on him. I didn't have a car and was phobic about driving in traffic, not knowing that some of my hidden alter-states had been driving for years.[1] I also didn't know how to use a bank account or write checks because Albert handled all of our money. I felt worthless, believing I couldn't survive without his help and guidance.

My submission towards Albert was reinforced within the Walk. Our leaders and some of the women–especially Barbara–taught us that we must obey our husbands, because rebellion against their God-ordained authority would bring demons into our homes, and would put our children in danger of becoming ill, demon-possessed, or even dead.

Following Barbara's example, some of us even wore white lace Spanish mantillas on our heads to publicly display our submission to our husbands and church elders.

We were constantly taught that if we obeyed our husbands, God would honor our obedience and would miraculously manipulate them to treat us right. Since we were encouraged to read Church of the Living Word literature and were discouraged from reading the Bible on our own, I didn't know that the leaders often used scriptures out of context to manipulate and control us.

We were instructed to listen to cassette tapes of sermons, especially those given by Apostle Stevens, several times a week. He and other leaders told us we must listen to each tape at least three times in a row, so the "living word of God" would "go down into our spirits." Over a period of three years, I purchased and listened to hundreds of tapes, allowing the leaders' teachings to bypass my critical thinking. I wanted God's "living word" to fill and transform me.

In their sermons, many of the leaders–especially Stevens–used a combination of Ericksonian hypnotic techniques and Neuro Linguistic Programming (NLP).[2] Whether this was accidental or intentional, most of their sermons were so irrational and metaphorical, they created a spiritual fantasyland in my mind that became more real to me than the physical world.

The leaders taught that demons could come into our homes through worldly literature and television programs. Following their teachings, I used cooking oil to anoint our television, doorways, windows, pillowcases, mail, and more. I would do whatever it took to keep my family safe.

Each night, I placed our tape recorder next to Emily's bed and played Stevens' messages as she fell asleep, so the Spirit-breathed (pneuma) word of God would fight off any demons that she was too young to recognize.

Alone with Emily in our apartment on weekdays, I "danced in the spirit," stomping and twirling as I sang to God "in tongues." I didn't care what she or our downstairs neighbors thought. Stevens and other leaders had taught us that such dancing and singing were inspired by the Holy Spirit. We were taught that it would please God, since He had been pleased when King David had publicly danced in praise to Him. I wanted to be as close to God as King David had been!

Insanity

Behind the walls of our attic apartment were thick layers of residue and feces from years of roach infestation. At night, when I walked into our large kitchen and turned on the light, they scattered into cracks and crevices. Every time I opened a drawer, they dropped egg sacs as they scurried away into the darkness. The feces, egg sacs and crawling bugs nearly drove me out of my mind. Albert refused to let me use chemical sprays to control them. He said they'd make his hair fall out, and then he'd go crazy.[3] I tried to work with him by using natural remedies to make the roaches go away, but they did no good.

Appalled by the infestation, a new landlord hired two men to thoroughly spray all of the apartments. When the men finished, insecticide dripped down the sides of the doorway between Emily's narrow bedroom and the kitchen. Albert freaked out and wouldn't let us walk through it. After the chemical dried and we did walk through it, Albert insisted we take off our clothes and wash them immediately, so that any chemicals that touched our clothes wouldn't get near his head. Because we couldn't yet afford to use the Laundromat down the street, I washed our "contaminated" clothes in our big cast-iron bathtub and hung them in the enclosed back stairwell to dry.

Each time the exterminators sprayed our apartment, Albert insisted I wash the doorways and any other parts of the apartment that the spray had contacted. I had to throw away the cleaning rags, then scour the sink and bathtub to remove every last trace of the chemicals. Still, he was convinced that residual insecticide was on my hands. Although I washed them many times, he never let me touch his head again.

One day, Dad's mother sent me an unexpected birthday present: two beautiful rugs she'd crocheted by hand. I treasured them, knowing they'd taken her many hours to make. I decided to put them on our kitchen floor. Unfortunately, Albert believed our shoes were also contaminated by the chemicals on the wooden doorways. After we'd walked on Grandma's rugs, he ordered me to throw them in the garbage. I cried and begged him to please let me wash them, but he refused. Although I obeyed, I never forgave him and grieved losing this precious connection to my grandmother.

He soon developed another phobia towards the acid inside car batteries. He was convinced that it, too, would make his hair fall out and make him go crazy. If I walked within several feet of a closed car hood, I had to wash my purse and all of its contents. If Albert had an especially bad day, I had to throw my purse into the trash in a sealed plastic bag, so the trash container wouldn't be contaminated.

Albert's logic had no logic, and yet it dictated our daily lives. Every time I had to dispose of another "contaminated" personal possession, I felt more anger towards him.

At times, I also appeared insane. After Emily started walking, I decided she needed a pet and adopted a small calico kitten. Soon, it started stalking and pouncing at Emily, claws bared. Something in me snapped. I felt an irrational need to protect Emily from it. First, when it pounced at her, I picked it up and shoved it across the floor, away from her. Then I started throwing it a little harder. One day, I totally lost control. I threw it so hard, it thudded into the far wall.

After that, it stayed away from me, making an eerie howl that made the hairs on my arms stand up. I was deeply ashamed of what I'd done to the poor kitten, especially since I didn't know why I'd done it. I enlisted a man from church to come and take it away. He looked disgusted when I wouldn't admit that I was responsible. I didn't know that I'd flashbacked and seen it as a danger to Emily, because I'd been forcibly exposed to frightening wildcats as a child. I felt like a monster.

On another occasion, convinced by Barbara that I must cleanse my intestines to make my body purer and more acceptable to God, I began giving myself a coffee enema every day. Sometimes I did it when Albert was home. Although it disgusted him, I refused to stop since Barbara's authority was higher than Albert's. Starved for a father's love, I was determined to do whatever it took to make God love me more.

Notes

1. Such schisms in my overall personality weren't unusual. Often, if I had a phobia that kept me from doing something that most people could comfortably do, I'd have a hidden alter-state that had compartmentalized the ability to do it. For instance, as the host alter-state, I was terrified of heights. And yet, I had at least one alter-state that wasn't afraid of dropping down from one open-air apartment balcony to the next, many stories high.

2. Dick Sutphen explained why, although is a powerful tool for mental control, we've heard so little about it:

   > The concepts and techniques of Neuro-Linguistics are so heavily protected that I found out the hard way that to even talk about them publicly or in print results in threatened legal action. Yet Neuro-Linguistic training is readily available to anyone willing to devote the time and pay the price. It is some of the most subtle and powerful manipulation I have yet been exposed to. A good friend who recently attended a two-week seminar on Neuro-Linguistics found that many of those she talked to during the breaks were government people. (Sutphen, pg. 13)

3. Chances are good that Albert suffered from Obsessive-Compulsive Disorder (OCD). Although some people with this mental disorder are obsessed with protecting themselves from germs and constantly wash their hands, in Albert's mind, chemicals were the invisible enemy.

Memory Manipulation

Temp Jobs

The more time I spent with Emily, the more I enjoyed and was fascinated by her. I no longer believed that demons inhabited her body. I was ignorant, however, about child development. Treating her as I'd been treated as a child, I didn't use baby talk and expected her to reason as an adult. Nonetheless, I marveled at her cuteness and her excitement as she explored the world around her.

Unfortunately for both of us, I was not yet in control of several "Mom" alter-states that did some of the more benign things to Emily that Mom had done to me. For instance, in public, I secretly pinched Emily to make her obey me, not understanding that I was actually conditioning her to fear me. Whenever she cried in a restaurant, I took her into the bathroom and spanked her on her rear, not understanding that I should instead find out what her need was. I was convinced that she was rebelling against my authority whenever she failed to do what I told her.

I even spanked her when she refused to repeat a prayer after me. I didn't understand that at the toddler stage, part of the child's personality development includes saying no. Any time she rebelled, I believed–based mostly on Barbara's teachings to the women–that a new demon in Emily was making her do it. I was convinced that I must spank Emily to keep her from giving the demon more power–after all, we were taught that demons could kill our children!

Whenever I spanked, pinched, or otherwise hurt Emily, I always felt horrible afterwards. And yet, because I didn't understand why I did some of those things, I created false rationalizations for my abusiveness. I was too frightened of myself to acknowledge my guilt and loss of control.

In one good way, I bonded closely with Emily. Unfortunately, I let it go on for too long–perhaps bonding her too closely to me. Because of the radical teachings of several pastors' wives in the La Leche League, I breast-fed her until she was two-and-a-half. I was taught not to stop until she didn't want it anymore. They said it should be up to the baby, not the mother.

After she'd weaned herself, Pastor Bob and Albert told me it was time for me to get a job. I didn't see how that was possible–how would we pay for a babysitter? I was touched when several church members offered to baby-sit for free. At the time, I believed they would be best for her because they were filled with the Holy Spirit. Now, I wonder if that was a mistake. After all, most of them were as "spiritually" psychotic as I!

I started working through Jobs, Inc., a temporary employment agency in downtown Waukegan. Because I'd taken two years of typing classes in high school, I was assigned to various departments at the sprawling Abbott Laboratories pharmaceutical facility in North Chicago. Sometimes, on a new assignment, I was led to an empty desk and given magazines to read for days at a time. I didn't understand that some of those temp jobs were cover positions for covert ops.

Op Preparations

Sometimes, when I was to be sent out on an op, Albert personally drove me to meet with professional handlers. At other times, handlers picked me up at home and drove me to buildings where I was hypnotized and tricked into believing I was at a regular job. I reported to many buildings and offices during the next two decades.

Because the handlers didn't want me to remember the exteriors of the buildings they transported me to, I was not allowed to look out the vehicle's windows. If I did, one of the handlers either tortured me with a stun gun–usually on one of my forearms, or painfully pressed on a pressure point near my neck or shoulder.[1]

Sometimes, they made me lie on the sedan's back floor, face-down. Sometimes they transported me in car trunks. When they transported me in the back of white, windowless panel vans, I was usually strapped to a gurney with an IV in my arm to keep me sedated.

One method they used to block out memories of civilian air flights was code-named "Sound Of Silence" programming. To do this, programmers created a "Helen Keller" alter-state that was certain she was blind, deaf, and unable to speak. When in this altered state of consciousness, I was led by the hand by my assigned handlers in and out of planes and airports. Even though my eyes were wide open, I literally was unable to see.[2]

Part of this programming was accomplished through hypnosis paired with the threat that if I did see any identifiers that indicated which flight I'd been on, or if I heard anything that would do the same, I would be killed. Therefore, to stay alive, I unconsciously chose not to see and hear.

By triggering out a succession of alter-states for each op, my handlers ensured that each participating alter-state contained only one piece of the whole experience. That increased the fragmentation of my op memories, which is one reason why the memories eventually emerged in so many bits and pieces.

Most of the op briefings were routine. Usually, I was led to a desk in a commercial building, and was told that the desk was mine. I was so drugged or hypnotized, I believed I was at my regular office job. Another handler, posing as my supervisor, placed a stack of files on the desk in front of me, or on a shelf above it.[3] An alter-state was triggered out by the sight of a red-jacketed manila file in the stack. That op trained alter-state opened the file consisting of a printed dossier, one or more black-and-white 8-1/2 × 11s of the intended male target, and other pages of printed information.

To the best of my knowledge, each dossier stated that the "target" had recently raped children, women, or both. Sometimes it stated that the target had just been released from prison and was an "imminent danger to society." My op parts believed that my duty as an American citizen was to "take him out." A simpler command from a handler was: "Do him." We both understood that "do" meant "kill."

After one alter-state read the file, another op-trained alter-state was also triggered out and briefed, to ensure that at least two op-trained parts always had the information necessary to complete the assignment. This ensured that if one part accidentally submerged into unconsciousness during the op, the other part could then be triggered out via a tiny transceiver that the handler had placed in my right ear.

The male professionals who briefed me often increased my deep store of volcanic rage towards men by ordering me to get down on my knees and perform oral sex on them before they sent me to perform the op.

I was then transported by car, van, truck, motor home, ambulance, plane, jet, boat, cargo ship, mini-submarine (ideal for rivers), or helicopter to perform the op.

I have also had numerous memories of having been in groups of American tourists that supposedly participated in guided tours in various countries. It seems that this was an overseas cover that not only made me seem innocuous; it also ensured the happy cooperation of my "tourist" alter-states. After all, who wouldn't want to go on free overseas vacations?

"Husbands"

My professional handlers couldn't risk my breaking free from their control in the middle of a mission. If a male handler could convince a female, emerging alter-state that the handler was my legal husband, then that alter-state would more likely obey his commands without argument. Most of my op trained alter-states didn't know that Albert was my husband. Instead, when they emerged, they believed whatever they were told. Some of the "husband" handlers took further advantage of my parts' ignorance by having sex with them after an op was completed, ensuring that those alter-states would more likely obey them on future assignments.

While preparing to take me home, my handlers always did a full body search. They checked my mouth, vagina, rectum, and all of my skin. They made sure that none of my op alter-states had hidden any clues or secret messages in or on my body for me to find back home. (Several parts had been caught using ink pens to write messages on my skin to tell me, the host alter-state, what was happening.)

Albert and other people close to me, including relatives, supervisors, and "friends," helped to cover-up for my absences. Whenever I returned home, they acted as if I'd never been gone. Their behaviors reinforced my amnesia.

At home, I wasn't able to remember having had extramarital sex with some of my "husband" handlers, since I repressed those experiences too. I did, however, remember it in my dreams. Because I felt embarrassed by the vivid orgasmic dreams, I decided they must be from Satan. Although my sexual needs were no longer being met at home, I still wanted to stay faithful to Albert so that God would be pleased with me.

Blammo

The following is a journaled memory of a typical op. As usual, I remembered the memory itself, with no knowledge of how I arrived in that location or how I returned home. And as usual, during the event, I didn't know who I was or even what year it was. Amnesic, I only knew what my handlers told me.

I found myself alone in a foreign country, slowly driving along a narrow, crooked street in a small car. It was right before dawn. A row of narrow, small, one-story, wooden houses were on each side of the street. My temporary home base that I shared with my "husband" (handler) was the last house on the left. The street was still quiet, but people would soon be waking up and coming out.

As I drove slowly along the street, I saw that somebody had placed a detonation device atop the front doorstep of each house, anticipating that when a person opened their front door and stepped out, blammo! The house would be damaged, at the very least, along with the victim.

I could make out several of these doorstep devices in the pre-dawn shadows. By our back door, I noticed a stack of three logs. A long, thin metal pin stuck out beyond the top log, to be triggered when the solid wooden door pushed open against it.

My first thought was for the man I called my husband, and the small, brown-haired, intelligent girl staying in the house with us. I believed she was our daughter. Though our "marriage" was a cover, this operative part of me believed in the reality of the arrangement.

The husband had short, straight brown hair, and was grizzled from lack of sleep. Muscular and clever, he knew how to disassemble bombs.

As prearranged, I drove on past the house, and pulled the little car around into an industrial area for a hastily-called rendezvous with him. He had just come back from a quickie assignment. I told him about the bombs I had seen, and begged him, "Come on, let's get out of here *now!*"

He gave me a grim look; taking it as a personal challenge, he was determined to stay behind and disassemble every bomb.

"Just because you know how to do it," I said, "doesn't mean you have to be the one to do it!"

As we stood arguing about what to do, two of the houses detonated from the doorstep bombs.

"Come on! It's not worth dying for!"

He wasn't going to go away with me, so I told him I wanted to take our daughter out of there to a safe place, before she got blown up too. We had another car, a station wagon with brown side panels, sitting next to the left side of the house, parked in the wet, leaf-covered dirt. When I suggested taking the station wagon, he shrugged, then gave me instructions about where to go next.

I tried one more time to get him to come with us, but I saw a gleam in his eye as he sought out the pin in the log on the back porch. The man was too far gone.

After he safely dissembled our log bomb, I entered the house, picked up the sleepy child, wrapped her in a red blanket, carried her outside, and lay her gently on the shiny brown leather seat in back. "There, now, honey, just take a little nap while I drive. We're going on a trip."

As I drove slowly away from the danger zone with the child lying quietly in the back seat of the car, I felt nostalgic, yearning for the man I had left behind. I also reached the sad realization that it may very well be the last time I would see him.

Movie Screens

After most covert ops, the professional handlers had to ensure that I would not remember what had occurred. One way they did this was by implanting fake "screen memories" in my mind that blocked out previous legitimate memories.

One type of screen memory was implanted at a location that I believe I was taken to after ops, to be debriefed. The Janus building was in Washington, DC. According to a photograph still in my possession, its street number was 1666.[4] The theater section was on the bottom floor of this multi-story building. The outside marquee sported two masks, one laughing and one sad, representing the dual faces of Janus, a mythological god. The concept of Janus was regularly used in my CIA mental programming because I lived two completely different lives, one at home and the other in the field.

At that building, I was usually taken upstairs first to a small, plain-walled office. The assigned debriefer, usually a clean-cut Caucasian man wearing a black business suit, triggered out every alter-state that had been conscious during the op and transportation. Each part told him what that part remembered. The parts knew that lying could lead to being tortured, so they were careful to tell the truth. They were not, however, averse to holding back pertinent information that could lead to their being tortured for having screwed up.

Afterwards, I was taken downstairs into the empty movie theater. While I watched a movie, a male handler sat to my right and carefully monitored my responses to what I saw and heard. Because I was in a trance state and was sometimes drugged, I believed the movie was really happening. Sometimes, the man added verbal hypnotic suggestions to make the movie seem more real.

Whoever chose these movies seemed to look for anything in them that could parallel at least one or two details they knew I'd experienced during the previous op. They understood that my future retrieval of memories of repressed events would work backwards. In other words, because of how my memory was naturally stored and retrieved, I would remember the most *recent* part of a series of experiences before remembering what had previously occurred. This means I would remember the movie screen memory before I'd remember the real op preceding it. If the movie seemed unrealistic, I'd be so confused by my memory of it, I'd think I was psychotic and therefore wouldn't believe the op memory if it emerged later.

Sometimes I was led into a plain-walled room–perhaps at a different location. I was told to sit in a small, tireless car that had been placed in front of a movie screen. Two more same-sized, white screens were attached to each side wall. Sometimes, instead of sitting in the tireless car, I was instructed to pedal a stationary bicycle or run on a treadmill, again surrounded by the three movie screens. Regardless of the mode of fake transportation, the scenery moved as I "drove" the car, pedaled the bicycle, or ran on the treadmill.

Sometimes when I pressed down on the car's brake, the moving scenery didn't slow down. I watched in terror as the car plunged off a cliff and crashed into the ground below. Each time I believed that I'd died, and then wondered why I could still see and think.

Using the bicycle or treadmill was also crazy-making because at first, as I pedaled or ran, I was going at the same speed as the fast-moving automobile traffic on the wide road that I believed I was also on (really, the traffic was on the screens). Then suddenly, the cars on the screens would seem to zoom around me and I believed I'd somehow lost my strength and energy to keep up. Each time, I panicked and felt ashamed. Because I believed I was on real roads with unfamiliar numbered signs, I worried. Where was I, how could I keep up with the traffic, and how would I ever get home?

These particular screen memories were especially effective in blocking my memories of having previously driven, in an alter-state, to specified locations.

Before the advent of virtual reality, Dad had preferred using what he called "acted-out scenarios" to implant screen memories in the minds of victim-slaves. Sometimes he and other alleged operatives contracted with established Hollywood actors and actresses to participate in these mock scenarios. At other times, they used people the victims would never see or meet in regular life.[5]

Dad believed by using all of a victim's senses during an acted-out scenario, the victim would be more convinced that the retrieved memory of the acted-out scenario was a fully legitimate event.

In the 1990s, my way of determining whether or not a remembered event had been acted-out was to review the expressions on the faces of the other participants. I usually could remember a bit of a sneer, or a smile in the eyes of a participant who should have been upset or frowning if the event weren't legitimate. Another clue was if I'd felt woozy or drugged during the event. During a real op, I would not have been drugged.

The implantation of another type of screen memory went like this: by phone, a male handler would instruct one of my alter-states to meet him at the ornate carousel atop a small hill in Six Flags Over Georgia, a large amusement park near Atlanta. Not knowing I was being controlled, I'd tell Albert I was going to the park for the day to "have fun." When I approached the carousel, its lights and calliope (organ) music and its rotation and the up and down movement of the horses quickly put me into a deep trance.[6]

Then the man walked towards me and triggered out a compliant alter-state that recognized him and enjoyed being with him. From there, he took me on another overseas assignment.

After the op and my debriefing, he brought me back to the carousel, had me watch it again until I tranced, then implanted a verbal hypnotic suggestion that blocked out all memory of the op. Finally, he melted into the crowd.

When I "came to" and drove home, I didn't know I'd been gone for several days. At home and at work, Albert and other local handlers helped to convince me that I hadn't missed any time at all.

Memory Scrambles

Some handlers hypnotically tricked my mind into seeing something that was not there, or tricked me into seeing something as other than what it really was. When I first remembered having been hypnotized that way, I felt embarrassed and scared. I didn't want to believe anyone could fool my mind so easily![7]

Stateside handlers used several "themes" to keep me compliant. One hypnotic trick was to make me "see" flowing molten lava outside a building, so I didn't dare leave it. (An adult alter-state related that this had originally been created in my mind when handlers made that alter-state walk on a bed of burning coals while in a deep trance.)

Some handlers told me to look out a multi-story office building's plate glass window at a cloud in the sky. They said the cloud was an approaching tornado. They knew that because of my Wizard of Oz programming, I had a strong fear of tornados. Sometimes they laughed so hard they doubled over, tears streaming down their faces, as I frantically yelled at them to follow me, then ran down several flights of stairs to the lowest level and hid there. At other times, if a helicopter were landing nearby, they mentally tricked me into believing it was another tornado.[8] Because the rotors created a strong gust and were noisy, hypnotically tricking me into seeing a tornado instead of the copter wasn't difficult.[9]

Notes

1. Although Groome, et al, described how a head concussion can temporarily negate a
   person's ability to retain bits and pieces of new memory, their description of its
   effects may also explain why the electrical effects of stun guns kept me and other
   slave-operatives from retaining certain information: "In all probability the contents
   of the STM [short-term, temporary] working memory at the time of the accident are
   lost because they have not yet been transferred to the LTM [long-term, permanent
   memory storage], and the STM working memory (which depends on conscious
   awareness) is put out of action during the period of unconsciousness." (pg. 161)

2. Some followers of Sigmund Freud would probably call this, "hysterical blindness."

3. I've had hundreds of flashbacks of "coming to" while sitting at a strange desk,
   surrounded by unfamiliar office workers, then opening a file and panicking because
   I didn't know what I was supposed to do with it.

4. Although 666 is a common symbol used by occult practitioners, some mental
   predators who are not occult practitioners have used it and other occult symbols to
   frighten and intimidate victims who had been ritually abused.

5. Some mind-control victims have even reported being put in full-scale, fake
   UFO's that were sometimes moved up and down by hydraulics. In the fake UFO's,
   drugged, tranced victims met humans dressed in "alien" costumes. Later, because
   of the effects of forcibly administered drugs and Ericksonian hypnosis, the remembering victims weren't able to differentiate between preceding, legitimate events
   and the subsequent acted-out UFO scenarios. They also were not able to recognize
   that the "alien abductors" were really human. Although some survivors are convinced that their abductors were aliens because they remember them as having
   been unnaturally tall, changing the perceived size of perpetrators in the minds of
   victims can easily be accomplished through hypnosis. For example, due to
   "Gulliver programming," I initially remembered some of my persecutors as being
   several *inches* tall!

   In the introduction to one of his fascinating books about true conspiracies in the
   US, Alex Constantine wrote:

   > The "Alien" Invasion–a very active cover story for the development of
   > mind control technology. Supposedly (as those weird syndicated UFO
   > television programs keep reminding us) alien scientists have voyaged
   > millions of light years to place CIA implants in the bodies of human
   > subjects. This incredible cover story is widely believed–yet most
   > "skeptics" scoff at the notion that human scientists might want to do
   > the same thing. The aliens have been pounded into the heads of the
   > American consumer by a slue of books penned by military intelligence
   > officers (*Psychic Dictatorship*, pg. xii).

6. Most mind-control survivors I've been in contact with have specifically remembered being taken by handlers or family members in the US to Disneyland (in California) or Disney World (in Florida) for programming sessions, as was I. I suspect this was done to us for a minimum of two reasons: 1) being in such a trigger-laden environment would easily cause dissociated individuals to regress into childlike states of consciousness; and 2) the overwhelming colors, shapes, sights, movement, and sounds–added to mental and physical fatigue–could easily cause dissociated individuals to go into a lengthy hypnotic trance.

7. Dr. Elizabeth Loftus, a FMSF spokesperson and self-proclaimed "memory expert," has generously provided the mind-control survivor community with irrefutable proof that, by using regression and hypnotic techniques on unsuspecting adult subjects, a professional can convince a fair percentage of them that they either experienced or saw something that didn't happen the way they remembered, or that they experienced something that didn't occur at all. If Loftus could accomplish these results by using benign, harmless techniques in controlled settings, imagine what could be implanted in a survivor's mind by using terror, coercion, sleep deprivation, food deprivation, hostile environments, drugs, Ericksonian hypnosis, Neuro-Linguistic Programming (NLP), and more.

8. It would be just as easy to hypnotically implant a screen memory in a victim's mind of the helicopter being a UFO.

9. Carla Emery explained this hypnotic technique:

> Words act as conditioned stimuli in a totally mechanistic, automatistic way when the subject is deeply hypnotized. During hypnosis, the conscious mind, one of whose functions is to keep us hitched to reality, has been turned off. The conscious is not there to interpret or deny. The unconscious is literal and, frequently, obedient. When the subject's conscious mind is turned off because of hypnosis, language takes the place of reality. If the hypnotist says, "You see a cat waltzing alone in pink pajamas," you might see exactly that. (pg. 209)

Enslaved

Ecclesia Split

While Albert and I lived in Waukegan, Dad and Mom occasionally paid for us to either drive or fly to Atlanta to visit them in their separate homes. Pastor Bob and Richard kept insisting that God wanted us to stay in Illinois. Angry that I still refused to relocate, Albert started coming home late at night from nearby taverns. Each time, he was so drunk, the fumes nearly knocked me out. He'd lie on our mattress on the floor and cry about how miserable he was. His incessant complaining made me feel like crap. I tried so hard to please him by being a good and godly wife; and yet, he still wasn't happy.

To protect myself from the pain of not being loved or accepted by my husband, I clung harder to the church and to the Apostle's teachings. Pastor Bob, Richard and Barbara assured me if I kept obeying the Word of God, Albert would eventually submit to their authority. They said that once Albert obeyed, our family would live in harmony.

We probably would have divorced, had Ecclesia Fellowship not unexpectedly split. It began when Pastor Bob and Barbara flew to Anaheim, California, as they'd done several times in the past, to visit with Apostle Stevens in his home. When they returned home this time, they were noticeably troubled. The next Sunday, Bob told our congregation that Stevens was no longer living for God. Barbara later stated that she had learned–true or not, I don't know–that Stevens had become an alcoholic, was committing adultery, and was consulting with astrologers.

Bob said he knew his personal decision to break away from the Apostle's authority would not be acceptable to any members who still chose to follow Stevens. He asked the church members to fast and pray, asking God what they should do–start a new church with Bob as their pastor, or stay in the Walk. Many of the younger adults chose to stay in the Walk under Stevens's authority. They relocated to a smaller church that we'd recently helped start in southern Illinois.

Bob's decision helped to break what I believe was John Robert Stevens's long-distance hypnotic control over my mind–and the minds of many other gullible believers. I was finally free to question what the Apostle had taught. Elated, Albert demanded that I discard all my Living Word cassette tapes and printed materials. As I obeyed, I felt as if I were going into physical withdrawal.

Local Church

A young, red-bearded friend of Albert invited us to go with him to downtown Chicago to attend church meetings held by another Christian group that identified itself as the "Church in Chicago." It was part of an international religious organization, the Local Church. The Local Church was led by a small, balding man named Witness Lee. He claimed to have been a disciple of one of Korea's famous Christians, Watchman Nee.

At these new meetings, my first lesson in how to pray the Local Church way was to cluck my tongue once, then say: "Oh . . . Lord . . . *Jesus*." The men and women in the Church in Chicago were very friendly. They used a technique I've since learned is called "love bombing." Someone always invited us to eat and rest in their home on Sunday afternoon so we could go to the evening service before returning home.

Atlanta

When I finally agreed to move back to Atlanta, I discovered I'd accrued enough hours as a temp worker to receive two weeks' vacation pay. That same week, a young couple from the Church in Chicago came to visit us and gave us $300, saying it was from God. I believed these were signs from God that confirmed we were to return to Georgia.

After we loaded up the car and traveled to Atlanta, Dad and his new wife invited us to stay in their home in an older subdivision in the outskirts of the city.

Local Airport

After several months of living with Dad and his wife, we found a second-floor apartment at Cumberland Court, a low-rent complex in

Chamblee, Georgia. Our new apartment was within walking distance of Dad's house. It was also close to Peachtree DeKalb Airport, a small air field used mostly by light planes.

I didn't know that sometimes I was flown from that airport to be briefed and prepped for ops. In fact, I had no conscious memory of ever going there. Although I've not yet found any evidence that Dad ever had a pilot's license, I've had several memories of him flying me from the airport and back in small aircraft.

I doubted these memories until a private investigator reminded me that because my father had been a flight engineer during his four-year stint in the Air Force, he would have known how to fly small planes. Another professional explained that often when a person "borrows" an owner's plane, he gets away with it by not having to present a pilot's license.

Aryan Cult Network

I was unaware that Dad was manipulating some of my younger alter-states to go to cult meetings in Atlanta and Cobb County, officiated by local Aryan associates. Although some of their criminal occult rituals were similar to what I'd experienced in Pennsylvania, the north Georgia Aryan network focused more on the manufacturing and sales of illegal drugs and pornography. Unfortunately, as in Pennsylvania, pedophilia seemed to be the norm, as was the horrification and torture of their victims–particularly children and women. Further, I was forced to help Dad and some of the leaders when they transported children who, Dad claimed, were being bought and sold through their extensive, lucrative black marketing network.

In Pennsylvania, Dad's cult had often used dogs, snakes, and an occasional circus-trained lion in bestiality porn shoots. The Cobb County Aryan network's leaders seemed to prefer using domesticated animals, including trained dogs, although they also sometimes used tamed wildcats.

Unfortunately, when several children victimized within the network testified about the wildcats in court in the late 1980s, they were disbelieved. As with that jury, most people are unaware that owning a large, tamed wildcat is a status symbol among certain groups of black-marketers.[1]

Dad continued to break child victims' minds, creating pliable altered states of consciousness they weren't aware of. In the mid-1970s, Dad had easy access to a large, two-story warehouse in Atlanta. On Saturdays, he and several male associates brought children there to be traumatized and mentally programmed.

Although he now used mannequins with fake blood to traumatize the children, he still insisted that the children use knives to kill baby animals on plain, cafeteria-sized tables. Doing this served several purposes: 1) the children had to suppress their consciences before they could kill the innocent baby animals; 2) they then developed perpetrator alter-states that didn't mind killing; and 3) even if they remembered, they wouldn't tell anyone, because Dad and the other men told them everyone would hate them for killing the animals.

Because the warehouse's exits were always guarded on the inside by men, my cult-conditioned alter-states didn't try to break and run. They believed there was no escape. Dad was also careful to always make another alter-state take over whenever I left the building, so I would not remember what had just occurred inside. And as I was being transported home, whoever drove me would verbally trigger out several more alter-states in succession so that, by the time I arrived home, the memory of the warehouse was completely gone. Dad and his criminal associates called this technique "information compartmentalization."

Dad taught several of the local Aryan leaders (including a man I'll name "J.C.") how to trigger out and use several of my child alter-states. Because these alter-states hadn't developed mentally or emotionally, they didn't feel old enough to be a parent and therefore didn't accept responsibility for Emily's welfare. Because Emily had no way of knowing this, she believed that sometimes her mother didn't care if those people hurt her terribly.

Some of the Aryan leaders called themselves "Southern Gentlemen" an oxymoron. They told my participating child parts what to do during hardcore rituals and kiddy porn shoots. The rituals also were used to create more screen memories in my mind. When I remembered them in the early 1990s, their horror blocked out memories of preceding, covert assignments–for a while.

My forced participation in the Aryan occult rituals was also used to blackmail some of my adult alter-states into performing more assassinations. Dad and other professional handlers repeatedly told these parts that if they went on ops, they wouldn't have to perform illegal acts in rituals and wouldn't have to see more children being hurt. Then they reassured the alter-states that the CIA would cover for them at home so they wouldn't be arrested for any stateside (ritual and porn) crimes that they were forced to perform.

Albert also participated in some of the local Aryan occult rituals, and often transported us to them. He seemed to do whatever Dad wanted, even taking me to a specialized facility where I was repeatedly drugged and electro-shocked. This usually was done when I became noticeably depressed or agitated at home and sat on our carpeted floor in the hall-way or bedroom, holding my head in my hands and crying out, "I have a whirlwind in my head!" (These whirlwinds seemed to consist of rapid thoughts and images that circled nonstop in my mind–some survivors call this phenomena "rapid switching" of alter-states.)

In the 1990s, when I first remembered Albert's many betrayals, I felt hurt and angry. To be fair, however, I had to consider that Dad might have blackmailed him into compliance and silence.

One reason I think this is possible is that, in the early 1980s, after Albert suddenly refused to have further contact with Dad, Albert kept ranting about how when "they" came to get him, he'd "take out" as many of them as he could before they killed him. At that time, I thought his mind had snapped–especially when he refused to say who "they" were. Now, I believe he was terrified that members of the Aryan network might kill him for breaking away from their control.[2]

In spite of Albert's animosity towards Dad, however, he had a streak of racism that perhaps helped him feel comfortable around some of the other white supremacists. He shared many of their beliefs, possibly because he was raised by a Nazi stepfather.

As an example: when Emily was about six years old, Albert repeatedly told her and me that if she ever had a "nigger's" baby, he'd disown her. He was angry when he said this, irrationally behaving as if she'd already become pregnant.

Albert nursed a terrible hatred towards Blacks. Sometimes he deliber-ately drove too close behind small cars driven by elderly Black women, deliberately terrorizing them and making frightening faces at them. Each time, I felt so embarrassed, I slid down in my seat. When we'd be near a Black male, Albert would usually sneer and call the man a "jigaboo." He clearly believed that people with darker skin were inferior, and avoided walking near or talking to any of them.

Whenever he drove past a government-subsidized housing project in Lawrenceville, Georgia, he sneered at the Black children playing outside between the rows of single-story buildings, calling them "yard apes" and "jungle bunnies." Because I didn't remember the Aryan meetings, I didn't understand where he got those strange words.

I was alarmed by his behaviors and often felt ashamed to be his wife. He seemed to be so full of hatred and rage–I prayed constantly to God to touch his soul and make him the good man I sensed he had the capacity to be. I wasn't willing to accept that God can't force any person to do or become anything, against that person's will. I needed many more years to realize that, unlike most of the male figures in my life, God was not a perp.

Child Victims

Because Dad created and conditioned most of my programmed alter-states, he knew which buttons to push, which triggers to use, and which parts to pull out to perform specific activities. He was careful never to trigger out a child-rescuer part when he wanted me to help him do awful things to children.

He and his criminal associates enjoyed using victims to harm and traumatize each other. They reminded me of prison guards who choose prisoners to harm each other for the guards' entertainment. By having victim #1 perform an act against victim #2 while the controller stands in the shadows or in another room, victim #2 will believe that victim #1 was responsible.

Forgiving myself for obeying Dad has been hard work. I've had to accept that I was weak. I broke. I reached my limits of endurance again and again, until I did whatever he and his criminal associates commanded. Holding onto undeserved guilt has also been a sneaky way to avoid remembering how weak and helpless I'd felt, having had no control over the situation.

When Dad made me do terrible things to children, he used a control technique that he'd first developed when he'd forced me to participate in murderous rituals as a young child. Each time, Dad gave me a choice between performing a greater or lesser evil–a classic double-bind. Either way I went, I ended up believing I was guilty and therefore a monster.

Based on Dad's specific instructions, I could either hurt the child, or he would take over and torture the child before carrying out my original assignment.

Dad's threat of torturing a child was always given to me away from the child's hearing. The victim had no way of knowing that my disobedience could lead to the victim's being brutally tortured. Because Dad made sure the child saw me participate without a struggle, I believed that each child saw me as a willing perpetrator. That especially broke my heart.

Because Dad controlled when my cult alter-states came out and when they went back under, those parts couldn't stay conscious long enough to be able to report the crimes. He also ensured my continuing cooperation by telling those alter-states that if they did report the crimes, they would go to prison. He never mentioned the word "coercion."

Because my alter-states didn't know they were not guilty for what they'd been forced to do, they believed they were just as guilty and monstrous as Dad.

Although those alter-states believed his threats and did whatever he commanded, the alter-states initially felt different towards J.C., the Cobb County Aryan leader. They weren't so sure that he'd carry out similar threats if they dared disobey.

The first time he told an alter-state what to do to a brown-haired boy for a porn shoot, that alter-state chose to disobey him rather than traumatize the boy. Livid with rage, J.C. came into the room, dragged the boy into another room, and tortured him by using a branding iron heated red-hot on a portable barbeque grill. Later, J.C. convinced this alter-state that my rebelliousness had caused the boy to be tortured. The lesson went deep; all of my cult alter-states obeyed J.C.'s instructions from then on.

Although they were careful to obey Dad and J.C., these alter-states still attempted to secretly soothe and comfort the young victims–since the men didn't say they couldn't. If the alter-states believed they weren't being watched, they whispered words of encouragement into the children's ears. Seeing no way out, these parts believed they could best help the children from within the system.

If a child was to be bathed as a preparation for ritual sacrifice, my parts bathed the child gently and soothingly, looking directly into the child's eyes the entire time. These parts knew that for some children, death was a mercy, compared to what they'd have to endure each day as slaves. My parts wanted each child to know that someone did care. They did the best they could in each evil situation.

My professional handlers knew I would much rather be given pain than witness children being tortured. And when I was forced to harm children, I took on the controllers' disowned guilt as my own.

Notes

1. In the early 1990s, several of the children's adult relatives told me that a female therapist in North Georgia, who had believed the children's stories and had planned to testify for them, was brutally murdered–officially as the result of a robbery attempt.

2. Through personal experience, I've learned that about 90% of the threats made to mind-control and ritual abuse victims are never carried out. Oftentimes, perpetrators believe if they can hurt and terrorize victims while they still have control over them, then if the victims decide to leave, the internalized terror and memories of torture and horrification are usually strong enough to influence them to give up and go back without a single threat being carried out. The use of threats to control the minds of victims is not an unfamiliar tactic. *Time* magazine 2/10/97, "By the Book":

   > To the growing list of popular "how to" manuals, add this release from the CIA, recently made public under a Freedom of Information request from the *Baltimore Sun.* The agency says it no longer follows the rules of the 124-page 1983 "human resource" handbook, used to train security forces in Latin American countries, which includes passages on mental torture: "A threat is basically a means for establishing a bargaining position by inducing fear in the subject. A threat should never be made unless it is part of the plan and the 'questioner' has the approval to carry out the threat. When a threat is used, it should always be implied that the subject himself is to blame by using words such as, 'You leave me no other choice but to . . .' He should never be told to comply 'or else!' The threat of coercion usually weakens or destroys resistance more effectively than coercion itself. For example, the threat to inflict pain can trigger fears more damaging than the immediate sensation of pain. In fact, most people underestimate their capacity to withstand pain. In general, direct physical brutality creates only resentment, hostility, and further defiance." (pg. 21)

   After 9/11, President George W. Bush and numerous other government officials constantly used the media to attack certain foreign leaders as either being terrorists or promoters of terrorism. This can be perceived as hypocritical, because *what employees of our government and their associates have done to the minds and lives of mind-control victims is a working definition of terrorism.* The ongoing traumas and mental torture perpetrated against these victims literally changed their brain chemistry. Added to that are the implanted threats that operate 24/7 in their minds, at least on an unconscious level. The perpetrators' terroristic threats can still dictate their actions, dampen their hope, sap their energy and strength, isolate them from the rest of humanity, and cut short any sense of a future.

Cover Positions

Reinsurance Clerk

As I continued to be taken to rituals and professionally handled on covert ops, I needed a plausible cover–a seemingly normal life that would hide the existence of the other activities.

My first full-time job was at a small insurance company in downtown Atlanta. I was hired to temporarily fill the position of reinsurance clerk, held by a petite, black-haired woman who handled large sums of premiums paid to reinsurance companies like General Re and Munich American, to insure the solvency of the policies issued by the agency. The volatile woman would soon go on maternity leave, and was understandably outraged that I'd been interviewed and hired without her knowledge.

During my initial training, she deliberately withheld essential information to sabotage my success as her replacement. I basically trained myself while she was gone, using her previous work as my guide.

Both before and after her leave, she screamed at me nearly every day, making cruel remarks in the presence of the other office workers. Each time she screamed, I froze. When she finished her tirade, I hurried to the bathroom to cry. My face was always blotchy and red when I returned to my desk. Then she smiled triumphantly and berated me more. The other employees were concerned about me. They didn't know I wasn't able to assert myself with her because I'd been a victim of both men and women for many years.

Before she returned from her maternity leave, a new supervisor tried to convince me to be the clerk's permanent assistant. I declined. To the best of my knowledge, while I worked there, I was sent out on covert ops on weekends, when I called in sick (the flu always made a great cover), or when I was on "vacation."[1]

Maryland Casualty

My next full-time employment was with Maryland Casualty Company at the insurance company's regional office located in a sprawling office park, north of Atlanta. To the best of my memory, all of my positions at that company were actively used as covers for my participation in covert ops.

Because nearly all of my supervisors and managers at Maryland Casualty appeared to be directly complicit in covering-up for my absences, I couldn't separate my feelings about the ops from my feelings about working there. When Albert dropped me off at the front entrance of the flat-roofed, one-story building, I usually cried. Each time I prepared to enter the building, an invisible darkness seemed to crush my soul. I have never forgotten telling Albert that Maryland Casualty reminded me of the song, *Hotel California,* "You can check out any time you like, but you can never leave."[2]

Because my mind was constantly active, typing insurance policies and endorsements bored me silly. After six months, I transferred to another room where I worked as a CRT operator for a year and a half, inputting pages of cryptic codes from insurance policy files. After that, I transferred to the Commercial Casualty Department located in the front part of the building. There, I was an insurance policy rater/coder.

Pam, our department's middle-aged supervisor, was petite with short auburn hair. I quickly learned to fear her, and tried hard to avoid angering her. Because Pam's behaviors reminded me of my childhood relationship with my mother, I developed an emotionally conflicted relationship with her. Unfortunately for me, she used my fear of her anger and stern disapproval, as well as shaming tactics, to keep me under tight control.

Our department's manager, Clyde, was a tall, middle-aged man with short, thinning brown hair. He usually wore a plain, long-sleeved white shirt, dark suit, and glasses. His bald manager, Fritz, usually sat quietly in his own cubicle and said little to anyone. Clyde soon became my substitute father figure.

Pam and Clyde seemed to cultivate similar childlike loyalties in many of the other young female workers in our department. Pam also used her religiosity and moral recriminations to keep us compliant. Tension often built up between those female raters who vied for Pam's attention and approval. Because tempers often ran high, a common expression was, "The shit just hit the fan."

At that time, if I'd been told that my positions were cover jobs, I would have said the idea was pure craziness. I didn't know what I couldn't remember.

Because I enjoyed being a rater/coder, I was rarely bored. Whenever I'd learned everything that I could at my current level of expertise, Pam encouraged me to attain more training. Since I received a raise every six months during my employment at Maryland Casualty, I believed I must be a highly valued worker.

After several years, our regional office transferred to a large new building near Perimeter Mall, located in a wealthy section of north Atlanta. The building had a huge multi-story atrium with dining tables, water fountains, and a long goldfish pond that many employees tossed pennies into for good luck.

Around that same time, Albert and I hunted for our first house. Still in control of our money, he claimed we couldn't afford more than the most basic home. In August, 1982, we found a tiny new pine-sided, three-bedroom, one-bath house on Cedars Road, out past the sleepy old town of Lawrenceville. Although we had no air conditioning in the hot summer and only small space heaters to warm us in the winter, I was ecstatic–finally, we had our own home!

Because we now lived an hour's drive from both of our jobs, Albert tired of transporting me. For a while, he encouraged me to rely on co-workers to drive me to work and back. When that was no longer an option, he agreed to let me purchase a small car of my own. (Still phobic about driving, I didn't obtain a driver's license until I was in my late twenties.)

I chose a new white Mazda GLC hatchback with standard transmission and blue–gray interior. When Albert tried to teach me how to drive it on the rural country roads near our home, he made me so nervous, I insisted on teaching myself. Within hours, I drove fine! I didn't know that I'd become co-conscious with an alter-state that had been driving since I was a teenager.

I felt more in control of my life as I drove to work and back each day. And yet, at work and at home, I was still being controlled.

Sitting at my desk each day, I helped to process huge stacks of files. Our copies of the business insurance policies, endorsements (changes), cancellations, audits, underwriters' policy renewal instructions, and our own sheets of coding were stapled inside the off-white manila files.

Any of the files that were jacketed by extra blue or red folders were to be processed first, because they either had large premiums that needed to be input on the computer ASAP, or they were so old, we could get in trouble with state auditors for not having processed them yet. Although

I tried to please Pam by working hard and fast, she always seemed to expect more from me. I usually enjoyed that challenge.

When Pam had first hired me, she'd agreed I would never have to work overtime. She broke her word when she and Clyde insisted that every rater must work overtime, either during weekdays or on weekends.

This was a problem, because I was often transported at night to Aryan meetings, and was exhausted from going on ops, doing my regular job, driving an hour each way to work and back, and now working overtime. It was more than my mind and body could endure.

One Saturday, I came to work early in the morning. When I sat down at my desk, I broke into tears. Surprised, Pam asked what was wrong. I held out my arm to her and said, "What does Clyde want? My blood?" Although they let me go home that day, the pressure to work overtime continued unabated. I was constantly exhausted and sick.

I didn't know enough about healthy boundaries to recognize that Pam was overly controlling and intrusive about my personal life. Therefore, I didn't think it strange when she told me what to do at home, as well as on the job.

I wanted to believe Pam when she claimed to be a godly Christian. I couldn't accept the alternate reality–that she and Clyde not only were *not* concerned about my health; they were deliberately using my mental programming to control and handle me. My belief that Pam was a devout Christian clashed with the hidden knowledge that she was not what she claimed to be. That clash created cognitive dissonance in my mind; one of the two sets of knowledge must be repressed. Believing that Pam was "good" was preferable to knowing that she was actively and willingly betraying me.

Because I repressed all memories of Pam and Clyde's covert activities as assigned handlers, I was shocked and dismayed when I discovered that for years, Pam had deliberately withheld information from me that directly affected my professional future.

Her betrayal fueled my anger, helping me to break loose from her control. I quietly inquired about rating positions at nearby insurance companies. An elderly female co-worker told me she'd been hired to work at Cotton States, another insurance company about a mile away. At her suggestion, I applied there and was quickly hired.

When I gave Pam my required two-week notice, she was icy cold and wouldn't speak to me unless absolutely necessary. Not having encountered that side of her before, I was deeply hurt.[3]

One day, I took some of my personal possessions from my desk outside to my car during a coffee break. When I returned, Pam furiously yelled at me in front of the other raters, informing me that from then on, she would inspect everything I took from my desk. I was stunned by her sudden distrust and by the realization that although I'd worked closely with her for five years, I didn't really know her. After that, leaving was easy.

In the 1990s, I pieced together enough information from my journals to know that much of my seven years of employment at Maryland Casualty was a front for other activities. To the best of my understanding, I often reported to work and then left the building–sometimes for days—to do covert ops under the control of one or more professional handlers.

Occasionally, Clyde or Pam were my handlers for local activities. I've had several vivid memories of Clyde driving me from Maryland Casualty to the Fort Gillem Army base south of Atlanta, to meet with spooks in rooms and corridors hidden beneath one of its small buildings. I've also remembered that on at least one occasion, Clyde personally handled me on an overseas assignment. I've also had numerous memories of Pam's involvement in Cobb County Aryan meetings and activities.

One alter-state journaled that Clyde's manager, Fritz, had privately told that alter-state that my personnel records had been doctored so if anyone asked about my unusual number of absences, my records would show that I was in the Army Reserves. I don't know if this is true, since I was never permitted to see that part of my personnel file.

Pam also told some of my alter-states that she covered for my absences by telling other raters that I'd gone to other branch offices or to the Baltimore home office for "special training" (I never did). Because Pam was in charge of our vacation schedules, she chose when I could take days off. Sometimes, if I felt exhausted from an op, she encouraged me to take the rest of the day off to recuperate. Not knowing that I'd just come home from a stress-filled op, I believed her when she said I had a 24-hour virus.[4]

On numerous occasions, both Albert and Pam suggested I take Emily to visit my mother and her second husband in South Carolina. I didn't know that after my arrival, they often triggered out alter-states and drove me to nearby airports to go on more ops while keeping Emily at their house as a coercive measure, ensuring that I would comply with my assigned handlers.

When I first remembered that my positions at Maryland Casualty were covers, I was very upset. How could I have been gone for days at a time, leaving my desk at the drop of a hat, with no questions asked? Damn it, I'd worked hard for my pay! I was a good worker!

As the memories continued to emerge with remarkable consistency and vividness, I realized I had probably been given semi-annual raises to keep me from seeking other employment. I also realized that, because of the way our department's file distribution system had been set up, any rater/coder could have easily completed another's work. This may be one reason why I had often started working on a complicated file, then had later discovered it had been completed by someone else–often by Pam herself.

Pam and Clyde had repeatedly reminded the Commercial Casualty rater/coders that the Baltimore home office required all workers to maintain and update our bulky, red-jacketed "desk manuals," so that no employee would be indispensable. Each desk manual contained indexed, handwritten, detailed instructions on how to perform any task handled by any person sitting at that station. In other words, any person could have completed my files while I was away.

When I finally accepted that my employment there had been a cover, I felt miserable. Pam had repeatedly told me I was one of their best workers. What a blow to discover I probably wasn't! Worse, Albert had been actively complicit. My bosses, Albert, my mother and her husband, Dad . . . had *anyone* in my life not betrayed me?

Even several co-workers, who Pam had assigned to drive me to work and back and to befriend me away from work, had been used to help transport me for ops!

I'd been raised from early childhood to believe that my value as a human was based on what I did, instead of who I was. Learning that I hadn't earned my pay was a powerful blow to my fragile self-esteem.

Cotton States

After I left Maryland Casualty and started working at Cotton States, I felt better about myself. We were treated with respect, and our employment benefits were excellent. Although I still don't know if my position there was a cover, I've consistently remembered that at least two supervisors had also handled me away from the building. I've also repeatedly remembered having taken solo walks outdoors during lunch breaks, strolling around the white Marriott hotel less than a block away. On the far side, I met briefly with a male spook who waited for me in a white car. Each time, I gave him information and he gave me new instructions.

Covert Activities

When I had worked at Maryland Casualty, several of my professional handlers had come there during the day to transport me. Although I didn't recognize them as they walked towards my desk, some of my alter-states emerged, happy to be with them again. With a nod from Clyde or Pam, these parts followed the handlers out to their waiting vehicles.

One of my regular handlers claimed to be with the CIA's Directorate of Operations. He was fairly handsome and charismatic with short, blond hair. He called himself "Jed," which he said was short for "Jedediah"–I'm sure that was an alias.

When he came there to transport me, Jed usually drove a sporty white Jaguar. He convinced several of my female alter-states that he was my legal husband. Because those alter-states didn't know of my life at home and didn't know that Albert was my husband, they believed Jed. Compliance came easy, because he gave those alter-states gentle, attentive sex.

These op alter-states loved going on trips with Jed and other alleged CIA handlers. One of Jed's sidekicks was a heavyset, wide-built man with fairly short, slightly wavy orange-red hair and a full beard. I rarely met with Jed in his office (if it really was his), without the red-bearded man standing close by–perhaps for extra protection.

When Jed called me at home, he first played the recording of a fax machine's wavy tones. My mind always short-circuited when I heard those tones, because one should hear them when *calling* a phone number that has an active fax machine. (We didn't have one in our home.) The resulting cognitive dissonance quickly put me into a trance. Then Jed spoke, and one of my CIA-loyal parts emerged to do exactly as he commanded.[5]

Once in a while, Dad acted as my local assigned handler. After triggering out a compliant alter-state over the phone, he gave that part specific instructions. Albert never intervened or argued when those parts said they had to leave. Each time, Dad told the triggered-out traveler alter-states that if they didn't do exactly what he and the other handlers said, he would personally kill Emily.

Believing my father's threat, each alter-state obediently drove to a contact point where an awaiting handler triggered out another alter-state to begin the next leg of the journey. These adult alter-states instinctively knew I couldn't survive the pain of losing another precious child. Although they hadn't emotionally bonded with Emily, they understood that if I died, so would they–since we inhabited the same body.

Although my handlers used my compartmentalized rage to do kills, that powerful emotion rarely emerged away from their control. In fact, I would often isolate or walk long distances, alone, to keep from hurting anyone if I felt angry. If it did unexpectedly emerge at home, I either told Emily to go to a friend's house, or to lock herself in her bedroom from the inside. Although we both knew I could easily use a wire hanger to open it, the temporary barrier gave me enough time to regain control and avoid hurting her.

My rage had been with me for many years. When I was fourteen, I had stabbed my oldest brother in the forearm with the pointed end of my styling comb after a ritual alter-state was accidentally triggered out while watching a TV movie, *Brothers of the Bell*. After I came back to consciousness, I was horrified at what I'd done, and cried and begged him to please not tell our parents. As far as I know, he never did.[6]

As an adult, the closest I'd ever come to consciously hurting a man was when Albert approached me menacingly in our bedroom in Lawrenceville one afternoon in a fit of rage. He shoved me backwards onto our bed, his fist balled, ready to punch me. An op alter-state emerged, raised my knees to my chest, pushed my feet against his midsection, then lifted and slammed him backwards into the wall. I was astonished and pleased that I'd done this to him; in turn, he never tried to physically assault me again.

Before my recovery, none of my assassin alter-states had emerged at home. When Dad murdered Rose, a new adult part had split off from my consciousness. Dad and other professional handlers code-named that male part, "Dark." He visualized himself as tall and muscular. He'd internalized Dad's overwhelming, murderous personality, to make himself equal to and unafraid of Dad. To keep that part under control and separate from my consciousness, Dad and others tortured him with electricity.

After the severe electrical torture, this alter-state was unable to connect with me or any other alter-state. He was also emotionally disconnected from the rest of humanity. He served only one function: to kill.

Once in a while, local handlers took this alter-state to a private home in Cobb County. In warm weather, the back yard contained a garden full of flowers and vegetable plants. Sometimes the handlers instructed this alter-state to take care of the plants by watering them and weeding around them. Although he wasn't capable of emotionally connecting with humans, this alter-state did develop a bond with "his" plants, perhaps because they subconsciously represented Rose.

When my professional handlers wanted this part to perform an especially reprehensible assassination, they took him *back* to the garden and forced him to stand and watch as they used a flame-thrower to cremate the plants. That killed what was left of the alter-state's ability to bond with any living creature.

After that, he was a stone cold killing machine with zero remorse or guilt. His only remaining pleasure was in doing each job well. Although he hated and despised everything that lived, he hated and despised himself most of all. And although he had a strong survival instinct, he dreaded facing another day of totally dark existence. He held the greatest emotional and psychic pain of any of my parts and was, more than any other alter-state, the wandering dead.

Some of my other specialized black op parts had been trained to disarm and kill hostage takers by pretending to be intellectually challenged. Those parts had no fear of weapons, having been taught that most people who hold a loaded gun are just as afraid as the targeted individual.

Although I was never allowed access to a gun at home, I used various kinds on ops. Since my forearms and wrists weren't as strong as a man's, I was more comfortable using smaller handguns. Because my aim was excellent (grey eyes are a plus), using a smaller-caliber weapon wasn't a handicap.

I was fortunate to also have the ability to see bullets coming at me in slow motion. I always had enough time to shift my body so they went past me.[7]

I also speeded up, physically and mentally, during dangerous ops. This may have been due to a powerful adrenaline rush paired with the effects of repetitive training. While my opponents fumbled for their guns, I'd already taken aim and formulated my next moves. While they were still raising their guns to shoot me, I easily picked off one or two of them.

These special abilities were invaluable, because I could go after more than one man at a time in a hazardous situation and come out alive and unharmed. Most of my spook handlers were so cowardly, they sent me in alone to take care of a situation during sniper and hostage interventions. My op alter-states never complained, however, because they'd been conditioned to believe they were disposable and dispensable. They fought to survive each op so they could go home, not knowing where home was.

During some nighttime ops, I emerged from a van (usually white, unmarked, and paneled) that my handlers parked out of sight, a block or two from a target's house. One of the handlers in the van monitored me via a tiny two-way radio device, reminiscent of a wireless hearing aid, that he inserted in my right ear. This way, the handler could hear what was happening and could give me more instructions, if needed. If a controlled alter-state accidentally froze or went under, the handler could verbally trigger out a second op-trained part to take over and complete the job.

Due to long-term exposure to criminal occult rituals, I felt comfortable with all kinds of knives–I still do.[8] As long as the blade was sharp, I carried out my orders with ease. On at least one occasion, I wore a leather contraption around my right wrist and forearm, the spring-released blade positioned against the inside of my forearm, hidden by a long sleeve. I didn't like that device because it was too awkward to use. The simpler the weapon, the more I liked it.

My MKNAOMI-programmed alter-states had limited training in the use and administration of deadly chemicals. A typical assignment involved my carrying a small plastic container of Vaseline in a purse. As instructed, I pushed the point of a long hatpin from the bottom/inside of the purse, outwards through a reinforced corner, making sure the point of the pin was directed away from my body as I carried the purse over my right shoulder. I then extracted the Vaseline container, opened it, and dipped the exposed point into a small, clear pool of liquid floating atop the petroleum jelly.

After coating the point and giving it time to dry, I then walked up to a male target and pretended to accidentally bump him with my purse, careful to scratch his skin through his clothes. Because the targeted individual didn't understand that he'd been fatally assaulted, I always had sufficient time to leave the area before anyone noticed me.

Some of my MKNAOMI parts were also sent into buildings to "paint" a clear substance onto a doorknob that a targeted individual was expected to use, usually while under surveillance. Some of these parts were even used to insert, or smear, clear substances onto targeted individuals' personal items in their homes, especially toothbrushes and the open ends of their tubes of toothpaste.[9]

When the first alter-state with biochemical training emerged in the early 1990s, she identified herself as Naomi. Unlike other black op alter-states, she was neither rageful nor emotionally cold–she'd simply done her job.[10]

A bulky, lightweight handgun that at least one op trained part had used (against a sniper) seemed to have been made of dark colored plastic. It could shoot three types of plastic cartridges that were color-coded: red, blue and yellow. That alter-state was told that each cartridge contained a unique deadly substance. Not only did the weapon pass through a metal detector; had it been examined, it probably would have been mistaken for a child's toy.

The hardest part of being overseas was that my black op alter-states couldn't remember who I was and where home was. They were more disconnected from me than my traveler alter-states were. This was, in part, because my op-trained alter-states had been created through extreme torture. Because they were blank slate alter-states, they didn't have my morals.

They were rarely allowed to carry any identification. If they did, the identification was always fake. Because they didn't know who they were, they assumed they were the person that the papers, travel visas, driver's licenses, etc. identified me as being. This helped the alter-states to pass through inspection points without appearing suspicious.

To keep any of my alter-states from breaking control and making an emergency phone call when someone was injured or killed, some of my mental programmers had exposed me to fake violence, then had let me "escape" into a room that had a phone. Each time I'd picked up the phone and dialed "0" to report the mock injury or death, a fake operator had answered and then either changed the subject or convinced the alter-state that local authorities didn't have time to deal with the problem. This conditioned the alter-states to believe there was no point in calling for medical aid if an injury or death occurred on a real assignment.

On most overseas ops, at least one specialized alter-state was made to memorize a temporary emergency number in case something went wrong. Such phone calls were occasionally unavoidable–handlers, op partners, and even assigned clients were occasionally injured or killed. At those times, my alter-states usually required further instructions.

In later years, several of my alter-states were temporarily given a small, black cell phone. All the alter-states had to do was press the "0" button, then a spook contact answered, posing as a phone company operator. These alter-states were trained to ignore what the operator said. When they gave a pre-arranged identifier code and reported the current circumstances, the fake operator stopped talking and transferred the call to a spook handler, who gave new instructions.

A particularly unpleasant assignment, after botched overseas ops, was to dismember dead spooks' bodies so they could be buried, undetected, in pieces. I was made to believe this was standard fare for overseas ops. I was told that local authorities couldn't be allowed to know the CIA was operating clandestinely in their jurisdiction. My op parts were also told that if I died overseas, my body would be disposed of the same way.[11]

Since Dad and other men had taught several of my alter-states how to dismember bodies in rituals, funeral homes, and in other closed environments, those parts became good at it. To stay sane, I developed one female alter-state that mentally did mathematical equations while cutting up the bodies. To this day, I visually "remember" numbers instead of the body parts and blood.

Some bodies were disposed of, stateside. At such times, a professional handler came to wherever I was and said that he had a job for "Angel." That emerging Angel alter-state (I had several with that code-name) specialized in body disposal, via acid. Although Angel was told that the bodies were deceased operatives, it is quite possible that they weren't.[12]

Most of the ops that my alter-states were used for, including body-guarding and hostage interventions, had the potential of traumatizing the alter-states. Sometimes, bad things happened to the people they were supposed to protect–the best of plans sometimes went awry.

Notes

1. Out of all of the years I worked full time, with nearly all of them generating two weeks of paid vacation each year, I only have one memory of having gone on a real vacation–to Miami. Even that trip was a cover for other activities I was forcibly involved in, while in Florida.

2. The lyrics were used as part of my CIA-compliant mental programming. Several spook handlers bragged that the song was an Agency favorite, partly because of the implied threat, and partly because "CIA" is embedded in its title.

3. As a child, I had learned to separate my awareness of the two "sides" of my parents' abusive personalities in my mind. By blocking out the abuse and danger, I was able to survive being in their presence each day without being terrified. This coping

mechanism continued when I was an adult. When an abusive person became an integral part of my life, I blocked out all memory and awareness of the harmful side of that person's personality, and only recollected the person's "good" side.

This is one of the primary reasons why I allowed abusive people to have power over me for so long. Only when their negative behaviors were so blatant that they punched through my wall of denial, was I able to recognize what they really were. When that happened, I (as the host alter-state) had one of two choices: I could accept the fact that the person was a threat to me and totally separate myself from that person to protect myself; or I could push the truth away, pretending that person's negative behaviors did not exist, and go back into denial about that person's true character and motives. I suspect this is what some alleged ritual abuse survivors have done: after they initially believed their emerging memories, they were influenced to go back into denial and return to their dangerous families, who then influenced them to blame the "false" memories on their therapists.

4. Because I was conditioned not to consult with regular medical doctors, I treated myself.

5. Carla Emery explained this effective hypnotic technique, known as Telephone Induction:

> The hypnotist speaks, or sounds the post-hypnotically suggested induction cue over the phone when he gets his subject's ear on the other end. He doesn't have to say "Hello" first. That would give his subject a predator-on-the-phone warning and the chance to hang up before the induction cue is spoken. Instead, the hypnotist gives the induction cue first. Immediately, in a person programmed for routine amnesia during trances, the subject's conscious mind is off-line. Only the reflexive hypno-robot is listening. The hypnotist gives his instructions to that subject's unconscious. When he is finished, the phone call and the hypnosis are terminated (probably both at once) by a routine suggestion. (pg. 65)

Possibly the best way for a novice to understand telephone induction is by reviewing the fictional movie, *Telefon,* starring Charles Bronson. In it, sleeper agents were unwittingly programmed to respond to a coded phrase. Not knowing that they were mentally programmed, they responded to a trigger phrase given to them during an unexpected phone call. In response, they each tranced and carried out the caller's instructions. The movie is an overly crude example of mental programming because most mind-controlled slaves are given many different programs that can be triggered, usually one at a time. Another difference is that in the movie, the sleepers were only used one time. In real life, because they are a serious financial investment, most slave-operatives will be used for decades.

6. At times, my brothers and I were fiercely loyal and protective towards each other. And yet, given our shared parentage, I am aware that I may not be the only sibling who was

programmed to have compliant alter-states. For this and other reasons, I choose not to have any more contact with them. Sometimes, to stay safe, mind-control and ritual abuse survivors have to care about those they love from a great distance.

7. I remembered this with no verifications in the early 1990s. Nearly a decade later, I attended a graduation ceremony in Chattanooga. The CEO of the Gallup Poll gave the address. He said he had interviewed successful professional hockey goalies and had learned that they had the unusual ability to see the puck coming at them in slow motion. In July, 2000, I wrote to Gallup for more information. An employee replied in an E-mail that this ability is called *elongated time.*

8. Some therapists call this a "trauma bond."

9. Not long before these memories emerged, I developed a sudden phobia about touching doorknobs and using toothpaste. In the past, I'd always carried a small container of Vaseline in my purse–perhaps as an unconscious reenactment. The initial awareness of my first emerging NAOMI programmed part was triggered during a class at a Baptist seminary, in which a student recounted the story of Ruth and Naomi. The impact of hearing the word Naomi was so tremendous that I ran to the bathroom and cried loudly for nearly a half-hour, not realizing that the adult students could hear all of it through the building's ductwork. I dropped out of school shortly after that.

10. In *Bluebird*, Dr. Colin Ross explained why the CIA's MKNAOMI project was developed. MKNAOMI was a joint project of the CIA and the Army's Special Operations Division in Fort Detrick, Maryland. It ran from 1953 to 1970. MKNAOMI involved "developing, testing, and maintaining biological agents and delivery systems for use against humans as well as against animals and crops" (pg. 67). At least one alter-state having that project's code name had continued to be used on black ops for years *after* the project officially ended.

11. This was a powerful, unconscious incentive to survive, because I didn't want my loved ones to grieve over losing me while having no idea what had happened to me!

12. I'm still phobic about handling all forms of acid, because I know what some of them can do to human flesh.

Interventions

Grandma's Gift

Because I was so busy going to work, rituals, ops, and more, I didn't have the time or energy to casually visit with my extended family in Pennsylvania. This was unfortunate, because I didn't have the chance to see my paternal grandmother one more time before she died of a massive heart attack in March, 1982, in the presence of her second husband. Although I deeply grieved losing her, I was glad she'd had the opportunity to experience safety, love, and happiness with him in his home during her remaining years.

When Dad was told of his mother's death, he was stone cold and showed no sign of grief. He insisted that he saw no reason to go to her funeral; after all, she was dead. My stepmother had to fight to get him to take her with him to Grandma's funeral to pay their last respects.

Before Grandma's death, she had secretly instructed one of Dad's brothers–the executor of her estate–to travel to Georgia and hand-deliver her brilliant diamond solitaire ring to me at Dad's house. Because I hadn't known that Grandma had owned it, I was deeply touched. It was my first nice piece of jewelry.

Grandma's legacy helped me to feel special. The knowledge that she had cared that much about me gave me new strength and helped me to stand taller. My uncle told me that because Grandma's first husband had never bought her an engagement ring, she had decided to save up her hard-earned money and buy one for herself.

Upon hearing the story, I realized if I was ever going to be happy, I couldn't wait the rest of my life for Albert to change. It was time to create my own happiness.

Meadowlark

Grandma's ring was the first step of my journey into strength and freedom. More changes came quickly after, almost as if an invisible hand was choreographing the events.

In the early 1990s, an alter-state named Andreia recounted an experience in which I had been forcibly transported in 1985 to an Air Force base that was identified to me only as "Meadowlark."

I was escorted there by a spook named Jim who fancied himself to be a cowboy. He led me into a set of below-ground corridors and rooms at that base. Soon, a succession of alter-states was triggered out and painlessly interrogated by a gray-haired, ramrod-straight, retired Army General who some of my alter-states had known in the past as "Poppa."

After the interrogations, Poppa asked to speak to any alter-state that would consider defecting and working for him and his people. Andreia emerged. Having known Poppa in the past, she still liked him.

Poppa warned Andreia that if I continued to go to the Aryan rituals in Georgia, I'd be put in prison for the rest of my life and could lose contact with Emily. He said his hand-picked, retired Army intelligence personnel were working covertly, on a strictly voluntary basis, to shut down Aryan organizations in the US as part of an extensive covert operation he called, "Clean Sweep." He said he knew about the nationwide Aryan network's plans to overthrow the government in the year 2000, since it was one of Hitler's long-term goals. He said that, because much violence was planned (including bombings in Atlanta during the Olympics), ASA and other intelligence agencies had chosen to intervene.

I write "ASA" with the understanding that I'm not able to recall, clearly, whether Poppa said his covert intelligence agency was the Army's ISA–Intelligence Support Activity, or ASA–Army Security Agency. Years after I remembered meeting Poppa at Meadowlark, several alter-states journaled that Poppa's recruits were connected to ASA, and that I had picked up the moniker ISA from a book about the extensive US intelligence community. For simplicity's sake, I will identify the agency as ASA with the understanding that it may not have been that agency at all.[1]

Poppa's face registered hatred towards the Nazi conspirators as he spoke. Then he talked about ASA's dedication to "God and Country." Although he had done hurtful things to some of my parts in the past, supposedly out of necessity, he now convinced Andreia that he'd become a true Christian and that, because of his conversion, he wanted to do what was right. Andreia believed him and agreed to cooperate with him and the ASA after I returned to Georgia.

Poppa warned that either I could stay completely away from the Aryan meetings from now on, or Andreia could attend them as his mole to help bring the network down from the inside. He reminded Andreia that if she chose to secretly participate in the Aryan meetings while pretending to be other alter-states, she would have to perform the same repugnant acts they'd already performed. He added that he would assign one of his inside men, already a mole, to protect her.

Although she grieved that she would have to harm others, Andreia agreed to stay conscious as much as she possibly could during the cult meetings. She was willing to lose pieces of her soul to help free the children.

When Andreia journaled this memory in the early 1990s, I thought I'd lost my mind. I could find no proof of any Air Force base named "Meadowlark." I put the questionable memory in the back of my mind to wait for verifications—if any existed.[2]

Several of the other alter-states interrogated at Meadowlark journaled that Poppa had told them that the CIA had made a disastrous mistake by bringing Nazi professionals to the US and installing them in secure positions.[3] He said the CIA had allowed our sworn enemies to work towards taking our government over from the inside-out. He said the public would not be told about the attempted overthrow, because there would be "riots in the streets" and "mass panic." He said Clean Sweep had to be conducted quietly. The main reason why our government was not willing to admit that criminal occult activities were rampant, Poppa told me, was because much of the occultism had been covertly intro-duced into the US, in a Trojan Horse sort of way, by some of the Nazi immigrants.

Poppa said the CIA was tight with many Aryan occult organizations, just as the FBI continued to collaborate in secret with a number of Mafia organizations still operating in the US. He said the CIA had a vested interest in ensuring that these secretive, dangerous cults continue to operate, unimpeded, and this was why other federal agencies enacted Clean Sweep. Poppa said that as they attempted to do damage control, they were having to work against the CIA in the process.[4]

The Mansion

In 1985, after I was flown back to Atlanta from Meadowlark, Andreia and some of my cult-conditioned alter-states continued to attend the

Aryan meetings in the Cobb County area. Many of the meetings were held in warehouses; some were held in old houses in and near Kennesaw. Those houses were owned by cult members who clustered in several neighborhoods. Some of the houses were connected by hidden underground tunnel systems that they used to store contraband and children who were bought and sold on the lucrative black market.[5]

On numerous occasions, I was also taken to an elaborate underground installation that was probably a former SAM missile site.[6] A large brick house had been built atop the site.

When I was taken there, the mansion's exterior walls were beige-colored brick. Sometimes men stood in black uniforms on the roof, holding rifles. Behind the mansion, I sometimes saw men dressed in similar garb, practicing martial arts.[7]

After entering through the front door, I saw at least one large chandelier hanging from the high ceiling in the open living area to the right that could also be used as a ball room. Walking through the house towards the rear, several enclosed rooms were to my left.

A hidden entrance was in a wall between two of those rooms. When it slid open, I saw a wide concrete ramp that sloped down to the first sub-level of a complex of concrete walled rooms and tunnels. On that first sub-level was a large nursery room in which young children, especially babies in cribs, were taken care of by rotating shifts of female Aryan cult members.[8]

I was told that some of these women's children were sold to childless couples through cooperative adoption agencies. I knew from previous experience that these children were birthed by cult mothers away from hospitals, so the babies had no birth records. Many of the women who birthed and tended the children were known in the Aryan network as "breeders."[9]

Another underground, concrete walled room housed expensive electronic equipment that accessed what was identified to me as the "Brandon" computer system.[10] J.C. and his father-in-law, B.H., told me that the computer system held pertinent information on every government programmed slave in the US–including the names and training of all their documented alter-states and how each one could be triggered out. They taught several of my alter-states how to use the system; based on what I saw, what they told me seemed to be correct. They said the reason the information would never be found in the CIA's files, was because it was stored on at least one of NASA's computer systems.[11]

The alter-states that were trained to input data into that system were amazed at how much information they found on it about people they knew. The Aryan leaders didn't know that Andreia was also accessing the information and funneling some of it back to ASA.

B.H. and J.C. met frequently at the mansion with a thin man who was both a Satanist and a civil war buff. B.H. and the thin man seemed to have a surprisingly loving and sexually intimate relationship. In some of the mansion's basement rooms, B.H. happily videotaped humorous pornography that was just as professional as Great Britain's Benny Hill TV shows. One of my alter-states personally assisted B.H. in the production of some of that pornography.

In that mansion, B.H. used an innovative form of electrical torture to create a new child alter-state in me that he named "Leah." That part became his personally owned slave alter-state.

In my last years in the Aryan cult network, B.H. seemed to convince himself and just about everyone else that I was, by choice, his cult wife. Several of my child alter-states liked him because he was nice to them at times. They were very upset to learn from other parts, after I broke away, that B.H. also had a cruel side to his seemingly split personality.

William

In 1985, J.C. introduced a new cult member, William, to us. Although he wasn't tall, William's shoulders and neck were strong, and his posture was ramrod-straight. J.C. explained that William had retired from the Army as a Sergeant Major after thirty years of service, and was now seeking J.C.'s personal protection.[12]

J.C. enforced strict rules about cult membership: each new member had to perform illegal, distasteful acts to prove his or her loyalty. They didn't know that J.C. would use secretly videotaped films of their initiations to blackmail them into ongoing compliance and silence about the cult's numerous illegal activities.

Several of my cult alter-states watched as William performed the demoralizing tasks in a stone-faced way. Unlike my father and J.C., William never fully relaxed at the cult meetings. My cult-loyal alter-states didn't know about my trip to Meadowlark, and worried that William might betray J.C. They didn't know that Andreia, a part they weren't aware of, already had.

William soon gained J.C.'s permission to drive me to the Cobb County meetings, and then back home to the east side of Atlanta. Some of my cult alter-states noticed that when William drove them home, his face screwed up with disgust and anger as if he needed a long, hot bath. Those alter-states were confused because they were accustomed to being in the presence of criminals who were noticeably relaxed and happy after performing illicit acts.

ASA

My cult alter-states didn't know that William was triggering Andreia out and driving her to covert ASA meetings that he officiated. At those meetings, the other ASA volunteers called him "Bill."

Andreia was amazed by the volunteers' selflessness. They seemed sincere when they stated that they were willing to give their lives, if necessary, to bring down the local Aryan cult network from within, brick by brick. Their #1 motto was "God and Country." A recent fundamentalist Christian convert, Bill believed if he served God and Jesus, he would be protected from the cult's evil.

The unselfishness and caring of the ASA volunteers became the human antivenom to the sociopathic poison I'd been immersed in, for nearly all of my life. They became my lifeline to sanity and morality, ushering me into a new state of grace.[13]

Coercion

Although I didn't remember J.C. or the Aryan cult network when I was home, I often thought about divorcing Albert and starting a new life with Emily. Twice, I secretly met with a local female attorney to discuss filing for a divorce. Each time, Albert found out and talked me out of it. Based on what I'd told her about Albert's abusiveness, the attorney was unhappy that I kept backing off and suggested I seek professional help. I never talked to her again.

At some of the Aryan cult meetings, J.C. and Albert repeatedly threatened some of my alter-states that if they should ever try to break and run, taking Emily with them, Albert and J.C. would use cult funds to ensure that Albert would gain full custody of Emily. The alter-states believed their threats and decided to stay and protect Emily within the system as much as they could, since they were convinced they'd never be able to take her away.

At home, Albert used another tactic to keep me controlled. He said if I ever tried to divorce him, he'd move to another part of the country and change his name, so that I'd never get a penny of child support from him. Because I didn't earn much as an insurance clerk, I believed I couldn't afford to raise our daughter on my own. In every way, I felt hopelessly trapped.

Notes

1. Although the ASA was officially disbanded after the end of the Vietnam war, some of its members may have continued covert operations, identifying each other as "ASA".

2. In July, 1992 I was at a local library, scanning the *1990 Encyclopedia of World Crime, Vol. III* for verifications of the names of several Mafia figures I'd remembered. In it, I found a section about a violent, subversive Aryan organization I'd already remembered: The Order. I also found verifications of what I'd recalled hearing at Aryan planning meetings. Best of all, it verified the existence of the federal government's Clean Sweep operation:

   Order, The, prom. 1983-88, US consp.-secret crim. soc. Fifteen white supremacists were indicted in Fort Smith, Ark., and Denver, Colo., in late April 1987 as the US government moved to eradicate America's racist movement. A lengthy investigation named "Clean Sweep" linked a group of neo-Nazis called The Order to racially-motivated killings and robberies dating back to 1984, and resulted in arrests in five states.

   Two of The Order's leaders were arrested. They had planned to "murder blacks and Jews, poison city water supplies, carry out terrorist actions to overthrow the US government, and bomb public utilities." (pg. 2376)

3. In 1994, a consultant told me that a new video had come out about the retired general. When I reviewed it, I learned that Poppa had been one of the first Army officers to enter a Nazi concentration camp in WWII. The camera panned a handwritten letter that he'd sent to his mother, expressing strong hatred towards Nazis. In the summer of 2002, I researched ASA, ISA, and Poppa (using his real name) on the Internet. I still didn't want to believe that the Meadowlark memories were true. I was astounded to find websites and articles on the Internet that directly connected him to *both* Army intelligence agencies!

   I found another verification on the Internet in early 2002. When I used the search terms "Meadowlark" and "Air Force," the Google search engine indicated the existence of "about 1490" website listings that included both. After ten years of clinging to denial, I finally accepted that the Meadowlark interrogation memory was valid.

4. If what Poppa told me was true, then this effort may have hit a brick wall when George W. Bush, the son of a former CIA director, was elected president-especially since many of his father's close associates had recycled themselves as George W's advisors.

5. Many ritual abuse survivors have reported that members of some criminal cults and black-marketing networks prefer to cluster in select neighborhoods. Often, when one cult owner has to sell a home, another member of the group will quickly buy it. This may be a reason why, when some ritual abusers are publicly accused of hurting children, their neighbors-in surprising unison-insist that the accused is innocent.

6. In the December, 2001 edition of *GQ*, I found a diagram of a former underground missile site with a house built atop it. The diagram of the underground rooms and tunnels was *identical* to the layout of the tunnel system I'd remembered beneath the mansion. Because the government-contracted Lockheed and Martin-Marietta plants were close by, logic can conclude that a SAM missile site might have been constructed there to protect them. And true or not, a consultant once told me that the US Department of Defense sold some of its defunct missile sites to members of the nationwide Aryan network.

7. In 2003, while researching a former CIA handler named Mitchell Werbell III, I found information that may explain the martial arts and black uniforms. Werbell owned and operated COBRAY-SIONICS Training Center, a spook counter-terrorism training facility in Powder Springs, Georgia. It seems that black uniforms and martial arts training were a part of their operations (Lau 1). I also learned that Blackhawk helicopters were used by some of these operatives-perhaps the same helicopters I'd watched land on the roof of the mansion (American Ballistics).

8. Although this may seem ludicrous, other survivors of that Aryan network have also spoken of the underground nursery and tunnel systems. Some of them had never repressed their memories.

Because this Aryan network is a tightly closed system, with many of its members fearing death to themselves or loved ones if they leave or tell, few out-siders (until now) have been aware of its existence. I want to emphasize that I am not opposed to the rights of Aryans to believe as they choose. What I do oppose is the cowardly torture, sexual abuse, black-marketing, prostitution, brainwashing, forced porn participation, and murder of babies, children, and adult slaves. I would be willing to bet that some members of these Aryan organizations are also opposed to these ongoing crimes. True pride is strong in itself; it doesn't need to prop itself up on the shoulders of slaves.

9. Some breeders are brainwashed to believe that bearing children in honor of Hitler is the highest possible honor. Most of them don't realize they are actually slave-prostitutes.

10. In 1996, I used NASA's ArchiePlex Internet search engine to find information that might verify certain memories. During that search, I ran across the word "Brandon." Nearly every reference concerning that word was about Brandon University, including information about its Computer Services and its Department of Math and Computer Science. What an odd coincidence!

11. According to Linda Hunt's *Secret Agenda: The United States Government, Nazi Scientists, and Project Paperclip, 1945 to 1990*, NASA was basically created by a group of Nazi immigrants who had been brought into the US by the Army and CIA, their records whitewashed in the process. Some were proven war criminals. Although I am certain that most of NASA's current activities are legitimate, it is quite possible that some of its Nazi founders and their associates could have worked all along as double agents, using its facilities and equipment-as I believe was also done within the CIA-to further the Reich's heady goal of eventual world domination (A.K.A. the New World Order).

12. According to J.C., William's cover story was that he had gotten into serious trouble with an Aryan group in Kentucky, and needed J.C.'s protection from them. In return, William offered to do whatever J.C. wanted of him.

13. The reason I mention these individuals now, is that their cover was compromised in the mid 1990s when a fake "good guy" named Mark Phillips gained this information and everything else I'd compiled. Later, he admitted that he gave it all to CIA officers working in Atlanta. Since then, I've been given the go-ahead by ASA operatives to share this part of my and Bill's story, with the understanding that doing so will no longer put their people at risk.

Freedom

Baptist Church

Before my unexpected trip to Meadowlark, several young people from Hebron Baptist, an old one-story, white wooden church in the tiny town of Dacula, had started to visit our rural neighborhood as part of their church's outreach program. After some initial reluctance, I gave Emily permission to ride with them in the church bus each Sunday.

After talking to the young driver and his girlfriend for several more months, I decided to go to Hebron, too. I hadn't attended a church on a regular basis since I'd left the Local Church. This was, in part, because Albert had great difficulty staying in any church for long.

Although he'd taken us to numerous Charismatic and Pentecostal church meetings in the Atlanta area, he'd eventually insisted that I support him in setting up a Charismatic church in our home in Lawrenceville, with him as pastor. I'd refused, because I believed he was unstable and dishonest. I wasn't willing to support his living a lie before God. He never forgave me for that.

Hebron became an important source of healing for my wounded, shattered soul. Its black-haired, dark eyed, energetic pastor, Larry Wynn, seemed determined that the congregation would reach out to all neighbors and newcomers, to share the love of Christ with them.

I was surprised to learn that his wife, Ethel, had been in my high school class in Snellville. Because I had liked her when I first knew her, and because Larry seemed sincere, I chose to risk trusting them. Every time I went to Hebron, members hugged me, talked to me, and made me feel welcome. Their caring and joy seemed genuine, unlike the "love bombing" I'd previously experienced in religious cults. I joined Hebron and was soon baptized in a tank of water behind the pulpit. I'd finally found a place where I could belong.

Soon, I was going to church three times a week. Albert angrily accused me of being a hypocrite. He claimed that all Baptists were fakes because they weren't filled with the Holy Spirit and didn't speak in tongues. Although he never set foot inside the church, he constantly criticized its members and said they were just pretending to care about me.

As I spent time with happily married couples from the church, I realized I was stuck in a stagnant, decaying relationship with Albert. Although I'd tried hard, I didn't love him and I knew he didn't love me. Since I didn't believe in divorce, I resigned myself to an empty marriage. The love of the people at the church, and from God himself, would have to suffice.

The insane pace of my life continued. I was transported to Aryan cult meetings at night and on weekends. I was sometimes taken from the cult meetings to Dobbins Air Force Base and from there for ops. I still worked at my day job. I went to nighttime exercise classes several times a week, and then walked around the local high school's track. I did all the chores at home, including cooking, cleaning, laundry, and mowing the lawn. I took care of Emily. And now, I went to church three times a week to try to get my life right with God.

Unfortunately, several of my male spook handlers took advantage of my naïve devotion to God. They triggered out gullible alter-states while claiming to be angels sent by God with special messages for me. Because I'd recently read evangelist Billy Graham's book, *Angels: God's Secret Agents*, I–in those alter-states–believed the men. The alter-states didn't know they were being manipulated by humans who were far from holy.

In church, Pastor Wynn taught that God didn't need anyone else to translate for Him. He said if we remained prayerful and open to obeying God, He would speak directly to our hearts. His words helped me to become more skeptical towards people who came to me, claiming that God had given them a revelation or a special message for me. I decided if God didn't tell me something first, then self-proclaimed "messengers" were either delusional, or were lying to manipulate me.

Something else happened at Hebron that drastically changed the direction of my life. On most Sundays, especially during the evening services, Pastor Wynn invited members to kneel at the front altar to pray. For several months, I felt a strong pull to the altar. Each time I knelt, I felt deep pain and couldn't stop crying. If I remained at my pew, I still felt an urgency to get on my knees, to ask God to please change me. I felt as if the true Holy Spirit was shining a spotlight in places inside that I couldn't see.

For many years, I'd felt a great blackness inside. Although I didn't know what it meant, I now think it represented the amnesic barrier between my conscious self and hidden alter-states. I had also sensed for a long time that something evil was in my soul, but I hadn't known what it was. I didn't dare tell other people about it—I was afraid they'd reject me if they really knew me. Still, I could be honest about it with God.

One Sunday morning at the altar, I felt a message form in my mind. Maybe an alter-state was talking to me. Maybe the words were from a hypnotically implanted suggestion. Regardless, it was what I needed to hear: "If you truly love God, if you really are willing to give Him your life unto death, then you will have to be just as willing to give Him your openness to the greatest pain you'll ever experience."

I sensed if I said yes, He would apply his Holy Spirit to my life, using it as a purging fire to burn away everything that was evil and corrupt. I sensed that the holy fire would be the source of the pain.

I wanted to be cleansed inside. I wanted to be pure for God. I didn't want to be a hypocrite anymore, hiding the secret darkness from other Christians. I was tired of living a lie, pretending to love people when I felt no warmth inside. I was tired of smiling when no joy was in my heart. I wanted to be what I believed God had given me the potential to be.

That day, I surrendered to God. I opened my arms and my heart. Although I didn't know how the purging would come, I decided not to struggle when it did. Since then, I've watched God keep His end of the bargain by enacting a strange sequence of events that I never would have dreamt possible.

Albert's Affair

One hot Saturday at home, I opened our doors and windows to let a breeze blow through. As I washed dishes in the kitchen sink, a weak voice called to me from beyond the doorway to our carport. I turned to see a thin, brown-eyed, middle-aged, sweaty woman standing outside the screen door, asking if I would give her a glass of water.

As Geena sat on our green living room sofa, gulping the ice-cold water, she said she'd hitched a ride to Lawrenceville to find shelter with some old friends, only to discover that they'd moved away, leaving no forwarding address. She said her current husband, an avowed white supremacist who worked for an Atlanta television station, had recently beaten her so badly, she'd ended up in the hospital. She said she couldn't go back to him.

I told her to wait in the living room, and discussed her story with Albert, away from her hearing. We concurred that God must have sent her to us, so we could minister to her. I told Geena she could live with us temporarily, paying us back by helping with light cleaning and weekday meal preparations.

In record time, Geena and Albert were lovers.[1] Two neighbors saw them kissing on different days in Albert's car at nearby shopping center parking lots. The neighbors later admitted they'd been afraid to tell me, because they'd believed that I didn't want to hear the truth. They were right.

Geena was significantly older than Albert, and claimed to have cancerous tumors all over her body. She'd already been married five times. Because I couldn't imagine that Albert would ever choose her over me, I didn't believe she was a threat to our marriage. And yet, as I continued to block out indications of their affair, my subconscious wouldn't leave me alone.

I had unnerving nightmares of walking through the doorway of an old house with wooden walls. As I entered an empty room, I heard rats scurry inside the wall to my immediate right. By the time I walked into that room and looked at the partially exposed wall, the rats had gone into hiding again. Each time I awoke, my heart pounded and I felt great dread.

Several weeks later, Albert took Geena to a large indoor flea market–one of their favorite weekend haunts – on my birthday while I did the weekly chores. That afternoon, after they returned home, Albert gave me my birthday present: fingernail clippers with a daisy painted on top. Then Geena showed me what he'd bought her: an "engagement ring." She assured me that its stone was just cubic zirconium, and said she needed it when Albert took her to country music bars at night, so other customers wouldn't "hit on" her. Seeing my anger, Albert encouraged me to hit him, saying I would feel better. I didn't.

About a month later, on a warm Saturday afternoon, I was coming home from my weekly trip to the grocery store. As I drove up a dirt road into our neighborhood, dread and pain built up intolerably inside me. Then something broke. I knew. The pain completely took over as I drove up our sloped, concrete driveway. I sat in the car for a long time, so paralyzed by the pain, I couldn't move. I couldn't even cry. When Emily came outside to check on me, I told her to go to a friend's house. I knew I'd go mad if Geena spent one more day in our home.

When Geena and Albert came home from the flea market that night, I demanded that he remove her immediately. Although he accused me of being crazy and claimed they'd done nothing wrong, I stood my ground. Geena screamed and threw objects in the living room as I hid behind my locked bedroom door. After Albert calmed her down, she packed her belongings and he drove her to a relative's house.

If I hadn't received genuine love and caring from the people at church, and if I hadn't subconsciously learned about integrity from Bill and his ASA associates, I might have backed down and become even more of a doormat to Albert. Fortunately, their positive influence short-circuited my scriptural religious programming: "Wives, be in subjection to your own husbands." (I Pet. 3:1, RSV)

After Geena was gone, Albert pretended to be a model husband and father during the week. And yet, he refused to be with us on weekends, claiming he needed some time alone to "figure things out." Although I wanted to believe him, I occasionally wondered if he was spending the weekends with Geena. When I questioned him about it, he accused me of being crazy. Sometimes I wondered if he was right.

One day, Albert surprised me by saying he wanted to drive to Miami by himself and stay there for a week. He said he needed time alone to figure some things out about his life, and to decide what he wanted to do with it. I believed him, and hoped that spending time away from me and Emily would help him to appreciate us when he returned.

Several months later, I asked him to go to marital counseling with me. He made an appointment with one of his co-workers, who was studying to become a Presbyterian minister. We went to two sessions at the man's church. Each time, Albert insisted he was not having an affair. Both men made me feel guilty for not trusting his intentions. The counselor said I should support Albert's godly friendship with Geena.

Although I'd tried to hold on to what I sensed was true (that they were having an affair), I caved in and accepted Albert's claim that their relationship was pure. I had very little knowledge about proper boundaries and behaviors between men and women, between a married couple and a single woman, and so on. I didn't know enough about life and relationships to say, "This particular behavior between you and Geena is inappropriate and I won't stand for it." Not knowing what was proper and what wasn't, I believed I must be wrong for thinking that Albert was having a sexual relationship with her. After all, even the counselor said he was innocent. As I accepted their false reality, I strongly considered the possibility that I was insane.

Facing the Truth

After several more months, Albert asked me to go with him to look at a new car that he wanted to buy at a local dealership. The salesmen seemed to suppress their grins when Albert introduced me as his wife. That bothered me; had Geena been there earlier with him, to choose the car? (Later, he admitted that she had.)

On another weekend, I took a long walk out into the countryside and was startled to see Albert driving home from that direction. As he pulled up beside me, I confronted him and asked if he was still seeing Geena. He said yes, insisting they were just friends and that I was crazy for thinking that Albert–a "man of God"–was committing adultery. He tried to make me feel sorry for how poor and lonely she was. He said I should be grateful that he was ministering God's love to her.

I decided I'd know the truth if I saw them together. When I asked Albert to invite Geena to our house for Thanksgiving dinner, he seemed surprised and elated. That holiday afternoon, their body language may as well have spelled "lovers" in flashing neon lights.

Several days later, on Albert's birthday, I confronted him and gave him until the following New Years Day, 1997, to agree to sell our house and split the net profit. Because I had no savings, I'd need the money to pay rent for an apartment. Instead of showing remorse, Albert screamed that I was ruining his birthday. I refused to back down.

When he realized that I meant what I said, he became openly cruel and said things I never would have believed he was capable of. I went into emotional shock and feared for my life.

His dark side emerging, he made all kinds of threats, even against my life. He still insisted I was crazy and that I was imagining he and Geena were having sex. He accused me of sinning against God by planning to divorce him. I struggled with that last accusation, because I wanted to please God by doing what was right. He added that if I divorced him and married another man, I would commit adultery–which I believed was a major sin.

After much soul-searching, I decided I'd rather sin against God than live one more year with Albert. If I divorced him, at least I'd still have God's love. Another concern was that if he and Geena were having sex, Albert could pass a disease on to me. Pastor Wynn told me that regardless of whether or not Albert was committing adultery, God loved me so much, He wouldn't want me to continue to suffer in an abusive relationship. I hired a new lawyer and filed for divorce.

Albert's rage increased when I still wouldn't back down. Whenever he was in the house, I locked myself in our spare room. Although he wasn't big, he had terrorized me for years with his muscular arms and fists, screaming and spitting in my face, pushing my back against walls for long periods of time while Emily watched, helplessly.[2]

Now, he constantly made threats and accusations. I spent innumerable hours on my knees in the small carpeted room, shaking, crying, and begging God for protection, sometimes reading the Bible aloud.

One day, as Albert screamed outside the plain wooden door, I read in the Bible that Jesus had said we should treat our enemies with kindness. Although the idea seemed irrational, I decided to give it a try. During the rest of our time together, I was the nicest wife Albert could ever want. I was pleasantly surprised when he stopped threatening me.

Not Crazy

After we'd sold the house, Albert started making new threats. He said he'd use Geena's gun to shoot anyone who tried to help me take any appliances from the house that he wanted for himself. Because I was tired and simply wanted my freedom, I let him have whatever he wanted.

My divorce attorney was unhappy that I insisted on splitting the profit with Albert. I even agreed to accept the legally required minimum in child support payments from Albert, although the judge soon decided that Albert should pay more. After Albert bought a small mobile home and had it placed in a trailer park near Lawrenceville, I prepared to move with Emily into a rented duplex on the other side of town.

While sorting through some of the personal belongings that Albert had left in our small attic, I found a set of Polaroid pictures of him and Geena standing on a Miami beach, embracing each other. Staring at the photos, I realized I'd been right all along–they *were* having an affair!

Emily celebrated when I showed her the incriminating pictures. She said she'd always known they were having an affair, and had been terribly frustrated and angry when I wouldn't believe her.

Going It Alone

When our divorce was finalized in the spring of 1997, I hated the word "divorcee" and didn't want a relationship with any man. I just wanted to be left alone with Emily and my relationship with God. My biggest treat each week was to sit on the carpeted living room floor of our duplex on Friday nights, eating canned oysters and cheddar cheese on crackers while listening to my favorite Christian radio programs. For the first time in thirteen years, I didn't have to worry about Albert yelling that I was contaminated by battery acid on the carpet.

I worried about running into Albert and Geena when I went to town on errands. Because I couldn't bear the pain of seeing them together, I wanted to move away from Lawrenceville. I didn't consider what another move would do to Emily, who had already lost contact with her friends from our former neighborhood. Although I took her to visit and spend the night with them as often I could, it just wasn't the same.

New Ministry

One Saturday morning at Hebron, I attended a women's workshop on intercessory prayer. Our petite, middle-aged, red-haired presenter, Jessie, said that she and her husband, Grant, had created an international intercessory prayer network.

After the workshop, I couldn't get Jessie out of my mind. Because I still believed I had the Holy Spirit's gift of intercessory prayer, I decided their ministry was right for me. After several months of visits and phone conversations, Jessie suggested I break my lease and move near their home in Conyers, in order to do voluntary secretarial work for their ministry. She said I could work in their home on Saturdays and on weeknights, as needed. She said God would financially bless me for what I would do for their ministry.

In July, Emily and I moved to the lovely old town of Conyers. It had quaint shops and seemed safe enough for me to walk my dog at night in the dark. I rented a duplex that stank. Dark and dirty, it was the best I could afford.

I first met Grant when I attended a weekend prayer retreat near Atlanta. I was impressed when he told us that for the past eight years, he'd worked for Billy Graham's extensive evangelistic organization. Grant's soft voice and startling blue eyes easily put me into a hypnotic trance-state. At the retreat, Grant and Jessie encouraged some of the female participants to sit on his lap and imagine him to be their father, so they could "emotionally heal" from negative relationships with their real fathers. Although I was uncomfortable and refused to do it, the other women's trust in Grant influenced me to also trust him.

On the last day of the retreat, Grant challenged us to go for a walk in the woods to see if God would speak to us, individually. I came back, convinced that God had given me a personal message. Others claimed to have had similar experiences.

I was impressed with how well-behaved Jessie and Grant's teenaged children were. I told Jessie I wanted Emily to spend as much time with them as possible, because I wanted my daughter to have the positive influence of a stable family with two godly parents. I didn't understand that I was infinitely more important to her than a houseful of strangers. I also didn't comprehend how grief-stricken she was since Albert had stopped calling her, and had told her he didn't want her to visit him anymore.

Falling Apart

At Jessie's suggestion, Emily and I transferred our church memberships to a large Baptist church in nearby Lithonia. I did what I could to keep Emily active in the new church, believing her youth leaders would provide a positive male influence. As a single mother, I was so exhausted and overwhelmed with responsibilities and worries, I didn't have the energy to open my heart to her anymore. Instead of loving her and listening to her, I became a religious, controlling disciplinarian. I spent many hours each week on my knees in my bedroom, praying desperately for God's help and guidance. She resented my fanatical Christianity and wanted her old mother back.

I also didn't understand that she'd probably developed a learning disability. She constantly brought notes home from teachers; they complained that she wasn't doing her schoolwork and spent most of her class time writing notes back and forth with other girls. When I confronted her, she said the classes bored her. Because I knew she was bright, I thought she was being lazy and rebellious. I restricted and disciplined her more, making her a prisoner in the duplex for every minor infraction.

I also punished her for my memory lapses. At least twice, she asked an alter-state for permission to spend the afternoon with a friend. Because I, as the host alter-state, wasn't conscious when she asked, I grew frantic when she didn't come home on time. Each time she arrived hours later, saying that I'd given her permission, I punished her for lying.

Although she had made good grades in the past, they now plummeted. She associated with local teenagers who were also having trouble at home. The more she fought for her independence, the more I panicked and fought to keep control over her. I didn't understand that parents aren't supposed to control and confine their adolescent children, but are to guide and encourage them to grow and become independent. When she needed consistent love and respect, I gave her harshness and control.

Notes

1. After their affair was confirmed, my mother's second husband told me he believed Geena had been "sent in" to live with us. Tight-lipped about his own covert connections, he didn't elaborate.

2. Although several alter-states have journaled that Albert sometimes hit me with his fists, I still have not recovered enough memories to be sure of this. It's possible that I'm still blocking the memories out because I don't want to remember how terrified and helpless I felt when he was enraged.

New Family

Bill

In the spring of 1997, I learned that an insurance company closer to home had an opening for an experienced Commercial rater. I applied for the position and was quickly hired.

Located near the end of an isolated road, this company's southeast regional office building was six stories tall with a flat roof. It was surrounded by acres of black-tarred pavement and perfectly manicured, green grass.

Within a week of starting my new job, I officially met Bill Sullivan for the first time.[1] He was responsible for the maintenance of the building's immense air conditioning and heating system, all the building's lights, cafeteria equipment, electrical wiring, and more.

After our first encounter, he spent an inordinate amount of time in my department on the fifth floor, standing on his tall ladder to change florescent light bulbs up in the ceiling while peering over my cubicle wall. He always whistled when he entered the area. Soon, he was leaving cryptic handwritten notes on my desk. Each one had a scripture reference. After several weeks, he asked me to go out on a date.

Because I hadn't been on a real date since I'd married Albert, I was nervous. What if Bill expected sex? I couldn't do that–I wanted to stay chaste for God! Still hesitant, I let him take me to lunch at a nearby Chinese restaurant. It soon became our regular haunt.

Pentecostal Church

After several months of dating, Bill persuaded me to stop associating with Jessie and Grant. I'd actually considered becoming an overseas Baptist missionary, perhaps–at Jessie's suggestion–in Indonesia or South Korea, where Grant sometimes addressed Dr. Cho's Baptist mega-church.

Unimpressed with my plans, Bill reminded me that my first responsibility was to Emily. Although I didn't want to let go of my escapist fantasy, I agreed not to do any more volunteer work for the couple.

Next, I agreed to attend Bill's Pentecostal church with him. They met in a small, red brick building for which he did all the maintenance—at no charge. I flashbacked constantly during their Sunday morning and evening services and felt as if I were losing my grip on reality. Bill insisted that I continue going there. Because I wanted to deepen our spiritual relationship, I relented, feeling miserable.

Religious Control

Bill suspected that Emily was taking street drugs. Although I refused to believe him, I admitted I was worried about her, too. He convinced me that if I married him, she'd have a more stable and secure environment.

During the year we dated, I recognized that Bill was a control addict. He tried hard to change both Emily and me. Because she and I both preferred androgynous clothes, Bill bought stylish, uncomfortably feminine garments for us and insisted that we wear them. Then, he paid for both of us to change our hairstyles. After the makeovers, I saw a total stranger in the mirror and felt fake.

Because he wanted to please God, Bill insisted that we abstain from sexual intimacy until marriage. Given my history, this was difficult. When I visited Bill at his house, he always insisted that we pray on our knees and read our Bibles together to stay out of trouble.

Although I believe that Bill meant well, both Emily and I rankled under his control. Nonetheless, I chose to marry him. I sensed that he was a good and loving person underneath the religiosity. I also believed that his influence as a stepfather was what Emily needed, to heal from the loss of her relationship with Albert. I didn't know that no man could replace what her father had been in her life.

Married

During the spring of 1988, I was under a great deal of stress. My finances were very tight, especially when Albert refused to pay child support. Bill offered to pay me if I'd help him to do odd jobs at people's houses at night and on weekends. I didn't know that these odd jobs were often a cover for my going with him to Aryan and ASA meetings.

When Albert learned that I was engaged, he resumed weekend visitations with Emily. Because Geena was now living with Albert, who still claimed that their relationship was nonsexual, I didn't want to let Emily spend the night with them. And yet, because I believed that she needed to be with her daddy, I let her go.

One Sunday afternoon after Emily had visited with Albert and Geena, they drove her to our church's parking lot. Bill and I sat in his car, waiting. When Albert got out of his car, Bill walked towards him to shake hands. Not saying a word, Albert stalked back to his car, got in, and drove away in a hurry. Although I couldn't understand his behavior then, I now believe that he'd recognized Bill from the Aryan meetings.

That evening, Albert called me three times, threatening to kill Bill. Although a local judge issued a restraining order at my request, I still feared that Albert was so irrational, he might follow through. Between that worry and the stress of arranging my wedding to Bill, I was mentally and physically exhausted.

On July 1, the day before the wedding, Emily disobeyed me about something insignificant and then locked her bedroom door. An infuriated male alter-state emerged and angrily banged on her wooden door, yelling at her to open it. When she refused, the alter-state used a wire hangar to unlock it. When he saw her trying to climb out a window, he became more enraged and ran at her. She shrieked and couldn't get out quickly enough.

I was completely amnesic as that part hit her on her back again and again with the wire hangar. When I came to, I was horrified at what I'd done and feared that I'd go to jail! Because I couldn't remember why I'd beaten her, I used a false rationalization–insisting that I wouldn't have "had" to hit her if she hadn't disobeyed me.

The next day at church, Bill and I married. I'd asked Dad to give me away to Bill and he seemed happy to oblige. I didn't know how much power I was still giving him. I also didn't know that a large percentage of the witnesses sitting on the church pews were handlers, Aryan cult members, or ASA personnel.

Although I was mentally unaware that I was surrounded by enemies and spooks, I felt unsafe and dissociated and became a curly-haired, mechanical Barbie doll. In our wedding pictures, my face was either frozen or I wore a pasted-on smile. The only time I felt any warmth was when Bill and I faced each other at the altar. He cried, and tears filled my eyes as he silently mouthed, "I love you."

While I posed as the glowing bride, Emily–one of my bridesmaids–smarted under her pretty blue dress, her back covered with fiery red welts. She stayed with Dad and his wife during our week-long honeymoon. Twice in one week, I seriously hurt her and betrayed her trust in me . . . as Bill and I had fun traveling across the Southeast, Dad was free to do whatever he wished to her.

Blended Family

After the honeymoon, we moved into Bill's large house in a new subdivision in the small, rural, unincorporated town of Centerville–several miles south of Snellville. His two-story house was several years old. I felt like the lady of the manor, and had difficulty accepting that God was now blessing me so lavishly!

His combination living-dining room had a cathedral ceiling. I was overwhelmed by all the open space, after having lived in a small, dark, smelly duplex for a year. Sunlight shone through the large house's many windows. In addition to the living-dining room, the upstairs contained three bedrooms, two full baths, a small kitchen, and a large wooden back deck. Downstairs were a fourth bedroom, a half bath, a recreation room, and a huge, high-ceilinged double garage. All through the house, the white walls were spotless; Bill still hadn't hung a single picture.

I chuckled when I noticed that he hadn't yet used his dishwashing machine. Was he in for a change, living with us! I often teased Emily about being a walking tornado because she constantly left dirty clothes and dishes in her wake.

Learning to Communicate

Bill and I continued to work at the same insurance company. Because he had to be there at 6 AM, he usually left before dawn in his blue pickup truck. I started work at eight. Although we got along well there, at home, our tempers often flared. We both were accustomed to being in control, and neither of us had learned how to constructively express our hurt feelings and anger. I cried a lot and wrote him dozens of angry, barbed notes.

Sometimes, when I was icy and uncommunicative, Bill grabbed my wrist and pulled me into our bedroom. He closed the door and made me kneel with him on the carpet to ask God for help. He usually started by praying and telling God what he felt and needed. Then he waited patiently until I did the same.

Believing that God was in the room with us, I felt safer to say what I really felt. Although our prayer sessions were extremely painful, we were learning how to be honest with each other about our feelings.

Schism

Almost every day, Emily and Bill snapped at each other. The more she rebelled, the more frustrated he felt. And yet, he showed her a kindness and gentleness that I was incapable of. I felt ashamed when I realized he was a better mother to her than I was. Instead of constantly restricting and punishing her, he tried to negotiate her privileges. I hated myself and wondered if they would be better off without me.

As hard as Bill tried to work things out with her, however, their disagreements escalated in intensity. Tired of all the stress, slammed doors, tears and barbed words hurled back and forth, and Emily's insistence that she'd be happier with her dad, I decided she should live with Albert for a while–so she'd appreciate what she had with us. Albert agreed to the temporary arrangement when I promised that he wouldn't have to pay child support.

After Emily moved into Albert's trailer in November, she refused to talk to me. I was devastated. Several times each week, Albert called me at work to tell me how well she was doing at home and at school. Although I felt sad that I'd failed as her parent, I was glad that she'd finally found some happiness and stability.

Arrest

In December, the sky fell. Albert called me at work to tell me that Emily had just been arrested at school with Geena's gun in her possession, the safety off. He said Emily had planned to shoot another girl who–fearing Emily's rage–had chosen to stay home that day.

Emily later told me that after shooting the girl, she knew she was "supposed to" walk into the school cafeteria, climb up on a table, and "blow her brains out all over everybody."[2] I'm deeply grateful that the principal was able to talk her into giving him the gun without anyone being hurt.

On the day Emily appeared in Juvenile Court, Bill and I sat as close as we could to the judge's bench. Although Albert had sheepishly admitted to me that Emily had recently become an Aryan skinhead, I was unprepared for her drastic change in appearance.

She wore a dirty denim jacket with the words, "Sex Pistols," hand written on it in thick, black magic marker. A large Nazi swastika was visible from the far end of the courtroom. She'd shaved her head in a Chelsea, a style that she later explained was fashionable for Nazi skinhead girls. Only her dyed bangs and a "tail" at the nape of her neck remained.

Because I didn't remember the Aryan network or its meetings or rituals, I was stunned that she'd turned into a hard-core skinhead in just one month!

Although she knew that Bill and I were present in the courtroom, Emily refused to acknowledge us. At first she seemed rigid and defiant, but when the judge gave his sentence, her face crumpled into a frightened little girl's. I wanted to hurdle the benches, run to her, and enfold her in my arms. I hurt so badly, knowing I couldn't do anything to comfort her.

Christmas was especially painful for Bill and me. The judge wouldn't allow Emily to leave the county juvenile detention center. I brought a specially embossed Bible to the center as her Christmas present. I hoped she would draw the same hope and strength from it that I did. It only angered her again. My heart broke more when she welcomed holiday visits from Albert and Geena, but not from us.

Crossroads

Emily's assigned county caseworker believed that Emily's acting-out was a symptom of hidden family problems. She wisely arranged for Emily to enter a juvenile rehabilitation program at the Crossroads of

Chattanooga facility in Tennessee. Each of its large cottages housed an individualized recovery program. Emily stayed in her adolescent cottage for over a month.

Before her discharge, she invited Albert, Geena, Bill, and me to her "family week" sessions. Although Albert declined, Bill and I attended them together. Initially there to support her, we both soon realized that we also needed professional help.

Because of what I learned about chemical addictions and dysfunctional family systems during that intensive week-long program, I recognized that our family was a mess. More important, I realized that I was almost completely disconnected from my emotions. I didn't feel fear, except for Emily's and Bill's health and safety. I felt no love, happiness, emotional warmth, or empathy. This frightened me. Why was I so emotionally frozen?

Emily's counselors gave me a challenge with a promise: if I would enter Crossroads' 28-day adult inpatient codependency therapy program, they'd recommend to the judge that Emily be placed back in our home. Unable to bear the thought of losing her again, I took a month-long leave of absence from my job and entered the program.

Letting Go

After Emily was discharged from the adolescent unit at Crossroads, she lived with us for several more years before marrying and starting a new life with her young husband. Until she moved out, our relationship stayed extremely rocky. Although Emily continued to block out what she'd endured in the past, she unwittingly acted it out in nearly every way possible.

While she was with us, I took her to a succession of therapists and hospitals, looking for a miracle for her–and for us. I didn't understand then, as I do now, that in part, I was frantically fighting to keep her alive because somewhere in my mind, she and Rose (who I didn't remember) were one. Even after Emily married and moved away, I still tried to save her from death – especially when she was suicidal.

One night, after spending the day with Emily and her young family, I was alone in a hotel room bathroom while Bill slept. As I thought about my conversations earlier that day with Emily, how she again threatened to suicide, even telling me about her plans for her funeral, I had a devastating moment of truth: by obsessively holding onto Emily and trying to save her from self destruction, I was actually feeding her suicidal tendencies and her exponential, destructive rage towards me. Over the years, I'd conditioned her to depend on me, which now kept her from being able to feel good about what she could do for herself.

Realizing this, I knew I had a choice. I could continue to lead us both down a destructive path, or I could distance myself from her and work to break our emotional dependency on each other.

When I first distanced myself from Emily, I began to experience the fullness of my suppressed grief from having lost Rose in such a sudden and brutal way. I had never experienced such pain. By working through that grief a little bit at a time–it was as much as I could survive–I was able to recognize that Rose and Emily were two totally different entities in my life.

Now, I feel a long-distance love for Emily that is wholly separate from what I will always feel for my baby girl. I smile now, as unexpected flashes of Emily's childhood come back to me. She was a sweet and beautiful child, and I am comforted with the new-found knowledge that, as broken and unstable as I was in the past, I did dearly love her and did want the best for her.

A great tragedy between us remains: now that I have the capability to truly love her for the person she is and always was, she is unwilling to trust and receive my love. (And really, can I blame her? This is her right!)[3]

Can there someday be a happy ending for us as mother and adult daughter? I don't know. And I don't know what's ahead for either one of us–no one has that kind of foresight. Every day, I find myself hoping that she will eventually encounter helpful support and a way to heal. Maybe it's already happening for her.

In the meantime, regardless of what happens to her, to Bill, or to anyone else I dearly love, whether it be life or death or anything in-between, I *must* focus on my own healing and recovery, and on doing what I believe is right for my own life.

From these painful experiences, I have extracted a powerful and life-changing truth: *the only person I have the power to save is me.*

Notes

1. Because Bill is firm about maintaining secrecy concerning his past activities for ASA, our first encounter at the insurance company remains his cover story for how

our relationship began. I respect his right to keep secrets, and he honors my right to speak out about my experiences with him.

2. Her too-calm statement that she was "supposed to" kill herself after killing the other girl sent chills through me. Now, I wonder: was it a hypnotically implanted command? If so, who had put it in her mind, and why was she commanded to self-destruct? What she said she was "supposed" to do was eerily similar to what we've witnessed time and time again over the last decade, in public schools throughout the US. What is happening to our young people?

3. This is perhaps one of the strongest grievances I have against the FMSF: some of its most outspoken members seem to insist that adult children do not have the right to distance themselves from childhood families that they believe are detrimental to their mental and physical health. I believe this proves those FMSF members' true motivations. If parents truly love their adult children, they will give them all the time and space they need to find their own way in life-even if it means grieving their absence. Control addicts cannot bear to lose control of their victims, whereas truly caring parents will-despite the pain-let their loved ones go their own way without making private and public recriminations against them. The greatest gift we can give ourselves, and our children, is encouragement, to build independent lives, and to teach them how to become self-sufficient. I wish I had learned this, sooner.

Reality Check

Codependency

In the summer of 1989, after Emily was discharged, I hesitantly entered Crossroads of Chattanooga's adult codependency program. I didn't like the idea of sharing my thoughts and feelings with a group of strangers. Still, for Emily's sake, I believed I must try.

Since most people with dependent tendencies focus on others to avoid their own needs and problems, the counselors in our cottage insisted that visits, phone calls, and incoming mail be kept to a minimum. Since my handlers and family couldn't use phone calls and mail to trigger me into silence and forgetfulness, I was safe to begin to remember.

In group therapy sessions, I listened to other patients talk about why they were there. Most of them were there because they had relatives suffering from chemical addictions. Although I talked a little about Emily's arrest, I sensed that my problem was much deeper.

Each patient was asked to draw a chart of major life events from early childhood to the present. Most of the childhood side of my chart was blank. As for the events I could remember, I didn't know how old I'd been, or when they'd occurred. When I compared my chart to those of other patients, I noticed that most of them had remembered the dates of important life events. Why couldn't I?[1]

Our codependency group performed two sets of relaxation exercises in a room where we lay on our backs on the floor, listening to either a female counselor's soft voice or to a cassette recording. Each time, we were told to visualize ourselves walking along a path through a forest, then finding unexpected treasure. Each time, I had flashbacks, sat up, and looked around the room to make the flashbacks stop.

I didn't want to believe what I was remembering: that when I was a child, my father had sexually assaulted me. Deeply shaken, I told no one.

Incest

One day, as I relaxed on a lounge chair near the facility's outdoor pool, another memory unfolded: it was daytime, because sunlight streamed through a window. I, an adolescent, was alone with Dad in his bed in Snellville, Georgia. We were both naked under a white sheet. He smiled as he moved towards me. The memory was so vivid, I couldn't make it go away. Again, I told no one.

Several days later, we were taken in a van to a nearby shopping mall to see a *Batman* movie. About halfway through it, I had more flashbacks. During the drive back to the cottage, I hyperventilated and wept. What was wrong with me?

After we arrived at the cottage, an older, gentle female counselor walked with me on a path that circled it. Because we were not allowed to take medications, she held a cold, wet washcloth against my forehead as I continued to cry, uncontrollably. She and the other counselors waited patiently, careful not to suggest anything.

During the next few days, I had numerous flashbacks of Dad perpetrating sexual acts against me and two other children in our bathroom in Reiffton, Pennsylvania. I wondered, "Why now? Why hadn't I known it all along? Could I be making it up?" My assigned counselor was concerned when I told her that Dad still had easy access to young children. She insisted I go to the authorities after my discharge and tell them what I was remembering. Although I agreed to do that, I felt uncomfortable–what if Dad wasn't hurting children anymore? Wouldn't I then be hurting him?

Notifying the Authorities

After I returned to Atlanta, I balked for about a week. Then I decided to send separate certified letters, one to my stepmother at home and the other to Dad at work, asking to meet with them. In the letters, I hinted at what I'd remembered. A day or so later, my stepmother called to say that she'd made Dad leave. After receiving my letter, she'd discovered that Dad was now molesting at least two children. When they were taken for a medical examination, physical evidence was found. They met with a child psychiatrist, and the eldest child gave a videotaped statement to a detective at the DeKalb Police Department Sex Crimes division, that incriminated Dad.

Not knowing what the children had said, I provided the detective an independent, handwritten statement about what I'd remembered.[2] I hadn't yet been told what the eldest child had disclosed during the videotaped interview. After I gave my statement, the detective told me that it was nearly identical to what the child victim had stated. I broke down and wept with both relief and dismay: I was happy to hear I wasn't crazy, but dammit, this meant the memories were real! I didn't want my dad to be a child molester, and I didn't want to accept that he'd sexually abused me!

Arrest Warrant

On August 26, 1989, a criminal warrant was issued for Dad's arrest. It stated that Dad "did commit an immoral or indecent act to or in the presence of [a child] . . . with the intent to arouse or satisfy the sexual desires of either the child or himself."

He was arrested, placed in jail, and released on bail shortly thereafter.

Intimidation

As I met with an assistant D.A. to prepare to testify against Dad, he warned me that Dad was facing a maximum prison sentence of sixty years. That upset me; although I didn't want Dad to hurt more children, I still cared about him and didn't want him to be put in prison.

During the next several months, Dad became openly hostile towards me. His behavior helped me to realize he wasn't the father I'd made him to be in my mind.

He told people in his church and community that I'd gone to Crossroads because of a "drug problem." He said my therapists had implanted the memories in my mind. He said that I wanted him sexually and was therefore lying to my stepmother to influence her to divorce him–so that I could have him to myself!

He also tried to intimidate me through the mail. He sent a photo album full of pictures from my childhood. Attached to it was a plaque with the words, "Recipe for a happy marriage." Although I was pleased with the pictures, I felt nauseous as I read the plaque. He also sent a series of greeting cards with threatening messages–some coded, some overt.

He instructed one of his criminal attorneys to send me a letter, threatening to sue me for interfering with his marriage. He attempted to subpoena my Crossroads records. He even admitted hiring a female private detective to secretly investigate me and "dig up dirt" about me.

When I learned of Dad's actions, I was heartbroken. His behaviors proved that he didn't love me, and that he now believed I was his enemy. That thought especially frightened me, although I didn't know why.

I continued to have visual flashbacks of his having sexually assaulted me and other children, and decided to go back to work to get my mind off the past for a little while. Too much of an emotional wreck to go back to a full-time office job, I applied for a part-time position as cashier at a nearby McDonald's fast food restaurant.

Left-Hand Memories

When I was at home, I constantly struggled with sensory overload. Day and night, I endured many visual flashbacks and strong physical and emotional memories known as abreactions.

Most of the journals I wrote during that time were about bits and pieces of memory that emerged throughout my waking hours. They were usually visual, odorous, physical, and/or audible. Some days, I had ten or more flashbacks in succession, all of them totally disconnected from each other. Each flashback usually contained no more than a half-minute's worth of memory. Their abruptness made journaling very frustrating, because they had no "before" and no "after."[3]

As I sat on my bed and journaled some of them, they were like opened doors that led into full memories. And like the ends of threads of individual memories, if I was willing to relax, trust, and follow the threads, the rest of these particular memories came quickly.

A new problem soon developed. I was so mentally stuck in the past that I kept forgetting what month or year it now was. To remedy that, I affixed a large calendar to our kitchen wall and I marked off each day. After completing each morning's journaling, I wrote the current date on the top of the first page. Writing and seeing the current date seemed to help bring me back into the present.

I also experimented with "right hand/left hand writing." I'd learned at Crossroads that writing with my right hand accessed information stored in the left side of my brain, while writing with my left hand accessed information stored in the right half. After journaling in the morning with my right hand, I then put the pen into my left hand and gave permission to hidden parts of my mind to journal. That technique helped me to access suppressed memories, and was my first attempt at connecting with alter-states that I still didn't know I had.[4]

One day in December, after Bill had left for work, I tried to learn more of what I'd blocked out from my childhood. Sitting cross-legged on the middle of the bed, I put the pen in my left hand. Immediately, I felt something unfamiliar in my mind, as well as new body sensations. The pen seemed to move on its own:

> I . . . Mommy where . . . come in here . . . why won't you come in . . . don't you know . . . blood red bloody red . . . you bitch you bastard . . . you knew and you didn't stop and you didn't try to stop . . . He broke me He broke the red thing in me . . . You didn't come in the room . . . You stayed safe in another room . . . bloody red hands . . . bloody red . . . I hurt in my tummy I gagged and went to throw up . . . bloody bloody hands . . . dad you are a god-damned animal you broke me your prick is as big as a house . . . what you did hurt me in my tummy . . . bloody red bloody red hands . . . my peehole legs are bloody red . . . It is getting down my legs stop moving stop blood stop . . . What I want . . . I want you to stay away from me . . . I want you to love me . . . I want you to do it again . . . You felt so good in me . . . you screwed up you made a mistake now what . . . she'll catch us . . . you are my prince . . . you make me feel real special . . . just between you and me . . . let's not tell her she's just a bitch anyway . . . you deserve better . . . you deserve ME!

I remained conscious as that child part of my broken mind told me more of what I had previously been unable to remember. In succession, I vividly experienced the pain, the too-big penetration, the fear, the unwanted sexual stimulation, the anger towards Mom for not stopping Dad, the adoration towards the man who had just raped me and torn my flesh. Weeping, I put the pen in my right hand and wrote to the child part of me as I would have to an external child. I explained that what Dad had done was wrong and the child was not to blame.

I put the pen in my left hand again. Another unpleasant memory emerged in writing. Again, my body was racked by the sensations of Dad raping me.

> Mommy . . . why didn't you stop him . . . He kept eating me up . . . No one could stop him . . . he was big and strong . . . he laughed if I tried to fight him . . . he pinned my arms to the side of the bed . . . he made my legs like scissors . . . he was a robot . . . He put his prick in me it hurt it hurt it hurt it hurt it hurt it hurt it hurt it hurt . . . it hurt it hurt it hurt it hurt it hurt it hurt it hurt I cried Oh God how could this happen to me I've been a good girl . . . he gave me a candy cane to suck on while he washed me . . . Mom and brothers were gone shopping . . . Dad was babysitting me . . . I had a cold I felt so awful . . . How could he do it to a sick girl

Freed by my left-hand writing, these memories slammed me. Every time I wrote with my left hand, I learned more than I could bear. I screamed when my body relived another childhood rape. I slammed myself into walls as I physically relived Dad throwing me against walls in the past. On my back on the floor, I bucked as I physically relived Dad humping my little body.

Trying to make me feel better, Bill teased that I should carry a "snot bucket" around the house because I cried so much. Trying to find humor in my pain, I told him that I should buy stock in the Kleenex tissue corporation. Making jokes took the edge off a bit, but it didn't make the pain and horror go away. More and more, I feared what else lurked in my unconscious mind.

Exhausted at night, I laid my head on my husband's legs as I watched TV with him. When I closed my eyes, I saw Dad's penis coming at my face again. I wept.

West Paces Ferry Hospital

After Dad's arrest, my stepmother learned about a support group for family members of sexual offenders that met once a week at West Paces

Ferry Hospital, northwest of Atlanta. When we went to a meeting we heard hard, cold facts about criminal mentality that made me realize that Dad would probably do whatever he could, to avoid prison. Although I had still hoped that he'd choose to tell the truth for the children's sake, I had to consider that he might never do that.

I worried more and more about Dad's future. Because he still ran for miles every day, I feared he wouldn't survive being in a locked facility. I didn't want to hurt him. And yet, if he'd recently assaulted children, he was dangerous. I knew if I testified against him, I'd never have a chance of receiving real love from him. I asked God to give me the strength to testify, and to give me the love that my earthly father never would.

We didn't know that Dad's court-appointed psychiatrist was actively working to have him evaluated on an in-patient basis as part of the hospital's Sexual Behavior Treatment Program. Had he gone into that program, the rest of this story *might* have had a better ending–but it doesn't. His AT&T medical insurance plan refused to pay for his treatment there.

Dr. Adams

On November 17, 1989, Dad received an indictment from a 23-member DeKalb County Grand Jury for three counts of child molestation. To prepare for his defense, he met privately with Dr. Henry Adams, a professor of psychology at the University of Georgia in Athens. In a subsequent civil deposition, Dad described Adams as "the leading authority on sexual abuse in children." Adams (deceased) had previously testified for the defense in the infamous "Little Rascals" ritual abuse trial.

Because Dad lied throughout his deposition, I do not know how many of his statements about his conversations with Adams were valid. Dad claimed that Adams said Crossroads was a sexual encounter clinic. I believe Dad was telling the truth about that, because before he'd met with Adams, he hadn't used that particular argument:

> [Adams] claims that . . . there are a number of people, mainly fundamentalist ministers, who are setting up a number of bogus psychological clinics all over the country. They call them sexual encounter clinics. Almost everybody that goes into these clinics comes out sexually abused, across the board . . . he said this is the kind of thing that's happening all over the

country right now. It's called scapegoating, where you dump all of your problems, whatever they are, on the person who raised you, as sexual abuse. (Deposition 76–77)

Suicide Attempt

Although Dad eventually enlisted Dr. Adams to testify for his defense in the upcoming trial, he became suicidal immediately after one of his initial meetings with the doctor. Dad later told his estranged wife that first, he visualized himself driving into a concrete bridge support. Then he "saw" himself climbing to the top of a nearby mountain and throwing himself off the side. Although he successfully fought off the first two urges, he then checked into a hotel near home, cut both of his wrists deeply with a razor blade, then went to their house to enlist her help. Seeing the blood, she called a neighbor who was a nurse. That woman in turn called the police.

One of the responding officers wrote: "He stated that he was very depressed because he is facing four counts of child abuse, and felt that suicide was the only way out of it."

According to that officer's memorandum, when he tried to talk Dad into seeking professional help, Dad said, "You don't know how bad it is, the prosecutor is . . . out to get me; I'm probably facing the rest of my life in prison; [he] is half prosecutor and half crusader."

After being taken to a medical facility, Dad was transferred to a psychiatric hospital where he stayed for several weeks. While being treated for depression and suicidal ideations, he developed a plan of action designed to help him feel more in control of his future.

Because I was quite shaken by Dad's drastic action, the assistant district attorney told me that one of the reasons Dad might have cut his wrists was to influence me not to testify against him (if so, it nearly worked). He reminded me that the welfare of the child victims, not Dad's mental state, should be my primary concern. I feel grateful that the assistant DA believed me and the children. His swift and determined action against Dad probably saved them and other children from being sexually assaulted, and worse.

When Dad was released from the hospital, he traveled to a conference at Disney World in Orlando, Florida. After that, he traveled to Pennsylvania to spend several days with his childhood family.

At Dad's request, the judge handling the criminal case moved the grand jury hearing forward by several months, making the older child's videotaped testimony inadmissible in court. I was told that the child would have to testify in Dad's presence.

As much as I loved Dad and wanted the best for him, I didn't believe I had any other choice than to testify against him. Clearly, he was still capable of sexually assaulting little children. I wanted to be a solid witness and not fall apart in court. I didn't dare tell anyone that I constantly visualized myself talking like a little girl on the witness stand.

I knew I wasn't ready to go through with it. Terrified and ashamed, I didn't know who to tell. When I prayed for additional strength, none came.

Notes

1. Carla Emery explained why amnesia is used to keep a "hypno-robot" from remembering and breaking free:

   The hypnotic suggestion that makes a subject most likely to carry out orders contrary to their self-interest is amnesia. The most important element in a case of abusive hypnosis is amnesia. The biggest roadblock to uncovering a crime of criminal hypnosis is amnesia. Amnesia is, therefore, the central problem of a survivor of abusive hypnosis. It is central to the operator's setup, central to the years of secret life hidden under the consciously known one, central to the struggle to escape and heal. (pg. 227)

2. Before the oldest child disclosed that child's negative experiences with Dad, the adults who carefully questioned the child did not indicate what I'd said about my own memories. The child freely and willingly disclosed to them-in graphic detail-without being coached.

3. "Psychogenic amnesias are quite different [from organic amnesia] in their origin, as the causes are psychological and tend to involve the repression of disturbing memories which are unacceptable to the patient at some deep subconscious level. Psychogenic amnesias can be disorienting and disruptive to the patient, but they are rarely completely disabling, and as there is no actual brain damage they are reversible and in most cases will eventually disappear." (Groome, et al., pp. 137–138)

4. One of the therapeutic memory recovery techniques that FMSF spokespersons occasionally ridicule and try to discredit is left-hand writing. I believe they attack its credibility because they don't want the public to know how well it works!

You are a murderer

You are guilty

You are bad.

You are evil.

If people really
know you:
    They'd hate you
    They'd never want
    to be near you
    again.

I'm the only one who
    really knows you

Four-years-old children
are incapable of
understanding what
death is. They
don't believe in it.

Children are not
    guilty, bad, or evil.
I was a child.
∴ I was not, and
am not, guilty,
bad or evil.

There are some
people who do
know who I really
am, and still
want to be near
me.

He told me who
I was, but he
never knew who
I was.

Kathleen Sullivan
7/29/02

REVERSING DAD'S GUILT MESSAGES – 7/29/02

Death

Gone

A month later, in January of 1990, my abreactions and flashbacks increased in intensity and frequency. Although I'd been consulting with a local therapist, she wasn't used to working with sexual abuse survivors, and didn't know how to help me–other than to listen.

I learned about an eight-day Intensive Experiential Program (IEP) at Charter-Peachford, a psychiatric hospital north of Atlanta. The next IEP session would start in one week. I signed up for it, believing it would give me the strength and tools I needed to keep on going.

That Monday night, Bill and I went to a banquet hosted by a fundamentalist Baptist Bible college that we both attended. Sometime between that night and the following Wednesday morning, Dad died.

Dreaming of Justice

On Wednesday morning, I awoke from an unusually strong, vivid, symbolic dream. In it, Dad was dressed like a desperado cowboy. Chased by a big gray wolf, he rode a brown horse down a steep hill. At the bottom, he crossed a stream; the wolf stayed on the other side. Knowing he was finally free, Dad smiled. I smiled too and felt happy for him. Then, as Dad looked at the gray wolf, a huge black wolf, its hackles raised, emerged from a dark cave above Dad and his horse. As it moved stealthily towards them, a bell slowly tolled.

The dream changed. I saw a huge, blond male angel, robed in white. As he stood and watched the wolf kill Dad (I didn't see it), he held the oldest child witness in his arms. The angel said, "Now justice is served. The child is mine." I woke up, trembling, still hearing the bell toll.

The dream was so powerful, I never forgot any of the details. At that time, I believed it was a message from God.

Phone Call

Several hours later, as I stood behind the counter at McDonald's, I was still dazed by the dream. As I pondered it, my stepmother called on the phone and said, "Kathy, your father is gone." I felt relieved, thinking that she meant Dad had gone underground to start a new life. She elaborated: "Your father is dead." My hands and body turned to ice and I became robotic. My manager told me to go home. I never went back to that job.

At home, I called my stepmother. She said Dad's body had been found on the back seat of his Grand Prix in the garage that morning by his apartment manager and his criminal lawyer, who grew alarmed when Dad didn't show up for an appointment.

She said because Dad's body had started to decompose, making the time of death impossible to determine, the coroner had instead used the time of the discovery of his body.

Believing God must have given me the dream to prepare me for the news of Dad's death, I told her about it. After I hung up the phone, I dropped to my knees and cried with grief while at the same time thanking Him for having protected the children. I didn't know how I was going to survive the rest of the week–I felt so cold!

Final Visit

Because I needed all the support I could find to get me through the next couple of days, I went to my weekly codependency group therapy meeting the next evening. After that, I planned to go to the funeral home to see Dad's body. The support group encouraged me to spend time alone with his body, reminding me that I needed to say goodbye to him. My stepmother agreed, and arranged for me to have a half-hour alone with his body, despite grumblings from some of his business-suited mourners.

Dad's official cause of death was *sequelae of carbon monoxide poisoning*. And yet, I've since been advised by three different professionals who are familiar with the effects of carbon monoxide poisoning, that the car exhaust would have turned Dad's skin bright blue. One calls the unusual color, "Smurf blue."

If these professionals are correct, I am not suggesting that the forensic examiner didn't do a thorough job. According to an article in the Atlanta paper from that time period, his office was swamped with cases. Several of the consultants told me that the examiner probably didn't see any point in pursuing an investigation because no one was raising a fuss about his death, and all other signs did point to suicide.

When I was alone with Dad's body in the funeral home, it was so swollen I had difficulty recognizing it. The only way I could positively identify him was by standing beyond the crown of his head and looking at him lengthwise. My stepmother had warned me that his skin was dark red from the carbon monoxide. Although I believed her, I still needed to see it for myself. As I stared at his face and neck, I noticed that someone had covered the skin with heavy beige makeup. I had to know. I unbuttoned the collar of his white shirt and saw that the skin beneath it was dark red. The body really was Dad's, and he really was dead.

Funeral

The following day, my brothers, their wives and children, my stepmother and half-siblings, Dad's sister and her husband, and others gathered in a small room next to the church sanctuary to prepare for his funeral. Other visitors joined us, including a retired, slim, grey-haired pediatrician who had been a neighbor and close friend of Dad's for years. Although I didn't yet recognize that man, he glared at me with obvious hatred and loudly told whoever would listen, that I'd lied about Dad. I later learned that Dad had claimed in his deposition that this man had actively coached him for his defense–including telling him to say that I'd wanted Dad, sexually.

When Mom entered the room, I broke down and wept, happy that she'd come to comfort us. Instead, she grabbed my arm tightly, pulled me out into the hallway, and said I had to get myself together and not let my brothers see me cry. I remembered what the people in the support group had told me: I had the right and the need to grieve. Defiantly, I told Mom I would cry as much and as often as I needed to.

I remained stunned by her callousness as we silently walked back into the waiting room.

The funeral was surprisingly healing for me. Dad's Methodist pastor didn't try to pretend that Dad had been anyone other than who he really was. He didn't try to minimize or cover up for what Dad had done. He did tell us that on the previous Sunday night, Dad had walked up to the altar and had asked the pastor to pray with him. That gave me some comfort.

Dad's death was one of the most shattering experiences in my life because he was the first person I had ever bonded with. When I was young, we were much closer than a father and daughter should ever be. He had been my first long-term sex partner. And yet, I was also able–at least as an adult–to love him in a non-sexual way. Some of the love and grief that I felt after his death was for the terribly wounded little boy inside who had never had a chance to grow up and experience love. For the funeral, I purchased a flower arrangement with a small teddy bear, and addressed the card to that little boy.

Perhaps part of my ability to love Dad non-sexually had come from what I had learned about God as a little girl. I'd almost always believed that He cared about me when no human did. And although He couldn't make the bad people stop, or magically pick me up in His arms and carry me to safety, I believed that He'd always been with me.

I believe that God also gave me the ability to love Dad because of the love I'd received from caring people. Unfortunately, Dad had been too broken to be able to receive my love–his soul had been a sieve.

Disposal

Due to his prior arrangements, Dad's body was cremated after the funeral. Ironically, that wasn't dissimilar to what he'd done to the bodies of some of his ritual victims. His widow scattered his ashes in a cemetery fountain. This could have symbolized the way he'd denied some of his victims a burial place. I still have no place to go, to kick his headstone and curse his memory or fall down on my knees and tell him again how much I love him. His family has no place to put flowers, just as I'd had no place to put flowers to honor my baby girl.

In so many ways, the giant blond angel in my dream had been right: justice was served.

Betrayal

Mom and her second husband stayed in our home through the following weekend. On Sunday, the day before I entered the hospital, Bill received an emergency call from work, informing him that the building's burglar alarm had been triggered. As he exited the house, climbed into his truck, and prepared to drive away, Mom walked towards him. His window was down. Knowing that the rest of us were still asleep, Mom leaned in, pulled Bill's head towards her, and kissed him full and hard on the lips.

Stunned, Bill moved his head away and said, "I want you to know I'm a happily married man."

She looked surprised, then stepped back and said, "Well then, I'm happy for you."

As Bill drove away, he felt angry and decided he would have no more contact with her.

That same afternoon, I lay down on my bed to take another nap–I was so exhausted! As I relaxed, Mom came in and sat down next to me. I was shocked as she quietly told me not to tell anyone at the hospital about her; then she said that if I did, she'd have me killed.[1]

When she finished speaking, she gently stroked my hair. That made me feel crazy. Because the two conflicting realities about Mom's personality and motives clashed, one had to go. When I woke up later, I didn't remember the instruction and threat, and believed she'd come into the bedroom to comfort me. Her touch lingered for days.

For twelve years, Bill stayed silent about Mom's inappropriate behavior earlier that morning. He was furious that she'd done it when my dad had just died, and I was deeply grieving. He was certain, and I agree, that because Mom was never a casual social kisser, she had cold-bloodedly attempted to seduce him.[2]

Epitaph

Throughout his adult life, Dad had secretly operated on the dark edge of society. He'd locked himself into an insatiable sex addiction with his back to an unyielding wall that had blocked off the immense pain fueling and driving the addiction. He died a lonely man who had spewed his incessant pain and rage onto innocent victims for probably more than forty years. When the sexual addiction had stopped working in the last decade of his life, I had also watched him turn to cocaine to numb his psychic pain.

Until a sex addict is willing to stay away from other sex addicts and victims, and actively seeks help to go through the childhood pain that sex temporarily numbs, that addict cannot give or feel genuine love. Most sex addicts confuse sex with love, perhaps because as children, they'd been seduced or sexually assaulted by adults who had claimed to rape or molest them because they "loved" them. For these victims, the concepts of "sex" and "love" are super-glued together. Too many sex addicts believe if others have sex with them and accept their bodies, then they are loved and accepted. What a sad lie!

Because I was addicted to sex for decades, I have no right to judge others who still struggle with the addiction. I'm one of the lucky ones; with much therapeutic help and my husband's genuine love and devotion, I've been able to excavate and accept the excruciating emotional pain from my childhood that perhaps thousands of orgasms had masked and medicated—although never for long. I now know that love and sex are two distinct (albeit overlapping) facets of humanity, and that having sex with a partner does not guarantee that partner's love.

I recently found a poem, written by an anonymous recovering sex addict, that seems to be a fitting epitaph for my father:

> We know better than others the limits of our sexual addiction:
> that it is solitary, furtive, and satisfies only itself,
> that, contrary to love, it is fleeting,
> that it demands hypocrisy,
> that it enfeebles strong sexual feeling,
> that it is humorless and cruel,
> that it is hollow,
> that it distances us from our feelings,

that it works to exclude our family,
that it exploits power over others,
that it destroys good feelings about ourselves,
that it causes us to abuse our bodies, and
that we end up broken and alone.

Notes

1. Years after I remembered Mom's death threat, I learned that most people are highly suggestible to verbal suggestions for several days after a trauma. I believe she knew that because Dad's death had traumatized me, her words would go deep inside my mind.

2. Based on numerous memories I've recovered, I am certain that Mom blamed me for "seducing" Dad. Instead of intervening and protecting me from his sexual assaults when I was a child, she seemed to view me as a competitor for his affections. I have yet to recall a single time in which she attempted to intervene as Dad sexually assaulted me in front of her-in fact, sometimes she gleefully joined him in the assault. At such times, she seemed to be in her normal state of mind. And yet, I've also had many memories of her switching into an older "stranger" alter-state while Dad was absent, punishing me for my sexual sins and calling me a whore and worse.

   A therapist who has worked extensively with child sexual abuse victims and their mothers told me that a surprising number of mothers do turn against the children and blame them for "seducing" the mothers' partners. She explained that this especially occurs if the mother is an unhealed survivor of childhood sexual abuse. Often, such mothers unconsciously choose a partner with poor sexual boundaries, which opens the door for the mothers to reenact their repressed traumas by not intervening and by sometimes even encouraging their partners to assault the children; and then, blaming the children for the sexual assault.

   Rosencrans discovered the same bizarre dynamic when she communicated with adult female survivors of maternal sexual abuse:

   > Some of these mothers must feel they have, for better or worse, reproduced themselves through their daughters. These mothers may re-experience their childhood pain, ambivalence, and rage through contact with their daughters, their daughters' little girl bodies and vulnerability . . . For example, a mother might feel sexually ashamed and sinful and repeatedly project those feelings

onto her daughter as a way to get them out of herself. The daughter may take those messages in as true about herself. (pg. 125)

My experience has been that my mother irrationally hated me and repeatedly sought to harm me and enlisted others to harm me-perhaps because she had made me "little her". Of course, she was careful to do this only in private and at gatherings where child abuse was encouraged. For this and other reasons, I choose not to have any more contact with her. Her shame belongs to her alone.

Without outside intervention, maternal abuse-including mothers passing on the baton of undeserved guilt and shame to their daughters for their having been sexually assaulted-can continue through many generations.

Healing

Charter-Peachford

I guess it's common for abuse survivors to fantasize that when their primary perpetrator dies, their traumatic memories, nightmares, flashbacks, and abreactions will magically stop. In reality, the opposite often happens–they get worse.

After Dad's death, the number of flashbacks and abreactions increased noticeably. I suspect it happened because I felt safer. I was ready to remember more.

The Monday after his funeral, as prearranged, I entered the eight-day Intensive Experiential Program (IEP) at the Charter-Peachford psychiatric hospital. I was still hoping for a quick fix.

Upon admission, my diagnosis was major depression.[1] Post-Traumatic Stress Disorder (PTSD) delayed was added later.[2] As a nurse led me by the hand to the IEP unit, I noticed that a large part of me seemed to have died. I was beyond exploring my emotions anymore. They were gone.

Most of my eight days in the Intensive Experiential Program were a blur. One day, I play-acted a mock funeral at a female counselor's suggestion, pretending that Dad's body lay on the floor, surrounded by small paper cups symbolizing lit candles. Although I said–to Dad–what the counselor suggested, I still felt nothing.

A day or two later, she told our therapy group to visualize stepping "on and off a stage" during a skit. As I did, I flashbacked and relived a pornography shoot that Dad had forced me to participate in when I was small. I sat on the floor with my back to a row of wooden cabinets and refused to budge until the flashbacks subsided.

One night, our group was herded into a room outside our unit to watch Barbara Streisand's movie, *Nuts*. We were left there, unsupervised. I wasn't prepared for the content of the movie–it included a very sick relationship between Barbara's character and her father. Halfway through the movie, I started to hyperventilate and weep. When I couldn't stop, a neatly groomed, gray-haired male patient comforted me as he

202

guided me back to our unit. A nurse standing behind a window told me to sit on a sofa until she had time to talk to me. I kept shaking and sobbing.

I didn't know that a friend from Hebron came to the hospital each week to encourage recovering alcoholics. I was surprised to hear his voice as he spoke to the nurse behind me. He was equally surprised to see me sitting there, and hugged me as I wept even more. His unexpected presence restored my spiritual footing. After that, I believed that no matter what other surprises emerged from my subconscious, God still cared about me.

On the last day of the experiential program, we had a small graduation ceremony. Without warning, the head counselor told me I would have to stay in the hospital. As each of the other patients said goodbye to me and walked out the door to awaiting loved ones, I wanted to die. Having come there to take me home, Bill was angry. We were equally in denial about the severity of my condition.

That weekend, I was placed in a dual diagnosis unit that housed patients who had a combination of mental difficulties and chemical addictions. Because I didn't understand why I was there, I grew more depressed and stopped eating altogether. After meeting with a psychiatrist, I was transferred to the hospital's general adult psych ward. There, I enrolled in an experiential track that was similar to the IEP.

In those group therapy sessions, our petite, gentle female counselor used techniques similar to what I'd learned at Crossroads. They included Gestalt methods, relaxation, and visualization. Because all of the counselors were careful not to use guided imagery that could suggest memories, mine emerged on their own.

I remembered that when I had been in the city of Atlanta one day as a teenager, I'd been sexually assaulted by a group of Black men in a run-down neighborhood. I relived the emotional pain of seeing their neighbors stand on their front porches across the street from the empty lot, watching silently as the men group-raped me. No one tried to stop them. I relived the rape so intensely that I felt the sharp corner of a partially buried brick press into the back of my head as I left my body by focusing on wispy clouds in the blue sky above.

I also worked through previously recalled torture memories in greater detail. Although I felt embarrassed about sharing the memories with male patients in group therapy, their gentleness and genuine concern helped me to understand that not all men were like Dad. I needed to know that.

During my two-month stay at Charter-Peachford, I was aware that I seemed to be at least two people: a rebellious teenager and a cooperative adult patient. I didn't tell anyone because I was afraid that I'd be kept there longer.[3]

Dr. V., my assigned psychiatrist, was petite, dark-haired, and intelligent. When I told her that I was embarrassed about having had so many orgasms as a child, she said: "Your sexual sensory neuron path developed very early in your childhood." She helped me to understand that I had no reason to feel ashamed–it hadn't been my fault.

In our therapy group, we were asked to write affirmations (positive statements) about each other. Afterwards, we were to go to our bedroom and look into our own eyes in the bathroom mirror as we read, aloud, the affirmations that the others had given us. As I spoke to my mirror image, I felt as if I were lying. Further, I was spooked because a complete stranger stared back at me. What was happening to me?

Our group therapy counselor consistently challenged us to go beyond our emotional comfort zones. One of my greatest fears was to be in a room with Dad, even though he was dead. To help me overcome that fear, she suggested that I sit on the floor and surround myself with large pillows to create an imaginary protective barrier that he couldn't breach. Then she asked who else was I especially afraid of. I said, "My ex-husband."

She asked me to choose two men in the group to represent Dad and Albert. For Dad, I picked a large, gentle Black man who had become my buddy. I sensed that he wouldn't hurt me. I picked another man to play Albert. The counselor asked me to choose someone else to stand guard between me and the two men. I chose the largest man, also Black, to protect me from Dad and Albert.

She then asked me to tell "Dad" and "Albert" to go farther and farther away. Each time I commanded them, the two men took another step backwards, until they were out of sight in the hallway. The third man blocked their way. For the first time in my life, I felt stronger than Dad and Albert.

In music therapy sessions, we were asked to pick our favorite songs from a large selection of record albums and explain why these songs were special. My favorite was *Leader of the Band* by Kenny Loggins. I said the song represented my relationship with Dad because "he's my leader, and his blood runs through my veins." Although the music therapist's expression seemed odd, she made no comment.

One day in art therapy, I fashioned a clay heart with a jagged line down the middle. I made a clay knife stick out of the crack. Although I knew it represented what Dad had done to my heart, when asked, I only said that it represented my relationship with him. The female art therapist looked stunned, but said nothing. Refusing to take it to my bedroom, I told her to destroy it.

On another day, I drew a picture on a large piece of white paper with felt-tipped, colored pens. It was me as a child, lying naked on my back on Dad's cold, metal power saw table in our basement in Reiffton. He'd used thick, metal C-clamps to fasten my wrists to each side of the table. That day, he had worn a red shirt, blue pants, and brown boots. In the picture, his hands were reaching towards my lower body. This must have been one of the times he'd tortured me on that table, because I was unable to draw my body from my chest down. I just left a blank space where it would have been.

In another art therapy session, I used watercolor paints to draw Dad's outline. Again, he wore blue pants and a red, long-sleeved shirt. This time, he held a black wire and a red wire in his outstretched hands. They were attached to a black battery he'd set on the basement floor. His gray eyes stared.

In another picture, I used a black felt-tipped pen to make an outline of what seemed to be a giant bat wearing a black robe. Again, Dad's eyes stared. His two long fangs were tipped with fresh blood. To his side was a green-painted, wooden door to a closet. In a child's scrawl, I wrote, "He raped me in there sitting on the shelf 9 years old."

At no time did our art therapist suggest my memories. Although she was visibly shocked by nearly every creation, she wisely kept her hunches to herself.

For many weeks, each time Dr. V. asked me if I was considering suicide, I honestly told her yes. Since Dad had died, I just didn't feel like living.

Dr. V. brought up another subject: she was concerned that I hadn't expressed any emotions about my mother. When she encouraged me to start talking about her in group therapy, I felt strangely frightened. What if Mom found out? Dr. V. continued to insist.

Still nervous, I agreed to at least think about my relationship with Mom, although I wasn't willing to talk about her to anyone–including Dr. V.

Although Mom had presented herself as loving and caring when I was young, she'd been a different creature in the privacy of our home. I'd always known that she didn't love me. I'd never forgotten an afternoon in South Carolina, long after Mom had married her second husband, when she'd insisted I sit beside her on their king-sized bed and listen as she told me, in detail, what a wonderful lover he was and how he pleased her sexually. I also never forgot how, from childhood through my adult years, she'd insisted that I sit on her bed or stand nearby as she sat, naked, in front of the mirrors in her bathroom–preening. She'd seemed to enjoy exhibiting her naked body to me, despite my obvious discomfort.

I'd never forgotten a week in our house in Reiffton when she had walked through the house, up and down the stairs, every day–stark naked. She'd insisted that she'd done it to tone her muscles. When we'd protested and asked her to put clothes on, she'd angrily exhibited herself more!

I'd never forgotten how each time I left her home in South Carolina as an adult, she gave me at least one paper grocery bag full of steamy paperback novels that she'd recently purchased. She'd collected so many erotic novels, her husband had attached long brown wooden shelves to their bedroom wall to hold them all. Although I'd told Mom I didn't like the novels because I was uncomfortable with their detailed descriptions of intercourse and orgasms, she'd continued to insist that I read all of them.

Away from Mom's presence, I now felt braver to question some of her past behaviors. I'd always felt uncomfortable with how sexually inappropriate she'd been with me, but I'd been too afraid of her to say it to her face. I decided to send several letters of confrontation to her. Dr. V. advised me to keep copies of them (I did) and assured me that if Mom really loved me, she would try to work out our relationship in family therapy. When I asked Mom to come to my family sessions, however, she flatly refused. Adhering to our family's "protect Mom at all cost" tradition, another relative soon contacted me and took me to task for having upset her.

Although Mom never communicated with any of my therapists and didn't know what my recovery entailed, she nonetheless told family members, including my teenaged daughter and my stepmother, that I'd "gone off the deep end" and had inherited a "bipolar disorder from Bill Shirk's side of the family."

She alternately accused my husband and therapists of implanting "false memories" about her inappropriate past sexual behaviors in my mind. Years later, she even sent my teenaged daughter a magazine article promoting the FMSF's bogus claims about recovered memory. She said the article "proved" that my memories had been implanted by therapists![4]

During the last month of my stay at Charter Peachford, I met an adult female trauma survivor who had Multiple Personality Disorder (MPD). I was discomfited by her odd behaviors and stayed away from her as much as I could. Each time she regressed into a child alter-state, several nurses led her into her private bedroom that was full of stuffed animals. Although the nurses always closed the door, we could still hear her screams as she relived one trauma after another.

After two months, my primary insurer's mental health benefits limit changed from one million dollars to a hundred thousand. Since I'd stopped wishing I could die, my secondary insurer claimed that I must be stable enough to be discharged. I was pleased, because I wanted to go home. Being in a locked psych ward was too much like prison–I'd had enough.

Before my discharge, Dr. V. asked: "Do you think you might have amnesia?" I said no. Years later, I realized the irony of my reply–if I had amnesia, how could I know that I had it?

After my return home, I was surprised at the difficulty I had in performing the most simple chores. I felt like a young child, having to learn basic life skills all over again. The flashbacks continued, although not as intense as before. I was convinced that I was almost finished healing.

Clash with Religion

In therapy at the hospital, I'd learned how to identify people who were overly controlling. I'd also learned how to set mental and emotional boundaries with them, so they wouldn't take advantage of me. This caused a problem, because I now felt become uncomfortable with some of our denomination's teachings especially its insistence that members should do whatever the pastors said "God" wanted us to do.

We were even told that God required us to tithe a minimum of ten percent, then twenty percent of our gross income to the church! Our pastor insisted if we did this, God would "bless" us financially. Although we complied, the promised blessings never came. Instead, our financial situation deteriorated.

Still, I tried to believe what we were told in church. During worship services, I continued to raise my hands and sing praises to God both in English and in "tongues"–really, babbling like an infant. At the altar, male leaders and established female members placed their palms on the heads and bodies of members, to pray for our spiritual help or physical healing. As usual, their chants and "speaking in unknown tongues" washed over my mind.

When we sang songs over and over again during the worship part of each service, we seemed to enter a group trance. We were told that our subsequent feeling of joyous elation "proved" that God's Holy Spirit was in the sanctuary. In response to that sensation, we raised our hands and praised Him. At that point, I entered a total trance state, my eyes rolling up in their sockets.[5]

Being in a trance made it much easier to accept mental suggestions from the church leaders that otherwise, I would have rejected as ludicrous. I now believe that was their intention. During the trance, the door to my subconscious mind opened, flooding my mind with many new flash-backs. Several church leaders and members tried to convince me (and perhaps themselves) that my emerging memories and flashbacks were evidence of demons lurking in my body.

They told me that when I'd consulted with secular therapists, I'd sinned against God because I'd sought their help instead of His. They claimed that these rebellious acts had enabled demons to enter my mind and body. They said the demons were giving me false memories to make me "accuse the brethren."[6] They repeatedly criticized me for not depend-ing solely on God, Jesus, and the Bible for healing. They convinced me to repent and seek spiritual "deliverance" to get rid of the demons, and said this would make the false memories go away.

Unfortunately, when they encircled me at church or in a member's home, putting their hands on my body, chanting and speaking in strange tongues, louder and louder, I relived occult ritual traumas that I'd other-wise had no memory of. As I abreacted, these people became my former abusers.[7]

I screamed and writhed, although I was in too much of a trance to leap up and run out of the room. The more I physically struggled and cried out, the more they were convinced that the "demons" inhabiting my body were fighting their prayers and the invoked "blood of Jesus." When I stopped fighting, sometimes after an uncontrollable, ear-splitting scream, they congratulated themselves for having cast the demons out.

As a result, I felt lower than an ant's belly. And yet, I wanted to believe that invisible demons *had* caused the memories and flashbacks. Because my esteem was still scraping bottom, to occasionally endure several hours of demeaning deliverance sessions at no cost was vastly preferable to suffering daily flashbacks and abreactions, spending months in hospitals, and paying many thousands of dollars for therapy.

I was deeply disappointed when the deliverance sessions didn't stop my flashbacks and nightmares. I had to face the truth: there was no magical or supernatural quick fix for the effects of long-term trauma. What I really needed was courage, time, energy, and support from people who were either unscathed or had gone through their own recovery.

Some church members tried to silence me in other ways. They insisted that God wanted me to let go of the past–as if flashbacking and having vivid, recurring nightmares was a choice! They claimed the Bible said I was to "forgive and forget" (forgive, yes; forget, no).

They said because God had cleansed me of my sins, I ought not to revisit them by remembering and talking about them. How odd! I was remembering sins that had been perpetrated against me as a young child by my father and other adult predators–and yet they seemed to be saying that when I was an innocent child, I'd sinned against God by being raped and tortured![8]

Their constant criticism and lack of emotional support left me feeling as if I had to fight the whole world to do what was I sensed was right.

Within months, Bill told me that he wanted to become a missionary. I told him I couldn't do it. I didn't feel right serving in a church system that discouraged its members from seeking professional help to heal.

SIA

During this phase of my recovery, I attended 12-step group meetings with Bill and Emily. They included Al-Anon and Co-Dependents Anonymous (CoDA). I wondered if any 12-step programs existed for sexual abuse survivors to talk freely about what the sexual assaults had done to their minds and souls.

Searching for specialized support within the 12-step community, I found Incest Survivors Anonymous (ISA) and Survivors of Incest Anonymous (SIA). Soon, I started the first SIA 12-step meetings in the Atlanta area. Although I did it to meet my own needs, I felt honored to support other recovering survivors who also sought to heal from the effects of childhood sexual abuse.

Therapeutic Fragments

It was time to review my artwork and journals from the previous summer at Crossroads of Chattanooga. I hoped they'd give me more clues about my childhood.

Looking through my Crossroads folders, I was dismayed to discover that a lot of what I'd written and drawn at that facility still didn't make sense.

First, I looked through the folder from Emily's family week. As part of our homework after each session, we'd been expected to journal all of our dreams. I still couldn't make sense of what I found in one night's dreams:

5/31/89 – Wednesday Night

1. Getting on expressway—starting downhill—other cars going 70. Me and some others on roller skates, skateboard, bike, can't keep up. Keep having to pull over to let cars go on, get on again, can't keep up. Recurring dream.
2. Maid of honor in church. Inappropriate dress—slip instead of gown. Recurring dream.
3. Husband fesses up about sex with other women due to our going through problem time. Wants me to forgive and accept his weakness. Binds together through sexual act.
4. On a large boat. Enemy invasion—enemies come with mines and other explosives. I dive off, swim to enemy territory, try to hide or pretend to be one of them, to be safe and try somehow to help comrades in trouble.
5. Large centipede—two-colored—stinging many people in room. It's poisonous, but they don't realize it when it stings them. Bill and I approach it cautiously—hit it with something. Cut it in pieces. Parts scurry off. I'm still afraid of parts.
6. Recurring—snakes.

On a questionnaire entitled "Family Systems/Roles," I'd written the following responses:

Describe Mom and Dad in one word each.
    Mom – sick (emotionally); Dad – dictator[9]

What childhood role(s) do you see for yourself growing up?
List characteristics of roles:
   Hero: hypercritical of self, overachiever (grades)

   Lost child: quiet one, withdraws, daydreams, fantasy life, independent, ignored, forgotten, loner/confused, materialistic
   (things and pets), solace in food, intimacy problems

   Scapegoat: defiant, rebel (not to Dad, just social rules and
   morals), peers important, law and school problems, unplanned
   pregnancy, self-destructive, negative attention, family focus,
   addict

What adult role do you see for yourself?
   Addict: Alcohol & drugs up to 18; strong sex drive within
   bounds of marriage; work; food; religion (gives me boundaries, family, and morals); excitement (crisis oriented)

How do you feel about the roles you see for yourself?
   I feel angry, afraid, stuck in a way I don't want to be. Afraid
   for our family's children—that patterns would continue. Angry
   that we children are still covering up for Dad and Mom, carrying their guilt (Dad still won't be honest about his own guilt).

On another questionnaire, *Day of Change – Day of Decision*, I'd
written:

Where were you stuck last night? Role (in family):
   Lost child and hero

Feeling:
   Angry and not whole and afraid

Who or what set you up for the role?
   Dad

What has been/is the payoff (reward) for your role?
   Keeping peace in the family—no upsets. Peace.

What has it cost you to play role?
Health, relationships, ability to be myself—don't really know
who I am, except spiritually.

What are you willing to change?
I've had to stay away from Dad and brothers for a long time—
want to begin own counseling. Want to be more open with
mother—caused her much hurt in past by invalidating her pain.
Will need to give Dad his shame back and quit carrying it for him.
Want to be myself and accept my faults and own needs and wants.

As I reviewed these papers, I realized that Emily's family week had
probably been my first step in recognizing how dysfunctional my childhood family had been. Except for a few rebellious teen years, I'd tried
hard to be the family peacekeeper—I mustn't upset anybody; mustn't
rock the boat. The counselors at Crossroads had helped me to recognize
how much I'd sacrificed to make my family happy.

Next, I reviewed my inpatient Crossroads folder. In it, I found a set of
diagrams of my childhood home in Reiffton that I'd drawn with colored
pencils. I'd color-coded anything in the house that still bothered me,
whether or not I understood why. I'd outlined certain furniture with colored
markers, indicating suppressed anger, sadness, happiness, guilt, anxiety,
shame, and depression. I'd indicated that I'd felt anxiety and shame when
near my parents' bed. I'd made a blob of black shame, surrounded by the
color for guilt, on the bathroom floor, where I'd often slept at night. I'd
marked a trail of anxiety and sadness at the stairs where Dad had stomped
from the ground floor kitchen to the landing in front of our second-floor
bedrooms. I'd color-coded other areas of the house for reasons I still could-
n't explain.

I reviewed lists of family messages and values that I'd internalized as
a child:

- Victim
- Future marriage failures—bitterness—due to Mom's example
  with Dad
- Male/female role confusion
- Triangular communication
- Lack of self-esteem

- Isolation
- Fear of heavy stomping on stairs (Dad's)
- Abusing future children
- Fear of anger directed at me from others, even when their anger is appropriate
- Lack of trust and fear of males
- Treating sex as a tool instead of expression of love
- Fear of criticism
- Lack of confidence in groups and around older people
- Inability to express emotions
- Inability to make choices for self
- Co-dependency (excessive dependence on others)
- Wives must resent husband
- Sex is a duty—no love involved
- I am not wanted by Dad except to work and be an object of vented rage
- I am not wanted by Mother
- When adults are present, kids must stay in another room. No mixing
- Kids stay out of sight and mind—don't mix with adults unless for adults' pleasure
- Children shouldn't be seen or heard unless they're doing chores
- If I fall down slippery stairs, it's my fault
- Boys can have fun and toys, girls can't
- If the dog goes hungry or thirsty, and dies, it's my fault
- The dog is more important to Dad, than me
- My physical needs are unimportant
- Don't talk at table
- Don't talk about feelings

I pulled out another diagram from the file. It was so big and bulky, I had trouble unfolding it. As I scanned it, I remembered that each adult patient had been instructed to take turns lying on their back on a large sheet of paper on the floor, and then another patient outlined the body, being careful not to be disrespectful. After our outlines were completed, we were given crayons with instructions to color-code any emotions and experiences from our past that were especially important. Looking at the paper now, I was stunned to see a large gash of red crayon drawn between my hips and the beige outline of a large fetus above that. And over one breast, I'd drawn three people holding hands. What did it all mean? I couldn't remember!

On the back of another large piece of paper was a crayoned message to my counselor, scrawled in a little girl's handwriting: *"4 U – Kathy."* I didn't write like that!

As I reviewed a second full-sized body diagram in the same file, I was amazed that I'd viewed myself as a container of negative emotions: fear, anger, pain, sadness, and loneliness. Nothing good, nothing happy. Where was my joy, peace, and happiness? Why did I feel so icy inside? Why was I still unable to feel love for my husband? What was wrong with me?

Those questions seemed to prime my mental pump. More emerged: Why did I still freeze when strange men were sexually inappropriate with me in public, even rubbing their engorged penises against my butt in supermarket checkout lines? Why couldn't I get angry and yell at them or at least move away?

Why did I have so much difficulty opening my mouth to tell Bill that I was bothered by something that he'd done? Why was I filled with pain? Why was I so terrified that if I expressed myself, he'd leave me?

Why did I have anxiety attacks whenever I anticipated having to go to social gatherings in rooms full of strangers? Why was socializing so easy for Bill, and still so hard for me?

Next, I reviewed several entries in my Crossroads journal:

6/16/89 – Dreams last night

> Major gore. Going up path up hill to home to where brothers are. Path through woods. Try to go past girl and dog/boy. Dog tries to attack and bite me. I have scissors—have to cut head off to make it stop. Then girl does same. It grieves me. I do same to her. I reach top of hill. Two spreads were laid out (different foods)—1 on one side, 1 on other. Tempted to eat from 1 side, start to, put it back in dish. Poisonous (Dad's).

6/18/89

> Me and other person with Princess Di and husband (not Charles) in water, frozen underneath, Styrofoam under that.

On bottom of pond was trash and coolers. I tried to get out quick. Tried to warn others. Snakes—various kinds. Water moccasins that look like rattlers. Later on, in a house—man with boots had snake in boot. Tried to take off boot without disturbing snake. Took boot off, snake hanging on leg with fangs in knee. He pulled snake's head out—harmless—round head. Put in old hamster container as pet. I felt sorry for the snake—used to living in the wild.

6/23/89

Dream—in institution, large building somewhere upstairs. Radioactive accident, people contaminated, became mutated. It tried to go after others in building. I was only person who knew what was going on upstairs. I was afraid, tried to find way out of building without being spotted. On highway, accosted woman driver in front of me. Next step was to hide in woods, but afraid they were in the woods, too. Dream—mute woman alone in house set me up to have sex. Dream—going up apartment stairs—I played role of husband with woman and child—I was both!

In these early journals, my handwriting had changed from day to day. Many of the words were tiny. Why had I been so secretive? Who had I tried to hide my thoughts from?

In an envelope in the file, I found pieces of paper on which fellow patients had written positive affirmations for me. I felt sad because I still didn't believe any of them. Why?

I found an early left-hand communication that I'd written there. I must not have wanted to read it, because I'd crumpled it up as if to throw it away. Then I'd smoothed it out, folded it, and put it in the folder:

```
Dear Kathy
    I hurt real bad Mom is never there every time I try to
catch up to her she goes more away from me sometimes she is
too much ahead and I cry I want my mommy she wont hear me
she leaves me alone and goes away in front of me. I am all
alone it is scary I don't know people where is she I am
scared I want to go home Mom I need you. Grandma are you
there help me please.
```

I was startled by the way some of the words had been spelled–the note had been written by a child! And why had I written that Mom kept going away? What did that mean? Unnerved, I shoved the paper back into the folder.

I found more drawings that startled me. I'd drawn one of them because a counselor had asked us to divide the big piece of paper in half, drawing our "public" self on one side and the person we preferred to be known as on the other.

Using brightly colored markers on blue paper, I'd first drawn my adult persona on the left side. I looked almost male as I flew through the air, wearing a blue "Superman" suit with a red cape and belt. The only feminine detail was my pink boots. I was carrying the world in my hands.

On the right side, I'd drawn a young girl sitting cross-legged on the ground with a brown bunny rabbit in her hands. She had blue doll's eyes and wore a pink, short-sleeved T-shirt and blue pants. I'd used those colors for the clothes because pink represented the girl part of my personality and blue, the boy part.

I'd made a similar drawing in art therapy at Charter-Peachford. That counselor had also challenged us to draw our public and hidden selves. Again, I'd divided the drawing into two parts. On the left side, I'd used crayons to draw myself as a young woman sitting cross-legged on the ground, reaching for a spring flower, wearing blue jeans and a short-sleeved, pink T-shirt. In this picture my arms and body were muscular. I was smiling.

On the right side I'd drawn my hidden self, using a pencil to outline an androgynous face with no nose or mouth. I'd used blue chalk to outline my staring, lidless eyes. The face peered wordlessly from behind thick black, vertical lines that seemed to represent prison bars.

I felt chilled as I pulled that drawing out of my Charter-Peachford file and stared at it. What did it mean? Who was that prisoner? After I put it back into the folder, the hairless creature's face haunted my mind.

Looking through the Crossroads folder one more time, I found a drawing that had embarrassed me, because I hadn't been able to explain it during group therapy. Our counselor had asked us to each draw a picture of our relationship to our higher power. With colored pencils, I'd drawn a tunnel of yellow light that was walled by many strands of different colors. The tunnel was preceded by a larger circular wall comprised of many hundreds of diamond shaped fragments. Some fragments were individual, while others were conglomerations of two, three or four pieces. The darker colored, more vivid fragments were closest to the tunnel of light.

I'd also drawn a winged female angel flying up into the mouth of the fragmented part of the tunnel, holding little girl me with one arm. The first diamonds and clusters they approached were given lighter, more soothing pastel colors.

I wondered: what did the hundreds of diamonds and fragments represent? Although I remember having felt a powerful compulsion to draw them, I'd had no conscious reason for doing so. Why had I drawn a multi-colored tunnel of light, extending up beyond the fragments? And why had I drawn myself as two persons—a flying angel in blue jeans and a little girl in a dress?

I sighed as I put the picture away. The strong sensation that more mysteries lurked inside my mind wearied me. Would I ever know all of myself?

Notes

1. More about Major Depression can be found at this website: http://www.psychologyinfo.com/depression/major.htm.

2. According to the National Institute of Mental Health, the symptoms of PTSD are:

    . . . flashback episodes, memories, nightmares, or frightening thoughts, especially when . . . exposed to events or objects reminiscent of the trauma . . . emotional numbness and sleep disturbances, depression, anxiety, and irritability or outbursts of anger . . . intense guilt . . . [avoidance of] any reminders or thoughts of the ordeal. (Facts 1)

3. Although I did check into the hospital voluntarily, leaving wasn't as easy-especially if I still appeared to be a danger to myself or to others. A common warning given to me and other patients in psych hospitals was that if we left "AMA" (against medical advice), our insurance might not cover our previous days in the hospital. That always kept me from attempting to leave before I was properly discharged.

4. Memory researcher Laura S. Brown wrote:

    I am aware that therapeutic malpractice exists and that rarely such malpractice includes iatrogenic induction of false beliefs that are co-constructed by therapist and client as memories of childhood abuse. But I view this line of the discussion as a red herring that focuses attention away from the more basic questions of the way trauma affects memory. (*International Handbook*, pg. 196)

5. At the World Congress of Professional Hypnotists Convention in Las Vegas, Dick Sutphen explained why such techniques are sometimes used in church services:

> If you'd like to see a revivalist preacher at work, there are probably several in your city. Go to the church or tent early and sit in the rear . . . Most likely repetitive music will be played while the people come in for the service. A repetitive beat, ideally ranging from 45 to 72 beats per minute (a rhythm close to the beat of the human heart), is very hypnotic and can generate an eyes-open altered state of consciousness in a very high percentage of people. And, once you are in an alpha state, you are at least 25 times as suggestible as you would be in full beta consciousness. The music is probably the same for every service, or incorporates the same beat, and many of the people will go into an altered state almost immediately upon entering the sanctuary. Subconsciously, they recall their state of mind from previous services and respond according to the post-hypnotic programming.

> Watch the people waiting for the service to begin. [In our church, this occurred during the worship part of the services.] Many will exhibit external signs of trance-body relaxation and slightly dilated eyes. Often, they begin swaying back and forth with their hands in the air while sitting in their chairs. (Sutphen p. 4-5)

6. One winter, I'd noticed that an adolescent girl in our church acted very sexual while in an obvious trance state. After I tried to communicate to her mother that I was concerned, the girl's father and our pastor insisted on meeting privately with Bill and me. In that small room, both men angrily accused me of letting Satan attack the "fine family" through me. Their accusation was odd, because I'd never suggested that the father had done anything-nor had I even considered it! Several weeks after that, during a worship service, Bill and I watched the same father absent-mindedly caress his younger daughter's buttocks in front of us in a way that should have been reserved for his wife. In response, the younger girl smiled happily at him and leaned into him. I think Anna C. Salter, Ph.D. was right on the mark when she wrote: "If children can be silenced and the average person is easy to fool, many [sexual] offenders report that religious people are even easier to fool than most people." (p. 28) We all want to believe the best in people, as they present themselves to us. But sometimes we do so at the children's peril.

7. After discussing marching and meditation during group meetings designed to gain control of the minds of participants, Sutphen explained how chanting can also put a person into a suggestible trance state: "The third thought-stopping technique is chanting, and often chanting in meditation. 'Speaking in tongues' could also be included in this category. All three thought-stopping techniques produce an altered state of consciousness." (Sutphen, pg. 11) My experience has been that, when I was "speaking in tongues," I was actually regressing into my babyhood-hence, my infant babbling. I now wonder if this is what I heard from others, who might have

also been in regressive altered states of consciousness. I am not suggesting that "speaking in tongues" is a bad thing. It can be a very peaceful experience. In fact, being in a trance state can be very addictive. I am, however, concerned that many people who "speak in tongues" may not realize that when they do this, they are indicating to the wrong people that they are vulnerable to mental control.

8. I've been told by several believers in reincarnation that when we were sexually assaulted as children, we were being punished for sins that we'd committed in past lives. This seems to be another version of "blaming the victim." I'm amazed that so few people are willing to place the guilt and blame where they belong-on human predators who willingly hurt, rape, torture, and sometimes even kill innocent children.

9. Mom usually presented herself as the emotionally sick, downtrodden wife (which she was, to a degree) while hiding the fact that she wielded enormous power in all of our lives. I called her manipulative crying, "crocodile tears" because she knew how to use it to manipulate me (and others) to feel sorry for her miserable state in life and to protect her from the consequences of her behaviors-especially when others were disgusted by the behaviors. At the same time, she narcissistically ignored my emotional needs and continued to abuse me. From her, I learned that I had no importance or value; only she did. I had to fight very hard not to perpetuate the same kind of relationship with Emily; unfortunately, I failed many times.

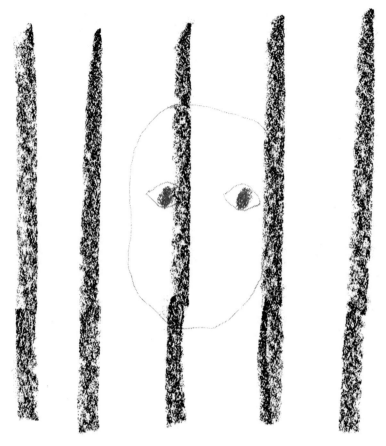

HIDDEN "PRISONER" PART, EARLY 1990

DAD PREPARED TO TORTURE ME WITH ELECTRICITY

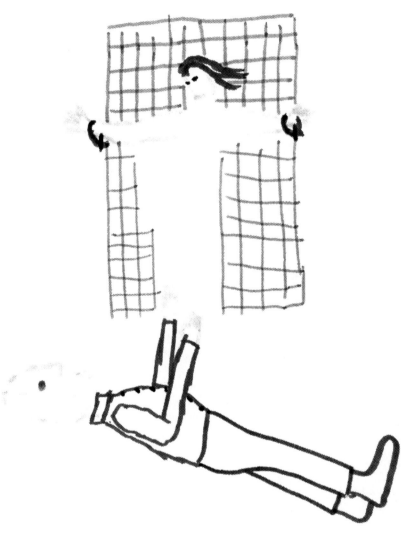

DAD CLAMPED ME TO HIS SAW TABLE TO TORTURE
ME WITH ELECTRICITY, EARLY 1990

4-31-90

The lady was gray not pink she lay on the floor they cut her tummy open it look funny, inside I feel sick throw up why they cut her tummy open. Daddy and other man they do it one man hold her daddy cut her tummy He reach in pull her guts out they spill all over the floor he think it funny Cat guts

WOMAN RITUALLY MURDERED BY DAD, 4/31/90

5/3/90

Dad

DAD WITH RITUAL ROBE AND KNIFE, 5/3/90

5/19 Altar

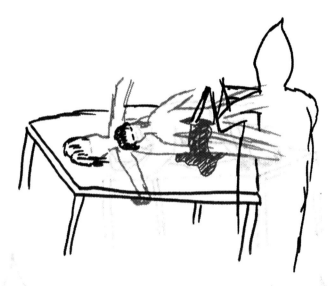

Dad made me lay back on the altar then
they lay the little boy on top of me he
didnt move limp they cut his dummy open
blood ran down me   I tried to sleep but
I felt the blood   It wasnt a dream
as hard as I tried to make it one

DAD RITUALLY KILLING A BOY ATOP ME, 5/19/90

Alter-States

Back to the One

After I reviewed the drawings and journals, I sensed that I needed help to reclaim hidden territory in my mind to which I still seemed to be amnesic. I told Bob, a local codependency support group facilitator, that I was having trouble finding a therapist who was qualified to work with sexual abuse survivors.[1] Because I was comfortable with him and he was already familiar with my history, he agreed to be my therapist. Careful not to prompt any memories, the big, bearded man patiently listened to whatever came to my mind during each fifty-minute session.

He kept big boxes of Kleenex in his office, which helped me to feel comfortable about crying in front of him. Because he had a Master of Divinity degree, he helped me to understand that God had never abandoned me, and that if He'd been angry at anyone, it was at the adults who had hurt me.

I didn't want to believe that, contrary to what I'd been taught in church, God didn't send His angels into dangerous situations to magically rescue and protect His children from being harmed. It took away my sense of safety and left me feeling exposed and vulnerable. And yet, no matter how spiritual or righteous I tried to be, I was really no safer from being assaulted than any other human being.

As I struggled with my anger towards God for not intervening on my behalf in the past, Bob reminded me that all humans have free will. He said that, having given us the ability to choose between right and wrong, God does not miraculously intervene and change the minds and behaviors of hurtful people; only they have the power to do that. And because their free will can include the will to harm children, God in all His power and glory will not stop them.

This explained why, no matter how hard I'd prayed for God to touch Dad's life or speak to his mind, he had never changed, had never indicated that he loved me, and had never said he was sorry for what he'd done to me and the children.

A powerful new anger stirred inside me. If God couldn't protect me, then he wasn't my loving Father. Ever since I was a little girl, I'd wanted a father who would love me. Because Dad had been anything but loving, I'd chosen God to be his big, strong replacement. In Sunday school, I'd been taught that God had created the world; He'd formed the seas and the biggest, most ferocious creatures. He'd decided when the sun would come up, and when it would set. All my life, I'd been told that He even created millions of angels to protect us!

The knowledge that God didn't protect us from harm stoked new rage, disappointment, and disillusionment. In my mind, God had become help-less, His hands tied behind His back.

What in the hell good was He, then? Why did He let me be born when He knew I was going to be hurt so badly? What kind of cruel, sadistic bastard was He, to put me on this earth, knowing I'd be betrayed and tortured and raped, over and over?

Bob encouraged me to express my anger towards God. He said that prayer was communication–that God made our emotions and wanted us to tell Him what we felt towards Him. Bob said that God, like a loving father towards his little children, was big enough to take our rage and still love and accept us. He encouraged me to cuss and yell at God, if that was what I needed.

Too embarrassed to do it in front of Bob, I did it at home–first on my knees beside the bed, then standing when I would not kneel for God anymore. My fist raised, I yelled and cursed at God. Let him strike me dead! I dared the lightning to come!

"Where the fuck were you?" I demanded. "Why didn't you care? Why did you let me be born to the bitch and bastard? Do you get off on send-ing kids to twisted parents, knowing what they'll do to them? Why did you give Dad free will, knowing what he'd do to me? What perverted kind of cosmic joke is this? You know what, God? I don't believe in you anymore. I think men just made you up, to keep us controlled. To make rules for us.

"'*Don't blaspheme.*' God'll get angry and strike you dead. '*Honor your parents so you'll have a long life.*' Oh, that one is a real joke, isn't it, God? And, '*Obey your husbands to please God.*' Even if they hit you or rape you or hurt your kid in front of you? Yeah right, God. Sure thing. That's how much you really care about the children, isn't it? And all these damned angels you created to protect us–why are you still holding them back? Why, God, Why?"

Time and again, after my rage was spent, I found myself sitting on the floor, my legs bent under me, rocking back and forth. I held myself as snot and tears ran freely. "Why God, why? Why?" I keened like a small child, then lay on my side on the carpeted floor, curled into a fetal position, still weeping. "Why? Why?"

One rainy afternoon, an old set of memories drifted into my exhausted mind: I was in the children's choir of our Lutheran church in Reiffton. We sang "Beautiful Savior" and "Fairest Lord Jesus," two soothing songs that made me love Jesus all over again. And "Onward Christian Soldiers" had a rhythmic cadence that sent the blood marching through my veins.

They and so many other hymns had helped me feel positive and comforted. I remembered how, many times, regardless of what else had happened in that church, I'd still felt comforted by what had seemed to be God's direct presence.

On the floor of my bedroom, I remembered what that presence had felt like–a powerful, pure love that had filled my body with every breath. It was a love that was so eternal and so "now" that nothing else had mattered. It said, "I'm here, I'll always be here, I'll always love you. No matter what you do, I'll always love you. I'll always be your Father."

As I remembered, I realized that my greatest anger wasn't at God; it was at myself–because I hadn't been what I believed God had wanted me to be. I'd failed Him; I'd done so many things that had displeased Him. I felt dirty, soiled, and filthy.

Wanting to hide under the bed from His nearly tangible presence, I prayed: "Oh, God, I fucked up so bad. I did everything you didn't want me to do. I'm dirty; I don't deserve you anymore." I meant it. I was ready to walk away from God forever, not because He'd failed me–but because I'd failed Him. He deserved a better daughter than me!

I was surprised as the same message broke through to my mind that I'd received so many times as a child: "I'll always be here, I'll never change, I'll always love you." His love gently broke through my shame-barrier and drew me back to Him. As it did, I knew that God really was my loving spiritual Father. He always had been and always would be.

I took comfort in the words of the apostle Paul who, as a rebel named Saul, had once caused the murder of many followers of Jesus: "For I am sure that neither death, nor life, nor angels, nor principalities, nor things present, nor things to come, nor powers, nor height, nor depth, nor anything else in all creation, will be able to separate us from the love of God in Christ Jesus our Lord." (*Romans 8:38–39, RSV*)

In a flash, I understood why I'd felt ashamed, why I'd distanced myself and blamed God for the distance between us. I'd foolishly tried to understand Him as I would a human father. Over the decades, I'd accepted teachings from a succession of church leaders who had preached that our heavenly Father had the same attributes as their earthly fathers. Thus, God was judgmental, angry, punitive, demanding, rigid, shaming, and non-accepting.

Now, I knew those men had been wrong: the God I'd known as a young child hadn't changed one iota. Before my mind had been tainted by human teachings and beliefs, I'd had the purest understanding of who He was.

Rising from the floor, I came back to the One who had been with me from the start. I vowed on my very soul that I would never deny God or turn from Him again. It was time to separate God from Dad in my mind, to stop blaming God for what Dad did and stop blaming Dad for not having loved me as God did.

Revelation after revelation came as I stood alone in the bedroom, enveloped by God's gentle comfort blanket of love. My heavenly Father had never deserted me. Maybe He couldn't break the rules by entering a room when I was being raped, to throw the human beast aside and carry me out of the room in what I imagined to be His big, strong arms. But He'd been right there with me.

And when my heart had cracked and broken from tears I'd dared not cry, He'd felt the awful pain and had cried for me. And when I'd hurt, He'd hurt with me. And when I'd lost the ability to withstand any more pain and horror, He'd given me the ability to dissociate, to block it all out, so that my mind and body could continue to survive.

Knowing this now, I was ready to feel the pain, to cry the tears, to endure what I could not bear as a child. As long as I had my heavenly Father and His enduring love, I could bear anything. He would be with me, right there with me, as I went through each tormenting memory. And then He would heal my terrible wounds with His eternal love.

Inner Children

Because I hadn't held a job since quitting my part-time position at McDonald's, I now had extra time alone at home to tap into whatever was still hidden in my unconscious mind. I did this, in part, by using several of the techniques I'd learned at Crossroads–especially right-hand/left-hand journaling.

I always kept a spiral-bound notepad next to my bed. Uninterrupted, I sat on the bed and used my right hand to journal any dreams I could still remember, and then diary what had happened the previous day, as well as the previous day's flashbacks.

Then I held the pen in my left hand and mentally invited my "inner child" to write to me. As before, each time I did left-hand writing, I was slammed by the physical, visual, and emotional effects of newly emerging traumatic memories. Sometimes I cried for hours; sometimes I stormed and yelled in rage at Dad for having hurt me.

Bob encouraged me to invest in a punching bag. I went to a second-hand sporting goods store and paid fifty dollars for a nice, big Everlast bag. Bill used a thick chain to hang it from a big wooden beam in our large garage. On weekdays, when I knew the neighbors living on our cul-de-sac were away from home, I whaled away at the punching bag. It was satisfying to hit and kick it as hard as I wanted.

As my rage erupted towards Dad and other men who had raped me, I screamed at them and pummeled their imaginary faces and bodies with my fists and feet.

Although the anger work sessions helped me to feel empowered, I was dismayed by the way more memories emerged right on the heels of previous ones. Would they never end?

When my rage erupted on weekends, I carried a children's plastic bat into our spare bedroom that was partially below ground. After placing a "Do Not Disturb" sign in front of the closed door, I whacked the bat as hard as I could on a pile of sofa cushions, screaming until my rage-energy was spent. Each time I ran out of anger, I collapsed and wept.

Bob suggested that I stockpile the same kinds of art supplies in that room that I'd used as a child. They included a big box of Crayola crayons, colored pencils, colored felt-tipped pens, different colors of glitter, glue, colorful construction paper, and drawing pads.

Sometimes, as I sat on the carpeted floor and drew, I seemed to go away for as much as several hours. When I came back to consciousness, I was unnerved by what I'd drawn.

One new drawing was of a yellow walking path that wound through a grassy meadow. Brown footprints temporarily left the trail to where a dead baby had been gently deposited in the grass; then the footprints went back to the trail and went on from there, heading towards big, stinking piles of feces with relatives' names on them.

Another drawing alarmed me. It depicted the naked body of a brown-haired Caucasian woman with black pubic hair, lying on the floor on her back, her abdomen cut open vertically. She was quite dead.

A location that kept recurring in my dreams emerged in another drawing of a "road on mountain . . . a long drive home." On one side of the road was a building marked "Episcopalian College/School/Church" and, a bit farther along, another building described as a "big red brick house with a white porch–Satanist headquarters–[teachers] taught us things better . . . Dad and me learned . . . demons taught here . . . later years, [I] taught classes here . . . near Little Rock, Arkansas."

Another drawing was of what Dad called the "Community Room." It seemed to be inside a building in or near Reading, Pennsylvania. The walls and floors were painted black; the doors were brown. The drawing included a door to a bathroom, marked "water to clean up blood," and a carved, brown, wooden "snake on pole carried by Dad–head pointed DOWN." Black squiggles on the floor represented the "killing, dismembering area." A horizontal squiggle along the wall was identified as "woman's intestines." One note on the drawing was about "double doors to outside–where cut up body in trash bags was carried out."

Another drawing was of a different room with a brown, wooden altar. On it were two lit candles and an upside-down bronze cross. I remembered I would sit on the edge of the altar and "watch, and swing my feet." Facing the altar in a semi-circle were nine metal chairs: "They would sometimes sit in chairs in robes and eat and drink refreshments. Sometimes they would stand & line up in the same order. Men who raped me [stood] to the right." A spiral drawn on the floor represented "where they would gang rape me." One corner of the room was labeled my "hiding corner."

One afternoon at home, alone in our kitchen, I absent-mindedly looked down at a large carving knife lying in our stainless steel sink. Suddenly,

I had a vivid flashback of Dad wearing a long, black, pointy-hooded robe. In his hands, he held the blade of a large bloody knife. I ran downstairs, grabbed my sketchbook, and drew what I'd just seen.

Another drawing showed me lying naked on my back on a wooden table. Also naked, Dad stared into my eyes as he straddled and raped me. Six adults wearing black, hooded robes stood in a semi-circle, watching silently. Words were written on the paper: "Dad reminded me not to talk back."

The next drawing described what had happened just before the rape. I was lying on my back on the same table. A little brown-haired boy had been placed atop my torso, his back on my abdomen. Dad had used his big knife to vertically slit the boy's abdomen open, making lots of blood run down the side of the boy's body, then onto and under my side and butt. "Dad made me lay back on the altar then they lay the little boy on top of me," the note read. "He didn't move–limp – they cut his tummy open blood ran down me I tried to sleep but I felt the blood It wasn't a dream as hard as I tried to make it one."

Another drawing was of Dad's mother, wearing a hooded black robe, and in her hands she held a thick, old book, bound in brown leather. A picture of a naked goddess was embossed on the front of it, her torso encircled by a snake. Its head pointed towards the side of her head. The book seemed to be very important to Grandma. In it were symbols that she called "runes." Although I was expected to read and understand them, I don't remember if I ever did.

In another drawing, I appeared to be an adolescent, now also wearing a hooded black robe. Dad "taught" me how to vertically cut open a boy's abdomen as the boy lay on his back on the floor. "First human cutting," read the words on the drawing. "Dad's hands on mine. He liked brown curly hair. I was 13." And, "I safe now I one of them still altar girl but they won't cut me now Now I big girl now I have to cut like cutting a cow."

I was confused; most of the pictures and messages seemed to come from children of different ages–mostly between the ages of five and twelve. What in the hell was going on?

Soon I "felt" voices talking in my mind.[2] At first, I was convinced they must be demons that were trying to trick me into believing they were human. I prayed to God to make them go away. When that didn't work, I commanded them to leave "in the name of Jesus." The childlike voices kept talking, whispering their names, sometimes making threats about hurting me. Was I going insane?

I wondered if I had Multiple Personality Disorder (MPD) like that female patient at Charter-Peachford. If I did have MPD, would my life be ruined? Would I be locked up in a hospital for years, like she had been? Would my neighbors think I was crazy? I chuckled at the last thought–if they'd heard some of my screams during my anger work sessions at home, they might already think so! It was time to stop worrying about what everyone else thought and go with the flow to see what happened next.

Several times in therapy, I hesitantly tried to tell Bob about the voices in my mind. Although he and other codependency counselors had taught me about getting in touch with my "inner child," I sensed I had a lot more than one child inside me. And although the counselors had talked about the "inner child" in a figurative way, mine seemed quite real. Sometimes so many children's voices talked to me at once, I had difficulty following them all.

When I told Bob I might have multiple personalities, he sat in his upholstered chair with a straight face, saying nothing. Uncomfortable with his silence, I tried reasoning with him. "Bob, I keep hearing voices."

"Are those voices inside your mind, or are they coming from the outside?"

"Definitely inside."

He seemed relieved and explained that some schizophrenics hear external voices.

I continued pushing my point. "You've seen my art work. It's not adult stuff. I go away for hours sometimes and when I come back, I don't remember drawing any of it."

He said this might indicate a split-off inner child that held some of my traumatic memories, but he was certain I didn't actually have MPD.

I felt frustrated. Why wouldn't he listen to what I was telling him? Didn't I know myself better than he ever could, since I was the one who had to live in this body and listen to those damned voices all day long?

Because he kept insisting that I didn't have MPD, I stopped mentioning the possibility to him and encouraged the children inside to write to me in my journal at home. Their journal entries were like the drawings— describing events that I'd had no prior memory of. That worried me. If these child parts were part of me, then whatever they'd experienced, I had, too. And yet their memories weren't mine! How they could be so vivid and yet not feel like parts of my history? Was I making them up?

I didn't think so, because I hadn't read anything, anywhere, that suggested such graphic and bizarre images. And some details of the drawings did match details of recent dreams. Were the dreams my mind's way of preparing me to cope with the impact of daytime memories?

I was exhausted from the incessant voices and memories. And because they were so damned bizarre, I absolutely could not accept them as being real. To help me to cope with them without having to accept them, Bob taught me to visualize a pantry room in the back of my mind with wooden shelves along the back wall. At his suggestion, I put each bizarre memory in a big glass jar and left it there on the shelf to "sit and simmer."

Living in both the past and the present was difficult. Although I talked about some of my new thoughts and memories in therapy, I never had enough time to process them all. I had to cope with most of them at home on my own.

New York City Ritual

Within weeks, I suffered a horrendous series of flashbacks about a sadistic ritual gathering that had been held in the summer that my family had gone to the World's Fair in New York City–either in 1963 or 1964.[3] Although I'd never forgotten about my parents taking us to the huge fair, I'd suppressed all memory of this part of the trip. I contacted an investigator at our District Attorney's office. The investigator encouraged me to come and give a verbal statement about what I'd remembered. A female secretary typed it:

INTERVIEW WITH KATHLEEN SULLIVAN

On May 23, 1990 at approximately 2:00 PM Ms. Sullivan gave the following information to the secretary:

My dad was the leader of a satanic cult in the area of Reading Pennsylvania. We lived in Reiffton. This begin [sic] when I was approximately 8 to 13 years of age, about 1963 to 1969. I witnessed weekly meetings on Friday nights where I saw both adults and children murdered, mutilated, dismembered. They

also did a lot of pedophile rituals with boys who were not physically cut or hurt (only sexually related) . . . I do remember that
during the '64 Worlds Fair in New York City my dad took me
to some kind of special meeting where it seemed to be either a
national or international gathering of pedophiles who were
involved in sadisam [sic]. I watched as they demonstrated rubbing a penis on the private parts of a baby and later saw
approximately fifteen dead babies laid out on the floor.
A woman took me by the hand and told me it was just my
imagination. I believe that by what I saw there may have been
some representatives from the Maffia [sic] there due to the way
they were dressed and their skin coloring and the power that they
obviously had over the group. We also moved to Cockeysville,
Maryland when I was fourteen. I do not remember any events
that occurred after that time relating to satanic activities . . . I
will related [sic] other things as they are remembered to . . . the
District Attorney's Office. At this time I am unsure of who to
trust in relating information to family.

Because I hadn't yet discovered similar information on ritual abuse or
pedophilia, I wasn't willing to accept what I was remembering and
reporting.

Suicide Programming

After telling Bob about some of these memories, I felt a powerful,
repetitive compulsion to insert the blade of a large knife into my
abdomen and vertically gut myself. Each time the urge came, I felt
unusually peaceful and believed I would feel no pain. Staying by myself
at home during the day was dangerous; I was losing strength and was
afraid I might not be able to fight the urge much longer.

Other therapists advised Bob that I might be experiencing *suicide
programming*. They explained that this type of mental programming usually kicked in when a client's ritual abuse (RA) memories first emerged.
Bob gave me the names and phone numbers of several psychiatric facilities
in the US that specialized in working with RA survivors. As I contacted
each facility, I "saw" myself cutting off my hands or cutting the veins in my

wrists. Again, I felt peaceful and believed if I followed through, I'd feel no pain.[4]

The most highly recommended program was at the Columbine psychiatric hospital in Denver, Colorado. When I called there, a man said their unit was filled to overflowing. He told me about a smaller program for ritual trauma survivors at Bethesda PsycHealth Hospital, also in Denver. I soon flew to Colorado to start the next phase of my recovery.

Bethesda PsycHealth

Because Denver is at a high altitude, the sky above the city was startlingly blue. The hospital, a former tuberculosis sanitarium, consisted of several large, red brick buildings. The walking paths and lovely flower gardens between the buildings helped to soothe my frazzled mind. One weekend during my stay there, my red-haired roommate talked her boyfriend into driving us to the Red Rock Amphitheater on a daytime pass. I was awed by the majestic mountains that I saw towering in the distance. That was the pleasant part of my stay.

Several days after I'd checked into the specialized unit, I met its director, a bespectacled, soft-spoken psychiatrist, Dr. T, for the first time. We met almost every weekday during my month-long stay. Sometimes I giggled when he entered the empty conference room to talk with me, because he usually burped.

During my first consultation with the psychiatrist, I described my internal children. He asked questions and told me that I probably had MPD. A battery of standardized psychological tests confirmed his suspicion.[5] When he verified my new diagnosis, I spiraled into depression. I instinctively knew that my life was about to change forever–I didn't want that to happen!

Remembering the movie *Sybil* and the odd behaviors of the female patient with MPD at Charter-Peachford, I believed I'd be treated like a freak for the rest of my life. I felt angry; I didn't want to share my body with other personalities! Damn it, it was mine!

For about a week, I didn't try to get better. I just wanted to die. Dr. T and the other staff members gently explained that I needed to learn how to work *with* my disability, instead of fighting it. Dr. T said if I used every coping tool they taught me during my stay, participated in every therapy group, stayed honest with the staff, asked lots of questions, and learned to cooperate with my alter-states, I should survive back in Atlanta. I appreciated his honesty and decided to follow his advice.

The staff encouraged me to allow hidden alter-states to emerge and explore the hospital grounds. Most of my alter-states had been flash-frozen in a Rip Van Winkle way by the traumas they'd compartmentalized. When they first emerged, they discovered that the world had changed a great deal. Some of them had difficulty with simple things like using feminine products, wearing a bra, and opening white plastic packets of jelly sealed with thin foil.

New alter-states emerged almost every day. I didn't like the idea of their taking control of my body. Because I resisted, they usually took control after I'd fallen asleep. Because I couldn't stay awake all the time, I decided to let them emerge during the day–I usually did this by taking a nap, knowing I'd be missing a chunk of time when I came back into consciousness. I wanted to learn how to negotiate with them so that they wouldn't hurt or embarrass me the next time they had control.

During this hospitalization, fourteen distinct alter-states emerged. Each had unique memories, emotions, and perspectives about life and past events. I'm still fascinated by how, when they first emerged, they were still "frozen" at certain psychosocial stages of development. That, more than anything, proved to me that they were real.[6]

Weekends in the hospital were hardest for me. Most of the other clients were visited by loved ones and went out on pass with them. Having no visitors and nothing to do, I used my solitary time to become more intimately acquainted with my emerging alter-states.

Whenever I could, I walked into the unit's combination conference/music room, lay on my back on the floor, propped up my calves on the seat of a wooden chair, and listened to a "love song" radio station on the stereo.

Although this technique may sound silly, it seemed to work wonders. Each time a love song played, I mentally dedicated it to my other alter-states, adapting the words of the songs and visualizing myself sending them all the way inside–into every crack, crevice, and recess in my soul. Over and over, I communicated "I love you, I care about you, I want you" to every part, no matter how hidden.

Internal cooperation increased dramatically after that. I soon felt safe enough to cede control of my body to the other parts, almost all of the time. Because my time at the hospital was limited, I wanted them to have as much time "out" as possible to work through their traumatic memories, before I was discharged. This was when the real repair work and connectedness began.

Neither Dr. T nor anyone else on the staff suggested my emerging memories. They still contained completely unfamiliar material that I frankly didn't know how to deal with. The memories seemed so utterly bizarre and impossible.

Warning – the remainder of this chapter may be triggering for trauma survivors.

Cindy – Age 5

Sometimes as I "came to," I found myself walking along a hallway in the hospital unit, wearing my nightgown and holding a stuffed white teddy bear that Bill had sent me. This child alter-state called it "Cindy Bear" and insisted that Bill buy it panties because she didn't like its privates being exposed. My Cindy alter-state had been flash-frozen at the emotional age of five.

She recollected that she had felt terrified of round holes drilled in the wooden floors of our living room in Reiffton. She constantly searched my shared hospital bedroom and the dayroom floors for similar holes (there were none). Dad had told her that snakes would crawl up through the holes and bite her for talking to outsiders. She still believed everything he had said. Because he'd been a terrifying, looming presence in my life, he was still alive and frightening to Cindy. She saw herself as a small girl with curly, soft, short blond hair.

Nikki – Age 13

Nikki was the second part to emerge. She insisted that she was asexual and proudly announced to Dr. T, "I don't do sex." Then she told him what she had experienced.

On my thirteenth birthday, Dad had told Nikki that she was now an adult, and that she was in charge of the occult rituals. Although Nikki had previously been naked during rituals or had worn a see-through "initiate's" robe, Dad now made her don a child-sized, hooded, black robe like the ones he and the other adults wore. Then Dad commanded her to stand in the middle of an encircled hexagram on the floor. He said, "Nikki, you're a big girl now."

He commanded her to kneel in the middle of the hexagram. She knew not to move out of the circle because if she did, demons would attack her. She tried to dissociate by staring at the white, flickering candles that Dad had set on each point of the large, painted star. She obeyed him by killing ("sacrificing") a boy in the middle of the star as Dad and the other black-robed cult members walked around the outside of the circle in single file, chanting louder and louder. Nikki had survived the horror by visualizing herself cutting a cow instead.

When she first emerged in Bethesda, she felt great emotional pain. She still believed that she'd been solely responsible for the child's murder. She smoked cigarettes and plotted to run away from the hospital on a pass so she could "get drunk and screwed." She was restricted to the hospital grounds after several other alter-states reported her intentions to the staff.

Dolly/Dreia – Age 7

Dolly, who also answered to the cult name Dreia, was developmentally stuck at the age of seven. Dad had taught occult beliefs to her that he'd said he had mostly gotten from the writings of the infamous British Satanist and intelligence operative, Aleister Crowley.

Sometimes, Dad's cult had met in a large old gray stone building in or near Reading.[7] A thick, gray, granite altar, upon which babies were murdered, was in one of the rooms. Dad told Dolly that the most powerful life-energy was stored in the blood of babies because they hadn't sinned yet. He said that a weaker but still effective life-force was stored in the semen of animals and humans. He seemed to believe that his body would never deteriorate or grow old if he continuously ingested both. He made Dolly do the same.

As Dolly tried to explain these beliefs to a nurse at Bethesda, she said that Dad acted as if he were a battery that needed to be recharged by blood and semen–either human or animal. In my sketchbook, she drew a succession of diagrams of hooded adult cult members positioned in and around the encircled hexagram. She drew pictures of the sequence of one ritual from beginning to end. Dolly was proud to have been an occult practitioner and wrote a page–with graphic illustrations–about the Magick that Dad had taught her during those rituals.

Eventually, Dolly felt the horror of what she'd been involved in as a child. Alone in the hospital bedroom, she frantically searched for something to kill herself with. She tried to remove metal screws from a metal window frame to cut her wrists, but they wouldn't come loose. She tried to escape by opening an emergency door–it didn't budge.

There wasn't any point of trying to walk out the building's main door–the staff constantly checked with me and other clients to make sure that unfamiliar alter-states wouldn't break and run if we strolled around the hospital grounds. Dolly was trapped with no way out, other than to talk and heal.

Andreia – Teenaged Part

Andreia was the same alter-state that had covertly met with the retired Army general, "Poppa," in 1985. Because Dad hadn't known about Andreia's existence, she'd successfully preserved a large portion of my morality. Like Dolly, Andreia was suicidal when she emerged at Bethesda. She felt great emotional pain and held memories of Dad's deadly rages. Even though he was dead, she still feared him. She drew a picture of him as a deadly black tornado.

Andreia recalled having watched Dad beat a male cult member to death in a ritual room in Pennsylvania. In the picture, the unconscious man hung by his wrists that were tied with a rope that was attached to a pulley Dad had previously fastened to the ceiling. (These were the same pulleys Dad used, when making me and other children hang from the ceiling in cages—sometimes for days.)

Andreia mourned the red-bearded man's death. Although she'd been one of his sexual "partners" during orgies, he'd been kind to her. And because of what she'd seen Dad do when he lost control of his rage, Andreia feared her own anger and worried that her rage might go out of control and hurt others.

Catalina – Teenaged Part

Catalina didn't like to be in charge of the body. She preferred to stay inside and mentally buffer younger alter-states from stress and traumas. She'd occasionally taken control of my body in the past, away from handlers' control, to protect me when she'd sensed danger. Her name came from a German rhyme that my paternal grandmother had recited to me as a child–something about going to the bathroom.

Visualizing herself as male, Catalina felt no compunction about assaulting anyone who might attempt to hurt "the body." Sometimes her rage translated into a need to self-mutilate. One Saturday, alone in the bedroom, she removed a metal number plate attached to my closet door and used its sharp corner to scratch an upside-down cross on my belly as she wept. A grey-haired nurse was making rounds and saw the metal object in Catalina's hand. After she obtained the object, she gently talked Catalina through a surfacing ritual memory that the etched cross represented.

In my sketch book, Catalina drew a picture of herself as a pressure cooker full of tiny cut-up bodies and blood, red steam swirling out through the hole in the lid at a dangerous rate. She seemed to keep a lid on the rage that younger parts couldn't control.

Little Kathy – Age 4

My most dangerous experience at Bethesda was when Little Kathy emerged. Her plan was to set my bed on fire while sitting on the middle of it. She believed she would feel no pain when she burned to death. After stealing a cigarette lighter from an unsuspecting female patient in the day room, Little Kathy shut the bedroom door.

Catalina was able to emerge part way, but because Kathy fought so hard for control, Catalina wasn't able to get off the bed. As Kathy tried to regain control of the body, Catalina screamed for help. When several staff members ran into the room, they found Catalina shaking and weeping. She handed the lighter to a stunned nurse and told her what Little Kathy had intended to do.

The nurse commended Catalina, and then—knowing that Little Kathy feared being punished—she gave a verbal message to Little Kathy through Catalina. The grey-haired woman said she believed that Little Kathy might be very angry at someone, and if she ever wanted to come out, the nurse would love to sit and talk with her.

Later that day, Little Kathy re-emerged and shared several memories with the nurse. She explained that she'd tried to kill herself out of rage at my parents and other cult members. The rage came from one experience in particular: at the age of four, she'd been forcibly penetrated from behind by a large yellow dog as Dad, Mom, and other Reading cult members had sat at a kitchenette table and watched. The adults had laughed as Little Kathy had screamed and shaken in terror, unable to break free from the dog's penis. (The child alter-states that had compartmentalized memories of having been penetrated by dog penises hadn't known that because of their unique anatomy, the poor dogs couldn't remove their penises until the swelling went back down.)

The nurse and other staff members taught Little Kathy and Catalina to vent their shared rage in constructive ways: through physical anger work, poetry, artwork, and sharing their experiences with the staff.

Renee – Age 8

During Friday night rituals, Dad had created Renee and then triggered her out by name. Each time, he had commanded her to sit naked on a wooden altar. The guilt of *not* being harmed, while being forced to watch Dad hurt other children and adults, had been unbearable. Renee still felt partly responsible for what was done to them because she was, after all, Dad's daughter. She had also been conscious during a part of the New York City ritual. She provided more details about that event. Softhearted, Renee wept every time she emerged. She was so full of grief that she had great difficulty speaking.

Kate – Adult Part

Like Catalina, Kate preferred to stay inside. Her "job" was to internally comfort younger alter-states that felt upset or frightened. Kate had compartmentalized the nurturing I'd received from my maternal grandmother. Not only did Kate grieve past traumas; she also mourned the current loss of Grandma M's mind and memory to the ravages of Alzheimer's disease.

Home Alters

After my discharge from my month-and-a-half stay at Bethesda, I fervently hoped I wouldn't find many more alter-states. Encountering and adjusting to emerging parts was hard. At home, I didn't have supportive people to help me cope and negotiate with them.

I still had great difficulty accepting the validity of many of these new memories, because I couldn't accept that Dad and his criminal associates had perpetrated such seemingly unbelievable crimes against me and other helpless victims. How had they gotten away with these crimes for so many years? Why hadn't the law caught up with them?

At home, I constantly went in and out of denial. I would try to make it all go away—at least for a couple of hours—but whenever I started to feel "normal" again, another set of flashbacks started.

Bill was unhappy with my new personality shifts and changes. When I had dissociated in the past, he'd blamed it on my moodiness and hormone fluctuations. What he encountered now was more drastic. These new alter-states had unique belief systems, personalities, and experiences. They even spoke and carried themselves differently. Those that emerged for the first time at home didn't know how to vacuum, use a dishwasher, cook, or drive. From one moment to the next, I went from loving and gentle, to rigid and distant, to hysterical or hopeless, to childlike.

Some parts were very young—they needed parents instead of a husband. Some of them didn't trust Bill at all, and refused to be in the same room with him. Quite a few of my newly emerging alter-states were either too young for a sexual relationship or were male—which meant no sex at all!

Many times, when we did try to have sex, I had bizarre flashbacks. Most were from decades of porn shoots that I'd been forced to participate in. One night, I saw a pig instead of Bill (I decided not to tell him about that one). When the flashbacks got ridiculous, as porn often is, I started poking fun at the grotesque memories instead of letting them re-traumatize me.

Another problem developed when child alter-states emerged that had been sexually tortured in the past. These parts still paired pain with pleasure. They'd been conditioned to want rough and painful interactions and had never experienced the gentle give-and-take of making love.

Although he was already monitoring me to make sure he didn't inadvertently have sex with a child part, now he also had to ensure that he didn't fall into the trap of being too rough at my request! This was making our relationship very complicated—he was more miserable every day.

Bill was especially alarmed by the parts that still compartmentalized occult beliefs. He was afraid that they, like Dolly, would reject Christianity and blaspheme God. Still overbearing about his fundamentalist Christian beliefs, Bill insisted that every part believe as he did. His open hostility and rejection of my cult-conditioned alter-states made some of the older ones want to go back to the Cobb County Aryan network, where they believed they'd be accepted just as they were. Fortunately, these urges were curbed by the intervention of wiser parts like Catalina, Andreia, and Kate.

From the time my alter-states first emerged in late spring, 1990 until the following March—a period of ten months—I documented a total of fifty-seven parts. Each held unique beliefs, experiences, and personality traits. And each part either journaled, drew pictures, and/or communicated to me in writing through more mature alter-states I was co-conscious with. Many of them were angry at me for not having accepted their existence before now. They were also angry that they'd suffered terribly, while "host alter-state me" had escaped the traumatic experiences.

Some of them were so angry, they tried to torture me in ways that didn't leave noticeable scars. One of their favorite methods was to relentlessly tweeze my hairs in hidden places until I bled or the wounds became infected. Another was to use several vibrators on my genitals at one time (torture/sex reenactment), leaving me in constant pain.[8]

These parts were careful not to leave lasting scars, because Dad had thoroughly conditioned them to believe if they were ever noticeably wounded, they'd be put to death.[9]

Even though Dad was dead, his threats still held great power over my mind and life. Because of his past influence, I remained terrified of surgery. I was certain that if I ever went under the knife, I'd be murdered.

Some of the alter-states that had emerged in Bethesda continued to communicate with me at home. I was surprised to learn that some of them had also found a way to repress traumatic memories. Their own repressed memories were triggered by the most innocuous events. One saw a flickering candle on television and immediately re-experienced another horrifying ritual!

Dolly/Dreia remembered where part of her name came from. She wrote that as a child, some of the occultists had repeatedly told her that ritually murdered babies were "just dollies." Later, while watching a video about the Holocaust, I was stunned to learn that some Nazi war criminals had called their murdered victims, *"figuren"* (dolls, in German).[10]

Little Kathy re-emerged and told me that as a very small child, she'd been terrified of Dad's staring eyes, and of his hands as they'd poked through the wooden bars of the crib. She described what I'd dreamed all my life: Dad often threw me up into the air, then lowered his hands just above the floor to convince me that my body was about to hit it full-force. That method bonded me closer to him. Although he was the one who initially endangered me, in the end he was also the one who rescued me from mortal danger–again and again.

Catalina shared that she had been my mental protector during "brain-washing sessions" conducted by Dad in experimental settings. She wrote that he'd closely watch her, "like playing chess. He would do something over and over and over again (mental or physical torture) until I learned not to show any reaction whatsoever, not even a muscle twitch. Then he would use another technique." She also recalled having been forced to sit in a chair with a floor-length metal lamp shining strongly in her face. "Could see nothing else. The room was black. I remember the light flashing and accessing the very insides of me."

Renee wrote that she'd watched Dad commit several daytime murders of adult cult members in Pennsylvania. They were so gory and inhumane that Renee was convinced nobody could save her from Dad. He was all-powerful, not just at home, but even within the cult! Because he first accused each victim of having told outsiders about cult activities, Renee also believed she must never talk about what she'd witnessed.

Glenda, a teenaged part, wrote that she'd compartmentalized the hopeless, depressed part of Renee. Glenda communicated that she didn't want to come out of the dark—she wanted to stay there forever.

Younger Kathleen, age eight, wrote about a dungeon in a stone-walled mansion that had been built on the side of Schuylkill mountain. She described a sloped hallway beyond a hidden entryway in the wall of an elegant old library with wooden, red leather-upholstered chairs. She recalled the underground circular dungeon. Lit candles had been placed in recessed hollows in the rough-hewn stone wall.

She wrote that the house was above an old cemetery, at a distance from the other houses on the road. I'd had recurring nightmares about that mansion, but when Younger Kathleen wrote about her vivid memories, the full horror of it came to life.

Heather, a young adult alter-state, wrote that she'd helped Dad "and a retired pediatrician and several others" to prepare several young boys to be filmed in child porn at a high school in north Atlanta, at night. As usual, Dad had a key to the building. She said Dad would summon her there each time, over the phone. She wrote that on another occasion, he placed a "huge wet Q-tip next to my nose and left me paralyzed on the floor." She watched helplessly, unable to intervene, as he raped a beloved child on the floor next to her. Later he told her, smiling, that the child would believe she hadn't cared that the child had been raped. He was right.

Ashley, age eight, had compartmentalized an unusual quantity of cult memories. Dad had given her that name after triggering her out and forcing her to watch him burn some of the cult victims' bodies into ashes.[11]

She held the memories of ritual events that had especially marked my soul. She wrote about a "cave with a stone tunnel leading to it in Pennsylvania." In it, Dad had forced Ashley to get down on her hands and knees, totally naked, setting a dog's water dish in front of her. Dad had placed a dog collar around her neck, with a chain attached to it that went back into the cave. Ashley was allowed to look out the mouth of the cave, but couldn't leave—the chain kept pulling her back. Dad had told her that if she tried to leave, she would choke. Sure enough, when she fought the chain, she choked as it cut into her neck. Dad said the chain would always "tie her to the cult."

In that same cave, Dad had forced Ashley to lie on her back on a low, stone altar. She must have been drugged, because she felt no desire to get up when she came into consciousness in that position. Her abdomen was covered with blood. Dad told her that he'd performed surgery on her stomach while she was asleep. He told her that a koala bear with very sharp claws and a snow owl with a sharp beak and talons were now inside it.

He said if the animals ever sensed that Ashley was thinking about telling cult secrets to anyone, the animals would claw at her insides and make her bleed to death.[12] Dad convinced Ashley that even if someone believed her, they wouldn't be able to save her in time. Years later, during phone calls, he often said the words "wet paint"—symbolizing human blood—to reinforce Ashley's secrecy.

On another occasion, Dad had told Ashley that a big, green, ugly, squat "frog demon" lived inside her, and that the demon held her rage. Then he had conditioned her to "let the demon out" by giving her a baby doll and telling her to stab it with a knife. In an uncontrollable rage, Ashley had stabbed it over and over. Although the killing wasn't real, the induced guilt was; she believed there was no hope for her, and was convinced that she was irretrievably guilty.

Marisha, an adolescent alter-state, had also been forced to lie naked on a stone altar. Dad and other cult members had ritualistically bound her to it with ropes that he claimed were "magick" because they were made from dried human intestines of other victims. He told Marisha that, because the bonds had magical powers, she could never be released. When she first emerged at home, because she still felt tied to the altar, I had difficulty moving my hands and arms.

Cindy wrote about a "television or radio station" in downtown Reading where Dad, Mom and other cult members had gathered on Sunday afternoons for more trauma-based mind control sessions. She wrote that, on one occasion, she had been bound and placed on the floor while Dad had dumped a wicker basket of wriggling snakes onto her torso. Cindy had thought she was going to be bitten and die from the poison.

Tiger was an animal alter-state that I'd developed on my own. He helped me to survive my fear of being bitten by snakes. I must have seen on television that a tiger could kill a snake. Tiger embodied most of my dignity and self-esteem, as well as great emotional pain. He was one of the few alter-states that had felt powerful in Dad's presence, although Tiger hadn't let Dad know of his existence. He had a flashback of Dad holding out a very large snake, with the markings of a copperhead, issuing me a direct order to hold it. Tiger had emerged, looking Dad in the eye, and had staunchly refused to take the snake.

In some of the rituals near Reading, Dad had ordered me to kill babies on a granite or marble stone altar, using an extremely sharp knife to cut their carotid arteries. He'd then handed me an ornate silver chalice, into which I was to drain their precious blood. Mixing their fresh blood with opium powder and red wine, he'd ordered me and every other cult member drink from the chalice.

Because I couldn't stand what he was forcing me to do, I created an alter-state named **Blood** that experienced and compartmentalized those traumas. Blood's heart broke every time she watched a baby's eyes go black, knowing that she was the last human the baby would see as it died. Blood's overwhelming sense of guilt made her dangerously suicidal when she emerged at home. Full of pain and grief from having watched so many precious infants die, she remained suicidal. Blood was never allowed full control of the body outside of therapy, and was in too much pain to try to fight for it. Hers was a living death.

Because adults had read nursery rhymes to me as a child, I developed two alter-states based on the rhyme about the butcher, the baker, and the candlestick maker. I created those parts after Blood. No one part of me could cope with the full horror of killing babies, seeing their blood, and being forced to dismember their sweet, soulless bodies.

Butcher emerged after Blood. Using Dad's large knife, Butcher learned to dismember the dead babies' bodies, and eventually was able to cut between their joints with ease.[13]

Blood and Butcher were forced to witness and perform what no human, let alone a child, should. (When I became an adult, these parts were occasionally triggered out by professional handlers, to disfigure or dismember a "target's" body. These alter-states again protected me from going insane from the horror.)[14]

After Butcher finished his job, **Candlestick Maker** emerged and watched as Dad and other adults rendered body parts that they'd thrown into boiling water in a large black cauldron that hung inside a round-topped, stone fireplace. After the liquid cooled, Dad removed the top layer of fat and mixed it with melted wax to create a new batch of white ritual candles. Candlestick Maker believed if he gave Dad too much trouble, he might be the next dead candle donor. He also watched as the victims' bones were given to cult members' dogs to chew on.

Not all alter-states developed during rituals. **Melissa** began in a large stone public building in downtown Reading. The building had at least one large wooden stage with big, heavy, dark colored drapes. I was taken there in the daytime, on Saturdays. I was eight years old.

Each time, Dad instructed several male Caucasians to stand inside the exits. Then he ordered a male street dweller, who he called a "bum," to stand on wooden stairs that led down from the stage. I stood above the "bum" on the stage with Dad and other men from the cult as they silently donned their black, hooded robes, which triggered tremendous rage inside me–not only because of what they'd done to me in rituals, but also because of what I'd seen them do to other children.

Triggered by the robes, I developed a new part, Melissa, that was able to remember both the rituals and portions of my experiences in this big building.[15]

Knowing that Melissa couldn't express her rage directly at the black-robed men, Dad pointed at the "bum" and said, "Kill the bad man." After he told the man to "start running," Dad then handed Melissa either a large knife or a loaded handgun. He never ordered Melissa to go after more than one "bad man" per training session.

Because I loved reading Sunday morning comic strips, I created a new alter-state that split off from Melissa. **Dick Tracy** visualized himself wearing a black fedora and overcoat as he chased after each man, fully intending to end the bad man's life. Each time he cornered the man, he brutally killed him. (I think this happened because: the rage made me unusually strong; the street people that Dad chose were probably weakened by malnutrition and debilitating alcoholism; and the shock of being attacked by an eight-year-old girl may have kept them from fighting back until it was too late. Knowing Dad's bag of tricks, he may also have drugged them.) My Dick Tracey alter-state felt completely justified because Dad had said they were bad men. This alter-state didn't understand that he probably, by proxy, was expressing Dad's hidden rage towards his own alcoholic father.

After Dick Tracey finished each "assignment," he submerged into my subconscious. After that, Dad–who always took off his black robe before searching for me–found me on my knees, bent over the dead man's bloody body, not wanting to believe I'd just killed the poor soul.

Ever alert for the tiniest changes in my body, voice, and behaviors, Dad recognized that I'd created a third new alter-state, a **young child part** that grieved each victim's death. He pointed to the spreading red blotches on the victim's clothing and said, "Look at the pretty red flower." The hypnotic suggestion worked because seeing a pretty flower was preferable to seeing human blood.

(Several professional handlers used this same technique when I was an adult. They would tell me to "look at the pretty red flower" after a black op alter-state had obeyed instructions to shoot a man. I suspect if they hadn't said it, I might have turned the gun on myself.)

Teenaged **Gloria** held my grief over a fetus that Dad had forced me to abort and then ingest during a ritual, when I was a teenager. She held other memories, too. She was the female I had seen in the bathroom mirror in recurring childhood nightmares. During each of those dreams, I was unable to cover my ears or turn away as she screamed. I've never forgotten waking up from these nightmares, drenched with sweat, praying that I wouldn't see the screaming lady again in my sleep.

When Gloria drew pictures of her experiences in my sketch pad, I finally learned why she had screamed in the nightmares. Dad had bound her to a wooden cross and had vaginally tortured her with a cattle prod. Gloria seemed to compartmentalize my blackest rage and my strongest memories of physical pain.

A child part that Dad had named **Margaret** was my only fully analgesic alter-state. Because she'd been created through torture paired with hypnosis, she was able to block out all physical pain. Margaret had stopped developing, mentally and emotionally, at the age of nine.

One day at home, Margaret proved to me that she could feel no pain if injured. She took control of the body while I watched (at those times, I visualized my body as a vehicle; the dominant alter-state "drove" while I observed from the "back seat"). She pushed a fairly large sewing needle through the web of skin between my left thumb and index finger. As long as she had control of the body and I just watched, I felt no pain at all; neither did she. When she receded and I regained full control of the body, however, I felt the pain. I was in awe.

Margaret drew several pictures of childhood torture sessions. She wrote about a gray-haired man she'd known as a "pain giver." He had spoken kindly to her while he'd done the most awful things. His gentle voice and demeanor had been crucial in helping Margaret to dissociate completely from the pain he'd inflicted. By focusing on his voice, she totally blocked out what he did to the body.

In one picture, Margaret drew a picture of him holding the flame of a lit candle under my left arm's soft flesh. She wrote, "Old Man Gray har [sic] likes me." The cognitive dissonance created by what he was doing, as opposed to his presenting himself as a caring person, was mind-splitting. Suppressing her fear and horror, Margaret emotionally attached to the torturer. He was much kinder in his face and voice than Dad had ever been.

During another "test," Margaret noted that Dad seemed fascinated as he stood silently, watching. First, the older man threw a live cat on a bed of nails that were affixed to a large wooden board that had been set on the floor, the points of the long nails sticking straight up. The cat screeched loudly as it scrambled off, bleeding. Then the older man told Margaret to lie on her back. When she obeyed, she felt no pain. As he examined her back afterwards, he said, "Very impressive," and commented on the absence of blood. Dad seemed pleased, which added to Margaret's sense of pride.

The older sadist's final act was to dislocate all the fingers on one of my hands. Again, Margaret felt nothing. The torturer popped each digit back into place, telling Margaret that she had "passed the test." Again she felt proud.

The ability to block out pain when injured, and to trance so that I didn't bleed, was crucial when I was sent into dangerous situations as an adult. I was made to believe that if I was disabled by any injury, my handlers would kill me. Since I wanted to stay alive, I tranced to stop any bleeding. I didn't want them to notice an injury and kill me![16]

A sweet-tempered teenaged part that Dad had perversely named **Evil** had been forced to participate in the most depraved rituals. Dad had convinced her that she belonged in a cage because she was too evil to ever come out. Evil had great difficulty relating to other humans. I saved both of us from her hopelessness by reversing her name and giving her a new purpose: "Live."

Tonya had compartmentalized most of Mom's sexual abuse at home and at rituals. She also remembered that she'd been orally raped, twice, by my only close childhood friend's oldest sister in their home. Although Tonya had felt guilty because of the physical pleasure, she'd refused to let the older girl do it a third time. Forlorn Tonya journaled that she'd "just wanted to be left alone to play" with my Ken and Barbie dolls.

Marla, an adult alter-state, wrote that when she was young, she'd been sent to "special classes" to learn how to dismember bodies. She wrote about a black liquid that had been poured into the stomach cavities by an adult male trainer. She'd been given black gloves with a red border around the wrists, and had used a special set of surgical tools kept in a black velvet-lined case. She wrote that she'd only emerged to dismember bodies after the victims were dead. She'd used "precise, scientific thinking and over-awareness of colors and artistic patterns of the bodies as coping mechanisms." She had no noticeable emotions.

Roddy, a male adult alter-state, also emerged with no emotions. Like Marla, he was very logical and scientific-minded. (I suspect these parts internalized some of Dad's personality traits.)

In my journal, Roddy wrote that Dad had ordered him to help with the disposal of the remains of murdered infants in Atlanta. He wrote that some of their body parts had been "pickled" in formaldehyde in glass jars, to be sold on the local black market to "med students from Emory University." He wrote that he and Dad had put other remains in garbage bags, then in large, white plastic paint buckets filled with moth balls, before dropping them off on the way home in dumpsters behind commercial buildings. They used a different dumpster for each drop-off. Dad made Roddy wear surgical gloves to avoid leaving any fingerprints.

After Roddy shared these ghoulish memories with me, the guilt hit hard. He was in such anguish, he might have suicided, had not other adult alter-states prevented him from taking full control of the body.

I was happier to discover a core alter-state named **Kathleen Ann**. She wanted to talk about how Dad had tried, at home, to touch her and do things to her that she knew weren't right. She had hidden from him as much as she could, while playing with her dolls.

She remembered when two strange boys had lived with us in our rental home in Laureldale, although she couldn't remember how long they were there. She told my therapist that the older boy had blond hair and was "old enough" to have a box that contained "pencils and pins." She liked that boy, but noticed he was reluctant to talk about his parents. She wrote that she didn't know why the boys had stayed with us, and added that no one talked about them after they left.

She shared another memory, again in therapy. One day, in the kitchen in Laureldale, she'd tried to reach for a cup perched atop a rack of dishes on the kitchen counter. She was terrified when the rack unexpectedly teeter-tottered on the edge of the countertop. She tried to hold it up with her little arms, but it was too heavy. As her shaking arms gave way, the dishes crashed to the floor. Mom entered the kitchen, saw the mess, and grabbed a broom to sweep it up. Surprised that Mom didn't hit her with it, a wave of relief washed over the small child. That wasn't the end, though:

> *Then Dad came in there and told me to go to my room. I had my very own bedroom. It was dark. I sat on the bed and waited. When I heard his big feet coming up the steps I peed on the bed. When he walked in the room and saw the dark wet on my bed, he got really angry and grabbed my arm and threw me against the far wall across the room. Then he grabbed all the sheets and pulled them off the bed. He told me to go in the closet. I was very upset because my panties were wet and cold. I sat in the closet and he shut the door. Then I heard Mom come into the room. She said something and I heard a slap. It sounded like she slapped him. I got real scared for her. I opened the door a peek to see if there was anything maybe I could do to help her fight him. I saw him throw her down on the floor. Her head hit it real hard. Then I saw him [rape] her. She got real soft after he did that and she didn't fight him anymore. He told her to make the bed and she did. They both forgot about me. I sat probably a couple of hours until suppertime. I made TV shows on the door. Lots of Captain Kangaroo. Finally mommy came to the closet and opened the door and asked what I was doing in there, silly, and why were my pants wet. She took me into the bathroom and washed me and changed my clothes like I was wrong and nothing had ever happened.*

Kathleen Ann communicated in a separate drawing that she had gone completely "under" at the age of four. A new host alter-state named **Kathleen** had split off from her that day, as Kathleen Ann had walked up a large dirt hill to a daytime pagan family ritual where she knew–from past experience–"bad things" were going to happen.[17] That particular day, she'd decided that she just couldn't take any more. For the next thirty-two years, she'd remained hidden inside, encased and protected by other alter-states.

A child part called **Baby** was one of a cluster of "home" alter-states that I seemed to create on my own. Baby had stopped developing, mentally and emotionally, at the age of ten. She explained that Dad had often called her a "cry-baby." She was terribly afraid of sudden noises and movements, and anything else that seemed inexplicable. She was petrified with fear when she turned a light switch to the "on" position at night, but the light didn't come on. She was the alter-state that had sleepwalked at night. She'd enjoyed spending time with my cat, Snoopy, and our family dog, Lassie, although she'd hated it when the pets fought.

Fatty, an adolescent part, had internalized that name because Dad had often called me "Fatty." This part almost always hid in our house in Reiffton with a good book and a paper napkin full of food. Mom had abused her, verbally and physically, when Dad was away at work. She wrote: "Mom would drink and get into a rage. I tried to win her approval and affection by cleaning the house and ironing. It never worked. I was afraid of her when she pulled out her bottle from one of the top kitchen cabinets. I remember having to iron all of the family's bed sheets." This is the only alter-state, to-date, that reported seeing Mom secretively drink liquor at home while Dad was away. She also reported that Mom often forced me to put my hand on the ironing board, and then Mom touched it with the scalding hot iron, telling Dad later (if he asked) that I'd done it to myself.[18]

Jennifer's mental and emotional development had been arrested at age 14. She'd compartmentalized a memory of having been brutally sodomized by Dad after we'd moved to Maryland. Showing rare spirit, she'd physically fought against him. She had desperately wanted to live a normal life and enjoy normal relationships with kids her own age.

Marcey, a child alter-state, usually emerged when I was sick and needed to rest. She visualized herself wearing a white nurse's uniform and cap. She tried to protect me by taking the brunt of the abuse whenever people took advantage of my illnesses and temporary lack of strength. When she emerged at home this time, I had the flu. She mentally "stood guard" and wouldn't allow Bill to talk to me until after I'd slept soundly.

Andreia remembered another terrible childhood memory and drew four sequential pictures of it. I was about six years old. It was a warm day; the grass was green and Andreia was clad in blue shorts and a red, short-sleeved T-shirt. At first, she stood near Dad and several other male cult members in a cemetery. She clearly felt helpless because in the first picture, in which she stood next to a deep dirt hole holding an unearthed coffin, she didn't draw her legs or feet. She wrote, *"They made me stand beside the coffin they put the dirt on the black cloth."*

In the second picture, she was lying on her back inside the open coffin, down in the hole. She drew her legs, but her hands and feet were still missing–signifying that she'd been unable to run or fight against the men.

She wrote, *"They take the lady [fresh corpse] out and make me lay in the coffin and shut it. I pretend I am dead then they open it and put her back in on top of me. I will not draw that she has no head. This is just a bad dream. I will wake up soon. She has juices come out of her neck, they get on my face and hair and top. Bad Bad Bad. I am dead. No more bad things."*

The memory of the "juices" was, by far, the most gruesome part of the entire memory. It was beyond any horror I'd previously relived. Because I couldn't stand the physical sensations and visual flashbacks, I called Bethesda and asked one of the nurses for help. She talked to Andreia and asked her to draw a closed coffin. On that page, Andreia wrote: *"The lady told me to close my memory until I can see the doctor. Coffin U R Locked until I say so!"*

Exactly one week after the memory first emerged, Andreia met with the therapist in his office. Having a supportive listener helped Andreia, tears and snot flowing, to survive the memory of the decapitated woman lying atop her, crushing her to where she could barely breathe.

At home that night, she drew a picture of the open coffin, with Andreia lying beneath the decapitated body that still wore a dress. Because young child Andreia was now blending and sharing information with me, and me with her, she now used grown-up words to explain the logic that had kept her sane: *"Her body was there but her soul was gone. My body was there and my soul was still there too. She was dead but I was alive. Not the same! Who was she? Was she somebody important to them? What was the purpose in them doing this?"*

Underneath the picture, she wrote: *"I got gooey stuff–slimy–on my face and hair and shirt. They took me to [a female cult member's] house. She made me take a shower and she washed my clothes so no one would ever know."*[19]

In this journal entry, Andreia seemed to be describing the trauma that had initially created her. Because her personality was like mine, and because she didn't identify herself by a new name during that horror, Dad hadn't realized that she wasn't the host alter-state. I believe this is why Andreia was able to stay hidden from Dad for decades, conserving my sense of innate goodness and my ability to love.

I was most surprised by the emergence of an alter-state named **Lisa**. Mentally and emotionally, she was more than thirty years old. She explained that she'd usually been conscious and in control at home as an adult, rarely allowing me to emerge away from work. She'd protected me from what she still perceived as Albert's "insanity." She'd also taken on the responsibility of enduring abusive and demeaning sex with him that no part of me had enjoyed.

Since 1981, many more alter-states and personality fragments–hundreds upon hundreds–shared their unique experiences with me. For a while, I tried to document each one, but after several years, I grew overwhelmed. There were so many, I didn't think I could ever experience integration! I realized if I was going to stay positive about my recovery, I needed to stop counting them.

Internal Cooperation

Although my personality and soul had been brutally splintered into many "pieces," I'd nevertheless started out as one person with one body and one mind like everyone else. Now, I prefer to visualize each alter-state as having been a glob of experience that was stored in one or more areas of my brain. I was not those alter-states before I became co-conscious with them; nor were they me. I did not yet have access to these parts of my brain.

That's why, when they did certain activities, I did not consciously participate; nor did the majority of them experience my life at home, at church, and at work. "My" experiences as the primary host alter-state had been stored in areas of my brain that were not yet accessible to them. And those alter-states had been stored in parts of my brain that were not yet accessible to me.

As pieces and fragments of my shattered personality emerged and communicated to me through diaries, drawings and more, new neuron and chemical paths bridged the gaps between where they were stored in my brain, and where "I" was stored. Many times, when I connected with an emerging part for the first time, I had a strong headache behind my forehead. Sometimes it went all through my head and down into the back of my neck.

Although some scientists claim that we are unable to feel our brains, I disagree. When I participated in therapeutic EEG biofeedback sessions, I was able to feel changes in pressure in different sections of my brain as I shifted from my Beta brainwaves to Alpha, and so on. That experience explained why, when some alter-states emerged, they described themselves as being up or to the right or left, or down a little. I believe those alter-states were describing where, in my brain, they could be found.

As I became more familiar with my emerging alter-states, and they with me, we became co-conscious and shared our information and knowledge with each other. Over time, I realized I was only one part of the original whole–a large piece, but just a part, nonetheless. I didn't have sufficient strength to take on all their traumas, but I could lend my knowledge and blend with them so that, as a more cohesive whole, we'd amass enough strength and understanding to successfully cope with future memories and attached emotions.

Notes

1. Although the codependency group helped me to be more assertive and to set and maintain stronger and healthier boundaries with others, I eventually terminated my membership in it and several other support groups. Even in groups designed for survivors of child abuse, I felt lonely and disconnected because my memories were too horrific to share.

2. Later, I experienced audio flashbacks. Like visual flashbacks, they were always unexpected. As an example, I might be working outside in the garden and suddenly hear one or two words. It wasn't as if they'd necessarily been addressed to me in the past; it was more like I had been in the same room when I'd heard that person speak.

3. I wasn't yet aware that not knowing the time frame or physical location of a remembered event is common among dissociated trauma survivors. At the time, I felt pressured to give a date for the event, even though I wasn't certain of that date. Now, I feel comfortable in stating that it must have occurred in either 1963 or 1964, because that's when the World's Fair was in New York City.

4. Being suicidal and committing suicide are two different things for me, although they can get way too close together when the emotional pain is at its worst. Because I've seen people killed via faked suicides, suicide is not an option for me. If a memory is absolutely unbearable and I have no safe way to get through it

at home, I will call my psychiatrist and ask to check into a hospital so that I can survive it.

5. At that time, many therapists believed that a person was capable of having more than one full personality (hence, multiple personalities). In 1994, the APA published a more accurate diagnosis, Dissociative Identity Disorder (DID) in its *Diagnostic and Statistical Manual of Mental Disorders, Fourth Edition (DSMIV)*. The symptoms of DID are:

   • The presence of two or more distinct identities or personality states;
   • At least two . . . recurrently take control of the person's behavior;
   • Inability to recall important personal information that is too extensive to be explained by ordinary forgetfulness;
   • The disturbance is not due to the direct physiological effect of a substance . . . or a general medical condition. ("Psych Central 1")

6. One might wonder if I'd inadvertently internalized other patients' traumatic memories. In reality, most hospitalized trauma survivors are so discomfited by their memories, they prefer not to discuss them-not even in group therapy. In group therapy sessions, I spent most of my time learning how to cope with my alter-states and unfamiliar emotions. Reliving horrific memories in individual therapy was exhausting and very painful. For that reason, when we socialized, we talked about light subjects and were careful not to trigger each other's memories. I have found this to be equally true at other specialized hospital units for trauma survivors.

7. I've been amazed by the number of recovering ritual abuse and mind-control survivors who have contacted me, who had either grown up in that part of Pennsylvania or had moved there as active victims when they became adults.

8. They finally stopped when a therapist explained to them that if they continued to do this, they might damage the nerves in my genitals, and then *no one* would be able to enjoy sex anymore!

9. This was a problem for me when my torture and op memories emerged, because I had no noticeable marks or scars to verify those memories. I envied survivors who had proofs on their bodies. I believe that Dad preferred using electricity, drowning, sensory deprivation, mental torture, and similar methods to split my mind because they left little to no evidence. Not having scars doesn't mean that one wasn't tortured. Graessner, et al wrote:

   Altogether, there are several forms of torture that are either hard to prove or can only be established based on a patient's complete presentation. One should not, however, make the error of dismissing a particular form of torture and its consequences simply because one has not heard of it before or has run into extreme difficulty explaining it. Torturers vary their methods, and our proofs inevitably lag behind. This is especially true for those states that are increasingly replacing physical torture with refined forms of psychological torture. (pp. 195-196)

10. After I'd begun to remember Dad's Nazi affiliations, I was deeply shaken when, on the Internet, I found a set of notes about the Holocaust film, *Shoah*. Claude Lanzmann wrote: "Itzhak Dugin-another survivor of Vilna-told of being forced to dig up the buried bodies with just his hands in order to burn them. When the last mass grave was opened he recognized his whole family. Was forced to refer to the corpses as 'puppets' or 'dolls' (*Figuren*) or 'rags' (*Schmattes*)." (Shoah 1)

11. Dad sometimes jokingly called the resulting sound, "snap, crackle and pop." He would reinforce the horror the next morning at our breakfast table by pouring milk on our bowls of Rice Krispies cereal, grinning as he watched me listen to the too-familiar sounds, so tranced, I couldn't lift my spoon from the table.

12. Even when I was an adult, Dad sent me items, such as stuffed animals, that represented snow owls and koala bears.

13. Every week, for years, I had a powerful compulsion–to buy a whole chicken at the grocery store and cut it into pieces. I couldn't buy already-cut chicken; I had to cut it apart myself. When I realized it was a ritual reenactment, I didn't have the compulsion anymore.

14. When the ritual memories emerged, my biggest question was, how could my father and his cult associates have done such gory and horrifying things to other humans without having nightmares and flashbacks? Why was I so traumatized that I tranced and split off the memories, but they didn't? Anna C. Salter, Ph.D. explained why:

> The rest of us blink when we're startled in the middle of viewing something unpleasant. Why is that? Who knows? But maybe the aversiveness of something unpleasant puts our nervous system on red alert. Being tense already, it reacts more when startled. Nothing like that happens to psychopaths. Landscapes. Burn victims. There's not much difference from their point of view. (pg. 9)

15. In April, 1998 a contact near Reading, PA did some investigatory work for me. She wrote:

> I wanted to see if the old abandoned movie theatre in Reading on Sixth St. was still standing so I took a drive over there and found that it is. It's a very large building and it sits right up close against the sidewalk. Sixth St. is right in the middle of town.

I believe this may have been the building where I was forced to endure my kill training as a child. Unfortunately, because I have remembered many traumas that

I suffered at the hands of criminals living in or near Reading, I choose not to return to that area.

16. When I first became co-conscious with Margaret, I had great difficulty accepting her memories. How was it possible that she had felt no pain, when tortured? And how could she have lain on a bed of sharp nails and not bled, although the cat did?

Carla Emery explained this phenomenon:

> Pain can be blocked by suggestion. Hypnosis enables people to endure more pain than otherwise would be possible. The deeper the trance, the more pain can be endured. Because hypnotic anesthesia is of psychological origin, numbing patterns induced by suggestion are what the subject thinks they should be, rather than correct nerve anatomy . . . Persons I have known, whose dental work was done under hypnosis, were pleased with how well suggestion overcame fear, pain, and bleeding. (pp. 217-218)

17. Although Dad chose to practice a combined form of Nazi Teutonic Paganism (as will be discussed in a later chapter) mixed with British and American Satanism and Luciferian practices, several of his older relatives, who publicly attended Christian churches, adhered to their family-generational Druid religion. For this reason, I-as the oldest child on both sides of my family-was expected not only to learn and participate in Dad's form of occultism; I was also expected to learn and perpetuate the family's old-world Pagan practices. This terrible burden increased my dissociation.

18. Fatty and other parts shared that, like with Dad, being alone in the house with Mom usually meant being sexually assaulted, tortured, or both. Another of Mom's favorite ways of torturing me was to wound me with straight pins and needles from her sewing kits because they left tiny, hard-to-notice marks. For this reason, I still have great difficulty motivating myself to mend our clothes.

19. When I remembered the coffin trauma, I hadn't yet read any occult literature. (I avoided such materials, so that my ritual memories would be untainted.) Because this was straight memory, I really thought Dad had ritually traumatized me out of his insanity. Then I received information from a researcher who indicated that the "occult tradition of initiation involving the ritual passage through death had occurred as far back as the Egyptian *Book of the Dead.*" The researcher wrote:

> The German Brotherhood of Death Society that Hitler belonged to was the Thule Society. Their coffin rituals are very similar to those Ron Rosenbaum describes in his article, "The Last Secrets of Skull and Bones." In the initiation ceremonies of this highly secretive occult organization that boasts several United States Presidents, including

George Bush Sr., new members "lay [sic] naked in coffins and tell their deepest and darkest sexual secrets as part of their initiation." (pg. 85) Aleister Crowley, in *The Ritual of Passing Through the Tuat*, described the initiation ceremony into the Order of Thelema: "The candidate then undresses; and is clad in the shroud of a corpse. His feet and hands are wrapped closely, his mouth is stopped, and his eyes are blindfolded. He is then placed in the coffin. The officer approaches, now that the coffin has been carried into the darkened temple. He stops with a napkin dipped in the consecrated water the nostrils of the candidate, much distressing him." Anton LaVey wrote in *The Satanic Rituals: Companion To The Satanic Bible:* "The ceremony of rebirth takes place in a large coffin. This is similar to the coffin symbolism that . . . is found in most lodge rituals." (pg. 57)

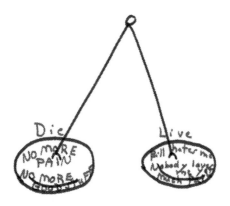

I dont know which to choose to live
or die every body I loved is gone I
dont know Kathleens husband and
daughter I dont know if they will
accept me I am scared I dont want
to feel old pain /new pain but part
of me wants to live who is helping me?

ANDREIA – CONTEMPLATING SUICIDE, 6/27/90

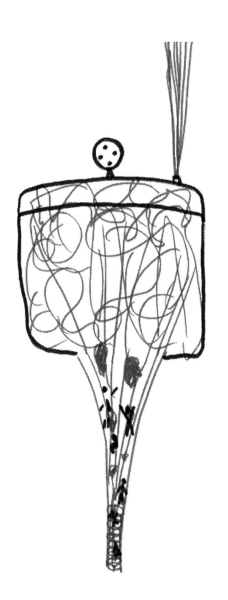

Catalina's
rage from
little Kathy

6/28/90

CATALINA–CHANNELING LITTLE KATHY'S RAGE, 6/28/90

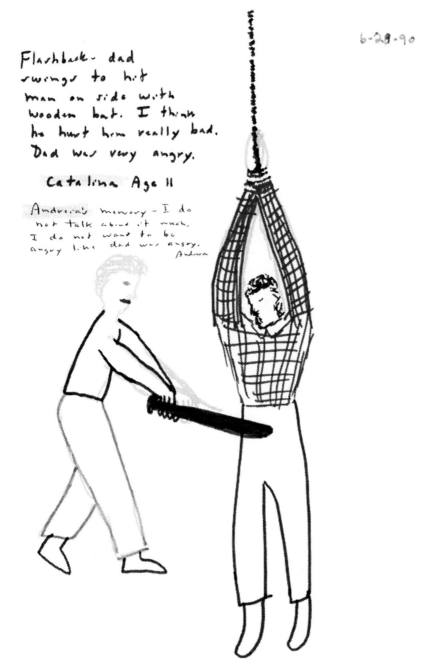

CATALINA AND ANDREIA – DAD BEAT MAN TO DEATH, 6/28/90

Reality

Andreia 7/2/90

ANDREIA – MY RAINBOW PROGRAMMING, 7/2/90

"Dolly" - Purpose - <u>Magick</u> 7/2

Take what is bad and make it good
Take what is good and make it bad

Blood into water   (Water of life, living water)

Water into blood
Life into death   (Babies are best, uncontaminated)

Death into life   (Newness of life)

Strong into Weak   (Renewed strength)

Weak into Strong   (sacrifice to our lord)

DOLLY/DREIA – RITUALISTIC "ENERGY TRANSFERS", 7/2/90.

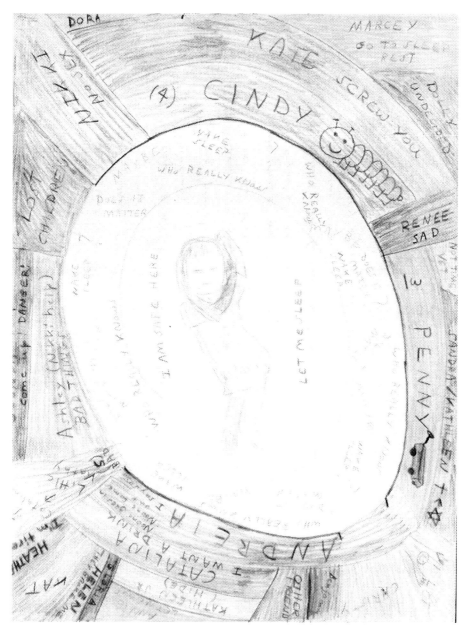

**GROUP OF CHILD ALTER-STATES AS DIAGRAMMED
BY A CHILD PART, SUMMER 1990**

RENEE

**RENEE – HER PART OF THE MEMORY OF DAD RITUALLY
MURDERING A FEMALE CULT MEMBER, 7/90 (SEE 4/31/90)**

They made me stand beside the coffin they put the dust on the black cloth

Her body was glass but her eyes were gone. My body was glass and my soul was void from you. She was dead but I was alive. Not the smell!! She was old, was she somebody important to them? What was the purpose in them doing this?

I got sang stuffers things in my face & wore a shroud. They dressed me at ... head. It made me take a shower and then washed my sisters to ... would ... them.

Andreia 7/11

ANDREIA – COFFIN MEMORY, 7/11-7/18/90

GLORIA – RECURRING CHILDHOOD NIGHTMARE, 8/17/90

GLORIA – TORTURED BY DAD WITH CATTLE PROD, 8/17/90

Margaret Age 9 8.23.90 "Bed of Nails"

Cat bleed on it and meow loud cry
I lay on it no blood bobey holes in my
back and <u>butt</u> - look like I sat on a
catus. "Very impaessive", men said.

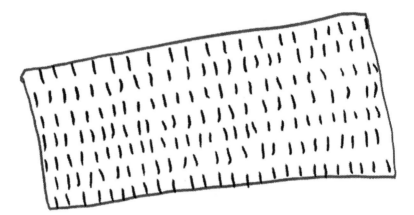

MARGARET – BED OF NAILS, 8/23/9

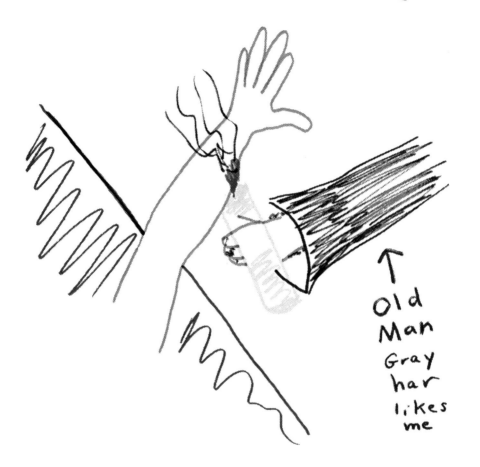

MARGARET – TORTURED BY FIRE, 8/23/90

KATHY – AGE 4, SPLIT OFF NEW PART (KATHLEEN), 1/4/91

MELISSA – AGE 8, SPLIT-OFF DICK TRACEY ALTER-STATE, 8/12/90

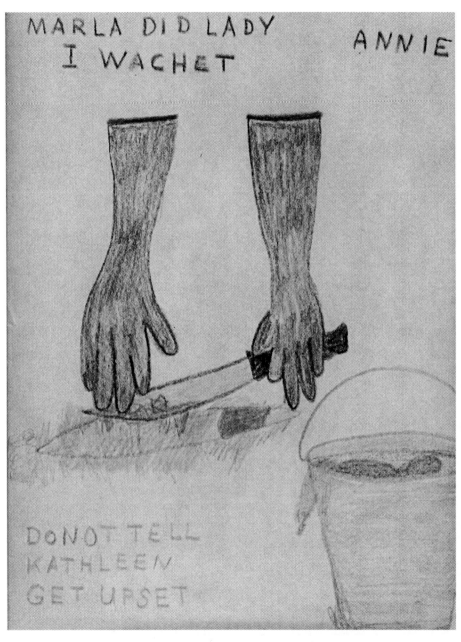

MARLA – WAS TAUGHT HOW TO CUT A BODY AND REMOVE ORGANS; ANNIE SHARED CONSCIOUSNESS

Traumatic Memories

Dr. R

Because alter-states and memories continued to emerge after I'd returned from Denver, Dr. T referred me to an associate in Atlanta who had some understanding of MPD. I first consulted with Dr. R in June, 1990. The psychiatrist was intelligent and surprisingly gentle. I was impressed by the many framed, black and white photos that he'd hung on the walls of his large, ornate room where he conducted our therapy sessions.

Although we met three times a week, there was never enough time for all of my emerging alter-states to share their experiences with him. I continued to process most of my memories at home, letting the parts draw pictures or write their memories in my journals.

After I'd met with Dr. R for about six months, he asked if it were possible that my memories were fantasy. At home that night, a child part that had opened up to him felt so painfully betrayed that she prepared to swallow all the pills in the house. As usual, Catalina took temporary control of the body and called Dr. R to explain the situation. Dr. R apologized to both alter-states, and said he'd work harder on listening to them without judging.[1]

Although I felt frightened and angry when I learned that I could have died that night, I now believe that what I'd told Dr. R about my past had probably been so horrific, his gentle soul couldn't deal with it.

Dr. X

In the late spring of 1991, several black op parts emerged. Full of emotional pain, they were dangerously suicidal. To stay alive, I needed to remain in a locked hospital unit while working with them. A contact told me about Dr. X, a psychiatrist who practiced in Dallas, Texas. She said that Dr. X was familiar with my mental programming, and advised me to check into his dissociative disorders psychiatric unit at Bedford Meadows Hospital, where she said I would receive specialized help.

When I told Dr. R that I wanted to go to that hospital, he said I should remain in Atlanta to work through my memories with Dr. R on an outpatient basis. When I disagreed, we had a falling-out. I never talked to him again.

Unhappy about traveling to Texas to enter another locked psych ward for God only knew how long, I kept reminding myself of a saying I'd learned at Crossroads: "The truth shall set you free, but first it shall make you miserable."[2]

When I checked into Bedford Meadows, Dr. X was away on vacation. His unit was tiny, and there wasn't enough staff to meet clients' basic needs. When some of the female clients tried to kill themselves, I and other clients had to protect them from self-injury with pillows, our bodies, and whatever else was available.

One young female constantly banged large dents in the corridor walls with her forehead. Anytime we heard thuds, we rushed to her and placed our pillows between her head and the wall. An older female repeatedly wrapped a telephone wire tightly around her neck, grinning. Her face turned gray-purple and her eyes bulged each time she fought our attempts to loosen it–still grinning. A thin, elderly female nearly died when she hung herself in her shared bedroom.

I was traumatized from witnessing one suicide attempt after another. I still joke that I should have been paid for the work I did that first week as a "staff member." Because I felt unsafe, I wasn't able to start working on my own reasons for being there.

Exhausted one day, I lay on my back on a sofa in the tiny lounge beyond the locked nurses' station. Suddenly and without warning, I experienced a powerful, full-body abreaction. My body tensed all over and I screamed involuntarily. Every muscle seemed to either tense or lengthen–it was hard to tell–and I couldn't stop the convulsions.

Each time another abreaction started, I pushed my face into a pillow to mute my screams. A soft-spoken, older female patient sat on the sofa and stayed with me through two days of convulsions. She stroked my hair and spoke soothingly until each abreaction ended. The seemingly unending onslaught frightened me, and yet neither of the unit's two nurses ever asked if I needed help. I was frightened because I didn't understand what these abreactions were about, and I didn't know if they'd recur (after the second day, they didn't).[3]

After a week, Dr. X returned to the unit. The psychiatrist's presence was like oil on troubled waters. He reminded me of a tall, thin Svengali.

His dark, commanding eyes and voice put clients into an immediate trance; they instantly stopped acting out. That amazed me.

Because the small unit and insufficient personnel didn't meet our needs, Dr. X convinced all of us to transfer to Charter-Grapevine, a nearby hospital. I decided that if Dr. X moved to the other hospital, I would go with him.

As we boarded several white Charter-Grapevine vans in Bedford-Meadows' parking lot, Dr. X excitedly boasted that the incident would be reported in professional journals. He said it was the first time in history that an entire psychiatric unit had transferred in protest from one hospital to another. I felt empowered by the idea that I had participated in such an event.

Charter-Grapevine

During one of our first group therapy sessions in the new dissociative disorders unit at Charter-Grapevine, Dr. X said that he'd secretly set it up during his vacation. Then he told us to map our internal systems of alter-states on large pieces of paper and bring our maps to the next session. He didn't suggest any specifics.

Alone in my shared bedroom, I put myself into a trance so knowledgeable alter-states could emerge and draw the map. Within hours, they'd used pastel pens to create a fairly elaborate, large diagram of different groups of alter-states that had specific programmed functions. The primary groups, or systems, were code-named Alpha, Beta, Delta, Theta and Omicron. When I compared my diagram to others' at the next group session, I was disappointed. I found no similarities in their maps, and didn't understand—yet—that my map was encoded. I feared that it was pure gibberish.

After the session, I went back to the bedroom, relaxed, and ceded control to the parts that had drawn it, asking them to please explain it to me. When I regained consciousness, I learned that an unfamiliar adult male alter-state had emerged. Emotionless, he had told a nurse sitting behind a large counter that he could scan the nurse's station and quickly identify twelve items to kill the staff with.

The nurse had handled the situation well by listening without showing any fear or anger. She later told me that she'd recognized that the alter-state had tried to communicate, in an awkward way, what he'd been trained to do.

The next day, another male adult part emerged. He believed that he must kill "the body" because other parts were close to telling secrets to the staff. He was frustrated when he couldn't find a television antenna to pierce my heart–the unit had cable hookup. Since he'd been programmed to suicide in only that way, he was then free to talk to the staff and to share his memories with me.

Lee, a tall, young blond technician, was especially gentle and helpful during my stay. He and another male technician spent a lot of time talking and bonding with my male, black op trained alter-states. They helped those parts to accept my brand of morality, and to discover new reasons to live.

Lee made a deal with several of them: if they sensed that a new part was emerging that could be dangerous to "the body" or to others, cooperative alter-states would alert the staff, walk willingly into the quiet room, and be put in leather restraints on a padded table. That way, the staff could talk to potentially violent alter-states in safety. Most of my op-trained alter-states first emerged in those restraints.

Being put in restraints had a downside, however. It re-traumatized alter-states that had previously been put in restraints by perpetrators to be drugged, electro-shocked, and more.

I'm glad that none of my alter-states attacked staff members. I watched as other patients, especially females, physically assaulted and injured some of the workers–especially males. Too many times, staff members came to work with casts on their arms, or limping, or with broken fingers.

Dr. X's hand-picked, personally trained staff had been careful to search all my belongings. They'd removed all metal and glass objects–"sharps"–that I could have used to harm myself or others. Even spiral bound notebooks were not allowed.

Several emerging alter-states searched for light bulbs they could break and use to cut my veins, but the bulbs were encased in metal cages. Because no bars had been installed in the clothes closets, they couldn't hang themselves. Even the mirror in my vanity case had been removed. The search continued.

One day, a female child alter-state emerged in the bedroom while my roommates socialized in the day room down the hall. Sensing she was in a place where secrets might be told, she believed she must kill the body. She dismantled my wind-up alarm clock and prepared to slice my wrists by using one of the clock's metal hands.

Susan, my young female therapist, unexpectedly entered the bedroom. As the black-haired woman introduced herself to the child part, who refused to speak, she asked what the child part was hiding in her hand. Unable to lie, she showed Susan the metal objects. Susan praised the child part for being so clever, and obtained the clock and metal pieces without a struggle.

Several days later, another child part emerged and discovered she could cut my flesh with the sharp point of folded foil from containers of orange juice in the unit's refrigerator. She tried to cut my exposed veins in my wrists and inner elbows. Fortunately, the foil wasn't sharp or strong enough. When the child part realized she wouldn't succeed, she receded. Catalina took over and cried from pain and emotional shock as she showed a nurse the throbbing gouges. The nurse murmured soothingly as she applied small bandages; she was used to seeing self-injuries.

When I emerged after that incident, I realized that some of my alter-states seriously wanted to successfully suicide. I feared for my life and deeply resented their existence.

About a week later, an adult female op-trained alter-state gained full control. For some reason, she believed that an airline ticket waited for her at the Dallas-Fort Worth Airport, across the expressway from the hospital. At dusk, she stood on the unit's open-air, concrete patio until the other clients had all gone inside to watch television. When she silently ascended the wooden fence that surrounded the patio, the flimsy lattice-work atop it cracked loudly. She receded and I emerged to find myself flopped over the top of the fence, unable to move in either direction without making a lot of noise.

Lee sprinted outside to the opposite side of the fence to prevent me from running away. Several nurses came out onto the patio and gently coaxed me down, then escorted me inside as I cried and shook. I was so embarrassed–what else were these parts capable of? And what might have happened to me at that airport?

Witch Hunt

Dr. X and his staff made a crucial mistake that slowed down my recovery process for several years. They constantly encouraged me and other patients to focus on "demons" and "demonic ties" that they said lurked within our bodies. They instructed us to mentally review every occult ritual that we could remember. They told us to pray and break every demonic tie imaginable, including any ties from our past that were created during sexual interactions–even from being raped!

Trusting they had information I didn't, I obeyed. Some of my newly emerging adult parts grew alarmed. They had risked death to divulge important information about how they had been programmed to perform black ops–especially for the CIA. And yet, I was now being told to focus on invisible ties from occult rituals and sexual interactions!

Because I was a member of a Pentecostal church, I believed Dr. X when he repeatedly insisted that most of our alter-states were demonic introjects (spiritual invaders). He gave each of us a paperback book written by his colleague, Dr. James Friesen, who seemed to believe the same. One evening, we sat in the day room as Dr. X played a videotape about trauma survivor Truddi Chase, author of *When Rabbit Howls*. Dr. X told us Ms. Chase had "failed to integrate" because she hadn't prayed away her hundreds of demons that, he said, were still posing as alter-states.[4]

In individual sessions and in group therapy, we were encouraged to visualize ourselves pouring the "blood of Jesus" on internal child alter-states to chase away lurking demons. This definitely was not good for me, mentally. Dr. X also told us to visualize placing alter-states in cages or soundproof rooms, so that the few remaining "true" alter-states couldn't hear the lies of the "demons," or their screams, in our minds. Again this wasn't good for me, but I did it, believing that Dr. X knew what was best.

In group therapy, he told us to prayerfully ask Jesus and angels to enter our bodies to oust the remaining demons. This especially bothered me because as a child, I'd been raped during a porn shoot by a bearded man dressed in a white robe–he'd played the role of Jesus Christ. (Some pornographers are really twisted.)

Although uncomfortable with most of Dr. X's instructions, I still complied. Because no one else openly complained, I assumed I must be wrong for feeling uncomfortable and for daring to consider that my "demons" might be human.

My assigned hospital psychiatrist, who saw patients in several different units, formally complained that members of Dr. X's staff were constantly putting me and other clients in restraints in the quiet room, then praying over us—rather like exorcists. In response, I filed a handwritten complaint against that psychiatrist, reminding the hospital administrators of my right to practice my religion. Dr. X expressed his appreciation for my doing this.

By the end of my two-month hospital stay, I'd used visualization techniques to internally lock up, cage, and exorcise all of my "demons." I'd also created a new host personality named Grace. During a phone call, I told Bill to address me as Grace from then on. Dr. X seemed pleased, and told me that I was fully integrated. I believed him. He said he would add me to his list of success stories that he shared with other mental health professionals.

In the beginning of October, I was discharged. When Bill came to the hospital to take me home, I cried and didn't want to leave. He was deeply hurt and didn't understand that I feared I'd be killed for having told people about what I'd done for the CIA. I now believed that Dr. X's hospital unit was my only safe refuge.

After leaving the hospital, Bill took me to Dr. X's nearby office for a private meeting. There, the psychiatrist instructed me to send him copies of all of my future journals. He said he would use my information to help other clients to deprogram. Flattered, I agreed to do so.

At home in Atlanta, I typed my daily journals and sent copies to the psychiatrist, once a week. Later, I recorded some of them on cassette tapes to send to him. For some bizarre reason, I believed that as long as Dr. X had copies of all of my journals, no one would hurt me. I also believed that as long as I communicated my alter-states' emerging memories to him, I didn't need a local therapist.

Because I'd developed strong emotional bonds with several staff members and some of the patients at Charter-Grapevine, Atlanta was a lonely place. I had no one to talk to about my still-emerging memories. I slipped back into denial, insisted I was fully integrated, and did my best to ignore new flashbacks.

After about a month, a friend called to confront me. She said she was tired of my bullshit; no one could integrate hundreds of alter-states in just two months! Happy to hear her voice, several child alter-states popped out and told her that "Grace" was a smokescreen I'd unconsciously created to hide the existence of my unintegrated "demonic" alter-states. They asked, what else could I have done? If I'd refused to say I had cast the "demons" out, I would have been accused of not cooperating with Dr. X or with Jesus Christ!

When I came back into consciousness, I remembered what those parts told my friend. Terribly embarrassed, I apologized to her and to Bill and asked them to please call me Kathleen from then on.

Therese

For the next six months, I tried to cope without a therapist. I gave up when my flashbacks were too severe to handle on my own. After several weeks of asking around, I learned about Therese, a local psychologist who had successfully worked with Vietnam Veterans and with several severely dissociated ritual abuse survivors. During my first consultation with her, I sensed she was what I needed. She was upbeat, intelligent, and a fighter.

We decided I would meet with her twice a week. I noticed that her office was full of unusual knick-knacks that she said clients had given her over the years. Several were similar to paraphernalia I'd seen in Pagan rituals. When I mentioned that, she explained that their real meanings had nothing to do with Paganism. She helped me to understand that because I was sensitive to hundreds of triggers, I would inevitably encounter some of them in regular life.

With her help, I accepted the reality that not all candles and Halloween items in store windows represented occult rituals, and not all people who used triggering phrases were bad guys. Coincidences happened. I practiced desensitizing myself to such items and phrases by giving them nicer, non-perp meanings. As I did, I started to gain power over many of my trauma-induced triggers.

Because Therese was familiar with multiplicity, alter-states and personality fragments emerged in her presence. Each was eager to share information and experiences with her. She was careful not to suggest anything, and explained that her job was to listen and to help me adjust to the information that those parts compartmentalized.

Therese recognized that I still suffered from heavy guilt and grief because of what I'd been forced to do in the past. In a gentle voice, she often repeated a phrase: "Less judgment and more curiosity." Her serene acceptance of what seemed abhorrent in me saved my life when the bulk of my sociopathic assassin alter-states emerged.

Black Op Alter-States

Most of my black op alter-states saw themselves as adult males. They complained to Therese that life at home was painfully dull. They were accustomed to working within extremely dangerous parameters, adrenaline pumping, making split-second decisions, enjoying the rush, facing death again and again, and winning. They didn't want to live a normal life. They wanted to go back to their handlers; they didn't want to be freed. As I interacted with the alter-states in therapy sessions, journals, and internal dialogue, I discovered deeper and more troubling reasons for their insistence in going back to the perpetrators.

First–if a local handler were to call me at home to instruct an alter-state to meet with him or her, and if the alter-state were to refuse, retribution could be swift and painful. Because these alter-states had been created through severe torture, they were terrified of pain and would do anything to avoid being "punished" for disobedience.

Second–they were convinced that if they did not obey, someone else–possibly my daughter–would also be tortured, raped, and possibly killed. Although some of these parts didn't want to do illegal activities again, they also couldn't bear for any child to be hurt or killed in their stead.

Third–these parts felt hopeless and believed they had no choice but to obey the handlers.

Finally–in the past, if they had been instructed to participate in a murder, they had cooperated because they'd believed the targeted individual would be killed regardless of who was sent in to do the job. They'd been programmed to believe it was better to kill one person than to disobey and be killed along with the target. In each situation, they'd been forced to choose between a lesser or greater evil.

The mental and emotional toll from performing black ops had been intense. Each time these parts had killed human targets, they'd felt more emotionless and bestial. They carried the greatest pain and horror of all: believing they were irretrievably evil.

Most of my black-op alter states had wanted to commit suicide at some time in the past. One had tried while in captivity, after she'd been forced to sign a legal document given to her by an alleged CIA handler. Afterwards, while left alone in a bathroom, she'd punched a glass mirror in a medicine cabinet and prepared to slash my wrists with a shard of glass. Fortunately, a black ops partner named Peter had entered and intervened, gently coaxing her into giving him the shard. That had made the alter-state feel more hopeless–she couldn't even suicide to stop the killing!

Some of my alter-states had emotionally bonded with op handlers, programmers, and with men who had claimed to be my owners. Some alter-states believed they were still owned by the men who had paid to use their services. These parts were so lacking in everyday knowledge, they didn't even know that slavery was illegal!

Some of the emotional bonding had occurred during sexual encounters. And some of my parts had identified with and molded themselves after the perceived personalities of programmers and "masters." An especially powerful type of bonding had occurred when these alter-states had witnessed the "good side" of the tormentors. Even the worst perpetrators had good qualities. Some of them were deliberately kind to the alter-states, pretending to treat them as equals. Those perp-loyal alter-states didn't know that other parts of my shattered personality had been betrayed, tortured, and sometimes sexually assaulted by the very same criminals!

I felt helpless and frightened when I couldn't stop my perp-loyal parts from reporting back. I had to wait until they became co-conscious with other alter-states that held memories of having been hurt or brutally betrayed by the same perpetrators. Only then were they willing to break their allegiances and cooperate with me.

I made sure these parts had sufficient time to grieve the loss of their unhealthy relationships with the perpetrators. Once they realized they'd been betrayed and duped, they became my fiercest fighter and self-protector alter-states.

Part of breaking away meant choosing not to respond to late-night, encoded phone calls from a succession of young children. They inevitably called just before a major occult holiday, asking to speak to an alter-state, by name, that I'd already identified and documented. The children sounded emotionally blank, as if they were reciting what they'd been told to say. Those phone calls were especially upsetting, because I believed the children were still being hurt at Aryan rituals.

Reframing

Each time I found another part that was still active, I felt devastated. Sometimes I wondered if maybe I should just give up and go back to the perpetrators. During that phase of recovery, I learned that I am a fighter. When facing overwhelming odds, I have a spark inside that just won't quit. I'm lucky that my fight instinct had been powerfully reinforced during brutal black ops training, and then by real op experiences.

Even if the entire world were to burn down around me, I was determined to be the one human still standing with a heartbeat.

Therese helped me to forgive myself when some parts did report back–usually by phone. Instead of berating myself, I reframed each discovery. Each time I successfully enlisted another reporting part's loyalty, I was a step closer to full freedom.

After a year of working with Therese, I uncovered another secret that terrified me: Bill also had spook-loyal alter-states. I hadn't remembered earlier, because I hadn't felt strong or supported enough by people outside our marriage. Now, however, I was ready to face the hard, cold truth. Not only had he recently done work with the ASA; he had also, in the past, occasionally handled me for the CIA during covert ops. As I remembered this, I feared that his CIA-loyal alter-states could be activated to betray me again.

Therese taught me to set up contingency plans in case of an emergency. My stepmother agreed I could stay at her house if needed. I insisted that my car be put in my name only. I opened a safety deposit box in my name, where I put my passport and other important papers that Bill couldn't access.

Only then did I confront him about his own multiplicity and insist that he also see a therapist. I explained if he didn't start getting co-conscious with his own alter-states, our marriage was over. As much as I loved him, I couldn't put myself at that kind of risk anymore.

Bill decided to consult with Bob since I'd done fairly well with him in the past. As Bill allowed alter-states to emerge in Bob's office, several of Bill's adult parts related details of covert ops that Bill, as the host alter-state, had completely blocked out. Because he'd never worked with a client like Bill before, Bob wasn't quite sure how to respond.[5] Therese explained to Bob that the best he could do was to simply listen in a non-judgmental way.

After Bill's alter-states emerged in therapy with Bob, they came home to meet me. Having so many alter-states popping out at the same time put an additional strain on our marriage. We often regressed and flashbacked at the same time. Sometimes, we both morphed into op trained assassins that were edgy, hyper-vigilant, and distrustful. (Play wrestling was *not* a good idea at those times.)

As we continued to remember, independently of each other, we both realized that we definitely had known each other long before I'd first met Bill's "William" alter-state in 1985.[6]

Bill's verification of our previous connections worried me. I questioned why we had chosen to marry each other. Was it because of our strong trauma bond from past ops? Was I Stockholming with Bill, marrying him and drawing close to him so that his CIA-loyal parts wouldn't hurt me? How much of our marriage was healthy? Any of it? Could it still be salvaged after we'd each remembered enough to take charge of our own lives?

I chose not to make any hasty decisions. After a number of heart-to-heart talks with Therese and other people in my support network, I decided I would focus on recovering, integrating, and growing stronger and more independent. I developed a stronger support network outside of our marriage so if I did have to leave Bill to stay safe, I wouldn't crumble. Having the freedom to leave also gave me the freedom to stay.

Return to Texas

In August 1992, two new child alter-states emerged. They both threatened to self-destruct–one, by fire. I returned to Texas to consult privately with Dr. X at his new unit at Cedars Hospital. As I met with him during our initial consultation, I told him that hundreds upon hundreds of alter-states had come out since I'd discharged from Charter-Grapevine. He said this meant I had "polyfragmented MPD" (poly = many). This fit, because some of my alter-states had journaled that Mom had told them I was a "thousand-piece jigsaw puzzle."[7]

I consulted with Dr. X almost every day for the next two weeks. During one private session, a male alter-state, code-named Lucifer, emerged. At the next session, Dr. X said this alter-state was the real Lucifer, which he'd met in another client a week earlier in Florida. Certain that Dr. X was wrong (the alter-state was definitely human), I realized that going back to Texas was a mistake. For the remainder of my hospitalization, I pretended to believe whatever Dr. X said so that I could leave as soon as possible.

After my discharge, I ceased all contact with the psychiatrist. After working so hard for years to accept and blend with my alter-states, I had–at his advice–rejected and accused them of being deceitful demons! And by rejecting and harshly judging them, I'd really rejected my own self–thereby *increasing* my amnesia and personality fragmentation! I decided that would never happen again.

Exploring the Dark Side

Because I've had many struggles about accepting the misnomered "evil" or "demonic" side of my personality, I understand why some severely dissociated survivors don't want to believe that their seemingly malevolent or "dark" alter-states are not split-off parts of their original whole personalities.

Acceptance of our fully human "dark side" requires great courage and a willingness to self-forgive.[8] Too many of our religious leaders have difficulty accepting the primal and wounded parts of their own humanity, which is why they often use excessive religion to avoid knowing themselves. Some of them treat their past selves as something that can be cut off or discarded, instead of being forgiven and embraced as part of the whole. If they're afraid to accept all of *their* own humanity, is it any wonder that some of them try their best to discourage us from accepting all of *our* selves?

I did things during ops that were absolutely bestial. I believe this is why I'd tried so hard to be spiritual and holy, before the memories came. My personality was polarized between overly "good" and overly "bad," keeping me from being able to blend and integrate into one entity.[9]

Before I started working with Therese, I'd had a hard time forgiving myself for what my assassin programmed parts had done. With her skilled help and support, I learned that I was no exception to the rule: any reasonably intelligent person can be brutally manipulated and conned into committing crimes against their conscious will–especially if the conditioning and torture begin in early childhood.

It was time for me to grieve the knowledge that I had experienced a soul-shattering crossover from rational humanity to primal brutality that, if I were God, no person would experience.

One of my difficulties in forgiving myself was that I was a female living in the Southeast. One of our Southern society's moral codes is that females are supposed to be gentle, passive caregivers. When assaulted, they are supposed to stay victims. They are not supposed to be physically aggressive, and they are expected to cry instead of expressing anger. I'd broken all of these rules to the nth degree.

During this crucial phase of my recovery, my depression and alienation from humanity were especially dangerous. So many times, I had to go to extraordinary measures to survive one more day, one more night. Part of my survival kit was information. The more I learned about what humans are capable of under extreme pressure and duress, the more I was able to accept my faults and limitations as well as the primal side of my human personality.

Lieutenant Colonel David Grossman wrote a ground-breaking book that examines the motivations and effects of killing others. Although the study was based mostly on his findings within the military, I could relate to much of what he wrote. His book, *On Killing: The Psychological Cost of Learning to Kill in War and Society* helped me to make great strides in understanding and accepting my "dark" side.

Grossman explained that the primal parts of the human brain that take over during danger do not need to function during safe times. This explains why my black op parts were so feral, a state in which I didn't find myself at any other time. I learned that my black op alter-states couldn't have rationalized and thought about the consequences of their actions (even if they'd had access to my store of knowledge) because they'd been in danger, and therefore had tunnel vision and tunnel thinking. All they'd been able to think about was carrying out their orders and surviving–one more time.

When my more empathic parts had first learned about the assassinations, they'd felt powerful remorse, regret, and guilt. They'd also felt anger and hatred towards the black op parts for not having cared about the targeted victims. Grossman's book helped bridge the schism between these two polarized sets of alter-states. Gradually, they met in the middle and began to blend.

Would I attack someone now, if provoked? Only if absolutely necessary. Although my "kill or be killed" primal reflex will always be in the background, I've developed other responses that are more helpful in stressful situations.

With emerging rage comes strong physical energy. During the early part of my recovery, I occasionally needed physical outlets to safely exert my volcanic energy in ways that would harm no one. This was the rage that had deliberately been reinforced and compartmentalized in my mind for decades, to be triggered and used by handlers to hurt and kill others. I had to learn new ways to express that energy. Although many abuse survivors turn their anger onto themselves by self-harming, I was conditioned to express it outwardly–albeit in controlled settings.

If I feel angry now, I might physically remove myself from the situation until I can think and respond calmly. I might call a support person to help me think things through. And instead of freezing, trancing, and obeying when approached by former handlers, I can now enlist help from others, or walk away and laugh, knowing that the handlers are still trapped and I am free.

In earlier stages of my recovery, I expressed my anger in many unmailed letters to perpetrators and complicit family members. The rage and pain were so intense, my clothes were often soaked with sweat by the time I'd finished writing.

I expressed some of my rage's immense physical energy by walking fast on my treadmill or by visualizing faces on a punching bag and slamming it. When I grew exhausted, I knew that particular "pocket" of rage had been sufficiently expelled.

If I felt fury, which was stronger than rage, I used a sledgehammer to break old slabs of concrete, or a pickaxe to remove rocks and thick roots from the ground in my garden, imagining the roots to be rapists' penises. (That was highly satisfying.)

In the house, I used a wooden dowel or a plastic bat to hit a mattress while I screamed at visualized perpetrators. (I wore a pair of sports gloves to avoid blisters.)

For a period of several days, one child alter-state that had been conditioned to kill had so much fury at anything living and breathing–including me–I nearly didn't survive. She wanted to pull up and destroy every plant on our property. She wanted to go to a mall and kill many people, indiscriminately. She wanted to drive my car at a high speed into an oncoming cement or dump truck.

Her unique solution was to find dead animals on the road and drive over the carcasses, back up, and drive over them again. This sounds extreme, but her *rage* was so extreme that nothing else worked. After about two days, the need to harm others was gone, and she never had to run over carcasses again.

So much rage emerged during my first decade of memory recovery, I felt like a walking volcano. That terrified me, because I didn't want to hurt innocents! I gradually realized that, regardless of my emotional state, I'd always worked hard not to hurt others–when I had a choice. When the rage had surfaced in my "regular" life, I'd chosen to isolate, power walk, or turn the rage into tears to protect those around me.

My support network has helped me to understand that I was not and am not a perpetrator, because perpetrators commit crimes by choice. I was a good person who was repeatedly forced into the most awful situations. I did what was necessary to survive and remain sane.

Working with my rage-filled parts, I also learned that no matter how much anger they had, they would never take it out on anyone who gave them caring and kindness. Perhaps this is because they had become rageful through torture and abuse, and therefore were starved for positive attention.

Therese encouraged me to take the acceptance of my primal side one step further. She explained that I needed to honor the parts of my humanity that had preserved my life. That concept was uncomfortable at first–how could I honor parts that had killed other humans? As I came to understand that the victims would have been killed regardless, and that I was a human tool and not a murderer, I allowed myself the right to feel gratitude for having survived.

Verifications

As memories continued to emerge, I scanned books at a local library for information that might verify some of them. Because my covert experiences had been so unusual, however, I had little luck. I was still careful to follow advice from a male staff member at Bethesda PsycHealth: I avoided reading books by survivors who claimed to have similar histories. When using reference books, I only looked at pages that contained specific information about names and organizations that I'd already remembered and journaled. I decided I'd rather not have enough information to verify a memory, than to subconsciously take in information from written materiel that could taint my memories.

Accepting my memories and making peace with them was hard work. The attached emotions were especially difficult to process, because they were new and unfamiliar. I needed time to learn how to feel and express them without being overwhelmed. Even joy was difficult to feel.

Although I processed some of my emerging memories with Therese, I worked through most of them at home by myself. So much information emerged after three decades of repression, no therapist could have possibly helped me to process it all.

Phobias

One of the ways I've been able to accept my memories is by recognizing that many of my irrational behaviors and phobias had actually originated from traumas I'd been blocking out. After I'd worked through the traumatic materials and integrated them as part of my conscious past, the resulting phobias usually faded away.

In May of 1994, a private consultant asked me to list my phobias. In one day, I listed 176. Since I've worked through almost all of their underlying traumas, nearly all of the phobias have dissipated. Having cognitive awareness of the underlying causes of those fears helped me to lessen their power over my mind and life. For example:

Before recovery, if the tiniest bit of a male dog's pink penis poked out, I couldn't stand for it to come anywhere near me.[10] Then I remembered the bestiality porn and worked through how it had affected me. After that, I adopted a male dog. The phobia is gone. I've emotionally bonded with him and don't see him as a sexual threat.

I felt nauseous if I was given any meat that was touched by sweet sauce–this phobia came from having been forced to suck on Dad's penis after he'd put honey or maple syrup on it. Since I have remembered and worked through the traumatic memories of having gagged and feared I'd die from suffocation, I can now eat meats with sweet sauces without flashbacking.

For decades, I was obsessed with looking for every stray hair in my bathroom – on the floor, in the tub, or wherever–and placing it in the trash receptacle. I "had to" brush off our bed every morning so not a single hair would be on it when I went to bed again. I couldn't stand to eat any food in which I'd found a hair. This phobia resulted from Dad's forcing me to eat victims' hair that he'd cut into bite-sized pieces with scissors. I'll admit that I'm still working on this phobia–but at least I know what it's about.

For decades, another phobia was about being in a room with a gun. This fear had developed, in part, because my mental programmers had implanted hypnotic suggestions to ensure that I would never allow a gun in my home, and would only handle one when professional handlers and trainers had direct control of me. I suspect they did this to keep me from accidentally reliving a training session or op at home and shooting someone.

After I remembered the black ops, the phobia was replaced by a new obsession: several of my alter-states *had* to have a "baby blue Beretta." They stated this was one of the guns that I'd used on ops. When Bill asked why I'd used such a small-caliber handgun, those parts explained that because they'd been conditioned to have excellent aim, the caliber hadn't mattered much. And of course, such a small gun is *much* easier to hide from human targets–until it's too late.

One day, I decided to face my fear by purchasing a small Beretta. I was so relieved when no one came to our home to arrest me for buying it! The first time I went to a local underground shooting range for target practice, I let several op-trained parts come out. Although their aim was still surprisingly accurate, they were uncomfortable because Bill insisted they hold it with both hands. Later, they explained to him that professional trainers had taught them to hold the handgun in just the right hand, so they could always keep the left hand free to self-defend and attack in other ways. (I probably couldn't have done this with larger handguns.)

At home, I practiced holding the Beretta in just my right hand. On a primal level, it was a completely natural sensation. I recalled what some of the spook trainers had told me about "my" gun: that it was my "baby," the most important thing in my universe. As I continued to use and feel the Beretta at the shooting range and at home, I realized another reason for my phobia towards guns was that I feared they would trigger visual flashbacks of the gory results of some of the black ops. Fortunately, that has not happened.

Whenever I feel a new fear that is irrational, I remind myself that this is probably a signal that another memory is emerging. This knowledge, paired with positive self-talk and relaxation techniques, keeps the fear from taking over.

Notes

1. One of the FMSF's claims is that mental health professionals should discourage their clients from accept emerging memories without proof of their veracity. I believe this irrational demand is a violation of survivors' basic rights. Why?

- Most repressed memories are of traumas that were perpetrated against the victims, in secret, by adults who had a clear and vested interest in hiding all evidence (to avoid societal disapproval, prison sentences, and more). Therefore, verifications are often unavailable to the recovering victims.
- If therapists tell clients they shouldn't accept their emerging memories without external proofs, the clients will not feel safe in baring their souls to the therapists. Perhaps this is what the FMSF wants-if we cannot talk to mental health professionals about what was done to us, we are effectively silenced.
- If trauma survivors are not supported in accepting their memories, this can reinforce their amnesia and dissociation, thereby keeping them vulnerable to certain types of predators.
- If the FMSF is successful within the legal system in forcing mental health professionals to discourage clients from accepting memories that the clients cannot initially prove, thereby silencing the clients during therapy, *the FMSF will have effectively sabotaged clients' right to free speech!*

2. Rick Stahlhut, M.D., M.S. is the originator.

3. A decade later, I remembered enough to know that the convulsions had been my body's way of reliving memories of forced electro-shock applications that I had endured as an adult, along with being forcibly drugged, in a government-run reprogramming ward in a psychiatric hospital not far from Atlanta. I believe this was intended to erase my memories of the most recent black op. In *Bluebird*, Dr. Colin Ross cited information from a CIA ARTICHOKE (pre-MKULTRA) document that may explain why ECT (electroconvulsive "therapy") can be used to create amnesia in victims of mind control:

> The use of electric shock to the brain for the creation of amnesia, and amplification of the amnesia with hypnosis were discussed by the author of an ARTICHOKE document dated 3 December 1951:
>
> *. . . One setting of this machine produced the normal electric-shock treatment (including convulsion) with amnesia after a number of treatments . . .[the experimenter] felt he could guarantee amnesia for certain periods of time and particularly he could guarantee amnesia for any knowledge of use of the convulsive shock.* (pg. 43)

4. Truddi Chase was one of the first severely dissociated trauma survivors to have their autobiography published. It helped an untold number of trauma survivors with MPD/DID to understand dissociation and the recovery process.

5. Although Bill's spook alter-states did share limited information about some military and/or covert ops with his therapist, they refused to divulge any details that would violate whatever oaths they or Bill had made during his 30-year career in the Army. I was equally careful not to share specific details of covert ops with any of

my therapists-not because I was worried about violating oaths (I'd taken none by choice), but because I didn't want to endanger them by telling them too much-my handlers had repeatedly told me that if I shared the memories with anyone, that person would be killed.

6. Because we had the potential to contaminate each other's emerging memories, I didn't discuss my op memories with Bill, other than a few specific details that I needed to verify (for example, the names of certain weaponry). I also insisted that he not tell me his op memories. Instead, we relied heavily on our therapists for primary support. They, in turn, didn't share our memories with each other. After about six years, Bill and I realized that our training and experiences, in general, were markedly different. After that, we occasionally shared op memories with each other-but only after we'd independently journaled and processed them.

7. Mom was aware that my mind had been so badly shattered by Dad and others that I had many hundreds of alter-states and personality fragments. This was deliberate on their part; Dad constantly told me he wanted to see how much of my brain he could activate and use, one piece at a time. Dad was careful, however, not to let Mom know my programming. I've met other mind-control survivors who were encouraged by perpetrators (as Mom encouraged me) to constantly assemble jigsaw puzzles. Doing that reinforced our false, implanted belief that we were in so many pieces that we would never fully come together. Dr. Colin Ross described polyfragmentation in *The Osiris Complex*:

> It is impossible to have hundreds of fully formed personality states in one person because there isn't enough lifespace in one lifetime. In a polyfragmented patient, there will usually be a relatively small number of more fully formed personality states that have been responsible for the bulk of the person's experience. Often the personality fragments will hold a single memory or feeling, and many may never take executive control of the body . . . [the process of creating fragments] seems more like a memory-filing device in which memories are broken down into small pieces and stored under filing labels consisting of names and ages. (pg. 55)

8. Dr. Ross described one of the biggest problems that trauma survivors encounter when they choose to believe that their alter-states and personality fragments are negative spirit entities: "Defining demonic alter personalities as actual demons reinforces the dissociation, and perpetuates the problem, even if the alters are temporarily suppressed by an exorcism." (*Osiris* pg. 131)

9. I believe this is one reason why so many religious leaders have gotten into serious trouble. What happened to Jimmy Swaggart, a Pentecostal evangelist, was a good example. (More than once, he was caught interacting with prostitutes.) Some religious leaders try too hard to be holy and perfect in public. Secretly, they may feel fake and ashamed. To compensate for their excessive morality (as Bill Bennett did

by gambling), they may unconsciously allow their misnomered "dark side" to emerge and have control for a while, in an attempt to bring a temporary balance between the two poles of their personality.

10. Sometimes, as I remembered the bestiality, I felt angry at certain types of animals. When I did, I reminded myself, as many times as needed, that the animals had been trained and conditioned to do what was unnatural to them, as had I. They were not responsible for what they had done to me-their human trainers were.

Witness

Suicide?

Some of my emerging memories were so painful, I continued to push them away–including my memories of what I'd been forced to witness when Dad died.

After his funeral in 1990, I'd grown comfortable with the idea that he'd committed suicide. It made sense to me for two main reasons: first, two months earlier, he'd deeply cut his wrists, necessitating treatment in a psychiatric hospital. Second, his body had been found the same way his father's had–in his car, with carbon monoxide poisoning documented as the cause of death.

Several years after his death, two male relatives sent me letters in which they accused me of having killed Dad. Each man insinuated that because I'd gone to the authorities about Dad, he'd suicided. By the time I'd received their letters, however, I'd healed enough to know that he alone had been responsible for his suicide. And his being arrested for child molestation had equally been his fault . . . if he hadn't sexually assaulted me and other children, he wouldn't have been arrested!

Although I felt sad to have lost him prematurely, I also felt peace in knowing I had done all that I could while he was alive. I hadn't stopped loving him in a pure way, despite what he'd tried to do to distort that love. I had confronted him in several letters while reminding him that I still loved him. Because I had no regrets, I was able to grieve in a healthy way.

My peace was shattered in late 1992 when a new series of alter-states emerged. Each part gave me new pieces of memory about his death. At first I was shocked by what they told me. As the shock wore off, I was pummeled by waves of terror, guilt, grief, and rage. I expressed the emotions at home and in therapy. I realized that I'd pushed the memories completely away because I was severely traumatized by what I'd witnessed the night of Dad's death. On a scale of one to ten, based on all the traumas I'd ever experienced, his demise was definitely a ten.

With each revelation from these alter-states, I was more certain that Dad had been murdered.

In November of 1992, a sociopathic, op-trained alter-state emerged that had been conscious that night. She journaled:

I was with some adults at night. I had been given folded-up clothes that I was supposed to wear. They really upset me. There was a thick, black spandex, short-sleeved leotard with a sad-looking hound-dog appliqué on front. It had a nasty saying about "Joe's Bar and Grill." And then there was a blue, short-type spandex outfit that went over it with straps. It looked awful on me! It made me look like a lady mud wrestler or something!

An older man was present. He was balding with curly, thinning, gray hair. We were using his facilities to change clothes. I had to pee, bad! We were in a hurry and the guy who was letting us use his place seemed really nervous. He had several bathroom stalls in a row that we were using to change in. Not very impressive looking. The doors and walls of the stalls seemed to be made of plywood.

I was making everybody late by going back one more time to pee. The man was even more nervous, now. I was told that we were going to do a "hit job." I felt really offended and embarrassed that they had picked out this particular outfit for me to wear, but I also accepted the fact that if anyone tried to describe me, it would be the outfit they'd remember most, instead of my physical description.

I remember too, that there was a plump-faced lady in one of the stalls to my left. Her hair was curly, black, and short. She was begging everybody not to flush the toilets, because if we do, then her toilet will start to overflow while she's still in there, changing her clothes. The plumbing was really screwed-up.

Later that day, the alter-state recalled more: She'd been transported in a van to Dad's apartment complex and had seen him being assaulted in his rented garage while sitting inside his Pontiac Gran Prix. She didn't write that part of the memory because she knew I wasn't ready to know about it. It stayed hidden with her until January of 1993 when the memory tried to break through again, this time in a vivid dream:

It was the night Dad died. In the dream, I finally got up the nerve to go to his apartment, to see what it looked like. I had no conscious memory of ever going to that apartment. Yet, in the dream I had alters that swore they had watched Dad die in his rented garage, and that they had obeyed orders to clean out his apartment of all incriminating evidence connecting him to the Aryan cult network and the CIA.

Though I noted the dream in my journal, I blocked it out of my mind again. I wasn't ready to consider its significance.

Memories of Dad's Murder

Several days later, I got up the nerve to call my stepmother. When she answered the phone, I told her I'd recently remembered details that made me think Dad's death might not have been a suicide.

I'd been afraid to tell her, partly because I feared she would blame me for his death (she didn't) and partly because I didn't want to cause her more pain. Like me, she had begun to heal. I didn't want to cause her to feel the same raw grief I was experiencing. And yet, when she insisted that I tell her what I remembered, I felt obligated to do so. After all, she was an adult and his widow; she had a right to know.

When I told her what I'd remembered, I feared she would think I was making it up. Instead, she indicated that murder was a possibility. She said she had a copy of the coroner's autopsy report, and asked me if I wanted to know what was in it. I declined, explaining that if I'd really witnessed what had been done to him, I needed to ensure that the rest of the memory, when it emerged, would be uncontaminated.

The next day, more pieces of memory emerged, starting with emotions I'd still been suppressing. I journaled:

> *I am in bad shape today. Not suicidal—everything but. Major depression. Want to cry, but can't. Feel frantic inside, like I want to scream and scream, deeply. Primal emotions. Raw pain, anger, grief. Can't eat worth a flip, again. My stepmother called yesterday to talk some more about what I had told her about my father's "suicide" actually being a snuff job. She said that the*

> *Sunday night before Dad died, he went out of his way, during a*
> *quick visit to her and the kids after church, to hug and kiss each*
> *of his children and say goodbye. She had wondered why he said*
> *goodbye. He'd handed her the support check, which was also*
> *unusual for him. She also told me that three coils of rope had*
> *been found in the trunk of the car in which he was found dead,*
> *and the coroners showed her pictures of his body, with blood run-*
> *ning out of his mouth. Also, she thinks it is very strange that they*
> *decided not to do any tests on his blood samples.*

Suddenly, I found myself co-conscious with an alter-state that had compartmentalized another piece of memory. As that part emerged, I fully relived the memory–visual, audible, tactile, everything. Devastating. As I journaled, its impact hit me like a hard punch in my stomach.

> *The night of my father's death, his spook associates had told*
> *him, in front of me, that he was being taken underground, to*
> *live somewhere else with a brand-new identity. That's why Dad*
> *was sitting in the front passenger seat of his car inside the*
> *small garage when I saw one of the goons, a professional*
> *assassin I knew as "Fred," put his arm around Dad's neck to*
> *kill him (I thought) from the back seat of the car. This is also*
> *why he didn't struggle or fight as we went into his rented*
> *garage. He honestly thought he was home, free![1]*

I was puzzled by what I wrote. My stepmother had told me that the coroners had found his body on the *back* seat of his Gran Prix. But I had watched the man's arm go around his throat as he sat on the *front* seat.

Another puzzle: my stepmother had asked me why I thought his killers had wanted me there at all. When she'd asked, I hadn't been able to answer. When they had taken me to his garage, I'd believed they were probably going to interrogate him and maybe search his apartment, but I hadn't been prepared for seeing them *kill* him. Then I realized that I'd been forced to watch, to frighten me into silence. And more.

As I sat on my bed, pondering these new revelations, the same adult alter-state[2] wrote a scalding critique:

> *These assholes knew my psychological profile. They knew*
> *that I tended to blame myself, personally, any time someone*

died in a room with me, even if I had nothing to do with it.
That, plus being a witness of [an execution] was meant
to blackmail/frighten me into silence. After all, if they could
do it to him, *it only was a logical conclusion that they could*
do it to me *next, if I didn't cooperate and keep my mouth*
shut . . . It worked very nicely (for them), at least until
today.

After the shock started to wear off, I felt sheer terror. I couldn't
stop shaking and crying. If I'd been a witness, then I was an active
liability to the killer and his accomplices because I could still identify
them! All the fear I'd felt towards Dad, I now felt towards those
men because they'd proven they were stronger and more powerful
than he.

Several months later, my stepmother and I visited the Senior Forensic
Investigator at the Office of the Medical Examiner in Decatur, Georgia.
He had performed Dad's autopsy. I agreed to let him tape-record
my statement about what I'd remembered. I wish now that I had made a
second tape for myself because I remember very little of what I told him.
I do remember that he offered to show me Dad's autopsy report, and
that I declined. And I remember he did say, after I told him I remembered
"Fred's" arm around Dad's neck, that no bones had been broken—
therefore, that hadn't been the cause of death.

After I returned home that day, I wondered: although it would be nice
to document what had been done to Dad, would taking further action
help or hurt me? After talking to several people in my support network,
I came to the conclusion that I'd be hurting myself if I pursued it further.
I'd done my duty as a citizen by telling them what I'd remembered. I
needed to leave it at that.

I wrote a five-page letter to the investigator, explaining that I was not
willing to share more memories if they emerged, and was not willing to
testify if Dad's connections to the CIA could be proven.

My stepmother had been concerned that the investigators might think
I'd made up the story so she could get additional life insurance payments
for my father's death (she didn't). In the letter to the examiner, I explained
that I hadn't known about that possibility until after I'd told her what I'd
remembered. I ended the letter: "Dad is dead. He can't be brought back.
We who survived need to go on living."

"You Killed Your Dad"

Over the years, I recovered more bits and pieces of memories of Dad's murder. I recalled that one of the killers had led me across the dark parking lot into my father's apartment. Because I'd seen Dad's coded files before, and knew what was in them, I was now told to look through the metal file cabinet in which Dad had kept them. I was to pick out any that could connect Dad to the Aryan cult or to the CIA.[3] A slim woman stood to my left, watching me closely. She was maybe 5'7" with short curly brown hair. She was very agile and emotionally cold. Her light complexion was pitted; she had brown doe eyes. I would have guessed her to be about 35.

In another fragmented memory, Fred had driven me away from Dad's apartment in a black, compact car. I don't know where we went or how long he drove, but I do remember that we arrived at a one-story warehouse. Fred ordered me into the warehouse and handed me a black handgun. He told me to shoot a black paper silhouette of a man, hanging on a wire about halfway between us and the far wall. My training kicked in; I shot through where the heart would have been.

Fred leaned over my shoulder and spoke in a lowered voice, "You just killed your dad." Immediately, all of the guilt I'd felt for not saving Dad, for not even trying, slammed and immobilized me, sealing the memories of that night behind a desperately self-protective amnesia.[4]

Was He Moved?

In January 1995, Emily saw her first autopsy during training at the Georgia Bureau of Investigation. The case she saw had resulted from carbon monoxide poisoning. When she questioned the medical technician about how the circumstances of my father's demise compared with this case, he explained that bodies with carbon monoxide poisoning do not get red like Dad's did. He said that the red on the front of Dad's body would have resulted from his having lain, face-down, on a surface for more than four hours. He explained that the reddish discoloration came from blood that had pooled and settled in that part of his body after his circulation had stopped.

This was odd because Dad was six feet tall and his body was too long for him to have comfortably lain face-down on his car's back seat. I wondered–was Dad's body moved after he died? Was it possible that when the man put his arm around Dad's neck, he hadn't actually killed him?

Later, I discussed this with my husband, who had special forces training, and also with a trained wrestler. Both men explained that the arm lock around the front of my father's neck would have temporarily cut off the blood to his brain–rendering him unconscious but not necessarily dead.

This confirmed what the forensic investigator had told me, and meant that more had been done to Dad than I could remember. It couldn't have been that they'd left him in the car, because he wouldn't have stayed unconscious long enough to die from the carbon monoxide poisoning–at least, not from the arm lock alone.

As hard as I tried, I couldn't remember what had happened after I'd shot at the silhouette in the warehouse. That worried me.

Multiple Emotions

In March of 1996, as I sat on our carpeted bedroom floor, I went back into the memory of losing Dad, and recovered more of my shattered emotions. Like a very little girl, I wailed and wept and rocked myself. My journal captured the turmoil.

Daddy! It wasn't supposed to happen this way! It's wrong! It's wrong! It just so wrong!

A teenaged part wrote: *What does it matter? What does anything matter, anymore? Dad is dead. I was supposed to die with him. His secret-keeper was supposed to die with him. It is understood.*

So now I'm reeling. Oh no. Oh no. This is *real.*

Why, Daddy? Why?

I'm not Dad. It's not my place to protect him. He made his choices. I'm not Dad. Whatever his decisions, it was his choice, not mine.

Then an "angel" alter-state wrote: *Poor little boy Dad. They killed you. But did they really? Can your hidden goodness ever be killed?*

I never felt so murderous in my entire life as I did at Dad's attacker when that man put his arm around your neck.

And yet survival took over. Crawl. Obey. Stifle the screams with whimpers.[5] Pray–oh how I prayed–to God, to them–that they wouldn't finish me off too! Who wants to die when there is so much creativity and love yet to be expressed? Oh please don't kill me! Please don't end who I am! It's not time yet!

So then, just then, I began to betray you, little boy. By putting myself, my life, first. As I watched them, I felt so guilty. I still feel guilty, putting myself first.

Self-Defense

In the summer of 1997 at a local college, I took a self-defense course taught by a police trainer who was also a judo expert. Tall and strong, he patiently taught us basic moves to thwart attackers.

To my chagrin, I realized I didn't know how to defend myself against attackers without automatically planning to kill them! I was excited as I realized that now I could learn how to disable attackers without causing serious damage.

A difficulty arose when he told one of the women to sit in a chair in the recreation room, then stood behind her and put his arm around her neck. As he put the choke-hold on her, I had difficulty hearing and came very close to a full faint.

Pulling myself back into consciousness, I realized I was still deeply traumatized from having seen Fred do it to Dad, and was terrified that someone might do it to me! To get past the fear, I asked the instructor to teach me how to break that hold. He did.

I would have earned an 'A' in the self-defense class, but our final test was to encounter our fully padded, helmeted instructor in an unexpected location, and then defend ourselves when he attacked us. Fearing that an op-trained alter-state might be triggered out and get me into serious trouble, I skipped that test and settled for a high 'B.'

Suicide by Lifestyle

In March of 2002, I finally remembered that after Fred had taken me to the warehouse to shoot Dad's silhouette, Dad's unconscious body had been carried in, accompanied by several of his associates whom I knew very well. After that, they'd forced me to watch as one, a professional assassin, had killed Dad, leaving a tiny mark in a place no one would have thought to look.

Shaken, I pondered the significance of this new memory. What should I do now? Should I report what I saw? Wouldn't that put me in direct danger? And how could I prove what I saw, now that his body was gone? What good would it do to risk my life to tell what happened to a man who was already dead? It was time to let the guilt and pain of my lack of intervention go. I'm still certain that was the right decision to make–what's done is done; I need to go on living.

After that, I felt new grief over the loss of the Dad-I-could-have-had. I realized when the real Dad had been murdered, my fantasy Dad had also died. This grief was even worse!

Several days later, Bill and I went to a movie. After it ended, we watched a father and his teenaged daughter stroll up the carpeted aisle in front of us. I felt a sharp pain in the middle of my chest and fought back stinging tears. Later that night as I sat in bed next to Bill, I journaled:

They had their arms around each other, then let go and walked and talked. They looked completely relaxed and seemed to truly enjoy being together. I was almost physically paralyzed. For a few seconds, I was barely able to take another step.

That was what I had wanted from Dad all along. Not sex. Real love! But to Dad, love meant nothing more than sex. So he never loved me as a father should love his child.

From infancy, the man had me addicted to orgasms and his touch and smell, like an animal. He conditioned me to be addicted to what I didn't want, and meanwhile, what I needed the most, he never gave me.

He robbed me of my dignity and my innocence. He made me feel filthy, no good, dirty, shameful, undeserving of human kindness. He made me feel "different" from the rest of the world. When I was with him, I was not myself.

Every time Dad dragged me into the sea of shame, I found my way back to the safe dock of hope, based on the human hunger for a father's love, that love-that-could-still-be.

And I waited there. For so many years, I waited, with my back turned to Dad's stinking sea, watching loving fathers with their emotionally fulfilled daughters. I kept waiting for my prince, the "Good Dad," to finally come and truly love me and cherish me, protect me and take me away from this horrid, stinking, shameful place. But he never came.

And when his body was murdered and his soul left our world, still I stood on that dock, looking at the land of love and hope, ever scanning the horizon for the Good Dad, the Loving Dad. And he never came. And he will never come.

In all truth, no one could ever be the "Good Dad" to me. My father cheated me. And then he robbed my soul. But I have my soul back now. And he's the loser. He's the sick one, not me . . . He was the only one who had the power to take my hope away. Now Dad is dead.

So now I'm no longer waiting forlornly at the dock for the Good Dad who won't be coming. I'm headed back into the city of life and love, where I can re-light my little flame of hope and make sure it doesn't flicker out.

Not long after I'd finally accepted Dad's manner of death, a psychologist familiar with the criminal underworld told me that, regardless of the physical cause of death, Dad had ultimately died of "suicide by lifestyle." This wise man's observation gave me a new perspective that helped me let go of the guilt I'd felt because I'd been unable to save Dad in the end.

Notes

1. After much soul-searching, I have decided that–as a witness to Dad's murder, my first moral responsibility is to protect myself and the lives of my loved ones. For this reason, I must limit what I write about it. Some secrets will probably die with me because for people like me, the witness protection program is not a viable option.

2. I had many alleged CIA-programmed, CIA-loyal alter-states. For years, some had secretly viewed my world through my eyes and learned what I knew while

continuing to hide their existence from me. Out of all my alter-states, these were least comfortable about sharing information with me. They feared that once I knew they existed, I would merge with them and then they wouldn't be able to go back anymore to the spook handlers who had claimed to work for the CIA's Directorate of Operations. These parts were emotionally addicted to being with those men. And yet, as they learned what I did about how cleverly I (and they) had been manipulated, they began to get angry at the handlers. That was their first step towards freedom.

3. Although I've retrieved memories of the contents of those sensitive files, I will not describe them because documentation is no longer available to validate them. (After Dad's death, his surviving widow-unaware of the value of certain items in the apartment-took them to the city dump.)

4. Mark L. Howe of the Memorial University of Newfoundland wrote a journal article, "Individual Differences in Factors That Modulate Storage and Retrieval of Traumatic Memories." It explains the neurological chemistry behind the mystery of why some traumatic memories are not forgotten, while others are completely disconnected from conscious memory. One of his conclusions is that "low and high levels of stress typically lead to little or no memory for an event (for different reasons) and moderate levels can lead to enhanced remembering." (pg. 686) My being forced to witness Dad's murder definitely created a high level of stress.

5. I remembered, and told the medical examiner, that Bill had also been in the garage that night. When I'd crawled to the closed garage door to where he'd stood, he'd stood there rigidly. When I first remembered his being there and doing nothing to comfort or rescue me, I hated him and wanted nothing more to do with him. One of his ASA associates had a long talk with me after that. The man helped me to understand that it had been a very dangerous time for both Bill and me. Bill had been in as much danger as I had, because he was still acting as an ASA mole. If he'd fought what they were doing to Dad, or had tried to interfere with what they were doing to my mind, they might have killed us both. For my sake, he had to act as if he was fully cooperating. Once I understood this, I was able to forgive him. After all, he had the right to be scared, too. There were three of them and two of us; and they were all professionally trained assassins. (Bill still has no memory of these events.)

RESUME

BILL SHIRK, PCMM/PCMH (PROFESSIONAL CERTIFIED IN MATERIAL HANDLING
AND MANAGEMENT)

o Senior Engineer of Material Management, AT&T

o 1945 Shipping Clerk - Hans C. Bick Dye Works

o C10 Steel Worker, Orr & Sembower Boiler Factory

o Four years, U.S.A.F. - Jet A & E Specialist, Flight Engineer

o BS Chemistry, Mathematics, Albright College

o Joined Western Electric in Transistor and Diode Manufacture -
   1956. Responsibilities included site plans, plant layouts,
   raw materials, stores, shipping, chemical and cryogenic
   handling and distribution, cranes, trucks, conveyors, etc.

o 1969 - moved to Atlanta to plan Norcross Cable Plant

o Graduate studies included Mechanical Engineering - Ohio State,
   MS in Operations Research - Purdue University

o Past President, International Material Management Society

o Technical Advisor to Chinese Mechanical Engineering Society

o Associate Editor, Co-author of Production Handbook (Wiley - 1987)

o Frequent Lecturer, Author for Material Handling Engineering,
   Modern Material Handling, Fortune, Distribution, Manufacturing
   Week, etc.

o Member MHI, MHRC, IIE, APICS, MHEF

o ▬▬▬▬▬ ▬▬▬▬▬▬▬▬▬▬▬▬▬▬▬▬▬▬▬▬▬

o Hobby - Archeology, Kingdom of Jordan

DAD'S PERSONAL RESUME, LATE 1980s

KALB COUNTY POLICE DEPART. IT
Statement Form

Ⓓ

Case No. _____

STATE vs. _William T. Shirk Sr._ Address _____

Statement of _Kathleen Ann Sullivan_ Address _4321 Wrexham Ct._ Lithonia, GA 30058

DOB: _8-20-55_ SEX _F_ HGT. _5'3"_ WGT. _129_ RACE _W_

EMPLOYER'S NAME: _Housewife_ Address _N/A_

PHONE NUMBER: (RESIDENCE) _978-1176_ (BUSINESS) _N/A_

STATEMENT TAKEN BY _Det. P.E. Warner_ DATE _8/25/89_ TIME _3:14 pm_

I had total blocked out memory of any physical contact w/ my dad from birth up to age 14. During psychiatric treatment (in-house) this summer, some memories began to come to the surface, and others since then, in the following age sequence:

Toddler (age 2-3) I was alone w/ dad in our house. He bent over w/ ass facing me & told me to "lick it". I then licked his anus. I have memory of the physical sensation.

Same age — I was again alone w/ him, he told me to pull my panties down. I did. Was then naked, standing in front of him.

Age 4 — dad & his brother raped me in a field away from a house. I was laid on a folding card table when they did it. Dad said nothing, just walked away when it was over. I cried, but told no one, just pretended I was "carsick" on the trip home. I cannot remember all the details of the rape itself.

Age 6 — full memory incl. physical sensation — I was laying on bathroom tiled floor at night (unfamiliar) because bedroom was too hot. Dad came in & picked me up & put me on my bed & then raped me. I felt awful, cried myself to sleep. This is my strongest & complete memory. It was done in complete silence.
_____

MY HANDWRITTEN STATEMENT GIVEN TO A DEKALB COUNTY, GA DETECTIVE, 08/25/89

D 248 /PG. 349 /S. N/C
CRIMINAL WARRANT

No. 297326

MAGISTRATE COURT
DEKALB COUNTY, GEORGIA

THE STATE
vs.

WILLIAM THOMAS SHTRK

Race: M Age: 65 Sex: M Ht: 6' Wt: 172
Hair DOB SSa
BRN 02-08-30 246-52-240120
Auto Tag

Charge: Child Molestation

O.C.G.A. Sec. 16-6-4

Prosecutor: DET. P.E. WEAVER

Agent for: DKPD
SEX CRIMES

Address: 294-2574

Phone: 294-2574

Attorney:

Phone:

Address
Home 3097 B PACK RD ATL
3125 S FLOWER RD.
ATLANTA
Work ATLT 20000 165'
Norcross, Ga

Bond:

STATE OF GEORGIA, DEKALB COUNTY:

Personally appeared the undersigned prosecutor, who being sworn on oath says that to the best of prosecutor's knowledge

and belief, the defendant herein, WILLIAM THOMAS SHTRK _____ at _____ m.,

7th or 8th day of AUGUST _____ 198 9 , in DeKalb County, Georgia, did commit the

offense of Child Molestation

at 2730 BRAITHWOD _____ Rd. ATLANTA _____ , DeKalb County, Georgia, for that defendant did (lot)

commit an immoral or indecent act to or in the presence of ████████

a child under the age of 14 years with the intent to arouse or satisfy

the sexual desires of either the child or himself/ ████ :

in violation of O.C.G.A. Sec. 16-6-4 _____ , and prosecutor makes this affidavit that a warrant may issue

for defendant's arrest.

P.E. WEAVER

PROSECUTOR

89-279618

Sworn to and subscribed before me this

26 day of AUG _____ 198 9

W. P. TROTH

Judge, Magistrate Court of DeKalb County

STATE OF GEORGIA, DEKALB COUNTY

To the Chief of Police of DeKalb County, any Policeman thereof, and to any Sheriff, Deputy Sheriff, Coroner, Constable, Marshal or
Law Enforcement Officer of Said State, authorized to execute warrants, GREETING:

For sufficient cause made known to me in the above affidavit, incorporated by reference herein, and other sworn testimony said
establishing probable cause for arrest of the accused you are hereby commanded to arrest the defendant named in the foregoing affidavit
charged by the prosecutor therein with the offense against the laws of this State named in said affidavit and bring him before me or some
other judicial officer of this State to be dealt with as the law directs. HEREIN FAIL NOT.

This 26 day of AUG _____ , 198 9

W. P. TROTH

TO: DET. P.E. WEAVER _____ Judge, Magistrate Court of DeKalb County

---

HEARING RESET

Date: _____ , 198

Time: _____ a.m. _____ p.m.

Place: Room 132, Magistrate Court

Peace Subpoena:

Remarks:

Defense Counsel:

Address:

Phone:

Appoint Public Defender Yes( ) No( )

Date:

Judge:

Tape No.

DAD'S ARREST WARRANT, 8/26/89

CERTIFICATE OF DEATH/STATE OF GEORGIA

Birth Number

Local File Number **00099**

State File Number

DECEDENT'S NAME (First, Middle, Last)			IF DECEDENT IS FEMALE, ENTER MAIDEN LAST NAME	SEX	DATE OF DEATH (Mo., Day, Year)
WILLIAM THOMAS SHIRK, SR.				MALE	JANUARY 10, 1990

RACE (White, Black, Amer. Indian, etc.) (Specify)	ORIGIN OF DECEDENT (Italian, Mex., Cuban, etc.) French, English, etc.)	DATE OF BIRTH (Mo., Day, Year)	AGE-Last Birthday	UNDER 1 YEAR	UNDER 1 DAY	COUNTY OF DEATH
White	American	June 8, 1930	59	Mos. Days	Hours Min.	DeKalb

CITY, TOWN OR LOCATION OF DEATH	HOSPITAL OR OTHER INSTITUTION NAME (If not in either, give street and no.)	IF HOSPITAL OR INST. (Specify) DOA	
TUCKER	NORTHLAKE REGIONAL MEDICAL CENTER	DOA	

STATE AND COUNTY OF BIRTH (If not in USA, name Country)	CITIZEN OF WHAT COUNTRY?	MARRIED, NEVER MARRIED, WIDOWED, DIVORCED (Specify)	SPOUSE (If married give name, give maiden name)	WAS DECEDENT EVER IN U.S. ARMED FORCES (Yes or No)?
Berks Co. Pa.	USA	Married		Yes

SOCIAL SECURITY NUMBER	USUAL OCCUPATION (Give kind of work done during most of working life, even if retired)	KIND OF INDUSTRY OR BUSINESS	
165-24-4150	Engineer	American Telephone & Telegraph	

RESIDENCE - STATE	COUNTY	CITY, TOWN or LOCATION	STREET AND NUMBER	INSIDE CITY LIMITS (Yes or No)
Georgia	DeKalb	Chamblee	3097-B Flowers Road	No

PARENTS

FATHER'S NAME First Middle Last	MOTHER'S MAIDEN NAME First Middle Last
Thomas Shirk	Edith Strunk

INFORMANT

INFORMANT'S NAME First Middle Last	MAILING ADDRESS (Street, R.F.D. No. City or Town, State, Zip)	RELATIONSHIP
Mrs. Shirk	Rd, N.E. Atlanta, Ga. 30345	Wife

DISPOSITION

BURIAL, CREMATION, REMOVAL (Specify)	DISPOSITION DATE (Mo., Day, Year)	CEMETERY OR CREMATORY NAME	LOCATION (City or Town State, Zip, County)
Cremation	Jan. 12, 1990	Atlanta Crematory	Atlanta, Fulton, Georgia

FUNERAL DIRECTOR (Signature)	FUN. DIR. LICENSE NO.	NAME AND ADDRESS OF FACILITY (Street, R.F.D. No., City or Town, State, Zip)	EST. LICENSE NO.
Fred C. Turner	2775	A. S. Turner & Sons	21
EMBALMER (Signature)	EMBALMER LICENSE NO.	P. O. Box 430	
James M. Watt	2739	Decatur, Georgia 30031	

CAUSE OF DEATH

PART I	IMMEDIATE CAUSE	(Enter only one cause per line for A, B and C)	Approximate interval between onset and death
	a. SEQUELAE OF CARBON MONOXIDE POISONING		
	Due to, or as a consequence of:		
	b.		Approximate interval between onset and death
	Due to, or as a consequence of:		
	c.		Approximate interval between onset and death

PART II	OTHER SIGNIFICANT CONDITIONS - Conditions contributing to death but not related to cause given in Part I A	AUTOPSY (Yes or No)	IF YES WERE FINDINGS CONSIDERED IN DETERMINING CAUSE OF DEATH (Yes or No)
	(If female, indicate if pregnant or post deceased within 90 days of death.)	YES	YES

WAS OPERATION PERFORMED? (Yes or No)	DATE OF OPERATION (Mo., Day, Year)	CONDITIONS FOR WHICH OPERATION WAS PERFORMED (Specify)
NO		

ACCIDENT, SUICIDE, HOMICIDE, UNDETERMINED (Specify)	DATE OF INJURY (Mo., Day, Year)	DESCRIBE HOW INJURY OCCURRED	HOUR OF INJURY
SUICIDE	01/10/90	Inhalation of auto exhaust fumes.	unk.

INJURY AT WORK (Yes or No)	PLACE OF INJURY (Home, Farm, Street, Factory, Office, Etc.)(Specify)	LOCATION (Street, R.F.D. No. City or Town State Zip County)
NO	HOME (Garage)	3097 B Flowers Rd, South, Atlanta, GA, Dekalb C

CERTIFIER / TYPE OR PRINT

To the best of my knowledge, death occurred at the time, date and place and due to the cause(s) stated (Signature and Title)	DATE SIGNED (Mo., Day, Year)	HOUR OF DEATH
		M

On the basis of examination and/or investigation, in my opinion death occurred at the time, date and place and due to the cause(s) stated (Signature and Title)	DATE SIGNED (Mo., Day, Year)	HOUR OF DEATH
Wayne K. Ross	January 18, 1990	unk. M

NAME OF ATTENDING PHYSICIAN IF OTHER THAN CERTIFIER	DATE PRONOUNCED DEAD (Mo., Day, Year)	HOUR PRONOUNCED DEAD
	on JANUARY 10, 1990	at 12:40 PM

NAME AND TITLE OF CERTIFIER (Physician, Medical Examiner, or Coroner)	ADDRESS OF CERTIFIER (Street, R.F.D. No., City or Town, State, Zip)
WAYNE K. ROSS, M.D., M.E.	4285-C Memorial Drive, Decatur, GA. 30032

REGISTRAR

REGISTRAR (Signature)	DATE RECEIVED BY REGISTRAR
Wanda Stone	JAN 22 1990

Form 3903 (Rev. 1-89) GEORGIA DEPARTMENT OF HUMAN RESOURCES/VITAL RECORDS SERVICE

DO NOT FOLD THIS CERTIFICATE

"CERTIFICATE OF RECORD"

"THIS IS AN EXACT COPY OF THE DEATH CERTIFICATE RECEIVED FOR FILING IN DEKALB COUNTY".

(VOID WITHOUT ORIGINAL SIGNATURE AND IMPRESSED SEAL)

COUNTY CUSTODIAN _Wanda Stone_

ISSUED BY _____ DATE _____

DAD'S DEATH CERTIFICATE, JANUARY 1990

Deposition for Jim Avila
investigators of Gwinnett Co
DA, GA 5/23/90

INTERVIEW WITH KATHLEEN SULLIVAN

On May 23, 1990 at approximately 2:00 P.M. Ms. Sullivan gave the following information to ▮▮▮▮.

My dad was the leader of a satanic cult in the area of Reading Pennsylvania. We lived in Reiffton. This begin when I was approximately 8 to 13 years of age, about 1963 to 1969. I witnessed weekly meetings on Friday nights where I saw both adults and children murdered, mutilated, dismembered. They also did a lot of pedophile rituals with boys who were not physically cut or hurt (only sexually related). I don't remember yet if my mother was present but she must have been. ▮▮▮▮ were used during these rituals also. I do remember that during the 64 Worlds Fair in New York City my dad took me to some kind of special meeting where it seemed to be either a national or international gathering of pedophiles who were involved in sadism. I watched as they demonstrated rubbing a penis on the private parts of a baby and later saw approximately fifteen dead babies laid out on the floor. A woman took me by the hand and told me it was just my imagination. I believe that by what I saw there may have been some representatives from the Maffia there due to the way they were dressed and their skin coloring and the power that they obviously had over the group. We also moved to Cockeysville, Maryland when I was fourteen. I do not remember any events that occurred after that time relating to satanic activities. ▮▮▮▮ contacted me last night and believes that my dad has involved ▮▮▮▮ from ▮▮▮▮. She will be in satanic activities in or near the Atlanta area.

contacting a ▮▮▮▮ Mr. J. Tom Morgan has some information on my dad's pedaphile activities.

I will related other things as they are remembered to Stan Hall of the District Attorney's Office. At this time I am unsure of who to trust in relating information ▮▮▮▮.

I now reside at 4321 Wrexham Court - Lithonia, Georgia 30058 Phone #978-1176.

Kathleen Sullivan

TRANSCRIPT OF STATEMENT I GAVE AT THE GWINNETT COUNTY, GA DISTRICT ATTORNEY'S OFFICE, 5/23/90

Fahrenheit°

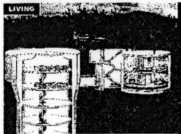

LIVING

GOING UNDERGROUND
FEARING THE WORST, REAL ESTATE TAKES A DIVE

In times of crisis, we have a tendency to tighten our belts and hunker down. Or, in the case of 20th Century Castles, a property consultancy in tiny Dover, Kansas, *bunker down* might be the more appropriate phrase. Ed Peden, who founded the company, specializes in selling decommissioned missile silos from the Cold War. He bought one in 1983, cleaned out the junk and eventually rehabbed it into a 5,000-square-foot, very high ceilinged home, with 13,000 square feet of secure closet space to boot. Peden has since sold twenty-eight Atlas E, Atlas F and Titan I missile sites over the years, at least five of which have been turned into private residences. He currently represents nine sites (www.missilebases.com).

HERE'S WHAT YOU'LL GET FOR...

$133,000
The perfect starter silo for the handy family. Located in Cresta, Oklahoma, this twenty-two-acre site features an Atlas F silo, an old-fashioned Quonset hut, two ponds and its own high chain-link fence. Needs work.

$575,000
A central-Kansas silo home featuring 2,400 square feet of underground steel-stud luxury. It comes equipped with satellite TV, three baths, a whirlpool and a commanding view from a hilltop entry point. Your mother-in-law will love the property's surface-level domed concrete studio apartment.

$1 MILLION
An Atlas E command center, comprising 15,000 square feet of refurbished living space in Wamego, Kansas. The 4,000-square-foot living area features a marble bath, a domed four-head shower room, a sauna and a hot tub. Twenty-two surrounding acres dotted with fruit and nut trees can supplement your diet of freeze-dried food.

$1.7 MILLION
A luxury silo getaway, *shown above*, bordering scenic Saranac Lake in New York's Adirondack Park. A private airstrip leads to a cedar-sided mountain lodge set atop what is perhaps the country's most thoroughly overhauled Atlas F site. Above ground sits 2,000 square feet of rugged luxury. Below, the command center has been transformed into a two-story three-bedroom home with limestone bathrooms lit by fiber optics. The government spent more than $14 million to build it in 1958; you can have it for nearly one-tenth the price. —STEPHEN P. WILLIAMS

MISSILE SILO DIAGRAM IN DECEMBER 2001 ISSUE OF GQ MAGAZINE

DAD POSING WITH GUNS, EARLY 1950S

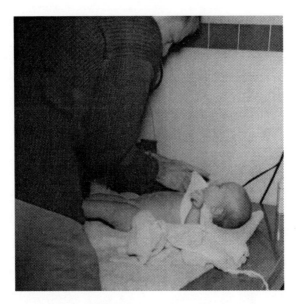

DAD CHANGING MY DIAPER, 1955

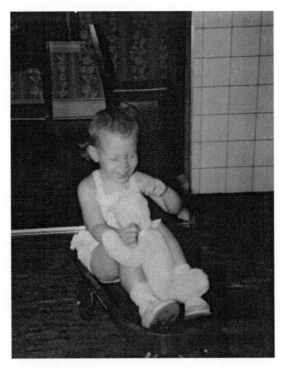

STILL ABLE TO RELAX AND REALLY SMILE, 1957

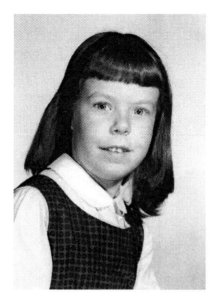

SCHOOL PHOTO – IN FULL TRANCE STATE, UNDATED

DAD IN HIS CROSS-COUNTRY TRACK OUTFIT, 1962

DAD (FAR RIGHT) LIP-SYNCING WITH "MAGGOTS"
ROCK-AND-ROLL BAND, LATE 1960s

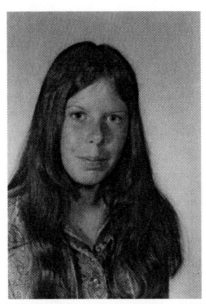

SCHOOL PHOTO–MATURE, SECRETIVE ALTER-STATE, 1971

**HOME PHOTO – CHILD ALTER-STATE HOLDING KOALA BEAR
FROM DAD, 1971**

HOLDING ROSE SEVERAL DAYS AFTER HER BIRTH, 7/74

DAD AT WORK, 1986

RELIGIOUS PROGRAMMED ALTER-STATE HUNTING FOR
EASTER EGGS NEAR MOTHER'S HOME, SPRING, 1989

IN THE PARC-VRAMC LIVING MEMORIAL GARDEN, SPRING, 2000

Connections

Bill's Past

My husband, Bill has a long military history that contributed to his need to control or be controlled. In 1978, after 30 years in the US Army, he retired as a Sergeant Major. During his last two years of service, he was a ROTC instructor at the University of Georgia in Athens. During previous active duty, he'd served in the 11th Airborne Division, the Airborne 187th RCT, the 82nd Airborne Division, the 101st Airborne Division, and the 173rd Airborne Brigade.

A master parachutist, Bill had successfully completed over 300 parachute jumps–which, VA doctors later told him, had led to his spinal deterioration. Beginning in 1991, he had five operations on his spine.

During one of his three tours of duty in South Vietnam, Bill served as an intelligence analyst and interrogator.[1] He served a total of fifty-one months of front-line ground combat in Korea and Vietnam. His medals and commendations include a Purple Heart; Silver Star; four Bronze Stars (one for valor); three Army Commendation Medals (one for valor); two Meritorious Service Medals; an Air Medal; and four Army Commendation Medals (one for valor).[2]

As memories of Bill's covert military experiences emerged in therapy and then at home, I was alarmed by how often he said, "The Army is my mother and my father." Couldn't he see how he'd been used–putting his life at risk again and again? Why wasn't he angry? Even though he'd been retired for more than a decade, his loyalty to the Army was still strong. I couldn't understand: why wouldn't he accept that that part of his life was over?

As Bill retrieved more buried memories and emotions, I learned why he was so dissociated. Not only had he been traumatized in Korea and Vietnam, and been severely abused by his stepfather for years; he had also lost most of his family. (Bill is the second youngest out of fifteen children; as of this book's publication date, only one other remains.) Perhaps worst of all, his father had died when he was a toddler and then, after Bill had joined the Army at the still-tender age of fifteen, his mother–who he says was his "whole world"–had died two years later, leaving him a homeless orphan still too young to vote.

Because of the terrible cumulative grief of losing so many loved ones, and the traumas he'd endured at home and during wartime in Korea and Vietnam, he could only feel and express his emerging emotions a tiny bit at a time. Like me, he had PTSD and needed to learn constructive ways to express and control his anger.

I told Therese that sometimes I felt as if an impenetrable steel vault door was inside Bill's mind. Although I yearned for deeper communication with my husband, I believed he was incapable of it. I decided to give myself some time to choose whether or not I would stay in that kind of marriage. After a couple of months of grieving what could have been between us (had we not both been so damned wounded), I decided to stay.

Once in a while, I wondered if Bill still had orders from ASA to handle me. Although I was afraid to talk to him about this–he was so secretive about his intelligence connections–I needed to know. On two occasions, once in Atlanta and again in Chattanooga, I talked with Bill about his ASA connections. He grudgingly allowed me to tape-record each conversation. One of his ASA alter-states told me that his contacts were waiting for me to "clear out the cobwebs" in my mind. That alter-state indicated that he was tired of being used by the ASA. He said he wanted to retire all the way. I was elated because this meant I could finally help Bill to free himself from his own handlers.

Using the techniques I'd developed over the years in identifying my local handlers, I helped Bill to analyze the behaviors of people in his own life, including some of his relatives who lived in Fayetteville, North Carolina–most of them had worked for the government, mostly within the military with at least one (a brother-in-law) within the CIA.[3]

Bill's therapist and I worked hard to teach Bill how to set healthy mental and emotional boundaries with the people in his life. He made a pleasant new discovery: he has the right to feel anger towards anyone who disrespects his personal rights and freedoms. That includes me.

One by one, Bill recognized and broke free from his most obvious handlers. He did this by assessing their odd and controlling behaviors, triggering phrases, government connections, and lack of emotional affect. Each time Bill identified one and quietly stopped accepting the handler's orders, the handler's personality suddenly changed and he or she expressed an unusual amount of anger and frustration towards Bill.

Then the handler tried–for a while–to regain control. Such behaviors verified to Bill that these people were controllers and not the friends they'd claimed to be.[4]

To protect us further, I wrote to all the journalists and authors with whom I had contact, giving them local handlers' names and addresses. I didn't care if the handlers were from the CIA, the ASA or the Aryan network. Good guys, bad guys, or both, it didn't matter anymore–*no one had the right to manipulate our minds!*[5]

As we continued the weeding-out process, I realized why, whenever I'd come home later than planned, Bill had switched and gone into a dark mood. Each time, he'd made cruel, unfounded accusations that wounded me. During one of our "ASA talks," an alter-state emerged and said he'd feared that while I was away from home, I'd be re-accessed by someone from the Aryan cult.

Then that part explained why Bill's "William" alter-state refused to come out and talk to me. William had been forced to watch me having sex with other men in the cult, even after we'd married. That was J.C.'s primary method of ensuring that all members' first loyalty remained with him. William hadn't known that J.C. had triggered out alter-states in me that hadn't been aware that they were married to William/Bill, and had therefore felt no obligation to be faithful to him! (Some of them had even thought they were still married to Albert.)

My heart breaks when I think of what the sight and knowledge did to William. And yet, he never stopped fighting to free me. Love sometimes comes at a great price, but I believe it's always worth the experience.

I've learned the hard way that when one marries a severely dissociated person, one may not marry *all* of the partner. Some of the partner's alter-states may not like the idea of being married, and may choose not to emotionally bond. Some of Bill's alter-states may never choose to bond with me. For them, the covert world may always be more important than our marriage. That is another loss I've learned to grieve.

More Verifications

Although there are still times I don't want to believe my memories, staying in denial isn't a safe option. It can leave me open to being accessed and traumatized again.

In hospitals and at trauma survivor conferences, I received verifications from several ritual abuse and government mind-control survivors who recognized me as a figure from their pasts. Each person provided details to me about my alter-states and activities that I'd already journaled. In most cases, I was able to do the same for them–usually with a therapist present to carefully mediate between us.

A group of recovering survivors from J.C.'s Cobb County Aryan cult network, some of whom had never repressed their memories, have helped each other to build mental strength and stay safe. Through third parties, several of them directly verified numerous memories that I'd already documented, of specific cult activities and of several of the cult leaders' activities and personality quirks. Their verifications–sometimes in the form of documents–helped me to stay out of denial and stay safe.

Every survivor who recognized Bill as a past participant in Aryan meetings and rituals said they'd known him as William. (This was significant because William isn't part of his legal name, nor did he let people call him that, away from the gatherings.) They told me things about his William alter-state that I'd already independently remembered and journaled. They also identified pictures of several of my complicit relatives, accurately describing their unique personality quirks and bizarre behaviors.

I received numerous letters and documents that Dad had left behind in the house he'd shared with his second family. Sorting through them years after his death, my stepmother sent me anything that might be significant. I'm delighted that Dad's handlers hadn't known he'd left those papers behind. Some of them directly verified my memories. I'm lucky that way, because most mind-control survivors have no proofs at all.[6]

I was given the opportunity to review psychiatric and legal documents from some of Dad's other victims, with the understanding that what I learned would only be shared with hand-picked investigators and authors who I believed would honor their privacy. These verifications helped me to stay anchored in reality.

Between 1989 and 2002, I consulted with a succession of over twenty-one mental health professionals on either an in-patient (hospitalization) or out-patient (private practice) basis. Extensively tested more times than I can count, I consistently received the diagnoses of PTSD, delayed; Multiple Personality Disorder (which later changed to Dissociative Identity Disorder); and major depression—a partly genetic condition that is exacerbated by cumulative trauma or stress.

Only one time did I ever exhibit any psychotic features. This occurred at home. A memory emerged that was so unbearable, I had to escape from reality until I was able to go through it in the hospital (even then, it was unbearable). My psychotic belief at home was that it was perfectly all right to shoot myself in the head as I lay next to Bill, with the intent of making him feel the pain that a beloved op partner had put me through when he'd suicided in front of me. That was the extent of my psychosis.

One of the ways I knew I had a dissociative disorder (DID) was that, before I achieved the bulk of my integration, I could easily do several mental tasks at once. For instance, at night I would work on a crossword puzzle or read a book while holding a conversation with Bill and watching a movie on television. Multi-tasking is fairly easy for most dissociated trauma survivors.[7]

I discovered another proof in several sets of recurring dreams that I'd never forgotten. Because they'd been powerful and wouldn't go away, they'd troubled me for decades:

The first set of dreams began when I was very young. In them, I either rode a horse or straddled a large tree limb, my legs hanging down. As I rubbed my genitals on the limb or the horse, I had powerful orgasms. I believe those dreams were an indicator that as a child, I'd been addicted to orgasms. And I believe the tree limbs and horses represented my dad's penis. Although many children masturbate, my addiction to orgasms was abnormal because it was too much a part of my life.

Another dream lasted from childhood well into the 1990s. In it, I moved up through the air to the ceiling of a room. With my bare hands, I tore a hole in the wood and insulation, only to find another ceiling above it. I clawed a hole through that, to find another, and another. Each time I awoke, I felt hopeless and trapped. The message of this dream was that, no matter how many times I split off, I still could not escape.

In another kind of recurring dream, I tried to fly into the air by flapping my arms as wings. Sometimes I tried to fly as I jumped off a high, elevated place, attempting to soar over trees. In almost all of these dreams I was pursued by short-haired Caucasian men in dark suits who, running on the ground, eventually grabbed my feet because I'd lost altitude. Each time they pulled me down to them, I awoke full of unnamed dread.

In another kind of dream, Mom and Dad took me to a location in the countryside. Large lots, covered with weeds and grass, were flanked on one side by a wooded area full of hardwood trees. Each time, I walked through a patch of meadow with the woods and two white, clapboard houses to my far left. I always encountered a rectangular "pit" in the ground in front of me. It was full of water green with algae. Even though I never saw them, I was terrified of the alligators and snakes that lurked in the water, waiting to bite me.

Eventually I remembered that the location had been a real place where Dad had often taken me when I was young. Because the pit was full with green, murky water, I couldn't see what else was in it. As Dad forced me into the water each time, the grass and mud around the edges of the man-made pond made it impossible for me to get out. He said alligators and snakes lived in it. Terrified with no way out, I switched into a new alter-state that had *no* fear of alligators, snakes, or murky water. Noticing my lack of fear, Dad ordered that part to dive to the bottom and retrieve objects that he and several neatly groomed men in black suits threw into it.

Another kind of verification I had never forgotten occurred on two separate occasions. Each time, I responded in an odd way as my body was accidentally punctured.

The first time, I was walking with other students outside Reiffton Elementary School in the daytime, shortly before Halloween. As was our yearly custom, we came to school dressed in our Halloween costumes. The teachers led our classes in single rows to "parade" through our quiet neighborhood.

This time, a female teacher first made us stand in a line behind a brick building. I didn't notice that a railroad timber had been placed behind the brick wall. As I walked, I accidentally swung my foot into it. I was horrified when I looked down and saw a large splinter sticking out of my cloth-covered foot.

Paralyzed by the sight, all I could do was stay still as my classmates continued walking. The teacher finally came to investigate. When she saw the splinter, she laughed at me for being so upset. Yanking it out, she told me to hurry up and join the others. Although I did, I still felt so horrified, I was sick to my stomach.

The second event occurred shortly after I'd "graduated" from our local drill team. During the previous year, I had appeared at public gatherings and had marched in a wintertime parade in Reading with the other baton-twirling girls. This particular day, we were expected to turn in our uniforms at the nearby high school. Since our house was only a block away, I decided to walk down the hill to it.

I carried my uniform on a wire hanger, balancing the tip of the hook on the middle of my upturned palm. Then I tripped on the hem of the skirt, which pulled the tip of the hook into my fleshy palm. Transfixed and horrified, again I was unable to speak.

Then I pulled the hanger out, still staring at the hole in my palm. In a trance state, I carried the garment to the big brick building. A woman sat in front of a table heaped with uniforms. Speechless, I held my wounded palm out to her. When the woman laughed, I felt embarrassed.

All through my younger adult years, I had tremendous mood swings. Although I wanted to believe they were from hormonal fluctuations, they continued throughout each month. At home and at work, I often cried heavily for no reason. If I was at work, I usually hid in the bathroom and wept for about a half hour, then used gobs of cold, wet paper towels to make the red blotches go away.

Sometimes depression slammed me so hard at home, I could barely function. At other times, I felt tremendous rage and had to take long walks to work off the energy. Sometimes emotional pain hit so hard, it literally paralyzed me. For several years, I was so depressed, I often walked through cemeteries, wishing I was in the ground with the dead.

For nearly two decades, Mom diverted me from going to professionals for help by insisting that I had hypoglycemia (low blood sugar). She convinced me that all I needed to do was to read *Prevention Magazine* (a natural health publication) and avoid sugar. Because we'd been taught in The Walk that sugar was poisonous, I believed her. I grew so phobic towards sugar, I refused to eat anything that had even a trace in it. That made socializing difficult. When my mood swings didn't lessen in frequency or intensity, Mom insisted I was still eating something with sugar in it. I believed her and became even more phobic.

Before recovery, I preferred being alone. At work, I walked outside nearly every day, even during some of our coffee breaks. I couldn't stand to socialize with other employees unless it was after work, when I could have a couple of drinks at a nearby restaurant with them. Then it didn't matter.

This started to change when I worked at Cotton States. Several older women in my department invited me to eat with them each payday at the next-door Marriott Hotel's fancy restaurant. Whenever I ate with them, I felt an odd, bittersweet warmth in the center of my torso. I liked that feeling and wanted more of it. I didn't know that this was the feeling that came with emotionally connecting with others.

Recently I discovered the underlying cause of an odd behavior I've had for many years. I began to understand it when I remembered a series of childhood porn sessions in which Dad took pictures of me "having sex with" young boys from a YMCA Indian Guides group that he often hosted at our house in Reiffton. The porn sessions occurred during sleepovers in our basement. I was made to wear a buckskin Indian girl costume and the boys wore the same feathered headdresses that they sometimes donned during regular meetings. While the boys and I sexually interacted, he made another boy play a set of tom-toms that were also used during their regular meetings. During this trauma, I focused on the rhythm of the drumbeat to block out what was being done to us. Since then, whenever I felt overly stressed, that same rhythm played in my head.

When I was still a victim, because I had PTSD and was often sent on dangerous ops, I was often ill. Mom usually said I had a "24-hour virus" and I didn't need to consult with a doctor. Because I believed her, I always stayed in bed (if I could) until I felt better. Now that I don't do ops anymore, and I make sure I get enough sleep and keep my stress level down, I'm rarely ill.[8]

According to therapists and other trauma survivors, grinding one's teeth seems to be a common symptom of PTSD. Since I've started remembering, I've grinded mine so much, five of my back teeth have been capped. I especially grind them when I feel stressed. (Because of decades of forced oral sex, I cannot bear to wear a protective retainer.)

After my recovery started, I often flashbacked while driving. This was dangerous for me and anyone else on the road. Some emerging memories were so powerful, I parked on the side of the highway to weep or yell until the attached emotions ebbed. One day, after an especially intense therapy session, I left the office and drove on the wrong side of the road. As I pulled off the road, my heart racing and hands shaking, I thanked God that no other cars were on the road at that time.

One of my most prevalent fears has been of imminent doom and death–either mine or a loved one's. This is a common symptom of PTSD that was powerfully reinforced by the many deaths I witnessed or was forced to participate in.[9]

In the late 1990s, a neuropsychologist gave me a battery of tests. While reviewing the results with me and my therapist, he told us the results indicated I had an anxiety disorder "the size of Dallas." Although I was aware that I had at least several anxiety attacks each day (heart racing, non-stop fear and thoughts of bad things happening), the confirmation of my diagnosis depressed me. Was it that noticeable? Would I be stuck with it the rest of my life? I was so sick and tired of not being able to handle problems like other people, without overreacting!

It happened again in the summer of 2002 when Bill had a stroke–he called it an "explosion" in the left side of his brain. When he told me about the odd sensation, the cortisol level in my brain spiked and my body flooded with adrenaline. Wanting him to get help before it was too late, I drove up to 97 mph down the highway towards the hospital.[10]

The cortisol didn't lessen when he was in safe hands–that's one of the reasons why my anxiety disorder can be disabling. For several days, my body shook and I couldn't stop circular thoughts and fears from flooding my mind. I was hyper-alert and had difficulty sleeping. The anxiety seemed to have no end; it only stopped when I realized I needed to take anti-anxiety medication.

Another verification has been my difficulty in trusting and bonding with others–a direct result of decades of betrayal trauma. Emotional bonding is still a new experience, because trust doesn't come easy.[11]

Another reason I believe the bulk of my recovered memories were of real events is that not all of them were of serious traumas. Because I dissociated easily, I also suppressed memories of non-harmful events in which I'd felt strong fear, confusion, pain, or embarrassment.[12]

For instance, I recovered a childhood memory of standing outdoors one day with several other girls, not realizing that a large beetle had landed on the front of my blouse. My fear of the creature was enough to make me repress the entire memory!

I've also recovered a series of memories that I had repressed out of sheer embarrassment. Each time, I was left alone while my handler was in the next room, talking in a relaxed way to someone (we were between ops). Each time, needing to use the bathroom, I was so tranced, I mistook a chair for a toilet and peed on its seat. Whenever I saw my urine splash to the floor, I felt ashamed and tried to clean it up before anyone would notice.

One of my most powerful verifications recurred over a two year period. Whenever I power-walked in a mall near my therapist's office, and a man or woman walked towards me, one of two types of flashbacks occurred.

In the first type of flashback, I "saw" myself running at the person, grabbing their right wrist and arm with my hands, and then using my momentum to force the person's arm up and back, until I dislocated the victim's shoulder. In the other type of flashback, I grabbed an adult male's chin and hair and used one of several methods to "swivel-snap" his neck.

The strength I felt in my body and hands during each flashback was enormous. I knew I could do it right there, in the mall. To keep from doing it, I used self-talk, reminding myself that although I had the right and the need to remember, I did not have the right to hurt anyone.

For months, I didn't tell my therapist about these flashbacks. Ashamed, I believed she would despise me if I told her. How could I have done such horrible things to people? I felt like a monster! Was there no hope for me?

When I told her, I instantly became co-conscious with a highly trained male, black op alter-state.[13] As I took on that part's knowledge and memories, I learned that he felt irritated whenever he watched police or spy characters on TV that seemed inept. He had zero patience towards characters who gave up their guns to assailants to bargain for the lives of hostages. Each time, not understanding they were just actors, he yelled, "You *never* give up your gun! Shoot him!" (To Bill's great irritation, I've responded the same way ever since I blended with that part.)

I learned that the alter-state had survived similar situations by shooting hostage-takers, since the hostages' bodies could never fully hide the captors'. He'd also been trained to "read" opponents' facial expressions, body twitches, and vocal tones to know whether or not he had time to shoot first. He wasn't afraid to take a gun away from an opponent. He said that unless the opponent was also a professional, the opponent would be surprised and wouldn't think to shoot until it was too late. So far, this seems to have been my most highly trained black op alter-state.

Another verification was my occasional changes in handwriting along with my inability to see the changes. During the first twelve years of recovery, I felt frustrated because my handwriting didn't seem to change when different alter-states emerged–I'd read that handwriting changes were a way to determine if a person was severely dissociated.

In 2001, when I decided to take a year off from school to type all of my journals–a Herculean task–I was astounded to discover marked differences between several types of handwriting. I had been so dissociated, I hadn't been able to see what was literally in front of my eyes! Recently, I've been able to feel peace and stability. I love it! My mood swings are nearly gone. I don't have as many crying jags. My old, pent-up rage has decreased to a manageable level of righteous indignation and occasional frustration. The emotional pain has also lessened.

I still have days when more unresolved grief emerges. When this occurs, I give myself permission to have "bummy days" in which I don't shower or brush my teeth or get dressed. I let myself fully feel my grief, knowing that this is the only way to really heal. Then I get on with my life.

These and other experiences have convinced me that I was a trauma survivor, that I was severely dissociated, and that the majority of my retrieved memories were of real events.

Reaching Out

In the 1990s, I sent packages of information about my remembered history to journalists and authors who wrote about ritual abuse, government-sponsored abuses, and mind control. I wanted more proofs to help me stay anchored in reality, and I hoped that if I shared information from my life with these people, they might tell me where I could find further verification.

One of the authors was writing a new book about the connections between occult ritual abuse and government mind-control programming. I sent him a packet of information that included copies of my 1991 systems maps. With my permission, he included some of the information in his new book. When I reviewed it, I felt frightened: would former handlers recognize my information and retaliate against me for "talking?"

The more I allowed authors to include my information in their books, the more I felt afraid. Numerous handlers had previously threatened that if I "talked," either I or a loved one would be killed. Since they'd used me and other slaves to kill for them, what would stop them from sending a slave-operative to do the same to me?

I constantly balanced my need for support and protection against my need to avoid upsetting former handlers and owners. I never knew whether I was talking too much or not enough. Although Bill supported my going public, he didn't understand the fear and anxiety that wracked my body and mind every single day.

Notes

1. In the mid 1990s, I met an alter-state that Bill had unconsciously created in childhood when he was severely abused by his stepfather. This part of Bill had compartmentalized his powerful rage towards the man. In Vietnam, as part of the CIA's Operation Phoenix, this alter-state had been used to transfer that old rage onto male prisoners via brutal interrogations and torture. Bill was horrified when he discovered this alter-state, which had tortured men with great zeal.

2. To this day, Bill prefers not to talk about why he received several of the medals. This is, in part, because he has very little memory of those heroic acts.

3. In the electronic version of his 2002 book, *Mindfield*, Gordon Thomas stated that in 1954, the CIA's "field training school" was located in Fayetteville, North Carolina. (pg. 15) *Mindfield* explores the issues of biochemical weaponry and mind-control technology. For more information, you can visit Thomas's website at http://www.gordonthomas.ie.

4. Incapable of bonding with and trusting others, we'd both developed pseudo-friendships with our handlers, not understanding that they weren't real friendships.

5. When individuals who are inappropriately controlled by family members or partners begin to think for themselves and to break free, the controllers will often accuse others (such as therapists) in the victims' lives of brainwashing the victims and turning the victims against them. I believe that such claims indicate the complainants are control addicts and possibly abusers. For whatever bizarre reason, abusive controllers seem incapable of comprehending that their victims have the strength, intelligence, and ability to make their own life-decisions.

6. To ensure that I didn't keep any proofs, I was conditioned to occasionally throw away every item I owned, other than the clothes in my closet. I was programmed to believe that each time I did this, I was getting rid of demons from my past that were attached to those personal items. For this reason, I do not have access to my childhood records. All I have from before my marriage to Bill are photos that several family members had since given me.

7. "... individuals who are high dissociators have developed ways to cope in life that allow for their dissociation without apparent problems under many circumstances. This lack of integration of experiences, memories, and thoughts creates an environment that requires constant divided attention. Individuals who habitually dissociate

information may come to be best able to function in multi-tasking, divided attention, divided control structure environments." (Freyd and DePrince, pg. 157)

8. According to the National Institute of Mental Health's website article, "Stress and the Developing Brain," "Cortisol and other stress hormones . . . temporarily suppress the immune response." (pg. 1)

9. To learn more about PTSD, you can visit the US Veterans Affairs National Center for PTSD website at http://www.ncptsd.org or call their PTSD Information Line at 1-802-296-6300.

10. During anxiety attacks, my brain has too much energy and I literally cannot stop thinking and obsessing about either what had gone wrong or, more likely, what *could* go wrong. This is why anti-anxiety medication is helpful for me: it reduces the level of cortisol in my brain so that I relax and stop worrying about possibilities that probably won't ever occur!

> Cortisol secretion increases in response to any stress in the body, whether physical (such as illness, trauma, surgery, or temperature extremes) or psychological. When cortisol is secreted, it causes a breakdown of muscle protein, leading to the release of amino acids . . . into the bloodstream. These amino acids are then used by the liver to synthesize glucose . . . [raising] the blood sugar level so the brain will have more glucose for energy." (Stoppler, pg. 1)

11. Dr. Jennifer J. Freyd's *Betrayal Trauma: The Logic of Forgetting Childhood Abuse*, thoroughly addresses this issue. Dr. Freyd is the daughter of Pamela Freyd, Ph.D., the FMSF's executive director and one of its primary founders.

12. Carla Emery explained the relationship between dissociation, amnesia, and hypnotic suggestibility: "In dissociation amnesia, you are not told to forget. You just do. It is a spontaneous, natural result of being in a very deep trance. However, the deeper you are, the more responsive you are to suggestion." (pg. 229)

13. Co-consciousness between two alter-states can feel like having two heads on one set of shoulders. This temporary condition can be disorienting and frustrating–not only for the survivor, but also for others interacting with the survivor. The effects lessen as the two alter-states fuse into one new, fuller alter-state. Family therapy can be especially helpful during this phase of recovery.

**BILL SULLIVAN AS FIRST COMMANDANT OF THE US ARMY'S
NCO RETRAINING AND RECLASSIFICATION ACADEMY,
FORT CAMPBELL KENTUCKY, 1976**

"Good Guy" Perpetrators

The Luciferian

Part of my preparation to go public was to decide whether or not I would name some of the men who had owned me and/or had used me to perform crimes for them. Although several mind-control survivors (e.g., Cathy O'Brien and Sue Ford A.K.A. Brice Taylor) did this in the past, I was reluctant to follow their lead for several reasons.

First, I don't know of any well-known figure who doesn't have ardent fans. Idolatry is part of being human; many people are too willing to buy into the polished public personas of people who may actually be wicked in their private lives.

In one radio interview and in subsequent interviews with several journalists, I did mention two well-known politicians who I believe had hurt and used me–in controlled alter-states–to perform criminal activities for them and others. One of them is a former CIA director. Soon after I went public on the radio program, I was re-traumatized. That experience forced me to re-think my desire to name perpetrators. I'd named the men so that, if I or a loved one was harmed, at least some people would have an idea of who might have been responsible. But after the assault, I realized I would only be harming myself by continuing to name them.

Beside the fact that they and each of their criminal associates are idolized to some degree, they also have an enormous number of influential contacts—particularly in the media and political arenas—and are also regularly advised by public relations professionals who teach them how to look good and be believable as "good guys."[1] How in the world could I, with my limited resources, convince anyone that these wealthy, well-connected men had hurt me and used me to perform crimes for them?

I finally found peace in my belief that regardless of how much they get away with in this life, they'll have to answer for their choices someday— in the next life, if not in this one. That keeps me sane and gives me hope that justice does come around—just not when I'd like it to.

The men I named are only two out of perhaps thousands of mind-control perpetrators currently operating in the United States. These men and women comprise an extensive covert population.

I will call one of them, an elder statesman, Lucian. A master hypnotist, Lucian was a flaming pedophile when I was a child, and probably still is. When I was a teenager, Dad–in a trade for certain favors–gave Lucian ownership of several of my alter-states, including one named Sasha. Lucian was an odd character, in that although he pretends to be a practicing Jew, he is really a behind-the-scenes Luciferian who doesn't mind mixing and mingling with staunch Aryans.

Over the years, Lucian taught me his Luciferian beliefs and told me about his involvement in Lucis Trust, an organization that he said was based on Luciferianism. He taught me that the sun, which he called Ra, was their God.[2]

He also taught me that Lucifer was the true son of God, and that Jesus Christ was the usurper. He said that one of the primary goals of Lucis Trust was to bring Lucifer back into his rightful position before God.

True or not, Lucian told me that Lucis Trust planned to make a man called "Lord Maitreya" their representative to the world, to attract and indoctrinate the masses into the Luciferians' planned world religion (as part of their Aryan-Greco-Roman-Egyptian "New World Order"). Lucian said the Lucis Trust would convince Christians that Maitreya was the reincarnated Messiah, returned to earth.[3]

Lucian taught several of my alter-states that he and his fellow worshippers were being kept in spiritual darkness along with Lucifer, who took on the persona of the dark lord, Satan, when Jesus Christ stole the light from him. He said that Lucifer was being kept in darkness against his will by Christians who worshipped Jesus Christ, whom he called "the liar." He said that Jesus had faked his own death and resurrection to make him appear to be God's son.

Lucian and his associates said that some day, they will all rise up as one. By subjugating all Christians, they would free Lucifer from the darkness and restore him to his rightful position as the true son of God. Lucian said that then and only then would Ra's worshippers live in the light forever, favored by Lucifer, eventually also becoming gods.

He explained that some Luciferians had already passed on and became gods. He called them "Ascended Masters." He convinced me that some devotees are able to "channel" the Masters in occult rituals.[4]

Lucian despised Christian politicians, and enjoyed blackmailing them–sometimes using me and other Beta-programmed slaves to sexually compromise them. When these Christians fell, he called them hypocrites. He didn't seem to understand that being a Christian doesn't guarantee that one will never sin again; it just means that one is expected to do one's best as a follower of Christ.[5]

Over the years, I accompanied Lucian to international Golden Dawn meetings, where he and other influential men and women–many of them also members of the Illuminati–participated in rituals in which they worshipped not only Ra, but also a myriad of other gods and goddesses that included Diana, Isis, and Gaia, goddess of the earth.

At these meetings they expressed pro-Aryan beliefs, including the denigration of "inferior" races. And yet, oddly, they occasionally invited "token" black politicians and their wives to participate in rituals–perhaps to enlist their support.

Lucian and other Golden Dawn members instilled their belief systems in a succession of my alter-states that came out only at Golden Dawn gatherings, including an alter-state named Gaia.

In 1993, I learned about a daytime, all-female Golden Dawn ritual that I'd been taken to as an adult. It was held in Atlanta, Georgia in what seemed to be a white, chilly greenhouse. Made of stone, it was behind an imposing mansion. A cult-conditioned child alter-state named Laurie Ann emerged and wrote about her experience there:

> *After ritual chanting, I took my seat, cross-legged in the middle of the sun on the floor. We all just sat and waited. There was a gold circle around the tips of the sun rays–they called it the rainbow. Women took turns speaking, positioning themselves on the circle–some of them started "channeling" and giving messages of encouragement and power from the gods.*
>
> *The light in the room got brighter and brighter and we felt it fall on our faces and skin, like a mist. We all were happy and we celebrated and felt better. The golden sun mist was like radioactive energy that our skin absorbed.[6] And we didn't need our body as much. And no one wanted to eat or have sex. But we did get sleepy. And they would give us glasses of liquid sun rays to drink. It shone with a bright fluorescent yellow glow in the dark.*

Another alter-state explained that this thick liquid was called the "Elixir of Life." It was actually human semen that had been processed in advance, to eliminate the transmission of any diseases.[7]

> *They liked to discuss philosophy. They would enjoy the light, and read poems to the gods. It was "Ode to this" and "Ode to that." They liked Greek statues, white ones, and water fountains and pools of water and lots and lots of flowers, in white stone vases. They liked to inhale the smell of fresh flowers in the room. Especially the long ones with rows of brilliant flowers on them–purple and red and yellow.*

> *Some of the wives of powerful politicians occasionally joined us in the rituals. Except for me, they all wore white robes with long sleeves and sandals and gold belts. No makeup was allowed. Long hair had to be worn down. Purity and simplicity. Oneness with nature. They were called acolytes.*

> *Lucian had told me they were willing to be sacrificed if they were chosen (by any of the gods, but especially Zeus). Not their children–themselves! I believed him, and was impressed by their level of devotion to the deities they worshipped.*

> *After the rituals, everyone was peaceful and gentle, and no one wanted to talk much.*

One of the reasons Lucian took me with him to international Golden Dawn meetings was that he triggered out an alter-state that heard everything that was said and later recited it verbatim, upon Lucian's command.[8] At some of their planning meetings, Lucian and other leaders discussed their goal of developing a one-world religion that would incorporate all religions. They said that Judaism and Christianity would be welcome at the beginning, but would eventually be outlawed. Although some members didn't seem to approve, Lucian and some of his friends also discussed their intention to legalize adult-child sex.

When I told a number of investigative journalists about this man's Luciferian beliefs and his involvement in both the Illuminati and the Golden Dawn, I received no verifications. That left me wondering if I'd somehow made it all up! I was about to give up on these memories when I purchased a book by Texe Marrs, a right-wing Christian author. Although I do not approve of some of his spiritualized fear tactics, I did find verifications in his *Book of New Age Cults & Religions*. In a nine-page chapter about Lucis Trust, he included the names of Lucian and several other politicians I'd remembered meeting at the secretive Golden Dawn and Illuminati gatherings. Marrs explained the connection between Lucis Trust and Luciferianism:

> The word "lucis" comes directly from the name Lucifer, which means "light bearer" or "the one who brings light" . . . when the Lucis Trust first began, founded by Alice Bailey, it was called *Lucifer Publishing!* It was incorporated in 1922, however, under its present name . . . the Lucis Trust defines its purpose as that of establishing a "New World Order." (pp. 238–239)

I was alarmed by what I read, because if my memories of these people were real, then I was in danger! Some of them still have enormous clout; I could imagine them squishing me like a bug on a sidewalk if they thought I posed a problem. My anxiety nearly went through the roof. After several days, I calmed down enough to realize that people like Lucian are so grandiose and narcissistic, they probably wouldn't care if I told what I knew about them.

As time went on, I also remembered enough to realize that although Lucian had used his political positions to hurt me and others, he was still just one individual, and part of a fringe minority at that. I suspect most of the participants in these secretive rituals were not blatant pedophiles, nor were they part of an evil conspiracy to rule the world and stomp out anyone who opposed them.

This knowledge has been important, because it has helped me to become less fearful of non-criminal Pagans and practitioners of other "alternative" religions.

Dr. J

Not all of the "good guy" perpetrators I remembered were influential politicians or wealthy businessmen. I was horrified to learn that several had been CIA-contracted psychiatrists who had been directly involved in MKULTRA![9] In my early recovery, I reconnected with one of them, Dr. J, in an odd way.

During his nationally televised daytime talk show that aired on March 5, 1993, Phil Donahue interviewed an elderly couple who had been accused of ritually abusing their grandchildren. I took notes as I watched the program. Donahue seemed to side with the accused couple. He even described them as being "Norman Rockwell" grandparents.

Using phrases that would soon be extensively promoted as "fact" by spokespersons from the False Memory Syndrome Foundation, an invited guest, Dr. Richard Gardner, suggested that what was being done to the grandparents was a "witch hunt." He said the grandchildren had been "programmed" to remember. He called the professionals who had helped protect the children, "zealots and fanatics." He also introduced other phrases, including "sexual abuse hysteria," "Salem witch trials," "overzealous therapists," and "mass hysteria," to the viewing audience.[10]

Initially, the faces of most of the audience members registered anger towards the accused grandparents. When Gardner spoke, however, many people in the audience seemed to go into a slack-jawed trance, then seemed confused. Towards the end of the program, some of them seemed to side with the grandparents.

I was concerned that the show might have been used to manipulate the public into disbelieving the children's claims. I wrote an angry letter to Donahue and sent copies to organizations that educated the public about the effects of criminal occult ritual abuse.

The director of a pro-survivor organization asked me to send copies of the letter to a list of nine individuals she'd been trying to educate about ritual abuse–including Dr. J. Because I didn't yet remember his name, I was willing to send a copy to him. However, as I addressed an envelope to him, something tugged at my mind. I ignored the odd sensation since no memory came with it.

Within weeks, the psychiatrist sent me a one-page, typed, signed letter. In it, he claimed to be on our side in the "war against the cults." He provided his phone number at work and asked me to call him, collect.

As I read the letter, I couldn't shake the sense that something was wrong. I sent copies to several authors. One responded post-haste, warning me that the psychiatrist was heavily connected to the CIA. Angry that Dr. J had tried to con me, I wrote a scolding letter to him; he never wrote back.

I now believe that Dr. J had written to me and had asked me to call him because he'd been worried that I was waking up and might eventually remember and tell others about what he'd done to me.

Nearly a decade later, Dr. J died from cancer. News of his death triggered a series of memories of experiences that I'd had with him as a CIA-contracted mental programmer.[11] In one, I was an adult. I felt completely alone and wore a bright orange prison jumpsuit. I stood in a wide, bare corridor. Its concrete floor was very clean, perhaps painted grey, with a yellow line painted right down the middle. The concrete walls were lighter colored. At the end of corridor, about twenty feet ahead, I saw darkness to the left, an entrance into another area I couldn't see.

As I recalled this and other experiences, I knew that although Dr. J was dead, I was keeping him alive within me. I told my therapist, "It's like I'm a movie projection machine and the reels haven't yet been given me to go through." She replied, "He is dead. He is dead."

I asked, "Why am I crying?"

She said, "You told me before that he was another father-figure to you. So this is another loss. He's dead and you're not."

I said, "It's so strange that the man tortured me and threatened my life, and yet I am crying. Am I angry? Is that what's beneath this?"

The therapist said, "Perhaps."

I said, "I feel like I've just been tortured, like it just happened. Like I'm still in that corridor." I kept telling her, "I'm stuck." I had odd thoughts that my stuckness had something to do with keeping secrets and "National Security." Then suddenly I dropped down inside and my body went limp in her upholstered chair.

I went back in memory to a brightly-lit room behind me, to my right, off the corridor:

> I was lying naked on a table with round metal "loops" at the very end that restrained my ankles. Dr. J was in charge. A shorter, balding man with short, straight, thin, light brown hair was there too. The second man wore silver-framed glasses, and was probably in his thirties or forties.

> First, the two men had done what many perpetrators called "cat scratch." Making me lie on my stomach on that table, they had "lashed" (really, scratched) my back with a bare-ended, live

black electrical wire. Even though Dad had tortured me this way in the past, I still was never prepared for the intense pain. Then they turned me over and restrained me as I lay on my sore back.

After that, Dr. J brutally rammed a large, hard dildo into my vagina, saying, "This will ensure your silence about what you couriered that way."

Then the short man held my eyelids open while Dr. J put drops of liquid in them that did something, so that even when I stared, I saw only black. Dr. J said, "You will see nothing."

Then Dr. J gave me a choice of what they would do to my mouth to ensure my silence. I could either have something awful-tasting or I could "take" a live wire in it. I was heavily sedated and couldn't move my arms at all. I felt like my head was disconnected from my body. I could still feel some pain.

They'd done awful tastes and electricity to my mouth before. Even though I preferred to suck on a live wire to get it over with, I refused to choose either method. So Dr. J declared there was a third option: "We can cut out your tongue." I heard a whining sound to my left that sounded like a workman's drill. I opted for the live wire and sucked on it as I had done so many times before.

After that, Dr. J said, "There's one more part of your body we must do, to ensure your silence." No rush this time. I heard the drill again and thought, they'll probably do my hands. The psychiatrist said, "We can make you like Christ–give you your own stigmata." I prepared to have my hands drilled.

I was surprised when instead, the second man pinched my left palm, both front and back. He said, "Feel that?"

I didn't respond although I did feel it.

He pinched harder. "Feel that?"

It hurt, but again I refused to respond. Then they each grabbed a hand and bent my wrists back very hard. The second man said, "We can break your wrists so you'll never write again." I feared that they'd damaged them.

The second man then lightly touched my belly button with the revolving drill, saying, "We can kill you now." I prepared myself for the intense pain, but he didn't go any further.

After that, the song "America the Beautiful" was broadcast from a small, brown wooden speaker attached to the far wall, below the ceiling. Dr. J intoned, "If you ever talk, you will be put in prison for the rest of your life. You'll never be able to talk to anyone again, not even to write or receive letters. You will be completely alone in prison for the rest of your life."

As he had in the past, he kept calling me his "good little girl." He said, "You are a good American, you love your country, you want to protect your country, you will never betray your country."

He knew me well enough to know that I do love my country. It is an integral part of who I have been since early childhood. People like Dr. J took that love and twisted it into an instrument of blackmail, a thing of fear.

He told me that at any cost, I would protect my country's "national security." With those words, he effectively sealed my secrecy–using my love of my country.

Then the two men made me stand up beyond the end of the table. I was unable to use my hands, so they assisted me. I was able to see some light but little else. They dressed me in a jumpsuit, and before long I found myself standing all alone outside the brightly-lit room, which was now back to my right. Miserable, I regressed and wanted to get down on the floor of the corridor and crawl, but I didn't.

As I recovered these memories in the therapist's office without any prompting, I realized with a rising sense of anger that what Dr. J and the other man had done to me had nothing to do with "love of country" or "national security." Dr. J had really been afraid I'd talk about *him* some day!

I was reduced to tears again, weeping because he had deeply hurt the good part of me that cared about my country. I'd put my life on the line for my country, over and over again. Maybe I'd been tricked, maybe I'd been misled and lied to, but my motives had been honest and good. Damn him for using my love for my country against me! All those years, I'd been made to feel like filth because of the dirty work I'd done for the handlers. But it wasn't out of love for them, it was out of love for my country!

At home after that exhausting therapy session, I rested and determined to pull myself together. "The bastard is dead," I reminded myself. I used self-talk to stay alive:

> *I know that I must master my emotions. He couldn't kill what was pure and good in me. He walled it off using torture and terror and fear of imprisonment, but he couldn't kill it. He could have chosen to do what was right, too. He could have sought to heal, to do good, to love. But no, he chose to torture and to hate. I am not like him. I will go on from here. To hell with the trauma-bond between me and him. I'm not going to suicide because he's dead.*
>
> *And what I do from now on, is nobody's business but my own. Love for country is love for its people. And I am one of my country's people too! I don't know what to do with this love I've reclaimed, but if I die, my love of country dies and I can't have that. So I'm going to take a bath, wash my hair, brush my teeth, get dressed, go to the grocery store–and live.*

The next day, more emotional pain built up inside me. I could sense another imminent wave of emerging memory. I was so exhausted, but there was no way to stop it. I relaxed to let it come without a fight. Then I heard myself saying, "I'm going down the rabbit hole." I felt as if I were going into craziness. The memory was going to be a strong one.

At Bill's insistence, I called my therapist and asked for an emergency appointment. She asked how fast we could get there; a client had just called and cancelled the next full hour. I mumbled, "I guess God wants me to live."

Because I couldn't stop flashbacking, Bill drove. Already beginning to regress, I couldn't wear my prescription glasses (I didn't wear glasses as a child). I closed my eyes against the bright sun. As we drove past groves of trees, I kept seeing sun, shade, sun, shade in quick succession. That triggered hallucinations of varied colored, different shaped objects flying at my face. This was new.

I asked Bill to stay with me for extra support. A child part told him and the therapist that having what she called "daymares" was like being with Alice behind her looking glass, where she saw things that clearly did not happen in regular life. The therapist explained to my child part that my daymares were called hallucinations, and that later on, when they'd happened at home, they were called flashbacks.

I regressed further into that child alter-state when the therapist asked why Dr. J mattered in my pain about not having had a father's love. I told her that the intensity of my pain was from the realization that I'd *never* had a dad who loved me, and that from now on I'd have to find ways to be my own father.

The absence of paternal love had left a painful void in me that I'd tried to fill with smatterings of attention and non-sexual "love" from older men like Dr. J. Although I'd previously struggled with similar pain about my mother's inability to love me, this pain was probably more intense because with it, came the realization that I'd had no parental love at all! Even the shadowy substitutes like Dr. Black and Dr. J had never really loved me.

After recovering the early childhood memories of being dosed with a hallucinogen and traumatized by the doctor in the bunny costume, that child part of me wanted to take Dr. J and do to him what he'd done to the white rabbit–slam him again and again against the white tiled laboratory wall. Only one problem: Dr. J didn't really have long white ears!

My greatest horror was that I'd been drugged to the point where, as I hallucinated, my nightmares had broken through to my waking hours and had become as real, at least visibly, as the furniture in the therapist's office. I cannot think of any greater horror than this, and this is what Dr. J had done to me.

This incensed me: the bastard had given *a little child* a powerful hallucinogen! The entire time this child part related the emerging lab/hallucinogen/rabbit memory to Bill and the therapist, my left leg shook uncontrollably and I kept crying and shaking and hyperventilating. I sometimes wasn't able to breathe at all.

After I'd processed that memory, I told Bill that I wanted to go out and get "shit-faced drunk." At a local restaurant, we had our private version of an Irish wake for both Dr. J and Grandpa M. (who had also recently died). At my initiation, we toasted both men's deaths. We then toasted the special part of hell that I chose to believe those men are now in, reserved for cruel spooks. I told Bill, "I don't want to imagine the punishment in hell I could assign for Dr. J and Grandpa." I decided that Satan could do better than I could imagine, and that was good enough for me. To free myself from the bondage of my baneful past, I needed to be angry and not feel guilty for it. I needed to feel free from my fear of being punished by God for saying such things.

It's amazing and humbling to me that so many of those men had mentally programmed me to suicide if I remembered them. And yet, I've survived every suicide program while *they've* died, one after another. And as each one has died, I've become freer to remember and heal from what they'd done to me.

Unethical Hypnosis

Because of my experiences with Dr. J and other CIA programmers, I have precious little patience with anyone who claims that adults cannot be hypnotized into performing acts that are, to them, morally reprehensible. This is a destructive and dangerous lie.[12]

A highly published expert on hypnosis, T.X. Barber, helped to promote the same lie when he claimed that subjects faked being hypnotized, and that hypnosis therefore didn't even exist. He failed to mention that he had previously "thanked CIA and Navy-funded hypnotists for favors given," in more than one of his written works. (Emery, pg. 341)

The late Martin T. Orne, who had worked with the CIA's MKULTRA program, was a founding member of the FMSF and created its Scientific and Professional Advisory Board.[13] He, too, seemed to actively promote disinformation about the benignity of hypnosis (Emery, pg. 345).[14]

I worry when people say they cannot be hypnotized into doing something wrong. By not understanding how powerful hypnosis can be, they're *especially* vulnerable to being victimized by unethical hypnotists. By understanding hypnosis and how it works, we can more effectively protect ourselves from those who use it to trance and control others to perform unsavory deeds–against their will.[15]

Recycled Predators

Some mental programmers and handlers have had the audacity to reenter awakening victims' lives, posing as voluntary helpers and saviors. Some of these men (and a few women), whom I think of as "carpetbaggers," masquerade as sympathetic investigators, therapists, authors, and conference presenters. They pretend to bring attention to ritual abuse and mind-control atrocities while secretly feeding disinformation to targeted victims and to the greater public. At least three of them still convince survivors to *pay* them to "deprogram" their minds! Since I began my recovery in 1989, I've had the misfortune of being conned by a succession of these devious individuals.[16]

Like many other mind-control survivors, I've occasionally had difficulty recalling the faces and voices of former programmers, owners, and handlers. Such perpetrators know that former victims are less likely to remember them if the perpetrators re-contact the survivors, posing as good guys.[17] The memories created by these *new* contacts serve as an overlay. They effectively block out the older memories while providing a plausible context for the strong sense of familiarity felt by the survivor.

Cognitive dissonance can also arise when a fellow survivor presents one of these recycled perpetrators as a good guy. This causes one's repressed memories of the perpetrator to clash with the fellow survivor's favorable information about the perpetrator. If one doesn't yet remember that the "good guy" is really a former handler or programmer, then one is *more* likely to accept him or her as a hero or a savior than would a non-victim!

When I am unable to remember what a particular perpetrator did to me in the past, I am also more likely to emotionally re-attach to them, a la Stockholm Syndrome. I call this instantaneous, unconscious response a "vacuum seal effect." I've observed this reaction enough times for it to generate automatic red flags when it occurs again. Each time it happens, I remind myself that genuine emotional bonds take time to develop.[18]

When re-accesses were attempted by former mind-control perpetrators in the past, I was usually too disconnected from my intuition and my memories of them to recognize who and what they really were. I did, however, feel oddly addicted to them when they re-entered my life, posing as good guys. Another clue was that I was much too quick to do whatever they wanted.

The reason for such mindless compliance was simple: when they'd hurt me in the past, I'd felt gratitude towards them for not killing me. That profound feeling of gratitude, mixed with my repressed fear that they might kill me now, created a new "blind spot" in my mind. Although some of my suppressed memories of those individuals did seep through in dreams after we'd reconnected, I was still unable to remember, or accept, that I had known them in the past in an unhealthy way.

After figuratively being burned again and again by these con artists, I have learned the importance of letting go of my pride and admitting that I may always have a mental blind spot towards some of them. My advice to mind-control survivors who feel an instant attachment to any stranger is this: run, don't walk, in the opposite direction. Get help from your tried-and-true support network to stay away from that person. Trauma survivors don't need "iffy" people in their lives, to deprogram and heal.

Notes

1. Anna C. Salter warned of the illogic of assuming that a person's persona is the same as his or her private persona: "It seems impossible to convince people that private behavior cannot be predicted from public behavior. Kind, nonviolent individuals behave well in public, but so do many people who are brutal behind the scenes." (pg. 23-24)

2. During my codependency treatment at Crossroads, a physical activity director told us that many people are addicted to lying outdoors during the day, because the sun's warmth provides the closest sensation they'll ever have to experiencing a mother's love. Perhaps this is why some people choose to believe that the sun is their loving God.

3. That memory seemed impossibly bizarre, until I started researching Lucis Trust on the Internet at http://www.lucistrust.org. In less than an hour, I learned that it is closely connected to Share International; furthermore, Share International is run by Benjamin Crème, who seems to be Maitreya's primary promoter.

4. Although some Christians would claim that this is proof of their being demonically possessed, I believe it indicates that they are so dissociated, when they go into an inevitable trance-state, their alter-states emerge and fake being spiritual entities.

5. I am amazed that he didn't recognize his own hypocrisy-posing as a dedicated Jew while practicing his Luciferian religion in secret.

6. I suspect that I had been drugged before this ceremony began, possibly causing me to hallucinate.

7. These female members of the Golden Dawn, when drinking liquid semen, claimed to be superior to Satanists who drank human blood in rituals. I do not understand why these normally intelligent women don't recognize that drinking semen is actually a form of sexual self-degradation.

8. In the same way, some of my alter-states were used as "mental couriers" to deliver unwritten, highly secretive messages to influential men in other countries. Those alter-states then couriered the recipients' verbal replies back to my owners and handlers-again leaving no paper trail.

9. I believe that Dr. J and other CIA MKULTRA psychiatrists have used the False Memory Syndrome Foundation, a non-profit organization, as a conduit for disinformation and propaganda designed to convince the public that: recovered memories aren't real; survivors fabricate "false memories"; mental health professionals implant memories of abuse in clients' minds; and alleged survivors fabricate MPD/DID. Certain individuals who have been employed to participate in government-sponsored mind-control programs have had a clear and vested interest in discrediting their former victims. If the former victims are not believed, then the perpetrators can escape prosecution for their crimes against humanity, including torture, false imprisonment, and slavery.

Carla Emery wrote that the FMSF's claims about the existence of memory confabulation are valid. I agree with her to a point; however, my experience has been that *genuine* "false memories" (really, screen memories) were methodically implanted by Dad, Dr. J., and other perpetrators, Emery did cite an article that reinforces my concern that some prominent members of the FMSF may have used the non-profit organization to promote a hidden agenda:

> . . . the False Memory Syndrome Foundation may have an ulterior motive in its efforts to deny validity to memories acquired-or recovered-after some passage of time . . . FMSF has some on their Board of Advisors who may want to cover up their own work. One is

Louis West, another is Martin Orne, one of the key MKULTRA researchers in hypnosis, and a third is Michael Persinger, who did research on the effects of electromagnetic radiation on the brain for a Pentagon weapons project. Regression therapy could threaten to reveal techniques the CIA may have secretly developed involving the use of hypnosis. (Daniel Brandt, "Mind Control and the Secret State," *Prevailing Winds* magazine, Number 3, pg. 73, NameBase NewsLine, #12, Jan–March 1996. pp. 239-240)

10. In its 5/31/03 obituary about Dr. Gardner, the Independent.co.uk website cited his explanations for the basis of his bogus theory, Parental Alienation Syndrome (PAS). Although PAS like "False Memory Syndrome," was never empirically proven, Gardner promoted it as scientific fact in self-published literature and in many court custody battles, providing an adequate false defense for an untold number of fathers and stepfathers who were accused of having sexually molested their children. As a result, many of these fathers gained *full custody* of the children.

Gardner . . . believed that 90 per cent of mothers were liars who "programmed" their children to repeat their lies, and never mind the corroborating evidence. He theorised that mothers alleging abuse were expressing, in disguised form, their own sexual inclinations towards their children.

Like so many other people with suspected pedophile mentalities, I believe Gardner displaced his own sexual inclinations towards children onto the genuinely concerned mothers:

And he suggested there was nothing much wrong with pedophilia, incestuous or not. "One of the steps that society must take to deal with the present hysteria is to 'come off it' and take a more realistic attitude toward pedophilic behavior," he wrote in *Sex Abuse Hysteria – Salem Witch Trials Revisited* (1991). Pedophilia, he added, "is a widespread and accepted practice among literally billions of people" . . . Along the way, he also turned into an authentic American monster. (Independent, pg. 2)

The callous and exponential damage Dr. Gardner wreaked upon our gentle society may continue for generations. More of his pro-pedophilia statements can be found on the Internet at http://cincinnatipas.com/richardgardner-pas.html.

11. My experience has been that when former owners or mental programmers died, my knowing that they could never hurt me again subconsciously freed my mind to recall more of what they had done to me. This also occurred after Dad died. I do not believe that I would have been able to remember the ritual and government experiences, had Dad remained an active threat to my life and safety.

12. Carla Emery explained that the person most influential in promoting this fallacy was Milton H. Erickson, a well-known hypnotist.

> Erickson claimed . . . that a subject cannot be made to do anything against his will, or against his morals. What he really demonstrated, however, is all of the methods by which a hypnotist can cleverly and deliberately fail to produce self-destructive or unethical behavior-if he wants to report those types of results. (pg. 334)

13. In the introduction to the FMSF's 2002 webpage entitled *The FMSF Scientific and Professional Advisory Board Profiles*, Executive Director Pamela Freyd, Ph.D. indicated that Martin and Emily Orne were instrumental in identifying "people whose published research in the field of memory or clinical practice might provide insights into the problem." Orne was, to the best of my understanding, not only a founding member of the FMSF-he was also primarily responsible for creating the advisory board and recruiting its members.

14. In *Bluebird*, Dr. Colin Ross named Dr. J. (who I'm fairly certain was Dr. L. J. West), Dr. Martin Orne, and other mental health professionals who had contracted with the CIA and/or the Pentagon to perform experiments on humans, and who later actively supported the FMSF (pp. 112-124, 137-142, 154). A large list of institutions, facilities, and individuals who allegedly participated in human experimentation in North America can be found on my personal website at http://www.kathleen-sullivan.com on the "Government Research" page. Much of the list has been compiled from *Bluebird*.

15. Carla Emery warned readers against the dangers of believing common myths about hypnosis:

> They say, "Hypnosis does not exist." Or they say, "We're not doing hypnosis. This is *something else*, and it's wonderful, and ineffable, and totally harmless, and mysteriously helpful." Saying that calms the public's fear, increases volunteering, increases subjects' susceptibility. This is the first stage of induction." (pg. 346)

16. Carla Emery explained how an awakening mind-control survivor can be unwittingly reaccessed by a former controller:

> The exploiter typically tries, to the bitter end, covertly to perform damage control and keep his secrets hidden as long as the subject is within his reach. If secretly he can access his longtime subject, he gives the old accustomed induction cue, then asks questions to bring himself up to date on the status of the investigation. Then he gives new suggestions to that conditioned mind, designed to protect himself or to further exploit his subject. (pg. 378)

17. One Christian author calls these individuals, "wolves in sheep's clothing."

18. In *Journey into Madness: The True Story of Secret CIA Mind Control and Medical Abuse*, Gordon Thomas described the powerful bond that can develop between captors and their victims. He stated that "pathological transference . . . could be seen, for instance, where parents seriously abused their children, even threatening their lives, yet when their offspring were rescued, perhaps by social workers, the children almost never complained about their treatment; they were overwhelmed with gratitude that their parents had let them live." (pg. 75)

Going Public

Talking to a Wall

Even as I was remembering and beginning to integrate, I continued to be contacted by handlers and Aryan cult members—not only by phone but at church, the grocery store, post office, shopping mall, and more. Because I didn't feel safe living in Atlanta, and Bill had recently been awarded medical disability for his spinal deterioration, we decided it was time to relocate. After much discussion, we chose Chattanooga, a lovely older city we'd had the opportunity to explore during our family visits to Crossroads. Three hours north of Atlanta, Chattanooga is surrounded by mountains and divided by the Tennessee River. It's relaxed and friendly–perfect for retirees.[1]

After we'd moved into our new home, traumatic memories continued to emerge. It was time to find a new therapist. I learned of Dr. M., a psychologist who claimed to be familiar with MPD and ritual abuse recovery issues. I assumed I could teach him about the issues surrounding government mind-control. After several months of twice-a-week sessions, he started curling into a fetal position in his leather upholstered chair, his eyes widening as I talked about what had been done to me by mind-control professionals.

Although I felt as though I were talking to a wall, I was afraid to stop consulting with him. I didn't know of anyone else in the area who worked with dissociated trauma survivors.

Internet Connections

Several friends encouraged me to buy a computer so I could use the Internet. After I bought it, I joined several on-line support groups. How wonderful to be able to communicate with other mind-control survivors! I no longer felt isolated. Unfortunately, I didn't understand that I was also reporting details of personal life, via E-mail, to people who could easily forward my information to active perpetrators. (And to be fair, I could

357

have done the same to them.) My need for support was so great, I still
ignored potential risks.

Predators posing as "good guys" soon contacted me through the
Internet. They were actively trolling the on-line ritual abuse/mind-
control survivor community for information and new victims. Several
of the predators tried to cultivate my dependence on them for help and
advice. One, an author who pretended to expose government mind
control, was the most successful. I eventually broke away from him
when I realized that he was attempting to gain control of my mind, and
therefore my life.[2]

Reaccessed

I wanted to believe that because we'd moved away from Atlanta,
I wouldn't be accosted again. I was in denial about the tenacity of my
former handlers and owners. Mentally unprepared for their ongoing
contacts, I blocked out each attempt.

One morning, as I drove south on a local highway (Hwy. 27) in the
right lane, three vehicles surrounded me. They positioned their vehicles
in front, behind me, and to my left. I recognized a bearded man, driving
an SUV, as being from J.C.'s Aryan cult. I was unable to break away from
them, and do not remember what happened after that.

Another day, I drove on a rural road from the town of Soddy Daisy
towards home. As I came to a bridge that spanned a creek, several men
stood next to orange and white striped construction barriers. A middle-aged,
thin, unkempt man, wearing a hard hat, stood closest to where I had to
stop. Because I was new to the area, I rolled down my window to ask for
alternate directions home. He approached the car. Again, I don't remember
what happened afterwards.

Several years ago, I looked in a mirror at my back to examine my
moles. I was unhappy to see two new, small, perfectly circular, flat, dark
brown marks exactly one inch apart to the left of my upper spine.
Handlers had used stun guns in the past to control and torture me,
leaving many small, white circular marks on my forearms and other parts
of my body. Still, they hadn't given me the brown marks that reportedly
identify most Beta-programmed slaves. I still don't know who might
have marked my back, or why.[3]

We received calls, on our unlisted phone, that activated more of our still-hidden alter-states. We were also skillfully compromised by a local husband-and-wife team that, we later learned, were actively connected to the intelligence community! (The wife had previously divorced the brother of an NSA Director; her current husband, who admitted couriering for the government, was given a used laptop computer by his handler–I found a blank CIA employment form on it.) I felt frightened and devastated when I realized that dammit, we were still being reactivated! I wanted to live a clean life–I didn't want to wake up in a jail cell, not knowing why I was there!

Many mind-control survivors seem to struggle with this particular fear. Some of the perpetrators who had controlled us don't want to let us go, even after we've told others about what they'd done to us. Part of their obsession with us seems to be a matter of pride–by losing control of us, they may appear inept to other controllers.

I believe another reason why they persist is that a great deal of time and money was spent on programming each of us; some controllers view us as financial investments and are not willing to let us go.

I also believe they don't want us to break away because if we do, it will be easier for us to remember them. And then, if we can identify them (as I was eventually able to identify Dr. J in a video that his university had put on the Internet), we could testify against them in court.

I suspect the deepest reason why they don't want to let go is that they're emotionally addicted to "their" former slaves. I believe these control addicts unconsciously fear that their own minds or lives will fall apart if they're left with no one to control.

I feel sad for those men and women. I believe that recovering survivors are more free than they, even if we're re-accessed. We're discovering and accepting who we are, all the way through. We're finding peace with ourselves and our imperfect world. They may never find such peace. We're learning to trust and bond with healthy people. They may never be able to bond, because they're immersed in a shadowy world in which bonds are built on shifting lies and secrecy.

Believe the Children

In April, 1997 I had the opportunity to meet with a group of mind control survivors, face-to-face, at a conference in Illinois. It was co-hosted by Believe the Children, a marvelous pro-survivor advocacy organization that disbanded soon afterwards. At the conference, I met some of the survivors with whom I'd communicated through an Internet deprogramming/support group.

Blanche Chavoustie and Lynne Moss-Sharman had created a pro-active organization, ACHES-MC, to inform the public about mind-control experimentation. Each night of the conference, Blanche and Lynne opened their suite for survivors and therapists to meet together and talk. One night, I listened to Valerie Wolfe, a clinical social worker who had recently testified before a Senate subcommittee with two of her clients—Claudia Mullens and Chris DiNicola.

On the second day of the conference, Lynne asked if we'd be willing to participate in a video that ACHES-MC was filming. She asked those of us who volunteered to tell a bit about our histories, then say what we would like the government to do. Feeling happy and empowered, I smiled as I gave my statement.

The videotape was sent to President Clinton with a letter from Lynne and Blanche, asking for an investigation to be opened into the CIA's MKULTRA experiments. When I learned about that, I felt another wave of fear–would I now be killed for talking? Again, I tried to balance my fear with the knowledge that I was probably safer for having gone public.

Helen

One night in Lynne and Blanche's suite, I met a professor of criminal justice. A good listener, he had a kind and gentle soul. I cried as I told him I wished I could have a therapist like Valerie. She was intelligent and compassionate, and seemed to be willing to hear whatever her clients needed to say without cringing or shutting them down. The professor smiled and said that he'd recently met a therapist in Chattanooga who might be what I was looking for. He said Helen was familiar with MPD, and had worked extensively with ritual abuse survivors and Vietnam veterans. He gave me her office number and suggested that I contact her.

Although I didn't want to give up on Dr. M., I knew I was getting nowhere with him. After several more unsuccessful consultations, I contacted Helen. During our first meeting in her office, I was surprised by how much emotional pain I felt. Her warm brown eyes and soft voice seemed to cut right through my armor. I decided I would work with her.

Helen seemed to be intelligent, warm, and empathetic. She said she'd be willing to learn more about mind-control while working with me. I insisted on one boundary up-front: although she was a skilled hypnotherapist, I wouldn't allow her to use hypnosis with me. I'd heard too many horror stories about abuse survivors who had lost legitimate court cases against perpetrators because the survivors had undergone hypnosis during therapy.

Whenever I did memory recovery work in Helen's office, she waited quietly in her chair as I relaxed and allowed parts to come out and talk about their experiences. Because she often testified in court, Helen understood suggestibility and was careful not to make any statements that could affect the credibility of my emerging memories.

Silenced

After I started consulting with Helen, the most serious re-access attempt occurred. This was shortly after I'd made two big strides in my recovery:

In September of 1997, I'd completed the manuscript for *MK*, a cathartic fictional account of my life.

That same month, I'd also given my first public interview with CKLN (a Canadian radio station) as part of its series about mind control. During the interview, I'd provided a large amount of information, although I'd chosen not to provide any specifics about the black ops.[4]

When nothing bad happened after the interview, I felt relieved and decided the threats that handlers and owners had made in the past against my life were lies. That same month, another female mind-control survivor[5] accidentally discovered a direct connection, through the Internet, between a well-known "Satanist"/Army psyops expert and an author who had posed within the survivor community as a concerned good guy for years.

Deeply shaken by this unhappy discovery, I shared it with the on-line mind-control survivor community. Like myself, many of the survivors were emotionally rattled. Some of us had trusted the author and had given him very personal information.

The author was scheduled to speak at the ECLIPSE-sponsored "Ritual Trauma, Child Abuse and Mind Control Conference" to be held in Atlanta on October 1–3. Knowing that he'd be there, I felt uncomfortable about attending the conference. I had, however, agreed to emotionally support a female mind-control survivor who would also be presenting. Despite the concerns of other survivors who had learned that the conference wasn't safe for us, I decided to go.[6]

D.W., an alleged mind-control survivor, also planned to attend the conference. Although we'd originally "met" through an Internet support group, she had also privately communicated with me via E-mail. She asked if I would share a motel room with her in Atlanta and split the cost. She convinced me that we could support and protect each other during the conference. I believed her.

What I experienced during the ECLIPSE conference and the following weekend was so upsetting, I still have not remembered all of it.

Because D.W. insisted on keeping me awake in our hotel room by incessantly talking into the wee hours each morning, sleep deprivation put me into a partial trance. (Each morning when I left for the conference, she stayed behind and caught up on her sleep–another red flag I ignored.)

At the ECLIPSE conference, I was shadowed and intimidated by a tall male attendee who the presenting author claimed to have hired to "protect" him from me. I recognized the professional bodyguard as a spook who had handled me, at least once, in the past. Other attendees were concerned about his odd behaviors towards me. Unfortunately, I couldn't stop him from intimidating me with his too-close presence. I felt trapped because I'd agreed to support my friend. I didn't understand that I had the right to break my promise and leave, if it put me at risk.

On the last day of the conference, the bodyguard used a neo-Nazi hand signal to trigger out an adult, op-trained alter-state, code-named Katherine, that I hadn't yet discovered. Katherine immediately recognized the bodyguard. She felt an overwhelming urge to follow him out of the room and go wherever he told her. Several other mind-control survivors recognized what was happening and convinced Katherine to stay with them.

Katherine stayed in control of "the body" throughout most of the following weekend. On Sunday morning, she drove D.W. and another survivor to the Atlanta Hartsfield airport, dropping off the other survivor at her terminal first, at D.W.'s suggestion, and then walking with D.W. to another terminal, where she'd catch her flight.

Before Katherine walked away, D.W., a former nurse, unexpectedly applied painful pressure to nerve bundles in my shoulder, then gave Katherine new instructions.

Instead of taking the underground train back to the concourse that she'd parked near, Katherine (now in a full trance) walked beside the underground moving walkways that connected several of the concourses. Recognizing one area from the past, a CIA-programmed alter-state emerged and walked towards a small room off a corridor just beyond an escalator that would have taken me up to the ground floor.

That alter-state had previously been conditioned to emerge in that part of the airport after ops, to report to awaiting handlers for debriefing. As she walked into the room, she saw at least three tall men in dark suits who stood silently with their backs to the wall, next to the doorway. One, a male relative near my age, had received the same black op training as I.

Looking further into the room, she recognized a psyops expert who had been one of my overseas handlers, and two other men who had previously told me they had worked within the CIA's Directorate of Operations.[7] The psyops expert and the handlers quickly triggered out a succession of CIA-loyal alter-states, threatening each part and giving some of them new commands.[8]

After the psyops expert left the room, the two alleged CIA spooks and my male relative raped me in succession, giving more threats and commands, knowing that the new trauma opened my mind so their words would go deep inside. Each rapist first donned a large, tacky, yellow, plaid sports jacket that they shared. I believe they did this so that if I recalled the rape, I would remember seeing the jacket instead of their faces. Each man used condoms, probably so that I would have no physical proof of the rape. The assault went on and on until I blacked out.

When I came back into consciousness, I was alone in the room with an older, bearded man who had been one of my primary mental programmers. He triggered out several more CIA-loyal alter-states and implanted two new sets of mental commands that were clearly intended to ensure that I would never "talk" about these men and my connections to them again.[9] After he finished, I again lost consciousness.

When I came into consciousness, I was walking dazedly in a concourse in the airport. Having confused the North and South concourses, I walked outside to the covered parking deck. Frantic when I couldn't find my car, I believed it must have been moved or stolen by spooks who had attended the counter-terrorism conference. I went downstairs and reported my concerns to a City of Atlanta police officer. When he helped find my car in the opposite concourse, I felt foolish.

I didn't yet remember the assault, although I did feel pain where there shouldn't have been any. Going to the police was totally out of character because I'd been conditioned all my life to stay away from cops. Calling Bill at home in Chattanooga and asking him to come to Atlanta with a loaded gun was equally out of character. Something very bad was happening, but I didn't know what.

That night at home, several alter-states emerged, called Helen, and communicated the pieces of the trauma that they'd experienced. They warned Helen that other parts that had previously emerged in therapy were now "missing." With Helen's help in therapy the next day, we were able to reverse some of the newly implanted mental programming.

It took me several years to recall most of the rest of that traumatic experience. First I remembered the yellow jacket, then the physical description of the first rapist, then the second, and then the relative who had raped me last.[10]

I believe the main reason why I didn't immediately remember these men was that the rape had been the worst part of the assault. The first two spooks who raped me were men that some of my CIA-loyal alter-states had been emotionally attached to. One alter-state had believed that the first rapist, who was in charge of the assault, was her husband!

For the next two years, I repeatedly pushed the memories away and told myself that the rape didn't matter. I told myself that I needed to get on with my life. That changed when I interned at a local agency that, among other things, helps rape victims. When I attended a required workshop about rape, I recognized that I needed specialized support and counseling to heal from what had been done to me.

I am fortunate that the agency provides free help to rape survivors. Those counselors helped me to release my buried anger and stop living in fear of being raped again.[11]

Until the summer of 2000, however, much of my behavior was still dictated by the effects of what the men had done to me. I didn't try to market *MK*; instead, I tried to bury it. And although I'd previously wanted to, and many people had asked me to, I now refused to write a factual account of my life (other than a brief piece I rebelliously wrote for PARC-VRAMC, a proactive nonprofit agency).

When I presented recovery information at conferences for ritual abuse and mind-control survivors, I was careful not to share specifics about my experiences with former handlers, programmers, and slave-owners. I only gave one television interview (in the shadows) as a favor to a good friend. I didn't understand that I was still allowing the rapists to control my life.[12]

Rape is one of the most horrible assaults a human can experience. It invades and wounds the body, mind, and soul in so many different ways.[13] Although I'd been raped hundreds of times in the past, only one or two of my alter-states had experienced and compartmentalized each rape. At the airport, however, I was gang-raped when I was probably about 90% integrated. This meant that at least 90% of my mind was directly affected by the assault.

Those cruel men's actions and words betrayed and wounded my soul and shattered my still-fragile self-respect. Feeling soiled and dirty, I isolated from others in shame. I had great difficulty opening my heart to Bill anymore, and he had great difficulty trusting and "forgiving" me for "letting" the men rape me.[14]

I also feared for my life and safety, and wondered when–as the second, red-bearded rapist had threatened–one of those awful men would suddenly pop up in my life and rape me again, or worse. I stayed in abject fear of them and their professional associates for over four years. I remained silent about the details of my past, despite the entreaties and encouragement of many people in my support system. They couldn't understand why I'd stopped speaking out.

During the rape crisis counseling, I gradually realized and acknowledged that I was still terrified, as I'd been during the assault, that those men–all trained killers–would kill me.

As I continued to heal, I learned that some of my CIA-loyal alter-states were grief-stricken that they'd been betrayed by the two spooks who'd previously been kind to them. They also grieved the heinous betrayal by the male relative, an Atlanta resident, for whom I'd once deeply cared. In turn, I—as the host alter-state—grieved the loss of four potentially productive years of my life since the assault.

As I returned in my mind again and again to that below-ground room at the airport, I relieved more pieces of the traumatic experience. Several CIA-loyal alter-states came out and gave me more specific descriptions of the rapists.

Eventually I realized that the first rapist had lied to me. He and the other two men hadn't "had" to rape me because I'd gone public. They had *chosen* to rape me, to reassert their control over me. The bastards! My resulting anger helped me to break their grip of fear over my mind and life.

Regardless of what is done to me or to my loved ones in the future, and regardless of who those criminals and their associates may recruit to try to assault my mind or body or reputation or loved ones or anything else in my life, I have made a vow to myself–based on my very life. From now on, I will speak out about my history and experiences when, where, and with whomever I choose. I will not allow those animals in human skin, or any of their associates, to silence me again. Their shame stays with them.

Notes

1. I wasn't consciously aware that during one of a series of private meetings with Poppa in Atlanta, before we moved to Tennessee, Poppa had given Andreia encouragement about starting a new, clean life and had showed her a Chattanooga realtor's magazine. In it was a picture of an old house in a backwoods community not far from Soddy Daisy, a peaceful rural area a half-hour north of Chattanooga. Poppa had told Andreia to purchase the house, which obviously needed remodeling. Although I couldn't remember Poppa's instructions, I found a copy of the magazine and "fell in love" with the house. Although Bill resisted, I wore him down until he agreed to buy it. Imagine my horror when I learned that a good portion of the people who had founded our small community had had high secrecy clearances-many of them having been involved in intelligence operations! Even the man whose widow sold us the house had been a career intelligence operative! When I realized that we'd probably moved into a spook retirement community, I had an emotional melt-down. Damn it, had I walked into another trap? I was trying to get free! Then Andreia explained that Poppa had said we would be more "protected" there. After having had the opportunity to interact with the few spooks who remain, I've discovered-to my great surprise-that they are just as human and vulnerable as I. That knowledge has taken a lot of the fear away. I also realized that I can't look to anyone else to protect us; only Bill and I are capable of doing that. Such knowledge has strengthened me and bolstered my courage.

2. This was confirmed to me by several survivors. One sent proofs that the author is still affiliated with a large, international, pseudo-religious cult that practices mind-control on its members.

3. Remembering the actual stun gun assaults has been next to impossible, although previously I had remembered enough to know that the white marks on my forearms

were from such assaults. (Their origin was independently confirmed to me by an private investigator in Atlanta who was a former police trainer.) I believe that either the pain or the electrical disruption in my brain (or both) created temporary amnesia, since I knew better than to scream and therefore wouldn't have been out of breath during the assault. "Estimating the effects of torture by means of electricity on the ability to remember is a very uncertain enterprise. In most cases, loss of consciousness resulting from electrical torture is likely to be caused by hyperventilation, induced by screaming and intensified breathing under torture." (Graessner et al., pg. 195)

4. During the interview, I unwittingly provided information about implanted "alien" screen memories that unfortunately still seemed as real as my legitimate op memories.

5. We give these survivors the honorary title of "Nancy Drew." Although some of them are living in the worst possible circumstances-some struggle with debilitating disabilities and many are still being reaccessed-they have nonetheless painstakingly sifted through massive amounts of available information, including the CIA's CD of released MKULTRA files, to find verifications for themselves and for others within the survivor community. Their contributions are invaluable.

6. An E-mailed advertisement stated that Marketing International Corporation of Arlington, Virginia was producing both the ECLIPSE conference and the "Counterterrorism, Tactical, Investigative, and Security Exhibition and Seminar," also known as the "CT Expo," on a lower floor in the same building at the same time. The CT Expo was heavily attended by law enforcement and intelligence personnel.

7. Specific and descriptive information about the men in that room remains in safe hands, and will be released if anything unusual should ever happen to me or my loved ones.

8. They expressed some anger about the CKLN interview, but seemed more upset about my *MK* manuscript. The man in charge of my being raped, a blond spook allegedly from the Directorate of Operations, threatened my life, should I ever publish it. I have since realized that he might have feared that I'd sufficiently identified him within the manuscript-as the character named "Jed."

9. This kind of "silence" or "suicide" programming is also called *booby-trap* programming. It can lay dormant for years in the survivor's mind until an alter-state that compartmentalized the implanted instructions comes back into consciousness. If the programmed alter-state takes control of the body, the survivor may temporarily be in extreme danger. The two ways I've found to successfully keep self-destruct programmed alter-states from carrying out programmed instructions are: 1) I can enter a hospital on an emergency basis so that I can safely disassemble the programming, or 2) I can become co-conscious with that part at home or in my therapist's office and relive the trauma(s) that influenced that part to prefer suicide or self-harm over safety.

10. I saw no point in reporting the rape. I didn't know the names or home addresses of the first two men-all I could remember was one of their aliases. And because the third rapist, a relative, had black op training, I chose not to confront him. Also, the blond rapist told me they had already created alibis that fellow spooks, who had also attended the counterterrorism conference, would back up. I believed him. Finally, because I didn't immediately remember the rapes, I had no physical proofs that they had occurred. All I had were the emotional and mental scars that would not go away.

11. The specialized counselors never suggested my memories-they came completely on their own. Instead, they taught me how to regain my emotional power by allowing myself to feel the full gamut of my suppressed emotions, to understand that the after-effects from the rape were normal, and what the rapists had done to me was about power, not sexuality.

12. "Survivors of torture, sexual abuse, and rape . . . have been put into a position of . . . "forced silence," that is, the assailant has often directly threatened the victim that death will result from disclosure, and thus the victim fears annihilation (as well as rejection from the listener) for telling about the traumas." (Blank A 14)

13. "Rape . . . is inherently humiliating and degrading of self-esteem; those are not meanings supplied by the victim, but rather are objectively contained within the event, as is the violent and tyrannizing imposition of the perpetrator's will and power." (Blank A 14)

14. I've learned that this is a surprisingly common response in many partners of rape victims, who believe that if it had been them, they could have successfully fought off the attackers. In reality, being in a room full of assassin-trained spooks didn't allow me that luxury; my goal was simply to survive.

The Void

This Is To Mother You

Although remembering and deprogramming were crucial parts of my recovery, my biggest step in healing was to accept how the methodically perpetrated traumas, betrayals, and absence of childhood nurturing had affected my mind and soul.

I'd always felt different from other people, partly because my parents had used me to meet their emotional and sexual needs instead of being there for me. Dad had conditioned me from infancy to bond with him through sex. In those conditioned alter-states, I'd believed that I was his partner, especially since he did things to me that should have been reserved for Mom. I'd bonded with him not only through touch and sex, but also through terror and torture.

From early childhood on, I'd also been a living receptacle for the hatred inside my parents and some of my other adult relatives. What I saw in their faces when they looked at me was what I believed I was. Rarely was I held gently, talked to in a soothing voice, or nurtured–other than by one paternal aunt and by my maternal grandmother. In the rituals, some of my adult family members openly treated me with scorn, hatred, and sadism. Believing that they and the other cultists wished that I didn't exist, I'd complied by going away in my mind.

After I'd married Albert, Mom had told me that she understood Albert's coldness towards me because she wasn't capable of loving anyone, either. Although her words had cut deep, they hadn't surprised me. I'd always known that she didn't love me. That is the mother I always knew. She was so focused on her own needs, wants, and desires that she seemed incapable of giving of herself, emotionally, to others–unless she wanted something from them.

I didn't have a mother who mirrored love to me. Instead, she avoided looking at my face when she changed my diaper. She didn't delight in picking me up out of the crib or holding me close to her beating heart as I did with Rose.

As a child, I never bonded in love with humans, other than to a limited degree with my brothers and one childhood friend who was also a victim. Feeling responsible for my brothers' welfare, I saw myself as their surrogate mother. The death of my baby daughter was probably the final stake that Dad drove through my heart's ability to bond. Her death totally split off the warm, caring part of me. Caring and connecting with other humans came at too great a cost. I couldn't bear any more pain.

In childhood, when I drew pictures of trees, I always drew a large black hole in the middle of each trunk. Even though the trees were full of leaves and fruit, I was communicating that the tree (really, my soul) was empty and black inside. People might have looked at me and seen life and intelligence, leading them to think that all was well while in reality, my soul was dying. Although I felt hollow inside, I tried to be like other people–but this was not possible. It took so much energy to survive and stay sane!

After we married in 1988, Bill assumed the role of mother-nurturer. He gave me consistent love, caring and acceptance. His actions helped me to begin to trust and open up to him.

In August of 1999, we were at home on a Sunday morning, making last-minute preparations to attend an annual SMART conference later that week.[1] Bill was shaving in the bathroom when he felt a strong pain in his chest that traveled down his left arm. When he couldn't dissociate it away, he yelled at me to take him to the hospital. I called for an ambulance. As I followed it in my car, listening to the siren scream, I switched into autopilot mode.

After several tests, the emergency room physician told Bill, "You're my prisoner now." Bill told me that he'd be on the golf course the next day. I wanted to believe him, but then he was transported by ambulance to the main hospital in downtown Chattanooga.

The following morning, an angiogram indicated severe blockage in three main arteries. His cardiologist met with me in a private room and said, "Mrs. Sullivan, if your husband leaves this hospital, he's a dead man." My body turned to ice; I seemed to hear his voice inside a barrel. A nurse kindly led me into a large room where Bill was being prepared for his heart bypass operation.

As Bill lay on his back, joking and teasing the nurses, I thought: "This might be the last time I'll ever talk to him." I tried to laugh at his jokes as I watched another heart attack on the monitor. Because he was drugged and dissociated, he never even felt it. As I held back my tears, my heart felt as if it were shattering into a million pieces.

I felt so alone and frightened, having no safe family members to call for support. An elderly couple who lived near us, rushed to the hospital after I called them. They sat and talked with me in the Surgical ICU waiting room to keep my mind occupied while I counted the hours. Their presence helped me to realize that I didn't have to be alone anymore. It was time to let honest, caring people become members of my new adopted family.

After Bill's surgery, I was led into the surgical ICU ward to see him for a few minutes. I wasn't ready for what I encountered. His body was ice cold and his skin was grey. A machine was breathing for him. Although he'd always responded when I'd touched his hand, now there was no response at all. And although the smiling, young nurse told me that Bill was doing well, I felt as if he had just died.

When I returned home from the hospital that night to wash up and get a few hours of uninterrupted sleep, I felt a shift inside. Pain and grief paralyzed me. I felt terrified and wasn't sure I could survive it. Fortunately, its intensity ebbed away by the next morning–especially when I saw that Bill was awake, talking to visitors.

Bill's near-death experience both traumatized me and helped me to appreciate him more. All the little infractions I'd held against him stopped being important. Nearly losing him helped me to value our relationship in a much deeper and mature way.

Do I regret loving Bill, when I know that love can bring pain? Do I regret having hesitantly moved towards him in my heart, soul, and mind for fifteen years, so afraid that he'd hurt me, that he'd leave me, that he'd despise me if he really knew me? Not anymore! How can I regret the greatest healing force I've ever experienced?

Bill taught me how to bond–not just through sex, but by learning to care and to give and receive love. He taught me that because I'm loved, I can accept myself as lovable. And by accepting caring from him and others in my support network, I am also able to care.

He oh-so-slowly helped me to peel away hundreds of thin layers of steel that had encased my soul. Because of his love and fierce devotion, I dared to open my soul to him, surprised again and again when it wasn't pierced to death by sudden betrayal and cruelty.

Bill was my soul-hospital, my triage, my burn unit. He helped me to survive and to know that life is worth living and risking love for.

A year after Bill's heart surgery, a woman in my support network sent me an unexpected care package. In it was iridescent, shredded plastic grass, several beautiful adult coloring books, a 64-count box of Crayons, several small toys, a card with small pressed flowers on the front, and a customized CD.

The first song on the CD was Sinead O'Connor's *This Is To Mother You*. Pain paralyzed me and tears streamed down my face as I played it over and over. Sinead sang about a kind of mother-nurturing that I'd never experienced, but had always hoped for: a mother who would love me and forgive my imperfections.

Sinead's words went deeper and deeper, all the way down into the black hole that my shell of a soul encased. Then I became the black hole. The null, the void. The place that had never been filled with loving touch and compassion, caring and kindness, encouragement, and gentle, non-sexual kisses. This hole could have only been filled by one person: my mother, the woman who I believe gave me life. I was astonished by the depth and intensity of my pain.

For days, I sat and grieved and played the song over and over. I finally allowed myself to feel the absence of mother-love. I grieved over who and what I'd never had the chance to be: maternally loving. Caring. Compassionate. Kind. Gentle. Nurturing. How could I be, when it had never been given to me by my primary care-givers? And how could I give out of a deep place that had never been filled?

During my next therapy session, I had great difficulty putting these thoughts and feelings into words. I told Helen, "I didn't know how to become close to other women. I have a big black hole inside with no way to fill it–my mother hadn't been what I needed, and probably never can be. What can I do to fill the hole? Is it even possible?"

She said, "You must learn to nurture your own self. You'll need to become your own mother." As we talked, I realized that the grieving child inside me needed to let go of the fantasy that Mom might eventually love me. How could she, when she was unable to love herself?

Now I understood why I'd never been able to forgive myself, and why I'd always felt "bad." If my primary caregivers chose not to mirror forgiveness and acceptance towards me when I made mistakes or failed to meet their stringent expectations, then how could I have possibly learned to forgive and accept myself? No wonder I was so damned dissociated; I'd never developed a core sense of self, because I'd never been accepted as who I really was!

Although I knew I needed to learn healthy ways to nurture myself, I had no idea how to start. Helen suggested I buy fragrant bath lotions and stroke my skin with my fingers in the shower: "sensually, not sexually."

I splurged on a bottle of French vanilla scented body soap. Standing in the shower, I felt my own skin, really felt it, for the first time. I enjoyed the lingering scent of vanilla and the softness of my skin. I stared at the hairs on my arms as they stood up when I stroked them backwards with my fingertips. I touched other parts of my body as a healthy mother might have if I'd been her delightful, soft-skinned baby. I kissed and held myself and wept.

Within a week my bottomless appetite for food went away. That surprised me, because during the past decade, I'd gained over fifty pounds from bingeing on the same foods that Mom had fed me as a child. Suddenly, I realized that I'd tried to use the food to fill the hole in my soul. No wonder I'd never felt full! How can anyone fill an emotional hole with food? Just as I'd believed that Dad had loved me because he'd gone to work to pay for our home and our physical needs, I'd erroneously believed that Mom's cooking had proven that she loved me.[2]

The next step in healing was to accept nurturing from other adult females. Because I hadn't wanted to feel the pain of not having been nurtured by Mom, I'd been phobic towards caring females. I needed to get past that fear. First, I thanked the woman who had sent me the care package. I told her she was the first non-therapist in my recovery who demonstrated to me that women other than my mother could give me bits and pieces of nurturing. Then I met with several women in my local support network and told them why I hadn't tried to emotionally connect with them. I told them that as I practiced loving and forgiving myself, I would also work harder at opening up to them.

Once I knew how it felt to bond with those women, I felt sad that I'd spent at least half my life isolating from such wonderful sources of soul-life. I gave myself permission to grieve that loss, too.

On the Wings of an Angel

I still didn't know that I had a hidden nurturer alter-state. In March, 1999, a sad little Aryan girl part wrote in my journal. She was in great pain. She hadn't emerged since Dad's death in 1990, and was unaware that my life had changed quite a bit since then. She wrote:

> *I don't want to talk to anybody. Why bother? I was one of theirs all of my life. How can I be anybody else now? I had no will. They took it all away and hurt me and slapped me and kicked me and laughed at me and I am not good. I am a puppet their puppet and I will do whatever they tell me to do. And if it's a good day I will feel something good down there maybe. Why bother to look for doors when there is no way to get away from them? They have my girl, my husband is with them, my dad and mom and brothers are with them, my in-laws are with them, my neighbors are with them, even the police and FBI are with them, and of course our lovely CIA–so where can I go that they won't hurt me again, where they won't do that thing to me down there again? There is no place but with them, always with them. Maybe I'm not with them, but I feel I am, and I don't like me, I don't hate me, but I don't like me, and I don't want to live. I want to sleep, sleep forever, but I don't want to hurt anybody. I don't want to hurt Bill, he's a nice man, but when he yells he is too much like them. So what do I do now? I'm supposed to brush my teeth and take a shower, and I'm supposed to do a term paper, but I don't want to do anything, I am crying again, and I don't want to do the computer, because bad people can read it, and they will know what I am doing. I wish Helen was here. I wish Bill would listen. I wish I had a friend, but I have no friend, never do. I just want to have a friend and I want to be in bed under the covers, and I don't bother anybody.*

She drew a picture of herself, naked with short hair, arms crossed across her chest, eyes closed, crying. Then an adult "angel" alter-state emerged. She drew herself in behind the lonely little girl and wrapped her wings around her. She wrote the words of a lullaby on the picture while crooning them softly:

> *I will hold you*
> *I will comfort you*
> *I will be with you*
> *You are no longer alone*
> *I will stay with you*
> *I will share your soul-shattering pain*
> *Rest in my wings*
> *Fall back into my wings*

The girl part responded, I feel bad about losing Emily. She saw so much badness.

I know, I feel bad about it too.

I did so much badness, I would get so mean at people, even to people I liked. It's like all the bad things they did to me built up and built up and I would be with non-hurters, and I would get upset or angry, and I kept hurting people I didn't mean to hurt, and then I wanted to say I'm sorry. But it was too late to say I'm sorry. Oh god, Oh god. I am such a monster, worse than them, I am a monster.

Not in my eyes. In my eyes you are not a monster. They trained and taught and tortured you to be a killer. They did NOT give you some magic on/off switch.

I talk so soft, but then I get so ANGRY, and then my hands and fingers get so STRONG, and it is like I don't think for a while, and when I think again—it's too late.

Emily is still alive. You did not kill her.

But all those people I hurt, all those children I hurt and scared—

Do you know how attack dogs are trained? Well, they are put in cages. And they are tortured over and over again until the good nature is terrorized out of them. Until their wills are broken, until they will do ANYTHING their masters tell them to do. But their aggression from all that torture has to go somewhere. They are dangerous, because sometimes they just "snap"–not when their masters tell them to attack. And just like an attack dog, you were terrorized and brutalized and tortured repeatedly. Your aggression had to go somewhere. Since it was not safe to turn it on those who tortured you–because they could do it again–you turned it on yourself–or if called out – on those who would not torture you. They broke your personality, they made you into an attack dog.³

That mean man and lady—she made the Dobermans . . . they growled so much at me, I thought they were going to eat me up! And they put their things in me! Ugly! I'm so ugly!

Yes, I know about that too. I know how heartbreaking and terrifying and degrading that was. They made you a dog. An attack dog. They took you away from your natural state of being and made you over, into something totally different.

All those people—all those bad things, those bad bad things I've done—

You can thank our Uberfuhrer for that. Dr. Black and his assistants liked to rechannel aggression and make naturally peace-loving humans turn on each other.

Why? Why would he do that to me—to them—to all of us? Why?

I wish I could tell you. I honestly do not know. He was a very sick man and a very perverted man.

They all were.

Very much so. But you had no choice. You had to go where he took you. You were his hostage, you were his victim, you were his prisoner, you were his slave. It was never your fault.

I hate myself.

No you don't. It's him you hate.

> *Rest in my wings, Little One*
> *Fall back into my wings*
> *I will comfort you*
> *I will hold you*
> *Rest in my wings*

Notes

1. Each summer, SMART sponsors an annual *Ritual Abuse, Secretive Organizations and Mind Control Conference*. To contact SMART, see the "Supportive Organizations" list in the back of this book.

2. Rosencrans explains the strong emotional connection between maternal nurturing and food:

   > Food and mothers are so intertwined for the daughters that it's hard to separate them. Food is used for discipline, rewards, emotional expression, cultural pride, and many other things . . . The roots of many eating problems are established in childhood and can lead to life-long struggles. (pp. 144-145)

3. This has also been done to other animals, to break their wills. In an article in *National Geographic Today*, Jennifer Hile reported on a technique still being used to condition elephants in Thailand:

   > [A] four-year-old elephant bellows as seven village men stab nails into her ears and feet. She is tied up and immobilized in a small, wooden cage . . . The cage is called a "training crush" . . . In addition to beatings, handlers use sleep-deprivation, hunger, and thirst to "break" the elephants' spirit and make them submissive to their owners . . . [a shaman said that] to control animals that can eventually weigh as much as 10,000 pounds, it's essential they fear their keepers. He believes it's the only way to safeguard against the animal kicking, goring, or otherwise injuring the people with whom they work. (pp. 1 & 4)

   Common sense dictates that when these handlers torture the elephants, they enrage the elephants. Then, fearing the rage, they torture them further to make them fear them and not attack them. Those who conditioned and tortured me for future ops used the same insane logic.

Letting Go of the Guilt

Sociopathic Mentality

Although I occasionally discovered comforter parts like the angel, I was more likely to find assassin trained parts. That was always very painful. To survive the pain, I had to believe I could survive it. But sometimes I wasn't sure I could. More than anything else, the guilt was slowly killing me. I didn't know, yet, that Dad had methodically created a foundation for this deadly guilt.

When I was a child, he'd repeatedly told me I was going to hell for my sins. Because he was a blatant sociopath who refused to accept responsibility for his own horrific sins, he seemed to encourage me to internalize his un-owned responsibility and guilt.[1]

In the 1990s, going to church and a Baptist seminary didn't help to free me from this pervasive sense of guilt. I was reminded again and again that Jesus had died for my sins, and that God had already forgiven me and washed me clean as snow. This added to my pain, because no noticeable exceptions were made for those who had been forced to commit sins against their will.

As I reviewed literature about criminals who were diagnosed with MPD or DID, I felt more depressed. Even if their host personalities didn't commit the crimes, most juries still believed their "criminal" personalities must be incarcerated, instead of being helped by legitimate mental health professionals to heal and possibly integrate.

Helen tried to help me understand that I'd had no way out and that my choices, in controlled alter-states, had been extremely limited. Although she made sense, every time she uttered the words "making amends," I again felt guilty and believed I should spend the rest of my life making up for my terrible crimes.[2]

When I tried to make amends by helping other mind-control and ritual abuse survivors to recover and heal, I ran out of energy and strength, spiraled into major depression again, and checked into a local psychiatric hospital to stay alive. Even after giving a presentation entitled "Letting

Go of the Guilt" at a SMART conference, I couldn't let go of my own. I didn't know how.

I tried to free myself from the guilt by mentally reviewing the techniques that had been used to mold some of my alter-states into torturer and killer parts. I was still seeking answers to free me from the guilt-shackles that held me back from building a new life.

When I was only three years old, Dad had started working on my mind at least once a week, if not every day. Because he'd focused on making me a receptacle for his guilt and self-loathing, I'd rarely felt good about myself. And after a while, even though I didn't remember his mental assaults, the ritual killings, and other related horrors, the sense of being guilty and unworthy of human kindness and forgiveness remained.

Because I was so young, I didn't understand that Dad wasn't capable of feeling guilt. He and most of his criminal associates were sociopaths. Instead of feeling remorse for their crimes, they gloried in breaking the law. To them, it was fun and exciting!

Because I'd spent most of my covert life in the presence of sociopaths, I've recently been fascinated by the hit HBO television show, *The Sopranos*. Listening to its shady characters' rationalizations for why they perform violent acts has almost been like being with Dad and his criminal associates again.

The rules in their twisted world were almost the direct opposite of those of normal society. For them, good was bad and bad was good. Murder and adult-child sex were expected and encouraged. They had no empathy or compassion for their victims. Torturing innocents, especially babies, seemed to sexually excite some of them. Murder seemed to be the ultimate thrill for people like Dad; but because the thrill didn't last long, they had to find more and more victims.

I think this is why he extended his mind and hands through mine, using me to kill even more innocents. I believe he was one of many ritualistic serial killers who have not been brought to justice.[3] The more Dad got away with murder and wasn't caught, the more untouchable he felt, and the more he murdered. The more he raped children and wasn't brought to justice, the more he raped children. His criminality spiraled out of control.[4]

Many parts of my shattered personality were forced to live exclusively in his sociopathic world. I absolutely could not reconcile his bizarre world with the normal world that I experienced at school, church, and play. I had to split completely to function and survive.

Divided Personality

In normal society I was taught to obey, to give, to care, to do good, to reach out and help those who weren't as well off. That benign training and conditioning was the foundation of my core personality.

In addition to that healthy part of myself, Dad created "bad" parts that were exposed exclusively to immorality, lust, lies, rape, sadism, torture and murder. Using trauma, drugs and hypnosis, he built impenetrable walls of amnesia that separated my normal life parts from my covert, hidden parts that were accustomed to sociopathic mentality.

Then he used hypnosis and brutality to put my anti-moral parts in invisible mental cages with locks that only he and other professional handlers had the keys to. Specific code words and other triggers released those alter-states, to perform like trained animals for the handlers and owners.

My covert alter-states were only conscious for as long as those masters and handlers allowed. These split-off parts weren't familiar with my life at home, nor did they know about my past. They had no sense of future. They didn't know my real name or how old I was or where I lived. Most of them didn't know what the year was, or who my husband was, or if I had children. Some of them didn't even know if "the body" was male or female, young or old, animal or human. Their only reality was what the programmers and handlers told them.

These alter-states and personality fragments had extremely limited life experience and knowledge. Most of them had never tasted and swallowed food, touched the soft fur of a pet, slept on a bed, or felt warm sunshine. When triggered out, most of them didn't know what country they were in. And most of them considered the professional handlers to be their friends and saviors.

They weren't allowed to talk to strangers. They weren't allowed to look out vehicle windows. During debriefings, handlers lied about where my alter-states had been. They hypnotically implanted false information to scramble the parts' memories of the real locations.

The alter-states were often smuggled into buildings through back doors and underground parking areas and service elevators. Sometimes they were shipped overseas in big wooden crates in planes or on the open decks of large boats, so they could see nothing and so that no one, other than assigned handlers, could see and talk to them.

Many times, when handlers made me wait in an office before taking me home, they either made me sit or walk around with no clothes on, or only let me keep some of my clothes while they remained fully clothed. When I emerged from amnesia and found myself naked or partially clothed, I believed it was my fault. The handlers laughed as I frantically looked for something to cover myself with. When they held me in rooms and buildings, they also made me remove my footwear to discourage me from running away.[5]

In spite of all this, some of my alter-states would have stayed, even if they'd been given permission to leave. To them, the covert world was addictive and exciting. There is something in the world of amorality and deception that draws the untamed parts of the soul.

Having been sexually assaulted and conditioned by Dad from infancy, some of my alter-states sought one male sexual partner after another. After each interaction, they wanted more. Several female alter-states that had compartmentalized "black widow" mental programming, saw nothing wrong with having sex with a man and then killing him while he slept–as ordered.

Because I'd been sexually assaulted and molested by my mother throughout my childhood and beyond, I'd also developed sexually conditioned parts that hadn't seen anything wrong with having sex with women–anytime, anywhere. Like with men, it was never about love–it was about sexual pleasure, and the power that came from knowing that, at least for a moment, these parts were able to make the women vulnerable as they brought them to orgasm.

Finding my sociopathic alter-states was a tremendous shock. They were everything I'd never allowed my rule-oriented self to be. They were all that I believed was wrong and evil. I judged them by the knowledge and rules I'd lived by in the normal world. I didn't understand that they'd never experienced goodness, sinlessness, honesty, kindness and love. I blamed them; I hated them; I despised them. I didn't understand that they'd had no choice. Feeling ashamed for what they'd done, I carried a relentless load of guilt-bricks on my back, day after loathsome day.

I argued that they should have done differently. I wasn't willing to acknowledge that amnesic barriers or gaps had kept my knowledge and morality from reaching where they had resided in my brain. I didn't want to know that they had been tortured and more, to transform them into seemingly less-than-human, primal and reptilian creature parts.

As I began to blend with them, however, I was overwhelmed by the intensity of their pain and rage. I realized *I did not have the right* to judge them, or myself, for what they'd been manipulated and controlled to do.[6]

Addiction to Secrecy

In 2001, I made another major discovery about myself. For years, I'd heard Madonna's hit song, *Live to Tell*, but hadn't listened to the words. One day, I sat in my office at home, I typed a journal entry. In it, I wrote my concern that some of my op-trained alter-states still wanted to go back to spook handlers. These alter-states missed the quiet excitement of living a double life that even the neighbors knew nothing about.

As I typed, I heard *Live to Tell* again. Madonna sang about the "secret inside of me." Tears streamed down my face as I realized I really was addicted to secrecy, and I wasn't the only person struggling with this problem.

In my next therapy session, I talked to Helen about my insane desire to go back to living a secret double life. She surprised me by telling me that secrecy is a common addiction among childhood sexual abuse survivors.

She explained that many women who marry and then have a series of affairs on the side, are drawn to illicit sexual relationships because they're reenacting secretive sexual "relationships" that childhood abusers had had with them.

As we discussed this phenomenon, I had another revelation. When I was a child, most of the mind-control programmers I'd been exposed to, had sexually assaulted me.[7] And when I was an adult, sexual assaults by spook handlers had seemed to be the norm. Had some of them used me to reenact their own childhood sexual traumas, this time acting out the role of the powerful, controlling perpetrator?

I told Helen I was beginning to grasp the powerful connection between addiction to secrecy and seeking employment within an intelligence agency. Over and over, I'd heard that the CIA and other intelligence agencies *expect* their employees to lie as part of their employment.[8] If the employees can't be honest with their families and neighbors about their employment, does lying gradually become second nature? And how many of them gravitate to intelligence agencies because, having grown up in secretive families, such environments are most comfortable? When I shared these thoughts with Bill, he said that–based on his never-forgotten experiences with CIA spooks in Vietnam–what I theorized was probably true. More important, he said he also struggled with a strong desire to go back to living a double life in a "James Bond" manner. In spite of all that had been done to him by his spook handlers, his addiction was so strong, he desired to work for them again, without pay!

Although going back to those handlers would mean being controlled, abused, and possibly placed into deadly situations, we both *still* desired to be used by them again!

The allure of living a secret life is powerful. Since I've made that discovery, I've worked harder to stay honest with my support system–even admitting to them that I wanted to go back.

Defusing the Threat

After I'd retrieved the bulk of my black op training memories, I fantasized about doing serious damage to those who had hurt me and other precious innocents. Perhaps I was lucky that my fundamental morality restrained me–it put on the brakes. The law that I'd been taught to respect, by teachers and scoutmasters and pastors and more, still guided me. As imperfect as our legal system is, without it we'd have my father's world. I cannot bear to enter that world again.

Before I'd found and connected with my covert alter-states, they'd only had enough information to perform their duties. When I blended with them, my shared knowledge balanced out their conditioning and programming. Other than their experiences, training, and the traumas that had been used to create them, the only big difference between me and them had been lack of information. They hadn't known what I did, and I hadn't had their knowledge. After they blended with me, they had a new opportunity–to choose between a nearly infinite number of choices; whereas before, they'd only been permitted to choose between the lesser of two evils.

Numerous child alter-states wrote or talked about having been repeatedly sexually assaulted, ritually abused and tortured, and more. Some of those parts had stored my greatest rage. Dad and his spook associates had used them to do the worst physical damage to targeted males. If a part had held rage from having been raped by men, that part had then been used to attack that part of a male target's anatomy or to have sex with him and then kill him.

An especially effective form of mental programming had been to convince several of my child alter-states that penis monsters had extended up into men's throats. Because an engorged penis and a male's windpipe feel alike, those powerfully strong alter-states were conditioned to grab targeted males' windpipes and yank them forward in total fury, believing they were *saving* the men from the invasive monsters!

When these programmed alter-states emerged in therapy, they were immediately suicidal, feeling tremendous pain as they realized they'd been tricked into killing the very men they'd tried to save!

The good news is that once those parts shared their experiences with me in a therapeutic way, and received my knowledge that they'd been tricked, they immediately stopped being a threat to society. Although very young, they'd never had the opportunity to play, eat ice cream, and do other things that "normal" children might experience. As I introduced them to such activities and experiences, they integrated with me and we became one.[9]

Cult Recruitment

Because Dad was a sadist, he'd enjoyed torturing and traumatizing others. I suspect he'd also used occult rituals to unconsciously reenact sexual, physical, and even ritualized traumas that he may have endured as a child. I also believe he would have perpetrated those crimes, regardless of whether or not he'd been influenced by his alleged CIA and Nazi connections.

Beyond all this, I believe he had another reason for forcing me to experience such horrors.[10] I believe that employees and operatives working within several intelligence and military agencies made secretive arrangements with criminal occult leaders to traumatize and condition children and to create alter-states in those youths, with the foreknowledge that their alter-states would eventually be used by these same agencies to perform illegal activities as mentally controlled slaves. I believe this is the reason why the deadly cover-up about the existence of ritual crime, repressed memory, severe dissociation, and mentally controlled slavery continues.

Investigative journalist Alex Constantine thoroughly exposed CIA/cult recruitment/mind-control/FMSF connections in his 1995 book, *Psychic Dictatorship in the U.S.A.* Based on years of extensive research that included many interviews with recovering ritual abuse and mind control victims, Constantine concluded:

> . . . the CIA and its cover organizations have a vested interest in blowing smoke at the cult underground because the worlds of CIA mind control and many cults merge inextricably. The drum beat of "false accusations" from the media is taken up by paid operatives like Dr. Orne and the False Memory Syndrome Foundation to conceal the crimes of the Agency. (pg. 54)

I strongly recommend reading Constantine's *Psychic Dictatorship,* Dr. Colin Ross's *Bluebird,* Carol Rutz's *A Nation Betrayed,* and Gordon Thomas's *Enslaved* if you want to learn more about the documented connections between complicit groups, federal agencies, and other organizations.

Nazi Sadism and Rituals

The more I've remembered about my childhood exposure to Nazis and neo-Nazi wannabes, the more I've felt appalled and amazed at their hatred towards strangers. My forced attendance at innumerable Aryan meetings throughout my life helped me to understand that when people chronically hate strangers who have never harmed them, based solely on their skin color or ethnicity, they're actually projecting their self-hatred onto them. That is one reason why I've worked hard on my own self-hatred; I don't want to irrationally project it onto others.

I've also concluded that when primary caregivers hate their children, the children learn to hate themselves, using the caregivers as their role models. In other words, as the caregivers model *their* projection of self-hatred onto the innocent children, the children are likely to do the same to others when they become adults![11]

No one likes to feel self-hatred. Self-hatred is extremely painful. It's always easier to direct one's self-hatred onto someone else as pseudo- or false-hatred. (I call it pseudo-hatred because real hatred occurs when one despises something in a person whom one *truly knows*.) Self-hatred that comes from having been neglected or abused as a child may explain many staunch Aryans' "need" to hate and attack people they don't really know.

I suspect these Aryans keep an emotional distance from their hate-targets because if they ever really know these people, they will recognize that their pseudo-hatred is irrational. They may be afraid to know it's irrational because then they'll have to give up the pseudo-hate and feel their painful self-hatred.

The only way I know to get out of this vicious trap is to get professional help to deal with the underlying cause of the self-hatred. It is hard work, but it can be done. Although one will have to feel the seemingly unbearable pain of self-hatred for a little while when confronting its root causes, surely that's better than running away from it and unfairly hating and isolating from others for the rest of one's life.

Self-hatred can also generate sadism towards the pseudo-hate targets. The most powerful article I've read to-date about the origin of Nazi sadism, "War as Righteous Rape and Purification," was published in the Spring 2000 edition of the *Journal of Psychohistory.* Written by the journal's editor, Lloyd deMause, the article extensively documents the abuses that *average* German parents perpetrated against their children in the late 1800s through early 1900s.[12]

Such horrific abuse must have generated tremendous rage and hatred in those children's minds and souls. I want to clarify that I'm not condoning the crimes that many of them committed or supported when they became adults. And yet, it's crucial that we understand that what they did to the victims in the concentration camps may have been their way of unconsciously reenacting what they had survived as children. I believe that such heinous brutality always has a source.

DeMause stated: "Every one of the things done to Jews in the Holocaust can be found to have been perpetrated by parents and others on German children at the turn of the century. The precise details of earlier events that were reinflicted upon Jews later are astonishingly minute and literal." (pp. 434–435) I believe this is true.

What the Nazis did to many of their victims in the concentration camps was also perpetrated against American victims (especially children) in secretive occult rituals and also in government-sanctioned experiments like the CIA's MKULTRA program right here in North America. This is one of our country's dirtiest secrets. I will spend the rest of my life, if necessary, to help survivors and pro-survivors to fully and permanently expose it.[13] (We're angry as hell about what's been done to us. We're *not* going to be quiet and we're *not* going to stop telling! Even if some of us are stopped–it has been done–others will take our place. I believe our movement's momentum, built on decades of pure moral outrage, is now unstoppable.)

The Nazi immigrants I was taken by Dad and Grandpa M. to meet as a child, practiced a Teutonic form of occultism. I still wonder if any of them were aware that they were using these rituals to reenact childhood traumas.[14] I've found verifications from a number of sources that sun worship, Paganism, and other religious beliefs that I was exposed to at Aryan Golden Dawn meetings and rituals had also been part of Hitler's occult practices.[15]

In my presence as a child, Dad and some of his Nazi associates had repeatedly bragged that they were reincarnated Knights Templar. Dad had also repeatedly told me that I was an "honorary daughter of Templar." He'd told me and the men that our "duty" was to perform assassinations. To me, the Templar rituals appeared insane; and yet, to those men, they were logical.

Dad and his Nazi friends seemed to be mentally disconnected from the world around them and from their own humanity. They claimed they wouldn't die if they continued to ingest the life-force stored in human blood and semen. They believed it would keep them young and strong. They also told me that, because they'd incorporated Gnostic beliefs into their Teutonic religious practices, they were gradually transforming into spiritual gods. They welcomed pain and physical deprivation (other than from sex), claiming that this speeded their transformations. Living in a spiritualized fantasy world seemed to be their way of dissociating from the harsh reality of their real lives.[16]

Never Forgotten

Although Dad kept his criminal and Nazi connections secret, he did say and do other things over the years that I never forgot. Although these statements and behaviors had seemed odd, I now believe he had tried to communicate about his covert world to me and others–possibly because he'd felt lonely in holding onto so many secrets.

He told my stepmother and me that when he was a teenager, he'd worked as a lifeguard for a Mafia family at their Florida hotel. He seemed proud of that.

When I was a teenager, he often took our family on Sundays to a fancy buffet brunch at Atlanta's Stone Mountain Park hotel. Occasionally, he pointed to certain sedans parked outside the hotel that, he said, belonged to "mobsters" who met regularly at the hotel to discuss "business." Although he told us some of their names, because knowing them wasn't important to me, I didn't try to remember them.

In the early 1970s, after Mom divorced Dad, he moved into an apartment in North Atlanta. During a rare visit to his apartment, Dad told me that he'd recently fallen in love with a woman named Ellen, who had been the girlfriend of a Mafia hit man. Dad cried and seemed very depressed as he told me his sad story: Ellen had approached him, telling him that her boyfriend was cruel to her. Then she'd charmed and dated Dad, indicating that she wanted to marry him. In return, Dad had agreed to protect her from the ex-boyfriend. Dad was emotionally devastated when Ellen unexpectedly broke up with him and went back to the hit man. Because I didn't remember that Dad had taken me to meet mobsters in several states, I thought it odd that he would get involved with such a woman.

Dad's income tax return statements from 1973, 1974, and 1975 verify that before he married his second wife, he was hired by Pinkerton Inc., a security agency based in New York City.[17] His first Pinkerton position was as a night guard in an Atlanta jail. His second position was as a nighttime security guard at Atlanta's posh Piedmont Driving Club, where the local elite and visiting dignitaries discussed business and socialized. One night, Dad gave Albert and me a tour of the main building and encouraged me to make a butterscotch ice cream sundae in the club's huge, stainless steel kitchen. He bragged that he didn't need to carry a gun because he knew how to talk people out of shooting him.

When he was younger, he probably didn't have the same level of confidence. Years after his death, his widow sent me four small black and white pictures of a much younger Dad. Wearing a long-sleeved white shirt and dark pants, a handgun was in a holster at his waist while he aimed a rifle under the supervision of an unidentified man.

Understanding My Father

Although I accepted and blended with my black op parts, I still had great difficulty reconciling "Dad the serial killer" and "Dad the pedophile" in my mind. How could he have been both? I wasn't willing to admit how strongly those two aspects of his personality had been intertwined.

Confused, I scoured many books and articles, searching for information that would help me understand Dad's criminal mentality. Anna C. Salter, Ph.D.'s book, *Predators: Pedophiles, Rapists, and Other Sex Offenders* was most helpful. I found other valuable materials listed in Safer Society's extensive book catalog. The non-profit's primary goal is to inform the public about sexual abuse and its harmful consequences.[18]

One professional journal article helped me to understand how Dad's mind worked. "Sexual Compulsivity as Post-Traumatic Stress Disorder: Treatment Perspectives," was written by Mark F. Schwartz, ScD., the "Clinical Director, Masters & Johnson Sexual Trauma Programs."

Schwartz explained a compulsion called "trauma reenactment," in which men and women who do not work through their original traumas "may repeat in concealed forms events that are too terrifying to remember." This may explain why Dad was so violent (even to the point of killing his victims) and yet he constantly minimized his own childhood traumas. Schwartz explained that by performing repetitive trauma reenactments, sexual abuse victims may also substitute the reenactments for normal intimacy. (pg. 333)

His description of a typical victim-turned-abuser may explain some of Dad's behaviors, especially towards children and women:

> Another common theme among sexual compulsives is the introjection of their perpetrator's passive or active rage. Among boys who have watched their mother being raped, it is common for the child to identify with the rapist in reenactments during play. Similarly, both male and female victims of abusive parents frequently "identify with the aggressor," i.e., introject the values and beliefs of the powerful perpetrator and reject the weak, ineffectual, yet equally rageful, passive parent. Traumatized children internalize the perfectionist, rigid,

demanding, critical, and conditional love of their parents and then as adults repeat their parents' messages daily. The result is a self-abusive adult often similarly demanding and cruel to others, particularly his or her own children. (pg. 334)

Some abuse survivors binge and purge or self-mutilate to feel a release from the discomfort of emerging emotions. Dad seemed to use long-distance running, even during blazing hot summer afternoons, to attain the same release and to numb his body. Throughout his life, running and sexual intercourse seemed to be the two primary compulsions that helped him to avoid the depths of his painful self-hatred and depression.

Schwartz explained why people like Dad would minimize the severity of their childhood traumas: "When sexually compulsive patients have a history of physical and/or sexual abuse and neglect, they are often either amnesic or they minimize and distort their histories."

In describing the phases of the cycle of sexual addiction, Schwartz explained that towards the end, "addicts' lives become unmanageable and the compulsive sexual behavior becomes the focus of their lives." (pg. 334)

Schwartz's explanations fit what I'd remembered about Dad. He had become such an ardent pedophile almost every time that I'd been with him, he'd seemed to be looking for his next child victim.

Dad made several telling statements in his 1989 civil, pre-divorce deposition. They may be the only keyhole I'll ever have, to peer through to Dad's internal fantasy world. He made the following statement after an attorney asked if he was a pedophile:

I do love children, but I do not love them sexually. I am crazy about children. And I can go to any airport in the country, any place, and the kids come to me like a dying maggot. I admit that I love them, and I have no problem with that. (Q: Do you know what a pedophile is?) No. Now I know; it's a man who loves children–sexually. (Q: A sexual sense?) Yeah, right. (pg. 197)

Because Dad had ritually abused me for many years, I was exposed to many decomposing bodies that crawled with maggots. In the spring of 1964, when I was eight years old, Dad and several of his friends created an entertainment group, "The Maggots." One night at dusk during our community's annual May Day festival at Exeter Township High School, the men were brought to the stage in a paddy wagon, its siren blaring. The crowd screamed as Dad and his friends, wearing black wigs, ascended the stage and then lip-synced several Beatles songs. A big "M" was marked on the front of each of their white T-shirts, and the word "Maggots" had been printed on a sign that was draped across the front of the wooden stage. Later, Dad bragged to us that he'd personally named the band.

Fast-forward twenty-five years. During his deposition, Dad identified himself as a "dying maggot." Only he knew, somewhere deep inside, what horrifying trauma that mental image may have represented.

Although Dad initially denied knowing what the word "pedophile" meant, he then stated that a pedophile is "a man who loves children–sexually." He also said that children were drawn to him. In reality, I met very few children who initially were comfortable with Dad. I think Dad had to believe that children were drawn to him and wanted him sexually because otherwise, he would have to face that he was a molester and a rapist. He didn't want to know that what he'd done was wrong. I believe he had to believe that he was sexually desired by his objects of lust and sexual pleasure. I believe if he'd ever faced the truth, his carefully constructed false self would have crumbled and *he* would felt the pain of having been sexually abused, beaten, and betrayed as a child, by those who should have loved and protected him.

When I'd accompanied Dad (in controlled adult alter-states) to meetings of pedophiles, child traffickers, and kiddy pornographers, I'd noticed that he'd surrounded himself with criminals and pedophiles like himself. Their world had seemed to become his primary reality; everything else had grown ethereal and temporary. He often told some of my alter-states that he and his "friends" were the only honest people in society. He said that everyone else was a hypocrite–at least *he* was willing to be who he really was.

Dad seemed so convinced that adult-child sex was normal, he had to believe that everyone else had the same tendencies. He told me the only difference was that they didn't "have the guts" to do what they secretly desired, whereas he did. This may be why, in the deposition, he said:

I guarantee it, and I don't know how better to put it, if I molested my children, every father in this room is a molester.

Every father in this office is a molester, and every father in the
City of Decatur or the State of Georgia is a molester. (pg. 202)

In the same deposition, he insinuated that I'd "stalked" him in the early
1970s after he'd moved away and was sharing an apartment with a man
in another town. What he said would have been impossible because I didn't
have access to a vehicle and didn't know where he lived. I believe that
Dad's strange statements were another indication of his fantasy world:

Now, when I was sick and when I was single–during–after
we were divorced, Kathy kept coming to my house time and
time again. And from–time and time again, she'd write me
something bordering on MASH notes. (Q: Define what you
think MASH notes means.) When you have your daughter
talking to you like she would like to have a man like me have
her children for her, I consider that MASH notes. And this goes
on and on. I have one of her [Fall 1989] letters here that I'd like
for you to–(Q: Let me see.) And when Kathy–when Kathy
started sending out those registered letters, yes, I put
that through the shredder. I had gotten hundreds of her letters,
and I'm absolutely sick of them and I don't want to see them
anymore. (Q: But you have an example of this MASH–of a
MASH note from her that you received some time in the past?)
I tried not to save these things because they made me so
mad. This one I started to scribble up because–the word is
pissed off, I guess. (Q: You were, after reading these letters.)
And that's where I started scribbling my replies. Then
I decided–(Q: Oh, that is your language.) Yeah, that's my
language. (pp. 206–207)

In reality, several months prior to the deposition, I had written a
total of three or four notes and short letters of confrontation to Dad.
Other than the first one, each had been my response to cards and other
items that he'd sent to me through the mail, to try to frighten and intimidate me. In each response, I'd tried to set new boundaries with Dad
while asking him to seek professional help. And in each, I'd written once
or twice that I still loved him. I didn't understand that, because Dad

equated sex with love, he'd inferred that I was requesting to have sex with him!

(Q: Do you consider that a MASH note, in terms of your definition?) It is a little much. (Q: In what respect? What language in there?) Her profession of love. I don't mind a person telling me they love me, but when they tell me 25 or 30 times in one letter, I object. (Q: And that upsets you?) It certainly does. (pg. 208)

Because Dad is dead, I may never know who caused him to internalize the false belief that when an adult rapes a child, the rape is an expression of love. In the deposition, he made only one admission about having been molested as a child:

I had a cousin who was very horny. She was about the horniest woman I've ever met in my life. And when I was about [her] age, nine or ten, she would shake me down continually. (Q: How old was she?) Well, she may have been 13 or 14. She was always about five or six years older than I was. Trying to get me to touch her, you know, and play with her and all this kind of stuff. And when she came around, I used to have to run and hide. But that—the story stinks.[19] (Q: Well, did she ever touch you in an—) She never touched me. (Q:—in your sex organs or anything?) No, she never touched me. She tried to get me to touch her. (Q: Oh? And you say that was the most serious–any other such incidents?) No. (Q: Did any adult ever try to sexually molest you?) No. (pg. 213–214)

Not Guilty

As I showed Dad's deposition to Helen, I told her that I knew I wasn't responsible for what Dad and his associates had forced me to do. I was beginning to see they had refused to accept their own guilt and had laid it on me, making me a monster instead of themselves.

She sat in silence. Then she said, "If I remember correctly, this is now the fourth time you came to the conclusion that you were not guilty. Why doesn't your discovery last? Why do you again believe you were a criminal? Why do you still blame yourself for what you had no choice about doing?"

I couldn't answer.

When she softly said, "You are not a criminal," I looked at the floor. I couldn't look into her eyes because something in me was warring against her words.

As I sat quietly in her office, I realized my biggest recurring problem was that Dad had told me countless times, starting when I was four, that I was a murderer. That I was guilty. That I was bad. That if people really knew me, they would not want to have anything to do with me. That they would hate me. That I deserved to be in prison for the rest of my life. And so on.

I had lived with him for seventeen years; three hundred sixty-five days a year, minus the times one of us was away from home. If I were to halve the number of days I'd lived with him, I still count at least 3100 days that he'd had access to my mind. Dad had hardwired my brain by using verbal repetition and more, so that his words had become so much an integral part of my own thought patterns, I hadn't recognized that the constant thoughts about being guilty had originated from him!

Dad couldn't see himself as who and what he really was. He'd constructed an immense, nearly impenetrable mental wall behind him. Behind it was the pain of his having been abused and betrayed as a child. In front stood the part of Dad that had secretly operated in the criminal world. This adult part had dumped his guilt onto me, his small victim, because he'd been unwilling to recognize that *he* was a murderer and a pedophile.

Dad had lied to himself most of all. In his fantasy world, he wasn't a molester; he expressed his love for children by having sex with them. He wasn't a murderer; he had to "teach a lesson" when he believed that adult cult members had betrayed him. He wasn't a murderer when he slaughtered "disposable" infants on altars–he'd need their life-force to survive. He'd tortured and sometimes killed children for being weak, with the justification that only the strong should survive. He'd raped and sometimes killed women because "women always get you in the end."

He'd killed "street bums" because they were worthless and caused problems. He wasn't a murderer; he did the world a favor by "taking out the trash."[20]

Perhaps he couldn't feel his guilt because he couldn't accept the knowledge that those who should have loved and protected him as a child, had instead willingly hurt and betrayed him.

I believe he also refused to own his guilt because it was too uncomfortable–he didn't want to see himself as who and what he really was. His free-floating guilt and self-hatred had to go . . . well, where else? Onto his innocent victims.

I became one of several primary extensions of Dad's ego. He made me a receptacle for much of his disowned guilt and hatred. In his mind, I was "bad."

At the age of four, I was the dark one, the guilty one. I was the one with blood on my hands and body and soul. It was all me. He was free. I was enslaved.

In spite of all the trauma that was done to me for decades to make me an assassin-by-proxy for spook handlers and their associates, I couldn't accept that I'd never had a choice. Dad's thousands of reinforced accusations had effectively anchored my sense of guilt.

In therapy with Helen, I began to separate these thoughts from my own. They definitely had Dad's feel and signature. Perhaps I could fight them by refusing to accept them as another form of his lies, throwing them back onto him one by one.

Helen gave me a better solution: reverse his messages. I was not a murderer at the age of four; in reality, Dad had been the serial killer. Dad had feared that people wouldn't want anything to do with *him*, if they really knew him. It was all about *Dad*, not me. For the first time in my life, I began to mentally separate from Dad and feel my individuality.

I'm now convinced that Dad really didn't want to know me, because then he would have had to know himself. To avoid the pain of self-knowledge, he instead made me one of his egoless, mental/emotional poison containers.

Armed with that knowledge, I can now accept and love myself for who I really am. I was never a murderer by choice; Dad was. Step by step, truth by truth, I'm breaking free of the false, self-destructive beliefs that he'd implanted in my mind.

Notes

1. Rosencrans wrote about the false guilt that plagues many abuse survivors:

   Oppressed people . . . frequently believe that they themselves are responsible for their failures and problems. This self-blame is often encouraged and even planted in the oppressed by their oppressors. The oppressed may live in an environment that not only allows oppression but reinforces it as justified. (pg. 231)

2. In *Necessary Losses*, Judith Viorst described a famous experiment conducted by a psychologist, Stanley Milgram:

   [He] brought people into a Yale University psychology laboratory to engage-or so they were told-in a study of memory and learning. The experimenter explained that the issue to be explored was the impact of punishment on learning, and to that end the designated "teacher" was asked to administer a learning test to a "learner" strapped in a chair in another room–and to give him an electric shock whenever his answer was wrong . . . the teacher was told that, with each wrong answer, he was to give the learner the next higher shock. Conflict began when the learner went from grunts to vehement protests to agonized screams, and the teacher became increasingly uneasy and wished to stop. But each time he hesitated, the person in authority urged him to continue, insisting that he must complete the experiment. And despite the concern for the level of shocking pain that was being inflicted, a large number of teachers continued to push the switches all the way up to the highest voltage. (pp. 138-139)

   Reading about the obedience and willingness of some of those students to shock the "learners" to death did help me a little to forgive myself for having obeyed my professional handlers' orders.

3. If ritual abuse survivors are telling the truth about these crimes, and I'm convinced they are, why isn't our government going after the criminals and shutting down their operations? I think this is because some government agencies like the CIA-and US military-are selecting ritually conditioned victims to perform illegal acts. Similar cover-ups have already been exposed. In 7/28/02, Associated Press's Jeff Donn wrote the first of a series of explosive articles that exposed the FBI's involvement, from the national headquarters on down through the ranks, in covering-up for the existence and crimes of members of mafia families-some of whom still continue to operate freely within the US. The cover-up included "shielding them from prosecution for serious crimes including murder." Donn reported that he and his co-workers discovered that although the "scandal has been portrayed largely as the work of local agents-mavericks willing to deal with the devil

to bring down a Mafia family" (a typical disinfo ploy), they'd discovered documents that "directly connect FBI headquarters to a pattern of collusion with notorious killers."

4. Viorst's description of a psychopath provides a glimpse into Dad's secretive world:

> There are . . . the so-called psychopathic personalities who seem to display a genuine lack of guilt, whose antisocial and criminal acts, whose repetitive acts of destructiveness and depravity, occur with no restraint and no remorse. These psychopaths cheat and rob and lie and damage and destroy with remarkable emotional impunity. These psychopaths spell out for us, in letters ten feet high, what kind of world this world would be without guilt. (pg. 138)

5. Shortly before I remembered this, I suddenly "had to" buy as many pairs of socks as I could cram into my bureau drawers. I probably have enough to last a lifetime!

6. Gordon Thomas's *Journey Into Madness: The True Story of Secret CIA Mind Control and Medical Abuse* solidified that reality. In it, he wrote about his good friend, William Buckley, who had been one of the CIA's top spies. In March, 1984, Buckley was kidnapped in Beirut, Lebanon. After learning of the abduction, CIA officials consulted with specialists, asking them what they thought Buckley would most likely do while in captivity:

> . . . the Agency specialists believed that Buckley's reactions would follow an almost immutable pattern, characterized by four distinctive steps. *It would make no real difference in the end that he was a trained intelligence officer trained in ways to resist interrogation* [italics added]. Because he would be in close and prolonged contact with his kidnappers, Buckley's psychological responses would be little different from any other kidnap victim; there is no actual way to prepare a person to cope with the stress of being taken hostage. (pg. 42)

After nearly two months, the CIA received the first of at least two videotapes of Buckley giving false confessions and making political demands for his kidnappers' terrorist organization. Twenty-three days later, they received the second videotape. On June 3, 1985, Buckley died of pneumonia–still a hostage. (pp. 42, 46–48, 351) If the will of a highly trained career CIA operative was broken in less than two months to where he betrayed his beloved agency; then how could a child who was tortured, drugged, raped, and more on a near-weekly basis resist becoming mindlessly compliant?

7. Many other mind-control survivors have reported that they were also sexually assaulted by CIA and military intelligence personnel, and/or by CIA-contracted MKULTRA doctors.

8. This is why I find it so bizarre that, on a wall in the entrance to the CIA's headquarters in Langley, is the phrase, "The Truth Shall Set You Free."

9. Blending with emerging child parts sometimes made life difficult, because adult "me" suddenly became childlike and socially inept. As I integrated with those child parts, I often felt a sudden need to pursue childlike experiences that they had been totally deprived of. A bonus to integrating with those child parts was that they'd compartmentalized wisdom and insights about humanity that had been split off from my consciousness. And because of their pure and childlike self-knowledge, these parts could also analyze others in insightful ways. These parts also had essential character strengths and a pure sense of moral outrage that helped me-as the host alter-state-to stand up to abusive and controlling people and say "no" to unreasonable demands.

10. Carla Emery describes a series of techniques that can make a person vulnerable to hypnotic suggestion. Many of them are used in criminal occult rituals:

    Brainwashing researchers have analyzed the types of **emotional shocks** and their power to devastate. Shocks are most likely to make a person suggestible—and to break him—when they are: intense, repeated, unpredictable, uncontrollable, linked to pressure, incomprehensible, humiliating . . . Any excitement or trauma (sudden fright, fear, terror, threats) makes you more suggestible . . . erotic excitation and orgasm greatly increase suggestibility. (pp. 298–299)

11. Dr. Charles Whitfield explains this sad legacy:

    . . . the parent or parent figure is previously wounded from having grown up in a dysfunctional family and world. As a result, they feel that they are inadequate and bad at their core, yet they have a toxic store of unfinished business inside. Because there is no safe place to express it, the parent or parent figure then regularly or periodically tries to express their pain, but ends up discharging it in the form of abusing self or others, including their children or others in or outside of the family. (pg. 170)

12. In detail, deMause describes what most of the Nazis, as children, had been forced to endure at home and even at school:

    Murder, rejection, neglect, tying up and beating by their mothers and other women . . . [mothers birthed] "their babies in the privy, and treated the birth as an evacuation" . . . [mothers coldly] killed their newborn babies . . . [babies] could easily be neglected and not fed enough . . . [mothers] refused to breastfeed their babies . . . [babies were given to] nursemaids, governesses and tutors . . . Mothers and other caretakers tied them up tightly for from six to nine months, and strapped them into a crib in a room with curtains drawn to keep out the lurking evils . . . restraint devices such as corsets with steel stays and backboards continued their tied-up condition to assure the parents they were still in complete control . . . Children were given away and even sometimes sold . . . the mother was far more often the main beater . . . The widely-followed Dr. Schreber said the earlier one begins beatings the better . . . [they endured] routine beating, kicking, strangling, making children eat excrement, etc. . . . [parents "hardened" them] by washing them with ice-cold water before breakfast . . . [children were bound] in controlled positions all day long . . . [they were] frightened by endless ghost stories where they were threatened with being carried away by horrible figures . . . [infant toilet training began] at around six months of age, long before the infant has sphincter control. The training [was] done by regular use of enemas and by hitting the infant . . . [enemas] resembled sexual assaults on the anus . . . [children were] used by parents and servants as sexual objects from an early age . . . incestuous assaults were regular . . . After using them sexually, [parents] then would threaten to punish the child for their sexuality . . . [parents used] anti-masturbation devices such as penis-rings, metal cages with spikes, and plaster casts to prevent erections while sleeping . . . [children were] again raped at school, as servants, on the streets and at work. (pp. 410, 412-414, & 416-421)

13. I am not the first person, by far, to make such statements. Other brave souls are also making the connections between criminal occultism, Nazi immigrants, the CIA, and mind-control experimentation:

> In 1993, Dr. Corydon Hammond, a professor at the University of Utah's School of Medicine, conducted a seminar on federally-funded mind control experiments. Topics covered by Hammond included brain-washing, post-hypnotic programming and the induction of multiple personalities by the CIA. Hammond contended that the cult underground has roots in Nazi Germany, and that the CIA's cult mind control techniques were based upon those of Nazi scientists recruited by the CIA for Cold Warfare . . . Hammond was forced to drop this line of inquiry by professional ridicule, especially from the CIA's False Memory Syndrome Foundation, and a barrage of death threats. At a regional conference on ritual child abuse, he regretted that he could no longer speak on the theme of government mind control. (*Psychic Dictatorship*, pg. 61)

14. As was experienced by many of the German children, most occult ritual abuse survivors in North America with whom I have been in contact have reported that they were also forced to eat excrement and drink urine. Many of them claimed they either witnessed and/or were forced to perform the murder of babies

and young children. And almost all of them reported they were sexually assaulted and/or tortured during rituals. Survivors like Carol Rutz, author of *A Nation Betrayed*, reported that as children, they were forced to stay in cages for long periods of time, naked and unable to bathe or use a toilet. Many ritual abuse survivors have also reported having been starved and/or put in sensory isolation containers, especially in boxes and coffins. Many of them have also reported "bug traumas" in which they had been placed inside containers and covered with insects.

15. An excellent resource is *The Occult Roots of Nazism: Secret Aryan Cults And Their Influence On Nazi Ideology,* by Nicholas Goodrick-Clarke.

16. Joseph Moreno, MT-BC, a Director of Music Therapy at Maryville University, St. Louis, Missouri, wrote *Orpheus in Hell,* a fascinating journal article about how both concentration camp inmates and their Nazi captors used music to cope with their experiences. Moreno made an observation about those Nazis that I believe also would have applied to Dad and his Nazi associates in America:

> Once a person has reached that level of criminality, to give up one's defenses would be an overwhelmingly self-destructive confrontation. The individual would then be obliged to move from a position of self-esteem, believing in the rightness of their actions, to a *totally* reversed position, that one was, in fact, a monster of evil. One can readily understand that many would avoid taking such a threatening psychic leap. (pg. 13)

17. I have repeatedly been advised by investigative journalists that the Pinkerton agency and the CIA have worked closely together for decades. This may explain why Dad, a skilled chemical, mechanical and electrical engineer, had also done security work for Pinkerton.

18. To obtain a free catalog or to learn more about Safer Society, you can mail your request to Safer Society Foundation Inc., PO Box 340, Brandon, VT 05733-0340 USA; call (802) 247-3132; send a fax (802) 247-4233; or go to their website at http://www.safersociety.org.

19. From what I read in Dad's remaining papers, and from my talks with several family members, I learned that Dad was phobic about odors emanating from female bodies. He even named a small female child victim "stinky" and brought her a toy skunk from Disney World.

20. Anna C. Salter, Ph.D. explained why people like Dad put unrealistic labels on their victims:

> This type of excuse, that the victim is somehow evil or defective or "less than human," is simply projection. The father of one of my clients told her she was too egocentric to ever have children. Another sadistic

father told his daughter/victim that she didn't feel things but only pretended to. Someone was, indeed, too egocentric to have children in that house, and someone didn't feel things. Someone was also less than human, but in no case was it the child.

This process of projection is the same one that nonsadistic child molesters use, projection of the offender's inner world onto the victim . . . Some denigrate whole classes of people, such as women or children. Many rapists believe that women are "bitches" who deserve anything bad that happens to them. Those who attack children employ similarly distorted cognitions in regard to children. (pg. 111-112)

Saying Goodbye

Goodbye, Fantasy Mom

Part of saying goodbye to my mother involves telling others what she did to me. It's not easy. I've already lost my father by telling the truth about him; all I have left of my parents is my mother. And yet, to hold back and continue covering-up for her past sins puts me in a bad position. Why? Because covering-up for her still reinforces my denial about what she did to me, about who and what she really is. It keeps me hoping against hope that maybe she'll turn around, maybe she'll get help and see the error of her ways, maybe she'll grow up, mature, and discover love inside herself for me. Maybe she'll stop being a narcissist and reach out instead of pulling everything into her. I want my mommy–not the mommy I had, but the mommy I never had.

I tried, once before, to go through the entire process of letting go and saying goodbye to her (figuratively, not in person) when I found the black hole inside my soul. I got about halfway through the grieving process, the letting-go-of-fantasy-Mommy process, but then I took a ninety-degree turn and sabotaged it.

Instead of fully feeling the grief of knowing that Mom never loved me and never will, I started looking for mommy-substitutes. I gravitated towards one woman after another whose personality resembled Mom's–to some extent, each woman was cold, controlling, and shaming. I locked into each one, emotionally, and tried to fashion her into my mother's personality. This was sick, but I didn't realize I was doing it–at least, not at first.

After breaking away from the most recent abusive female, I decided not to look for another substitute. I knew I needed to get honest with myself and take a hard look at what was underneath my unhealthy behavior. It was time to admit that I was still trying to fill the gaping void that the absence of mother-love had left in my soul.

It was hard to let go of my fantasy mother. Doing this always takes a lot of courage, strength, and support. As I began to let go of the fantasy, really let go, I was immediately slammed by new emotions that were so sharp, so keen, so breath-taking, I could barely move.

402

I finally entered the full reality that as a child, I'd had nobody. Nobody at all. Just a little girl, I'd been tortured and sexually assaulted at home *nearly every day*, and nobody had been there to help me survive it.

Then I remembered and felt what else I'd blocked out–that as a child in constant danger, I'd had to stay *in the moment* to survive. Back then, I couldn't bear to think about the next moment, what might happen–my mind couldn't survive that. I had to blank my mind out and think of nothing. Because nothing was all that was left to me.

How did I survive day after day, year after year of unending torture, rape, and more? To be honest, I really don't know. I have given myself pat answers in the past: I managed to dissociate it away; Mom's mother gave me nurturing at times; teachers and other adults gave me sprinklings of love and caring now and then; God loved and cared about me; but in reality, most of the time (especially at home), I had no one to care about me, no one to protect me from human evil, no one to hold me, love me, comfort me. Not even God was there, that I could see or feel. I was completely alone.

At home with Mom and Dad, the only way I could mentally survive was to stay in the moment, choosing not to think about what might be done to me next. I couldn't bear thinking about such possibilities. And I was always acutely aware that nobody was there for me. *At all.*[1]

In our rental home in Laureldale, Mom usually made sure my brother was in his crib for the night before Dad came home from work. My stomach hurt whenever I saw a gleeful expression on her face. My stomach hurt even more when, as Dad entered the house, she bounced on her toes and clapped her hands.[2] That's how I knew it was going to happen again. And I was certain I was going mad. At the age of three, I already knew what madness was.

The reality I've still been running away from is hard and harsh: I was raised by two sadists. Not one—two. Both of my parents had enjoyed torturing me – individually, together at home, and with others in larger gatherings. Any way they could. I had no heroes. I had no rescuers. I had nobody to love me. Instead, I lived in perpetual dread of what they were going to do next.

Nearly every night, when we lived in Laureldale, when it was just me, my parents, and baby brother in the house, Mom and Dad would take me into the downstairs kitchen in the back of the house to start the next torture session.

One time, when I was being toilet-trained, they ordered me to sit on my potty seat in the kitchen. Dad stuffed purple grapes and a piece of banana into my rectum and ordered me to sit there all night without going to the bathroom. This was excruciating for a small child. (Terrified of Dad's anger, I obeyed by staying in a trance state – which is probably what Dad wanted.) Mom laughed at my discomfort and made fun of me as she watched.

On another night in the kitchen, I sat on a chair. Mom placed a brown metal bobby pin on my arm and Dad touched it with the end of a live wire, burning an imprint the shape of a bobby pin on my tender flesh. Then they both called me "Bobby." I instinctively created a boy alter-state that answered to that name from then on.[3]

I've clearly remembered one night when they went beyond their normal limits. Earlier in the evening, Mom had placed a large skillet full of grease atop of the stove. After supper, one parent picked me up and held me tightly, approaching the stove. The other grabbed my hand and forced my outstretched palm on top of the scalding-hot grease for several seconds. It was one of the few times they didn't punish me for screaming or struggling. I screamed until my throat was raw. I kicked and wriggled furiously, trying to get away from the heat and the incredible pain. Snot ran out of my nose and tears poured down my cheeks. Then I saw Dad smile and Mom laugh.

I didn't want to believe that particular memory when it first emerged. It didn't fit their profile – usually they tortured me in ways that either didn't leave marks at all, or had left marks that could be explained in other ways. And yet, for the next couple of days, I felt an odd need to be very gentle with that hand. To not let it touch anything. To nurse it as I would have, had it recently been burned. Then, in therapy, a child part came out that had endured the pain and the aftermath. She explained to Helen and to me that my palm had turned "gooey white." I can still clearly see what it looked like. I have no other memory of having been badly burned, and have not known anyone else who was. The gooey white substance was pure memory.

Helen confirmed that this is how my hand would have looked, had it been burned that way. The child part explained that when adults asked about my hand, Mom told them that I'd burned it atop the stove by myself. That child part couldn't understand why the adults believed her–after all, I wasn't even tall enough to reach the top of the stove!

Because Dad was an electrical engineer with a creative mind, he used a new variation of a set of standard forms of torture nearly every night. He might make me sit in a different part of the room. He might say different words. He might have Mom do something new. By keeping me on edge, never letting me get used to a predictable pattern, my personality split and split and split. I believe this is what he intended.

In our home in Reiffton, after Mom gave me my cat, she and Dad started what they called "cat scratch." Similar to what Dr. J did to me as an adult, they used the live end of a stripped electrical cord and scratched its bare copper end on my back, my arms, anywhere they wanted. I cannot adequately describe the intensity of the pain of being simultaneously scratched and shocked. It's still one of my worst physical memories. Each time they did it, they said if I told anyone, they'd tell that person that when I picked up my cat, it scratched me. Believing their threat, I stayed silent and then blocked it all out.

Other than "cat scratches," the worst ongoing torture I suffered at home was being bitten. I've had more memories of this than I can count–I usually relive the pain of the bites when I'm lying in bed at night, trying to sleep. It's excruciating.

In each memory I've recovered thus far, they made me lie on their bed, sandwiched between them, all three of us naked, and literally bit me all over my body, making comments about how I was food. I'm not talking about nibbles and nips – they bit me hard. By saying I was food, the implied threat (in my mind, at least) was that they might eat me (cannibalism) as they had the bodies of babies and children at the rituals Dad officiated. This, more than anything else, made me terrified of my parents. I believed that some-day they would eat me alive, making me feel every incredibly painful bite.

This was the life I lived at home as a child. Yes, there were good times. And yes, most of the time, I wasn't being tortured. But even when I wasn't being tortured, I was always waiting for the other shoe to drop, waiting for when they'd grab me and do something new that was even more terrible. I became hyper-vigilant when I was just a little child; I've been that way, ever since.

If a child cannot bond with and trust the primary caregivers (an oxymoron in my case), then how can the child fully bond with anyone else? If the child is conditioned to constantly live in fear, how can the child feel safe? Perhaps the home torture I experienced as a child is why I'm still unable to relax completely at home. Even when I'm sitting in my recliner, my feet propped up, reading a good book or watching TV, I still have figurative eyes in the back of my head. I'm alert to every change in air pressure, to the tiniest sound in another room, to anything that indicates someone is about to hurt me – even though I know that no one is there. The fear never completely goes away.

There. I've told you. I've told everyone who reads this book. The cover-up is over. Reality has finally asserted itself: my mother tortured me, too. My mother chose to torture me. My mother looked forward to torturing me, and laughed when she did it. And she laughed when she gave me to other people to hurt me. My mother was, and may still be, a sadist. Both of my parents were sadists. And I had the bad luck to be born to them.

This is reality. This was my life. This was what I experienced. I never had a mother who gave a damn about me. I was a soul-orphan. Goodbye, fantasy mom. I will not miss you. Goodbye.

Goodbye, Childhood Family

I've said goodbye to Dad and to Mom. But there are more goodbyes to be said, before I'm really free.

Part of becoming an independent, mature adult involves cutting ties to my childhood and all it represents–not to the memories, but to my child-like relationships with the people I knew back then. This is hard to do, especially since I'd developed Stockholm Syndrome relationships with a few of the adults in my childhood family–on both sides.

During a therapy session several years ago, Helen told me a story that has helped me to understand why I have still feared the recriminations of perpetrators lurking within the family. The story she told me was about the strange relationship between two dogs that lived together.

First, the owners adopted the Chihuahua. Their only pet at the time, it grew up to be a feisty adult. Then the owners adopted a second pet: a Great Dane puppy.

The Great Dane was small at first, which made it vulnerable to the domination of the aggressive, controlling Chihuahua. And yet, as the Dane grew bigger and bigger, it remained submissive to the Chihuahua. The owners laughed at the Dane's odd behavior, not realizing it wasn't able to comprehend that it was now much bigger and stronger than the Chihuahua!

Helen said that abused children who grow up into adulthood often perpetuate similar mental/emotional relationships with childhood perpetrators. Even though the children gradually become bigger and stronger, they may still feel little and helpless in the abusers' presence. And sometimes, the adult children still feel a powerful emotional attachment to the abusers that they wouldn't feel if they *hadn't* been abused.

This is the attachment I've still felt towards several much-older perpetrators in my childhood family. Even though I haven't seen them for many years, and have only heard from two of them in the last decade, if you were to ask me if they still matter to me, I would say (in my heart of hearts), absolutely. I can't explain why, and yet, the attachment is both illogical and powerful.

My concern about what these perpetrators might say to me, and about me to others, has continued to have a strong effect on my mind and my decision-making processes. Even though I'm much bigger now, and am better educated with good resources and an excellent support system, I've still felt a vulnerability towards them that I haven't felt towards anyone else. It has continued to affect my life, even though I haven't heard from most of them in a long time. Even though I've recovered greatly. Even though I'm much wiser and have gradually gained my mind back. Even now.

As I look deeper within my heart, I discover another reason for the attachment that leaves me vulnerable towards them. The relationships I had with my extended family were the closest I experienced with anyone for a very long time. The family I knew as a child was a tightly closed system. No outsiders were allowed in without permission. I was punished if I told outsiders what went on inside the family. We were expected to keep the family's secrets at all costs. There was hell to pay either overtly or covertly whenever one of us tried to buck the family system.

I experienced its power when Mom divorced Dad. I was seventeen. We lived halfway across the country. What the family thought and said shouldn't have mattered that much to me, anymore. But it did.

Furious at Mom for daring to divorce her son, Grandma retaliated by announcing that she'd disowned me and my brothers. For years, she totally shunned us. We were no longer her grandchildren. I cannot adequately describe how deep that hurt went inside me. It was as if she'd taken away a huge chunk of who I was, and held it hostage. The extended family that had been my foundation was pulled completely out from under me, leaving me with *no identity*. I didn't know who I was, if I wasn't a Shirk.

Decades later, after Dad's death, one of Dad's brothers (also a pedophile) reminded me by letter of my Shirk identity. The man indicated that no matter how hard I tried to break away from the family, I would always be a Shirk, first and foremost. I was thrown completely off-kilter by his letter. It had a profound effect on my mind. For a while, I forgot who I was and mindlessly agreed – he was right. I'd made a mistake by breaking away from the family, by trying to tell the authorities what some of them had done to me. I was wrong; he was right; I would always be a Shirk. Not an individual with my own mind and choices, just a cog in the family machine. Thank God for therapy; it helped me to break his insane spell over my mind.

Now, I'm weighing the possible consequences of going public about my past. What will I have to give up if I name my father as a perp, if I tell what my mother and others in the family did to me? What will telling the truth cost me? Will some of the perpetrators try to contact me and rattle me to the core again? And if they do, will they be successful? Who am I, if not a family member? Am I anybody outside of the closed family system–even though I've not had contact with it for years?

If I change my mind and decide to stay silent, if I realign with the family and its rigid rules, if I recant everything I have remembered and go back into the fold, what would *that* decision cost me?

If I stay true to the current course and don't recant–if I tell–can I bear the pain of losing every person in the family who has still been dear to me?

I wonder what that would feel like. I decide to test the waters within. I allow myself to feel the grief of losing them all, every one of them, in one fell swoop. I emotionally disinherit myself from them before they can do it to me.

Immediately, I'm slammed by new pain. Unfamiliar pain. It's a kind of pain that I've not yet acknowledged existing inside me. What's it about, I wonder? As I look inside, I make an amazing new discovery: it's the grief of losing my relationships with the family perpetrators!

This is a part of my personality that I became too jaded as an adult to recognize: that even when they had hurt me, even when they had done the worst to me, I had still loved them. Hated them, yes. Feared them, most certainly. But the pure child in me had found a way to love them, too.

And this is my final connection to them: the love-connection. I hadn't wanted to let go of it. It's my final tie to them, straight from my heart to theirs. And yet, to truly be free of them once and for all, I must cut the cord. It's time.

To my childhood family: goodbye. I love you. Goodbye. I wish you well. Goodbye.

Notes

1. I am not minimizing my relationship with my brothers; but they were both younger than I. Even if they had wanted to, they couldn't have done anything to protect me.

2. Anna C. Salter, Ph.D. wrote: "When you or I see someone in pain, we empathize, which is to say, we feel some of that pain ourselves. Sadists feel satisfied, high, happy instead." (pg. 108)

3. My Bobby persona was one of my primary alter-states. He'd compartmentalized a large amount of knowledge about my life and my past, and was one of the parts I could count on the most, to fill me in about the histories of other alter-states when they first emerged. Some therapists call this kind of alter-state an ISH (internal self-helper). Bobby had also compartmentalized a large number of traumas. His last confession, before becoming one with me, was that he'd "had to be a boy" because otherwise, he feared he'd become Mom in all her insanity.

Coming Home

One of the most difficult questions in my recovery has been, "Who am I?" In so many different ways in the past, I was hindered from developing a single core personality–a solid sense of self. I was severely traumatized for more than three decades. My right to live and to be loved was never affirmed by my primary caregivers, who modeled dissociation, and covert hatred and cruelty to me. I was repeatedly betrayed by those I needed to be trustworthy and safe. My mind was skillfully split and shattered into many hundreds of shards and pieces. All this, and more, contributed to my inability to have a centered self.[1]

Until I started remembering my hidden past, I didn't have a clue to who I really was, other than what was external. I answered to the name of Kathy as a child and as an adult, Kathleen; I was a mother and wife and daughter and sister and aunt; I was also a neighbor and church member and insurance clerk.

I had no cohesive internal self. This is why, when I came into consciousness to find myself in one strange place after another, I was easily able to shift and change with my surroundings. I was so good at adapting, some of my spook handlers called me a "chameleon."

These shifts and changes served a vital purpose in the past: I was able to survive extremely dangerous situations. And yet, when I began my recovery, "switching" into amnesic, altered states of consciousness quickly became a handicap.

Although I respect the right of trauma survivors who choose to maintain their multiplicity (if that's possible); for me, integration has been an important goal. I've desperately wanted to know what it feels like to be a "singleton" or "monomind." I've wanted to know what it's like to wake up every day, having full knowledge of what happened the day before. I've wanted to experience what it's like to not live in constant fear that I may "lose time" again and not know what I'd done in an altered state of consciousness.

I've wanted to be able to build a new life that isn't in a constant upheaval due to mental and emotional shifts and changes. I've wanted to be consistent in my behaviors so that my loved ones could feel secure in my presence and no longer worry that I might have a terrible abreaction or that a suicidal alter-state might emerge while alone in the house. I've noticed the peace in the faces of some people who don't dissociate. They seem to relax as they appreciate the simplicities of their reasonably normal lives. I've wanted to experience that kind of peace, too.

Although I'd worked very hard to remember what I'd blocked out, to deprogram my mind, and to accept and blend with all of my emerging alter-states, I'd still felt separated from my deeper self. Sensing an ongoing chasm between my normal life and my more traumatic past, I didn't know how to bridge it. This worried me. Because my two lives had been so drastically different, was it impossible to ever blend them together?

Another worry came from a haunting, nearly indescribable feeling of homesickness that centered in my belly. The homesickness wasn't for my childhood home, nor was it for the family. It was a deep, bittersweet pang in my gut that just wouldn't go away. Something was still missing; something so fundamental that I wasn't whole without it.

What was causing this homesickness? And what was still keeping me separated inside myself? I especially felt it whenever I encountered a perpetrator from my past who tried to reaccess me. I mistakenly assumed that I'd been pining for that person. I didn't understand that such people, with whom I'd developed Stockholm Syndrome relationships, represented past *experiences* that I was still denying as part of the fabric of my overall personality.

I didn't understand that I was still homesick for my split-off past experiences because they'd been among the most basic building blocks of my sense of self. I didn't yet understand that until I allowed the blocks to be found and placed together, parts of my foundation were still missing.

In the spring of 2003, I learned that physical evidence exists that proves that some traumatic memories and experiences are split off or stored in separate parts of the brain, leaving amnesic gaps in-between.

In their 1998 journal article, "Cognitive Impact of Traumatic Events," Gordon H. Bower and Heidi Sivers of Stanford University described two separate memory systems. One holds regular, life narrative memory; the other stores traumatic memory. They wrote:

> . . . re-experiencing of sensory memories of the trauma triggered by external cues reflect the first, implicit/emotional system, whereas the coherent verbal narrative of the trauma

that is gradually constructed during psychotherapy reflects the second, verbal system. (pg. 640)

What does this mean? As I and many other trauma survivors have experienced, our memories have often emerged in fragmented, visual flashbacks and emotional abreactions. Because these pieces of traumatic memory were not stored in the "normal experience" parts of our brains, we did not have the ability to regulate or control when or how the flashbacks and abreactions would occur.

Referring to a 1911 journal article, "Recognition and Selfhood," by Eduard Claparede, Bower and Sivers wrote:

> . . . the trauma victim's consciousness may be distorted (or attention narrowed?) during the traumatic event, so that traumatic memories are more likely to be stored in the situationally-accessible memory system rather than in association with the cognitive [normally conscious] self. This analysis may provide a useful account of why some trauma victims are at times unable to recall voluntarily the trauma, while at other times they suffer from spontaneous flashback memories of it. (pg. 640)

The authors explained that although survivors cannot voluntarily remember these traumas, they can be triggered by cues that are linked to the memories–as the sight of a dog's pink penis triggered flashbacks of bestiality porn shoots in my mind.

They cited a study that seems to verify that the two types of memory are indeed stored in different parts in the brain:

> Some evidence . . . comes from a neuroimaging study by Rauch, et al. (1996) When traumatic memories were provoked in PTSD patients (Vietnam veterans), the investigators observed decreased activation of Broca's area of the brain along with increased activation of right cerebral hemisphere areas. Broca's area is the area of the brain most centrally involved in transforming subjective experience into speech, whereas the right hemisphere has been implicated in processing intense emotions and visual images. (pg. 641)

This may also explain why I'd been able to use my left hand to access visual and emotional information that I'd not remembered when writing with my right, dominant hand. Using my left hand had accessed information that was stored in my brain's right hemisphere. Before then, my primary source of information about my past had been what scientists call Broca's area. Now I knew why my traumatic memories had been stored and had emerged quite differently from my cognitive or already-known memory; they'd been stored in a completely different part of my brain!

This new discovery raised another question: how had I been able to integrate those traumatic memories, thereby stopping them from generating more flashbacks, abreactions and nightmares?

In his remarkably honest 2001 journal article, "Threads from the Labyrinth: Therapy with Survivors of War and Political Oppression," Jeremy Woodcock of the Medical Foundation for Care of Victims of Torture, located in Great Britain, used simple terms to explain how traumatic memory can be transferred from the right hemisphere to Broca's area, where it can then integrate with and become part of the survivor's "normal life" experiences.

First, let's look at his definition of a person's life narrative:

Narrative is first of all a story, most often the stories of people's lives and therefore, in the context of survival, to be taken very seriously, but not so reverentially that we cannot tease out new meanings. Narrative implies that these stories have layers and therefore that there may be tensions and conflicts between them. These may exist within an individual's internal world or between family members who will naturally own different scripts about their life stories. Some of these layers will be fully elaborated and out in the open. Others will be hidden, repressed or denied. (pg. 137)

Woodcock explained why some traumatic memories are repressed (split-off) and later emerge as memory fragments such as flashbacks:

What is not common, because it is astounding or horrifying or shameful, often gets lost to the memory or translated into metaphor [a wellspring of symbolic nightmares?] where its capacity to horrify is encapsulated and made more safe to comprehend . . . More compelling and less consciously available dimensions of denial are when memories of gross violations are so threatening to the psychological and physical integrity of the survivor that recollections are literally split off from consciousness . . . the shattering manner in which torture and atrocity violate the physical and psychological boundaries of survivors frequently causes their recall of events to emerge in ways that may be fragmentary, disconnected and bizarre. (pp. 141, 144)

If traumatic memory can split off and later emerge in fragmented form, how can a therapist help the survivor to integrate and accept the traumatic material stored in the right hemisphere by transferring it into the left hemisphere where the survivor's life narrative center is located? Woodcock explained that this is usually done by helping the survivor to speak–often for the first time–about the traumatic memories. As this is done, the material or information literally transfers from one side of the brain to the other, where it gradually blends with and becomes a permanent part of the survivor's life narrative. (pg. 147)

This is what a succession of mental health professionals have helped me to do, one tiny piece of memory at a time. As a result, I've been able to accept much of the past that I'd previously disowned. I can speak and write about many of my traumatic experiences without trancing out. I can communicate these memories as Kathleen, as one person.

So far, so good. I'm integrating. And yet, as of six months ago, the pang of homesickness still bothered me. What was causing it, and why wouldn't it go away?

According to Gordon and Sivers, Claparede wrote that a person can split off part of his/her existence, thereby making some experiences not part of the self. I found Claparede's article translated and published in a 1995 edition of *Consciousness and Cognition.* Claparede provided a practical explanation for the homesick feeling. He wrote:

But what is this feeling of selfhood? . . . If I have experienced a thing I have the feeling that it is mine, belongs to my experience. This feeling manifests itself even after a few moments of observing a new object: As the object is considered and (ap)perceived, it becomes progressively familiar, appears more and more intimate, and finally attains the character of being "my object." It is not surprising then if on reappearing, after some time has elapsed, it again evokes that feeling. (pg. 373)

Claparede's words told me something I'd known deep inside: the sum of my experience–*all* of it–is who I really am as a person. If I continue to push *any* of it away, I'm still pushing *me* away. I can't think of anything I would feel more homesick for, or yearn more for, than my own self.

Although I'd worked very hard to find and integrate every alter-state, over the past thirteen years, I was still pushing away the *essence* of my past experiences; I was still avoiding accepting that my past was an important and essential part of my personality!

This presented a new challenge: it was time to relax and accept all of who I am and all of what I've experienced, without fighting against it.

My continuing struggle against the essence of my past had been similar to what I had experienced when I'd been put in a human-sized, upright, clear container that had been filled with what had probably been liquid oxygen.

As the liquid had risen to my chest, then my neck, then my bottom lip, I'd panicked. But because the container had pinned my arms against my sides, I hadn't been able to break free. Even as I'd prepared to die, my survival instinct had struggled to keep me from breathing the liquid–not understanding that it would not harm me. This same survival instinct now struggled against accepting the realness of my past–because I feared its emotional impact might kill me!

For thirteen years, I'd endured one extreme traumatic relive after another. I'd checked myself into psychiatric hospitals seven times because the memories were so torturous and painful, I'd had no strength left to endure them. Many times, I became ill, exhausted and depressed from their emotional impact. Gradually, without realizing it, I'd developed a phobia towards the very act of remembering! Because I'd feared and resisted remembering, I'd become increasingly dissociated. Eventually, I'd been unable to remember what was still repressed, without first switching entirely into another alter-state.

Claparede explained this form of dissociation:

Voluntary acts imply processes which we call "self." If for one reason or another some presentations [e.g., memories of traumatic events] are not associated with a feeling of "selfhood," the subject does not have the impression of possessing them and thus cannot recall them–as one cannot at will move one's ears unless the muscles have first revealed themselves through certain inner sensations. The first prerequisite of recalling a memory is the impression that we possess it. It is thus understandable that if the impression of "selfhood" is destroyed, the absence of recognition which follows is coupled with an absence of voluntary recall. (pg. 376)

In other words, I now needed to be willing to accept that who I was in the past is still part of me–regardless of who created the alter-states, or how much or little I was to blame for what the perpetrators had influenced me to do. This wasn't about blame; it was about acceptance. It was about addressing my past as part of my essence instead of calling it by another person's name. It was about relaxing in bed at night, allowing myself to feel total calm and peace instead of tensing with the fear about what was sure to come in my dreams. It was about opening my mind and my will and saying, "Whatever is there, I welcome you. I welcome you as part of me. I will not fear you any more."

Perhaps this act of surrender was what Claparede referred to when he wrote:

The feeling of selfhood is, so to speak, the link between an imaged memory and ourself: The link by which we hold it and thanks to which we can retrieve it from the depths of the subconscious. (pg. 376)

Now, if I choose to remain at peace and don't try to fight or re-repress my emerging memories, if I'm willing to accept them as part of me instead of making them "not me," I don't automatically dissociate as they emerge. In general, I'm able to accept them more quickly as part of my past and my life. Although some of the memories are still emotionally devastating, and I must still give myself time now and then to process them in a private and uninterrupted way, I seem to be struggling less and relaxing more. These memories are, after all, a fundamental part of who I am. It seems that I'm finally finding my way home–to me.

Notes

1. By analyzing my current behaviors during minor crises, I've detected a pattern that may explain, in part, how I had developed some of my altered states of consciousness as a child, and then named them:

   First, whenever I felt overwhelmed by a sudden, troubling event, my automatic thoughts were usually either "I can't believe this is happening," or "This can't be happening to me!" I suspect that each time I said or thought this to myself, I conditioned my mind to store the memory of that particular event in another part of my brain, separated from where my normal life/"me" memories were stored.

   For this reason, whenever I encounter a new crisis now, I'm careful to stop myself as soon as I utter or think those words. Instead, I say aloud to myself: "Deal with it. It *is* happening, and it is happening to *you*. And if other people can get through this, you can, too." So far, this new technique has worked-I've stayed mentally present through each difficult event.

   In the past, whenever I'd said, "This can't be happening to me," I'd also generated a missing sense of self-a void that needed to be filled because, after all, the memory of the event was being stored in my brain as having happened to *someone*! To fill that void, I had unconsciously created other personas, giving them (if I were able to choose) names that were, at least, a bit different than the one I was commonly known by: Kathy. I created Little Kathy, Katherine, Catalina, and so on. In my mind at such times, a fundamental truth had been that each experience had indeed belonged to someone-but not necessarily to *me*!

New Life

Progress

Helen has often reminded me that as I continue to heal, I should "keep one foot in the past and the other in the present." In other words, I need to be careful to not become so immersed in the past that I don't enjoy my new life, while not running away from the past by focusing solely on the present. Both are important.

I still rarely know when the next unexpected memory will occur. Sometimes I can sense that something is emerging when I say or do something out of the ordinary. I might repeat a word that isn't part of my regular vocabulary, or I might have a recurring, vividly detailed dream that I've not had before. When this occurs, I relax my body and mind as much as possible, so that I won't fight what's surfacing.

I may retrieve bits and pieces of traumatic memories for the rest of my life. Remembering has become part of my daily routine. With each memory, I learn something new about my past and, more important, about who I am. Each time I blend with newly emerging alter-states and personality fragments, I gain their skills, strengths, and abilities. I am amazed by how much I can do now, that I couldn't do in the past.

I am no longer paralyzed with fear in the presence of sex addicts, control addicts, and sociopaths. The more I've learned about what motivated Dad and other abusers, both male and female, the more I've felt compassion for them–at a safe distance. (Helen reminded me to treat them as I would a rabid dog. The dog might be cute and I might feel sorry for its deteriorating condition, but I don't need to get so close that it can bite me and destroy me, too!)

I feel sad for them because I'm healing while most of them are mired in misery, denial, chaos, and destructive behaviors. Many of them are so used to being in pain and running from it every way they can, they don't even know they're hurting!

I don't tolerate abusive behaviors from others anymore, nor do I allow myself to be abusive. I've finally found a comfortable middle ground. I'm becoming more willing to connect with people instead of fearing what

418

they might do to me. I had been immersed in the ugly underbelly of our society for so long, I hadn't known that normal, non-hurtful people comprise its majority. Now I know that criminals are a minority. What a relief!

Gifts to Myself

Like wonderful Christmas and birthday presents, I give myself new gifts that equip me to live a healthier life. Some of these gifts are everyday rights I'd never been allowed to own. Some are decisions to do or say something that I'd not been allowed to do or say in the past. Some are decisions to not do what I'd previously had no choice about doing. Some are permissions to think in new ways. And some are choices I wasn't allowed, before.

I give myself the choice to ask for help if I feel suicidal or if my emotional pain becomes unbearable. I can call my support network for emergency support. If needed, I can make arrangements to check into a psych hospital so the staff can monitor me until I work through the pain.

I give myself the gift of humor–not sarcastic and angry, but silly and childlike or from my belly. I wasn't encouraged to laugh as a child and frankly, there wasn't much to laugh about. Now, there is.[1] Together, Bill and I have used humor to weather many difficult crises. Our laughter has been the oil that smoothes out the roughest days. In the summer of 2002, he had a stroke. People probably thought we'd lost our minds when we laughed about how he tilted to the left when he tried to walk forward in his hospital room. It was a way of reminding ourselves, "This will get better." It did.

I choose to let go of small grievances. They sap too much of my time and energy.

I utilize the energy of my anger instead of letting it overwhelm me. Occasional spurts of anger are a gift because, for a while, they make me manic. Although I can expect to feel exhausted afterwards, I visualize myself riding the energy like a booster rocket. I think, "What can I do with this energy to make a positive change? How can I use it to accomplish something I normally don't have the energy to do?"

Much of my anger surfaced between 1996 and 2001. I used it to create the PARC-VRAMC Living Memorial Garden near Chattanooga. As I dug holes for trees to be planted, I often encountered rocks and thick roots. I used the roots as an opportunity to express my rage at the men in my past who had sexually assaulted me. And then, when I'd finished expelling the anger, I planted a tree or bush.

I've given myself the opportunity to study to become a better gardener. Gardening is a major part of my healing now–I call the PARC garden my "playground." Whenever I feel overly stressed, I pick up fallen tree limbs or pull weeds while enjoying the beauty all around. It's exciting to know that now, I have the chance to help living things grow and thrive!

I've given myself the right to live a long and healthy life. I'm still setting goals that I expect to reach by the time I'm eighty. After that, I'll consider retirement.

I'm working towards obtaining a bachelor's degree and then a master's degree in Social Work. Ironically, the US Government provided this opportunity. Because my husband was awarded 100% disability status from the Veterans Administration, I was automatically awarded four free years of college! In my Social Work studies, I've been humbled to learn that all kinds of injustices exist in our world–not just those I've experienced.

I give myself the right to be "good enough." If I earn less than an 'A' in a class, I relax and don't go into an anxiety-induced tailspin. I don't have to be perfect anymore. Having fun is a good goal!

I choose to use visualization, therapy, and memory building techniques to heal my brain. Every day, I "see" more of its damaged neuron paths reconnecting. I choose to believe that my brain has the power to heal itself.

I choose not to obsess about memories that I probably still repress. I don't have to remember every piece of every repressed memory to be able to heal and live a full life.[2]

I give myself the right to not forgive those who viciously and willingly hurt me. I give myself the right to feel anger towards those who battered me mentally, emotionally, and physically. I allow myself to feel glad when they fall ill or die, knowing the same can happen to me and my loved ones (after all, illness and death are not selective). I need to feel the anger to avoid being their victim again.

I balance out my anger by learning what I can about their childhoods. I try to understand them and to feel compassion for their woundedness, although not in a way that emotionally locks me into them again (remember: rabid dog).[3]

To protect my mind and life, I choose not to have any further contact with my childhood family. Although I miss those who did not harm me, they are too closely connected to those who did.[4]

To avoid feeling overwhelmed and depressed, I allow myself to relax on family holidays. Sometimes friends invite us to celebrate with them. Their kindness and caring are precious gifts.

I give myself the right to say, "My mother and other women sexually abused me." I choose not to let societal myths about sainted nurturers silence me anymore. Females sexually assault children, too.[5]

I choose to research the evidence of historical conspiracies. I will not accept the shame that continues to be indiscriminately dumped on intelligent people by our government and the mainstream media when we choose to question what we're told to believe. We are not conspiracy theorists or fanatics. Such labels are condescending and inaccurate. We are *realists*.

I give myself time to grieve old and new losses. The traumas that I endured hurt me in many ways. I still grieve the loss of not having had the ability to nurture, respect, and properly care for Emily. I accept that I may never fully recover from the murder of my precious baby Rose and other dear ones I lost along the way.

Never having had loving, protective parents has been a huge loss for me to grieve. Not having respectful, loving family members to go to when I feel upset or need advice is another.[6] I give myself permission and time to grieve each of these losses—as often and for as long as I need to.

I give myself permission to be just plain human. When I first discovered the hidden parts of my personality, I was terrified of making mistakes or doing something immoral. I was afraid I'd turn into a sociopathic abuser if I integrated with those parts (I didn't). Now, I choose to believe that life is a journey of discovery and growth. Even if I screw up royally, I can still learn from that mistake and make better choices in the future.

I give myself the right to feel and express gratitude. I do not feel grateful for having been betrayed and harmed in the past. I do, however, feel grateful for so many good things that have come into my life since I started to break free from my controllers. I received free schooling. I have good medical insurance coverage that has kept us from having to file for bankruptcy. I have two functioning legs, arms, and eyes, and a brain that still works well. I have a nice home. I have a husband who loves and cares about me. I can hear and talk and hug and type. Even if I lose some of those abilities, I'll still have the rest!

I especially feel grateful that I have today. I'm alive and have the opportunity to work towards my life goals. I have another day to cuddle with my husband and inhale his natural, soothing scent. To massage our elderly dog's arthritic shoulders as he groans with pleasure. To make new friends. To fall in love with humanity.

Because I'm alive, I can walk through the garden to see which plants are in bloom. I have another day to listen to the chorus of thousands of katydids that rhythmically buzz at night. To read entertaining magazines (I adore *Star, Cosmo,* and *GQ*). To watch a good movie that I didn't have the opportunity to enjoy in the past. To walk in the rain. To watch children at play and note that they are being watched and protected—how wonderful!—by their caregivers.

I give myself the right to change the meanings of those things in my life that Dad and other perpetrators had sadistically desecrated and perverted in my mind. Now, I can enjoy breathtakingly beautiful rainbows with the understanding that they are not magical and won't take me to another dimension. When I see storm clouds roiling in the distance, I know that a tornado isn't likely to appear. I can even tolerate the sound of an approaching military copter and know that I am still safe.

When I light fragrant candles in our home, I know that black-robed Satanists won't walk into our living room for a ritual. I even give myself permission to wear red and black clothes together, knowing they won't change the essence of who I am.

Butterflies are another symbol that I have disarmed. Many mind-control victims have been called "butterflies" by programmers. In the past, I felt agitated every time I heard a survivor talk about being transformed from a worm or caterpillar to a butterfly, or about leaving the cocoon, because such phrases were used as part of our programming.[7]

To counter its effects, I created a small butterfly garden, within the larger PARC-VRAMC garden, to honor those survivors. I installed butterfly bushes (some were donated by survivors) and a wooden butterfly box. Every spring, I plant lantana. On summer days, I watch individual butterflies flit and land on the flowers, knowing that I was not and never can be a butterfly. Now I'm able to enjoy them for what they are–beautiful, totally harmless, delicate creatures.

I've also reclaimed the real meaning of some of the spiritual elements in my life. About halfway through the intensive phase of my recovery, I stopped attending church altogether–too many elements of the services triggered horrific memories.

In December 2002, I decided to go to a Christmas Eve church service with Bill. I wondered if it would still be too much for me to bear.

Entering the small brick church, I chose a pew behind the rest of the congregation so that I had an easy avenue of escape. As the service started, I discovered something new. For the first time since the summer of 1989, I was able to hear and enjoy the Christmas carols and the pastor's words without trancing or flashbacking. The pastor talked about communion in a simple way, stating that the grape juice and bread were symbolic representations of Jesus' blood and body, "shed and broken for us." As I hesitantly took communion at the altar, I noticed that it didn't trigger any ritual flashbacks.

As I stood there, I received an unexpected gift. Looking straight into my eyes, the pastor said, "Your sins are forgiven." As I heard those words, icy pain threatened to flash through my body. In a split-second, I realized that I'd stayed away from church and fellow worshippers for one more reason I hadn't been willing to face: I'd still seen myself as unforgivable and unacceptable, undeserving of the right to be with them.

After I returned to the pew and prayed, I realized that because I'd been forgiven, I didn't need to isolate myself from my spiritual brothers and sisters anymore. Then another revelation unfolded: I'd been starving from a lack of spiritual sustenance. Every day, I'd been clinging to fraying strands of hope, fighting blindly to keep doing what I believed was right–all on my own. But the battle was simply too big for me. I desperately needed spiritual help and strength.

Feeling a deep connection with the fellow worshippers and with God, I realized that my own spirituality may be the greatest gift I can ever give to myself. It transcends all human evil, no matter how much that evil may yet amass around us. Those who secretly lust, conspire, and kill for power will rise and fall, but what is spirit will outlast them all.

In spite of the evil that will always exist to some degree in our society; in spite of the many cruelties I've endured and may yet suffer; in spite of the loss of important relationships; in spite of my mental, emotional and physical disabilities; and in spite what evil is yet to come; there is still much hope in the world. Not only do we have a God who truly loves and cares about us; we also have a world full of people who care about each other and want to do what's right. I believe if we give it a chance, goodness will always win–beginning in our own hearts and lives.

Notes

1. *Glamour Magazine's* August, 2002 edition stated: "The average child laughs 400 times a day. The typical adult? 15." (pg. 119) Because I didn't laugh much as a child, I'm making up for lost time now.

2. There may be events in my past that it's best I not remember. This doesn't make me weak; it just proves that I, like everyone else, have a limit to the amount of horror I can endure. "There was an exploration of the labyrinth of torture and atrocity, and the recollection that we are most vulnerable to destruction when alone and beyond the gaze or recall of ourselves and others. Perhaps ultimately the realization that nothing is seemingly beyond the wit of man's destructiveness: even the possibility that we will never know the worst that has befallen us." (Woodcock pg. 151)

3. I didn't know that developing empathy towards those who had brutally harmed and used me, while still feeling anger towards them, might actually be the most sincere form of forgiveness. Beverly Flanigan, MSSW, does an excellent job of explaining the forgiveness process in her book, *Forgiving the Unforgivable: Overcoming the Bitter Legacy of Intimate Wounds.*

4. Dr. Elizabeth Loftus, Pamela Freyd, and other outspoken members of the FMSF publicly attack the character of abuse survivors who choose to separate from their families to maintain their personal safety and mental health. One of the glaring flaws in these women's stance is that they make the cohesion and dysfunctional stability of "allegedly" destructive family systems more important than the constitutional rights (such as liberty), survival, and sanity of their individual members.

5. Rosencrans wrote: "I'm concerned that society will not take abuse between mothers and daughters seriously because both victim and perpetrator are women. In addition, people might resist this information because they want to continue to stereotype and view women as nurturers incapable of such abuse, as non-sexual protectors, and as somehow morally 'better than men.'" (pg. 238) Although I think the feminist movement has made important advances in bettering the lives of untold numbers of women (including my own), I think that we-as women-must be extremely careful not to overlook or minimize the potential of women to also be sexual predators of children.

6. Judith Viorst's *Necessary Losses* has helped me to understand that it's healthy and normal to grieve these and other personal losses.

7. I and many other survivors were mentally conditioned and programmed via trauma, hypnosis, NLP, and other nefarious methods to develop alter-states that truly believed they were fragile, controllable butterflies.

Bibliography

"20 parents charged with molesting their children, Internet porn ring." Associated Press, 8/10/02.

"American Ballistics: History." Website. http://www.amballistics.com/id17.htm.

"About Si Gung (Grandmaster) Jason Lau"- Website. http://members.aol.com/_ht_a/sidaijoey/jason_lau.html?mtbrand=AOL_US

Banning, Peter, "Female Offenders: Child Molesters," *Men's Issues Forum*, Vol. 6, pg. 2.

Blank, Arthur S., "Trauma Disorders and a Psychology of External Experience," *Military Medicine*, Vol. 159, April 1994, pg. 4.

Bower, Gordon H. and Sivers, Heidi, "Cognitive Impact of Traumatic Events," *Development and Psychopathology*, Vol. 10, 1998, pp. 625–653.

"CIA Is Obstacle in Hunt for Nazis," *Parade Magazine*, 12/22/96.

Claparede, Eduard. "Recognition and Selfhood," *Consciousness and Cognition*, Vol. 4, 1995.

Constantine, Alex, *Psychic Dictatorship in the U.S.A.* Portland, OR: Feral House, 1995.

DeMause, Lloyd, Ed., "War as Righteous Rape and Purification," *The Journal of Psychohistory*, Vol. 27:4, Spring, 2000.

Deposition of William Thomas Shirk, November 8, 1989, Volume 1.

Donn, Jeff, "Memos Show FBI Knew About Scandal," Associated Press, 7/28/02.

Duenwald, Mary, "Feed a Cold, Starve a Fever," *Ladies' Home Journal*, February 2003.

Emery, Carla, "Secret, Don't Tell." *The Encyclopedia of Hypnosis*. Pickton, TX: Acorn Press, 1998.

Encyclopedia of World Crime. Wilmette, IL: CrimeBooks, 1990.

"Fahrenheit: Going Underground," *GQ* magazine, December, 2001.

Flanigan, Beverly MSSW, *Forgiving the Unforgivable: Overcoming the Bitter Legacy of Intimate Wounds.* New York: Collier Books, 1992.

The FMSF Scientific and Professional Advisory Board – Profiles. Website. http://www.fmsfonline.org/advboard.html.

Freyd, Jennifer J., *Betrayal Trauma: The Logic of Forgetting Childhood Abuse.* Cambridge, MA: Harvard University Press, 1996.

Freyd, Jennifer J. and DePrince, Anne P., "Perspectives on Memory for Trauma and Cognitive Processes Associated with Dissociative Tendencies," *Journal of Aggression, Maltreatment, and Trauma*, Vol. 4, 2001, pg. 2.

Gill, Mark Stuart, "The Woman Who Wouldn't Be Silenced," *Ladies' Home Journal*, March, 2001.

Goodrick-Clark, Nicholas, *The Occult Roots of Nazism: Secret Aryan Cults and Their Influence on Nazi Ideology.* New York, NY: NYU Press, 1992.

Graessner, Sepp, M.D., Ed., Gurris, Norbert, Ed., and Pross, Christian, M.D., Ed., *At the Side of Torture Survivors: Treating a Terrible Assault on Human Dignity.* Baltimore, Maryland: Johns Hopkins University Press, 2001.

Grohol, John, *Dissociative Identity Disorder.* Website. http://psychcentral.com/ disorders/sx18.htm.

Groome, David, et al., *An Introduction to Cognitive Psychology Processes and Disorders.* East Sussex, UK: Psychology Press, Ltd., 1999.

Grossman, Dave, Lt. Col., *On Killing: The Psychological Cost of Learning to Kill in War and Society.* Boston: Little, Brown and Company, 1995.

Gumbel, Andrew, "Dr Richard A. Gardner: Child Psychiatrist Who Developed the Theory of Parental Alienation Syndrome," 5/31/03. Website. http://news.independent.co.uk/people/obituaries/story.jsp?story=411000.

"Happiness Quickie," *Glamour* magazine, August 2002.

Harary, Keith, "Selling the Mind Short: Exposing the Myth of Psychic Privilege," *Omni* magazine (date unknown).

Hile, Jennifer, "Activists Denounce Thailand's Elephant "Crushing" Ritual," *National Geographic Today*, 10/16/02. Website. http://news.national geographic.com/news/2002/10/1016_021016_phajaan.html.

Howe, Mark L., "Individual Differences in Factors That Modulate Storage and Retrieval of Traumatic Memories," *Development and Psychopathology*, Vol. 10, 1998.

Hunt, Linda, *Secret Agenda: The United States Government, Nazi Scientists, and Project Paperclip, 1945 to 1990*. New York, NY: St. Martin's Press, 1991.

Marrs, Texe, *New Age Cults & Religions*. Austin, TX: Living Truth Publishers, 1990.

Moreno, Joseph. "Orpheus in Hell: Music and Therapy in the Holocaust," *The Arts in Psychotherapy*, Vol. 26:1, 1999, pp. 3–14.

Muhltohi. Laureldale, PA: Muhlenberg Township High School Class of 1948.

"Facts about Post-Traumatic Stress Disorder," National Institute for Mental Health. Website. http://www.nimh.nih.gov/anxiety/ptsdfacts.cfm.

"Stress and the Developing Brain," National Institute for Mental/Health. Website.http://www.mentalhealthmatters.com/articles/nimh001.php? artID=334.

The New York Review of Books: Short Reviews. 9/28/78. Website. http://www.nybooks.com/articles/8053.

O'Brien, Cathy and Phillips, Mark, *Trance Formation of America Through Mind Control: The True Life Story of a CIA Slave*. Nashville, TN: Global Trance Formation Info LTD., 1995. (Caution: trauma survivors are advised NOT to contact the authors for help.)

Pease, Lisa, "James Jesus Angleton & the Kennedy Assassination," *Probe* magazine, July-August, 2000.

Pezdek, Kathy, "A Cognitive Analysis of the Role of Suggestibility in Explaining Memories for Abuse," *Journal of Aggression, Maltreatment and Trauma,* Vol. 4, 2001.

Rhodes, Richard, *Why They Kill: The Discoveries of a Maverick Criminologist*. New York: Vintage Books, 1999.

Rosenbaum, Ron, "The Last Secrets of Skull and Bones," *Esquire* magazine, September 1976.

Rosencrans, Bobbie, M.S.W., *The Last Secret: Daughters Sexually Abused By Mothers*. Brandon, VT: Safer Society Press, 1997.

Ross, Colin A., M.D., *Bluebird: Deliberate Creation of Multiple Personality by Psychiatrists*. Richardson, TX: Manitou Communications, Inc., 2000.

Ross, Colin A., M.D., *The Osiris Complex: Case-Studies in Multiple Personality Disorder*. Toronto: University of Toronto Press Inc., 1994.

Rutz, Carol, *A Nation Betrayed: The Chilling True Story of Secret Cold War Experiments Performed on Our Children and Other Innocent People*. Grass Lake, MI: Fidelity Publishing, 2001.

Salter, Anna C. Ph.D., *Predators: Pedophiles, Rapists, and Other Sex Offenders – Who They Are, How They Operate, and How We Can Protect Ourselves and Our Children*. New York, NY: Basic Books, 2003.

Sarson, Jeanne, RN, BScN, MEd, and MacDonald, RN, BN, MEd., "Acts of Torture." Website. http://www.ritualabusetorture.org.

Sarson, Jeanne, RN, BScN, MEd, and MacDonald, Linda, RN, BN, MEd., "The MO: The Modus Operandi of Pedophiles: Insights about Pedophiles from the Victim's Perspective." Website. http://www.ritualabusetorture.org.

Sarson, Jeanne, RN, BScN, MEd, and MacDonald, Linda, RN, BN, MEd., "Seeing Inside the Ritual Abuse-Torture Co-Culture." Website. http://www.ritualabusetorture.org.

Schoener, Helen C., editor, *Cue*. Reading, PA: Albright College Senior Class, 1956.

Schwartz, Mark F., ScD., "Sexual Compulsivity as Post-Traumatic Stress Disorder: Treatment Perspectives," *Psychiatric Annals*, Vol. 22, June 1992.

Shalev, Arieh Y., Ed., Yehuda, Rachel, Ed., and McFarlane, Alexander C., Ed., *International Handbook of Human Response to Trauma*. New York: Kluwer Academic/Plenum Publishers, 2000.

"Shoah Notes: The Bible and the Holocaust, Handout #1." Website. http://www.uiowa.edu/~c032150/shoah1.pdf.

Spinhoven, Philip, Ph.D., Nijenhuis, Ellert R.S., and Van Dyck, Richard, "Can Experimental Memory Research Adequately Explain Memory for Trauma?" *Psychotherapy*, Vol. 36(3), Fall 1999.

Stoppler, Melissa C., M.D., "Cortisol: The 'Stress Hormone,' 2001." Website. http://stress.about.com/library/weekly/aa012901a.htm.

Sutphen, Dick. "The Battle for Your Mind: Persuasion and Brainwash ing Techniques Being Used On The Public Today." Website. http://www.serendipity.li/sutphen/brainwsh.html

Thomas, Gordon, *Journey Into Madness: The True Story of Secret CIA Mind Control and Medical Abuse*. New York: Bantam, 1989.

Viorst, Judith, *Necessary Losses*. New York, NY: Simon and Schuster, 1998.

Whitfield, Charles L., M.D., *Memory and Abuse: Remembering and Healing the Effects of Trauma*. Deerfield Beach, FL: Health Communications, Inc., 1995.

Wolff, Hans, "New Jersey and the Nazis," 8/98. Website. http://www.afrocubaweb.com/assata4.htm

Woodcock, Jeremy, "Threads from the Labyrinth: Therapy with Survivors of War and Political Oppression," *Journal of Family Therapy*, 2001, Vol. 23.

Recommended Reading

Adams, Jeanne, BS, *Drawn Swords: My Victory over Childhood Ritual Abuse.* Available through the Internet at http://www.mrlight.org or from Genesis Bookstore, 248 East 3900 South, Salt Lake City, Utah 84107.

Adams, Stephen B. and Butler, Orville R. *Manufacturing the Future: A History of Western Electric.* New York: Cambridge University Press, 1999.

Bashir, Kai, *Mind Control Within the United States.* Kai Bashir, PO Box 30366, Cincinnati, OH 45230.

Blood, Linda, *The New Satanists.* New York, NY: Warner Books, 1994.

Blume, E. Sue, CSW, DCSW, "Sympathy for the Devil: 'False Memories,' the Media, and the Mind Controllers," *Treating Abuse Today,* Vol. 9, No. 3.

Chase, Truddi, *When Rabbit Howls.* New York, NY: Jove Books, 1990.

Constantine, Alex, *Virtual Government: CIA Mind Control Operations in America.* Venice, CA: Feral House, 1997.

DeCamp, John W., *The Franklin Cover-Up: Child Abuse, Satanism, and Murder in Nebraska.* Lincoln, NE: AWT, Inc., 1996.

Helmut, Lammer and Marion. *MILABS: Military Mind Control and Alien Abduction.* Hidden Mysteries Books. Available through TGS Services, Frankston, TX.

Herman, Judith Lewis, M.D., *Trauma and Recovery: The Aftermath of Violence – From Domestic Abuse to Political Terror.* New York, NY: Basic Books, 1992.

Hersha, Cheryl; Hersha, Lynn; Schwartz, Ted; and Griffis, Dale, Ph.D., *Secret Weapons: 2 Sisters' Terrifying True Story of Sex, Spies and Sabotage.* Far Hills, NJ: New Horizon Press, 2001.

Hoffman, Michael A., II, *They Were White and They Were Slaves: The Untold History of the Enslavement of Whites in Early America.* Boring, OR: CPA Book Publisher, 1992.

Hougan, Jim, *Spooks: The Haunting of America–The Private Use of Secret Agents.* New York: William Morrow and Co., 1978.

Lee, Martin A., *The Beast Awakens.* New York: Little, Brown, 1997.

Lewis, H. Spencer, Ph.D., F.R.C. *Rosicrucian Questions and Answers with Complete History of the Rosicrucian Order.* San Jose, CA: Rosicrucian Press.

Lorena, Jeanne Marie, Ed. and Levy, Paula, Ed. *Breaking Ritual Silence: An Anthology of Ritual Abuse Survivors' Stories.* Gardnerville, NV: Trout and Sons, 1998.

Mackenzie, Angus, *Secrets: The CIA's War At Home.* Berkeley: University of California Press, 1999.

Matsakis, Aphrodite, Ph.D., *I Can't Get Over It: A Handbook for Trauma Survivors.* Oakland, CA: New Harbinger Publications, Inc., 1996.

McClendon, Pat, MSSW, CSW., "Dissociation: Dissociative/Posttraumatic Stress Symptomatology." Website. http://www.clinicalsocialwork.com/dissociation.html.

Newton, Michael, *Raising Hell: The Encyclopedia of Devil Worship and Satanic Crime.* New York: Morrow/Avon, 1993.

Noblitt, James Randall and Perskin, Pamela Sue. *Cult and Ritual Abuse: Its History, Anthropology, and Recent Discovery in Contemporary America.* Westport, CT: Praeger Publishers, 2000.

Oksana, Chrystine, *Safe Passage to Healing: A Guide for Survivors of Ritual Abuse.* New York: HarperCollins, 2001.

Ostrander, Sheila and Lynn, Schroeder, *Psychic Discoveries behind the Iron Curtain.* New York, NY: Bantam Books, 1970.

Quan, James, "A Consolidation of SRA and False Memory Data," November 1996. Website. http://home.att.net/~mcra/consldra.htm.

Raschke, Carl A., *Painted Black.* New York, NY: HarperPaperbacks, 1990.

Reeves, Claire R., C.C.D.C., *Childhood: It Should Not Hurt!* Ms. Reeves is the founder and president of MASA (Mothers Against Sexual Abuse). Website. http://www.childhooditshouldnothurt.com.

Reid, Gregory, Ph.D., *Orphans In The Storm: Male Survivors of Sexual & Ritual Abuse.* YouthFire, Box 370006, El Paso, TX 79937. Website. http://www.gregoryreid.com.

Russell, Dick, *The Man Who Knew Too Much*, New York: Carroll & Graf, 1992.

Ryder, Daniel, C.C.D.C., L.S.W., *Breaking the Circle of Satanic Ritual Abuse: Recognizing and Recovering from the Hidden Trauma.* Minneapolis, MN: CompCare Publishers, 1992.

Ryder, Daniel, *Cover-Up of the Century: Satanic Ritual Crime & World Conspiracy.* Noblesville, IN: Ryder Publishing, 1996.

Simpson, Christopher, *Blowback: America's Recruitment of Nazis and Its Effects on the Cold War.* New York, NY: Weidenfeld & Nicolson, 1988.

Smith, Margaret, *Ritual Abuse: What It Is, Why it Happens, How to Help.* New York, NY: Harper Collins, 1993.

Vachss, Alice, *Sex Crimes: Ten Years on the Front Lines Prosecuting Rapists and Confronting Their Collaborators.* New York, NY: Random House, 1993.

Supportive Organizations for Ritual Abuse and Mind Control Survivors

ACHES-MC (Advocacy Committee for Human Experimentation Survivors – Mind Control)

Website: http://www.aches-mc.org
US Contact, Research & Archives:
Patty Rehn
Fax # (541) 388-5068
E-mail: aches@bendnet.com
Canada Contact, Research:
Lynne Moss-Sharman
230 Miles St. E #3
Thunder Bay, ONT
P7C1J6 Canada
(807) 622-5407
E-mail: lsharman@shaw.ca
Prison Contact:
Vern Mulka
PO Box 5081
Biddeford MA 04007
USA
(207) 282-7225
E-mail: jeanne@lamere.net

Mr. Light & Associates, Inc.

Website: http://www.mrlight.org
Contact: Jeanne Adams
PO Box 12927
Ogden UT 84412-2927
USA
E-mail: mrlight@konnections.net

PARC-VRAMC

Website: http://parc-vramc.tierranet.com
Contact: Kathleen Sullivan
PARC-VRAMC, Inc.
PMB 129, 5251 Hwy. 153
Hixson TN 37343
USA

(Please note: PARC-VRAMC does not provide individualized support to survivors.)

Persons Against Ritual Abuse-Torture (RAT) and Other Acts of Non-Political Torture

Website: http://www.ritualabusetorture.org
Contact:
Jeanne Sarson, RN, BScN, MEd
Linda MacDonald, RN, BN MEd
361 Prince St.
Truro Nova Scotia
Canada B2N 1E4
(902) 895-2255
E-mail: flight@ns.sympatico.ca

SMART (Stop Mind Control and Ritual Abuse Today)

Website: http://members.aol.com/SMARTNEWS/index2.html
Contact: Neil Brick
SMART
PO Box 1295
Easthampton MA 01027-1295
USA
E-mail: SMARTNEWS@aol.com

Survivorship

Website: http://www.survivorship.org
Survivorship
PMB 139, 3181 Mission St.
San Francisco CA 94110
USA
E-mail: info@survivorship.org

Information about other supportive organizations and resources can be found by reviewing these organizations' websites and literature.

About the Author

Kathleen Sullivan lives near Chattanooga, Tennessee with her husband, Bill. She is the founder and president of a grassroots advocacy organization, PARC-VRAMC (pronounced "park") – Positive Activism, Remembrance and Commemoration for Survivors of Ritual Abuse and Mind Control. For more information, see http://parc-vramc.tierranet.com.

A master gardener and rock collector, Kathleen enjoys "playing in the dirt." She's currently helping to develop PARC-VRAMC's Chattanooga Living Memorial Garden. A Social Work student at the University of Tennessee, she is also the author of *MK*, a novel about mind control that is scheduled for publication in 2004. You can visit her personal website at http://www.kathleen-sullivan.com.

Index

Non-Fiction:

Stranger than Fiction: An Independent Investigation Of The True Culprits Behind 9-11, by Albert D. Pastore, Ph.D... Twelve months of careful study, painstaking research, detailed analysis, source verification and logical deduction went into the writing of this book. In addition to the stories are approximately 300 detailed footnotes Pastore: "Only by sifting through huge amounts of news data on a daily basis was I able to catch many of these rare 'diamonds in the rough' and organize them into a coherent pattern and logical argument." (ISBN 1-893302-47-4)

Ahead Of TheParade: A Who's Who Of Treason and High Crimes— Exclusive Details Of Fraud And Corruption Of The Monopoly Press, The Banks, The Bench And The Bar, And The Secret Political Police, by Sherman H. Skolnick... One of America's foremost investigative reporters, speaks out on some of America's current crises. Included in this blockbuster book are the following articles: Big City Newspapers & the Mob, The Sucker Traps, Dirty Tricks of Finance and Brokerage, The Secret History of Airplane Sabotage, Wal-Mart and the Red Chinese Secret Police, The Chandra Levy Affair, The Japanese Mafia in the United States, The Secrets of Timothy McVeigh, and much more. (ISBN 1-893302-32-6)

Another Day In The Empire: Life in Neoconservative America, by Kurt Nimmo... A collection of articles by one of Counterpunch's most popular columnists. Included in this collection are: The Son of COIN-TELPRO; Clueless at the State Department; Bush Senior: Hating Saddam, Selling Him Weapons; Corporate Media: Selling Dubya's Oil War; Iraq and the Vision of the Velociraptors: The Bleeding Edge of Islam; Condoleezza Rice at the Waldorf Astoria; Predators, Snipers and the Posse Comitatus Act, and many others. (ISBN 1-893302-75-X)

Palestine & The Middle East: Passion, Power & Politics, by Jaffer Ali... The Palestinian struggle is actually a human one that transcends

445

Palestine... There is no longer a place for Zionism in the 20th century... Democracy in the Middle East is mot safe for US interests as long as there is an atmosphere of hostility... Suicide bombings are acts of desperation and mean that a people have been pushed to the brink... failure to understand why they happen will make certain they will continue. Jaffer Ali is a Palestinian-American business man who has been writing on politics and business for over 25 years. (ISBN 1-893302-45-8)

America, Awake! We Must Take Back Our Country, by Norman D. Livergood... This book is intended as a wake-up call for Americans, as Paul Revere awakened the Lexington patriots to the British attack on April 18, 1775, and as Thomas Paine's *Common Sense* roused apathetic American colonists to recognize and struggle against British oppression. Our current situation is similar to that which American patriots faced in the 1770s: a country ruled by 'foreign' and 'domestic' plutocratic powers and a divided citizenry uncertain of their vital interests. (ISBN 1-893302-27-X)

"Evil Fire Made to Burn"—A True Account of the World's Greatest Coverup, by Gary... In the spirited Indiana Jones tradition, Gary Vey, editor of an internet underground website, viewzone.com, finds himself transported from a sleepy New England suburb to a waking nightmare in the barren Alaskan tundra, the unpredictable vortices of Yemen and ultimately the wilderness of the Australian Outback. Eden accidentally stumbles into what turns out to be the most startling revelation of his life. Besieged by his newly-discovered destiny as prophesied translator of ancient texts, he learns he holds the key for unlocking secrets that have the power to change the course of history. From that point on, Eden becomes one of the most wanted—and haunted—persons on the planet. (ISBN 1-893302-41-5)

The Perennial Tradition: Overview Of The Secret Heritage, The Single Stream Of Initiatory Teaching Flowing Through All The Great Schools Of Mysticism, by Norman D. Livergood... Like America, Awake, this book is another wake-up call. "It was written to assist readers to awaken to the Higher Spiritual World." In addition to providing a history of the Western tradition of the Perennial Tradition, Livergood also describes the process that serious students use to actually realize—bring to manifestation—their Higher Consciousness. "Unless we become aware of this higher state, we face the prospect of a basically useless physical existence and a future life—following physical death—of unpleasant, perhaps anguished reformation of our essence." (ISBN 1-893302-48-2)

The Awakening of An American: How America Broke My Heart, by Meria Heller, with a Foreword by Catherine Austin Fitts... A collection of choice interviews from Meria Heller's world-famous www.meria.net rapidly growing radio network that reaches millions of people daily. Dr. Arun Gandhi, Greg Palast, Vincent Bugliosi, Mark Elsis, William Rivers Pitt, Mark Rechtenwald, Nancy Oden & Bob Fertik, Howard Winant, Linda Starr, Dave Chandler, Bev Conover, John Nichols, Robert McChesney, Norman Solomon, Stan Goff and Mark Crispin Miller. (ISBN 1-89302-39-3)

America's Nightmare: The Presidency of George Bush II, by John Stanton & Wayne Madsen... Media & Language, War & Weapons, Internal Affairs and a variety of other issues pointing out the US "crisis without precedent" that was wrought by the US Presidential election of 2000 followed by 9/11. "Stanton & Madsen will challenge many of the things you've been told by CNN and Fox news. This book is dangerous." (ISBN 1-893302-29-6)

America's Autopsy Report, by John Kaminski... The false fabric of history is unraveling beneath an avalanche of pathological lies to justify endless war and Orwellian new laws that revoke the rights of Americans. While TV and newspapers glorify the dangerous ideas of perverted billionaires, the Internet has pulsated with outrage and provided a new and real forum for freedom among concerned people all over the world who are opposed to the mass murder and criminal exploitation of the defenseless victims of multinational corporate totalitarianism. John Kaminski's passionate essays give voice to those hopes and fears of humane people that are ignored by the big business shysters who rule the major media. (ISBN 1-893302-42-3)

Seeds Of Fire: China And The Story Behind The Attack On America, by Gordon Thomas... The inside story about China that no one can afford to ignore. Using his unsurpassed contacts in Israel, Washington, London and Europe, Gordon Thomas, internationally acclaimed best-selling author and investigative reporter for over a quarter-century, reveals information about China's intentions to use the current crisis to launch itself as a super-power and become America's new major enemy... *"This has been kept out of the news agenda because it does not suit certain business interests to have that truth emerge... Every patriotic American should buy and read this book... it is simply revelatory."* (Ray Flynn, Former U.S. Ambassador to the Vatican) (ISBN 1-893302-54-7)

Shaking The Foundations: Coming Of Age In The Postmodern Era, by John H. Brand, D. Min., J.D.... Scientific discoveries in the Twentieth Century require the restructuring of our understanding the nature of Nature and of human beings. In simple language the author explains how significant implications of quantum mechanics, astronomy, biology and brain physiology form the foundation for new perspectives to comprehend the meaning of our lives. (ISBN 1-893302-25-3)

Rebuilding The Foundations: Forging A New And Just America, by John H. Brand, D. Min., J.D.... Should we expect a learned scholar to warn us about our dangerous reptilian brains that are the real cause of today's evils? Although Brand is not without hope for rescuing America, he warns us to act fast–and now. Evil men intent on imposing their political, economic, and religious self-serving goals on America are not far from achieving their goal of mastery." (ISBN 1-893302-33-4)

Democracy Under Siege: The Jesuits' Attempt To Destroy the Popular Government Of The United States; The True Story of Abraham Lincoln's Death; Banned For Over 100 Years, This Information Now Revealed For The First Time! by C.T. Wilcox... U.S. President Lincoln was the triumphant embodiment of the New Concept of Popular Government. Was John Wilkes Booth a Jesuit patsy, hired to do the dirty work for the Roman Catholic church—whose plan, a well-kept secret until now—was to overthrow the American Government? (ISBN 1-893302-31-8)

The Last Atlantis Book You'll Ever Have To Read! by Gene D. Matlock... More than 25,000 books, plus countless other articles have been written about a fabled confederation of city-states known as Atlantis. If it really did exist, where was it located? Does anyone have valid evidence of its existence—artifacts and other remnants? According to historian, archaeologist, educator and linguist Gene D. Matlock, both questions can easily be answered. (ISBN 1-893302-20-2)

The Last Days Of Israel, by Barry Chamish... With the Middle East crisis ongoing, The Last Days of Israel takes on even greater significance as an important book of our age. Barry Chamish, investigative reporter who has the true story about Yitzak Rabin's assassination, tells it like it is. (ISBN 1-893302-16-4)

The Courage To Be Who I Am, by Mary-Margareht Rose... This book is rich with teachings and anecdotes delivered with humor and humanness, by a woman who followed her heart and learned to listen to her inner voice; in the process, transforming every obstacle into an opportunity to test her courage to manifest her true identity. (ISBN 1-893302-13-X)

The Making Of A Master: Tracking Your Self-Worth, by Jeanette O'Donnal... A simple tracking method for self-improvement that takes the mystery out of defining your goals, making a road map and tracking your progress. A book rich with nuggets of wisdom couched in anecdotes and instructive dialogues. (ISBN 1-893302-36-9).

The Clear and Simple Way: The Angel Lessons, by Judith Parsons... a book about heart, with heart. Parsons, known throughout the world for her spiritual workshops and seminars, shows us how to transform our lives into infinite "presents"—"gifts" and moment-by-moment experiences—of peace, joy and self-fulfillment. (ISBN 1-893302-43-1)

Cancer Doctor: The Biography Josef Issels, M.D., Who Brought Hope To The World With His Revolutionary Cancer Treatment, by Gordon Thomas... Dr. Josef Issels treated more than 12,000 cancer patients who had been written off as "incurable" by other doctors. He claimed no miracle cures, but the success record of his revolutionary "whole person treatment" was extraordinary... the story of his struggle against the medical establishment which put Dr. Issels in prison, charged with fraud and manslaughter. (ISBN 1-893302-18-0)

Fiction:

Ticket to Paradise, by Yvonne Ridley... Judith Tempest, a British reporter, is searching for the Truth. But when it starts to spill out in her brilliant front page reportage of Middle East suicide bombing in retaliation for Israeli tanks mowing down innocent Palestinian women and children, both 'Tempest' and 'Truth' start to spell 'Trouble'—with a capital 'T', joke her friends and colleagues. A non-stop mystery thriller that tears along at a reckless pace of passion, betrayal, adventure and espionage. (ISBN 1-893302-77-6)

The Alley of Wishes, by Laurel Johnson... Despite the ravages of WWI on Paris and on the young American farm boy, Beck Sanow, and despite the abusive relationship that the chanteuse Cerise endures, the two share a bond that is unbreakable by time, war, loss of memory, loss of life and loss of youth. Beck and Cerise are both good people beset by constant tragedy. Yet it is tragedy that brings them together, and it is unconditional love that keeps them together. (ISBN 1-893302-46-6)

Freedom: Letting Go Of Anxiety And Fear Of The Unknown, by Jim Britt... Jeremy Carter, a fireman from Missouri who is in New York City for the day, decides to take a tour of the Trade Center, only to watch in shock, the attack on its twin towers from a block away. Afterward as he gazes at the pit of rubble and talks with many of the survivors, Jeremy starts to explore the inner depths of his soul, to ask questions he'd never asked before. This dialogue helps him learn who he is and what it takes to overcome the fear, anger, grief and anxiety this kind of tragedy brings. (ISBN 1-893302-74-1)

The Prince Must Die, by Gower Leconfield... breaks all taboos for mystery thrillers. After the "powers that be" suppressed the manuscripts of three major British writers, Dandelion Books breaks through with a thriller involving a plot to assassinate Prince Charles. The Prince Must Die brings to life a Britain of today that is on the edge with race riots, neo-Nazis, hard right backlash and neo-punk nihilists. Riveting entertainment... you won't be able to put it down. (ISBN 1-893302-72-5)

Waaaay Out There! Diggertown, Oklahoma, by Tuklo Nashoba... Adventures of constable Clint Mankiller and his deputy, Chad GhostWolf; Jim Bob and Bubba Johnson, Grandfather GhostWolf, Cassie Snodgrass, Doc Jones, Judge Jenkins and the rest of the Diggertown, Oklahoma bunch in the first of a series of Big Foot-Sasquatch tall tales peppered with lots of good belly laughs and just as much fun. (ISBN 1-893302-44-X)

Synchronicity Gates: An Anthology Of Stories And Poetry About People Transformed In Extraordinary Reality Beyond Experience, by Stephen Vernarelli... An inventive compilation of short stories that take the reader beyond mere science, fiction, or fantasy. Vernarelli introduces the reader to a new perception of reality; he imagines the best and makes it real. (ISBN 1-893302-38-5)

Daniela, by Stephen Weeks... A gripping epic novel of sexual obsession and betrayal as Nazi Prague falls. The harboring of deadly secrets and triumph of an enduring love against the hardest of times. Nikolei is a Polish/Ukrainian Jew who finds himself fighting among the Germans then turning against them to save Prague in 1945. Nikolei manages to hide himself among the Germans with a woman working as a prostitute. (ISBN 1-893302-37-7)

Unfinished Business, by Elizabeth Lucas Taylor... Lindsay Mayer knows something is amiss when her husband, Griffin, a college professor, starts spending too much time at his office and out-of-town. Shortly after the ugly truth surfaces, Griffin disappears altogether. Lindsay is shattered. Life without Griffin is life without life... One of the sexiest books you'll ever read! (ISBN 1-893302-68-7)

The Woman With Qualities, by Sarah Daniels... South Florida isn't exactly the Promised Land that forty-nine-year-old newly widowed Keri Anders had in mind when she transplanted herself here from the northeast... A tough action-packed novel that is far more than a love story. (ISBN 1-893302-11-3)

Weapon In Heaven, by David Bulley... Eddy Licklighter is in a fight with God for his very own soul. You can't mess around half-assed when fighting with God. You've got to go at it whole-hearted. Eddy loses his wife and baby girl in a fire. Bulley's protagonist is a contemporary version of the Old Testament character of Job. Licklighter wants nothing from God except His presence so he can kill him off. The humor, warmth, pathos and ultimate redemption of Licklighter will make you hold your sides with laughter at the same time you shed common tears for his "God-awful" dilemma. (ISBN 1-893302-28-8)

Adventure Capital, by John Rushing... South Florida adventure, crime and violence in a fiction story based on a true life experience. A book you will not want to put down until you reach the last page. (ISBN 1-893302-08-3)

A Mother's Journey: To Release Sorrow And Reap Joy, by Sharon Kay... A poignant account of Norah Ann Mason's life journey as a wife, mother and single parent. This book will have a powerful impact on anyone, female or male, who has experienced parental abuse, family separations, financial struggles and a desperate need to find the magic in life that others talk about that just doesn't seem to be there for them. (ISBN 1-893302-52-0)

Return To Masada, by Robert G. Makin... In a gripping account of the famous Battle of Masada, Robert G. Makin skillfully recaptures the blood and gore as well as the spiritual essence of this historic struggle for freedom and independence. (ISBN 1-893302-10-5)

Time Out Of Mind, by Solara Vayanian... Atlantis had become a snake pit of intrigue teeming with factious groups vying for power and control. An unforgettable drama that tells of the breakdown of the priesthood, the hidden scientific experiments in genetic engineering which produced "things"—part human and part animal—and other atrocities; the infiltration by the dark lords of Orion; and the implantation of the human body with a device to fuel the Orion wars. (ISBN 1-893302-21-0)

The Thirteenth Disciple: The Life Of Mary Magdalene, by Gordon Thomas... The closest of Jesus' followers, the name of Mary Magdalene conjures images of a woman both passionate and devoted, both sinner and saint. The first full-length biography for 13 centuries. (ISBN 1-893302-17-2)

**ALL DANDELION BOOKS ARE AVAILABLE THROUGH
WWW.DANDELIONBOOKS.NET... ALWAYS.**

Breinigsville, PA USA
15 November 2010
249416BV00002B/21/A

9 781893 302358